350

4/24

Fundamentalism and American Culture

Fundamentalism and American Culture

Second Edition

GEORGE M. MARSDEN

2006

OXFORD
UNIVERSITY PRESS

Oxford University Press, Inc., publishes works that
further Oxford University's objective of excellence
in research, scholarship, and education.

Oxford New York
Auckland Cape Town Dar es Salaam Hong Kong Karachi
Kuala Lumpur Madrid Melbourne Mexico City Nairobi
New Delhi Shanghai Taipei Toronto

With offices in
Argentina Austria Brazil Chile Czech Republic France Greece
Guatemala Hungary Italy Japan Poland Portugal Singapore
South Korea Switzerland Thailand Turkey Ukraine Vietnam

Published by Oxford University Press, Inc.
198 Madison Avenue, New York, NY 10016
www.oup.com

Oxford is a registered trademark of Oxford University Press

Library of Congress Cataloging-in-Publication Data

Marsden, George M., 1939–
Fundamentalism and American culture / George M. Marsden.—2nd ed.
p. cm.
Includes bibliographical references (p.) and indexes.
ISBN-13: 978-0-19-530051-2
ISBN-13: 978-0-19-530047-5
1. Fundamentalism—United States. 2. Christianity and culture—United States. I. Title.

BT82.2.M37 2006
277.3'082—dc22

2005053920

9 8 7 6 5 4 3

Printed in the United States of America
on acid-free paper

To my students with thanks for all they have taught me

Preface to the Second Edition

Several days after the reelection of George W. Bush in November 2004, my editor, Cynthia Read, contacted me about updating *Fundamentalism and American Culture* in the light of recent events. I am delighted to do so. It is especially pleasing that this volume has remained in use for a quarter century and that its usefulness might be enhanced in this way.

Since the original seems to have stood well on its own as a point of departure for understanding the emergence of American fundamentalism, I have left that text intact as it was published in 1980. Subsequent scholarship has shown that there are many additional things I might have said and has pointed to limits in my angle of vision; nonetheless, this version of the story has apparently proven illuminating both to scholars and to general readers. I have been particularly gratified by the scores of people who over the years have told me that this book helped them immensely in understanding the religious community in which they grew up. So rather than tinkering with something that has served well, I have updated this edition by adding a substantial supplemental section. In it I have reflected on the fascinating question of what the differences and similarities are between the fundamentalism in America since the mid-1970s and the fundamentalism of the 1920s.

In some ways it may have been an advantage that I was able to draft most of the first edition of this book before fundamentalism had reemerged as a conspicuous part of American politics at the end of the 1970s. What I wrote was not driven by the sorts of political and cultural concerns that have dominated our views since then. In other respects writing in advance of these past several decades of fundamentalism in American life was a disadvantage; the recent events might have alerted me to dimensions of the movement that I did not see or think were especially important. In any case, I now have the opportunity to reflect on the comparison of the fundamentalisms of the two eras and have found that a most fruitful exercise.

Part Five, the result of that reflection, has been a communal exercise. First, I have learned a great deal from the many fine works on early fundamentalism that have appeared in the past twenty-five years. Second, I have depended on the large secondary literature interpreting recent American fundamentalism and evangelicalism. Finally, as I have worked through several drafts of this update I have been tremendously helped by the comments of many readers. Most of these have been my graduate students or former students who are better informed than I on many details of recent developments. I am also grateful to the history department of the University of Illinois for an opportunity to discuss a draft of this paper with them. Many thanks also for all the comments from the discussions in my graduate class on evangelicalism and fundamentalism, at the Colloquium on Religion and History at Notre Dame, and at the conference on this topic held at Michilinda Lodge in June 2005.

Those whom I wish to thank for written comments, or for particularly memorable verbal ones, include Thomas Bergler, James Bratt, Joel Carpenter, Cliff Christians, Jonathan DenHartog, Darren Dochuk, Raully Donahue, Danielle DuBois, Kristin Kobes DuMez, Timothy Gloege, Michael Hamilton, Thomas Kidd, Michael J. Lee, Kathryn Long, Patrick Q. Mason, Sarah Miglio, Richard J. Mouw, Kurt Peterson, Glen Ryland, Brett H. Smith, William Svelmoe, David Swartz, John G. Turner, Grant Wacker, and John Wigger. I am also grateful for many other comments from those whom I have neglected to mention here.

I wish once again to express my gratitude to the Peter B. and Adeline W. Ruffin foundation and to the McAnaney family for their generous support of the Francis A. McAnaney Chair in History at the University of Notre Dame. I am also grateful to my colleagues and to the staff of the Notre Dame history department, especially to John McGreevy, the current chair, for their ongoing support.

I also wish once again to thank the staff of Oxford University Press—Ruth Mannes, Director of Editorial, Design, and Production—especially Cynthia Read, who has worked with this book since its publishing beginnings and has contributed much to it.

As always my great personal debt is to Lucie, whose continuing loving friendship and support is invaluable. Everything I said about her in the Preface to the original addition remains true.

Preface (1980)

The scholar and the fool, as a colleague pointed out to a college "honors" convocation, are in Renaissance Christian imagery often equated. Anyone who has spent many days secluded on a project like the present volume can sympathize with such an identification. Though Christian scholars often find it difficult to be fools for Christ, we have at least as much aptitude as other scholars for simply being fools. We must be reminded, then, that there are many virtues greater than that of forsaking the world in order to write about it.

Yet this book, for all the isolation it has involved, is not solely academic or detached in its purpose. It is addressed not only to the scholarly community, but also to an audience of thoughtful Christians and other observers who are interested in a dispassionate analysis of the development of a significant Christian tradition in an American cultural setting. While I have attempted to assume a stance of detachment and to avoid using history as a tool for partisan debate, this study represents a definite point of view and set of interests. Since these give it direction, they are best revealed at the outset. This is an essay in distinctly Christian scholarship, an attempt to present a careful, honest, and critical evaluation of a tradition not far from my own. My sympathies may be described most succinctly by saying that I greatly admire two American scholar-theologians, Jonathan Edwards and Reinhold Niebuhr. In the theology of Edwards—especially his sense of the overwhelming love and beauty of God revealed in Christ, in Scripture, and constantly communicated through all creation—I see a starting point for the attempt to comprehend reality and to see our place in it. In the ethics of Niebuhr I find a way of understanding the pretensions, limits, and folly of even the most admirable human behavior. Particularly, his analysis reveals the inevitable ambiguities in Christians' relationships to their culture.

These perspectives, especially those associated with Niebuhr, can be found implicitly throughout this study. "Culture" and the relationship of Christians to it are prominent concerns. By "culture" I usually have in mind the collection of beliefs, values, assumptions, commitments, and ideals expressed in a society through popular literary and artistic forms and embodied in its political, educational, and other institutions. In most cultures the prevailing formal religion has been an integral part of and support for the dominant beliefs, values, and institutions. Although this has been largely true in Western civilization during the long era of "Christendom," the relationship of Christianity to Western culture has always been complex. Some Christian groups have equated culture with the "world" which must be shunned; others have virtually identified Christianity with the values and progress of culture. As H. Richard Niebuhr has pointed out in *Christ and Culture* (1951), there is a spectrum of middle positions which can claim ancient lineage. This perennial tension has been accentuated by the dramatic secularization of Western culture in recent centuries.

My interest in these issues led to the questions and themes that shape this study. The central question involves the degree to which the fundamentalist versions of evangelical Protestantism (as defined in the Introduction) were shaped by the American cultural experience. The question of fundamentalists' own attitudes toward American culture is closely related. My conclusion, which finds expression in a variety of specific ways, is that fundamentalists experienced profound ambivalence toward the surrounding culture. Perhaps the same might be said about almost any group. Yet the fundamentalist experience strikes me as unusual in at least one respect. These American Christians underwent a remarkable transformation in their relationship to the culture. Respectable "evangelicals" in the 1870s, by the 1920s they had become a laughingstock, ideological strangers in their own land. Their traditions, the ways they maintained them, and the ways they modified them are all understood better in the context of this collective uprooting.

This narrative is designed to serve as a general history of the rise of fundamentalism, but it has been shaped more by interest in analyzing the issues just mentioned than by desire to cover everything that happened in textbook fashion. Throughout I have attempted to choose a strikingly representative person, group, or event to illustrate a general phenomenon. This method is, I think, not widely advocated in academic disciplines other than history and the arts. In recent years two perceptive colleagues, one in philosophy and one in the social sciences, have spoken to me of their dismay concerning the historian's procedure. They have argued that one cannot prove anything about general phenomena by picking out a few examples. They are right, of course. No matter how long or impressive or varied the footnotes, to a degree it must require an act of faith on the part of the reader to believe that the instances selected capture the true spirit of the endless information which bears on any subject and which the historian has presumably surveyed. Like many fascinating things, however, most of history is too complex to be susceptible either to genuinely comprehensive treatment or to definitive scientific analysis. In the final analysis it can be understood and illuminated only by sympathetic insight.

Christian scholarship is essentially a communal enterprise. I have written this book with a strong sense that it grows out of the brotherhood and sisterhood that make up the body of Christ. I am especially grateful to other scholars in that body at Calvin College. They have set high standards, shaped much of the tone, and suggested a good deal of whatever insight is found herein. My friends in the history department have been especially helpful in listening to and criticizing parts of the manuscript. This supporting community has extended to my neighborhood, which fortunately is not made up entirely of scholars and which includes academics who are not unrelievedly scholarly. Here I would thank Sandy and Dale Van Kley, Phyllis and Richard Mouw, and Karen and Peter De Vos (who also lent me study space in their home for several years).

Thanks are due also to my friends and colleagues at Trinity Evangelical Divinity School and to its administration for their cooperation during the year of my stay there. They helped the progress of this work in many ways.

The administration and board of trustees of Calvin College have been generous in supporting this project, providing a sabbatical leave as well as time released from teaching. The librarians at Calvin, especially Conrad Bult, Peter De Klerk, Jo Duyst, and Stephen Lambers, have always been extremely helpful.

No formal acknowledgment can adequately convey my personal gratitude to another group of scholars who deserve considerable credit for this book. Joel Carpenter, Mark Noll, Harry Stout, and Grant Wacker all took a great deal of time from their own pressing schedules to read versions of the manuscript and to comment in detail. Donald Dayton and Richard Mouw each gave advice during the course of the enterprise, read the manuscript, and furnished important insights. Martin Marty also helped at crucial points. Cy Hulse and Barbara Thompson, each my research assistant for a year, provided sophisticated aid and insight. I am indebted also to C. Allyn Russell, whose fine work on this subject has preceded mine, and whose friendship, advice, and encouragement I have valued. He is the tennis champion among historians of fundamentalism.

I also wish to thank the National Endowment for the Humanities for generous support during 1971–1972 when I began this project. I am indebted to the librarians of a number of institutions for their cooperation. I thank Jill Los and Nelle Tjapkes for typing the manuscript and Paul Stoub for helping with the illustrations.

I am grateful to many students of American culture and Christianity whose work and insights I have borrowed. My acknowledgments and comments appear in the notes, which are indexed to serve as a critical bibliography.

Most important is the support I have received from my family, Lucie, Gregory, and Brynn, three witty and enjoyable people who hardly ever complained about the time invested in this enterprise. Of Lucie it might be said, as Meredith wrote in *Diana of the Crossways,* "A witty woman is a treasure; a witty beauty is a power." She has provided me with love, understanding, advice, and humor. I wish to thank her especially for her effort in beginning to read my earlier book, which was dedicated to her. This has inspired me to attempt a work in English prose interesting enough even for philosophers. But now I am back to foolish pretensions.

G. M.

Calvin College
Grand Rapids, Michigan

March 21, 1980

Acknowledgments

Parts of Chapter XXV are a revision of parts of "Fundamentalism as an American Phenomenon, A Comparison with English Evangelicalism," *Church History* XLVI (June, 1977), pp. 215–32, © 1977, The American Society of Church History, reprinted with permission.

A portion of Chapter XXII closely follows a section of my "From Fundamentalism to Evangelicalism: An Historical Analysis," *The Evangelicals,* David Wells and John Woodbridge (eds.) (Nashville, Tennessee, 1975).

The illustrations by Clarence Larkin on pp. 52, 58–59, and 64–65 are reproduced with the permission of the Clarence Larkin Estate.

The illustrations from *The King's Business* on pp. 154, 155, 157, 163, 209, and 213 are reproduced with the permission of Biola College, Inc.

The illustration on p. 218 is used by permission from the May issue of *Moody Monthly.* Copyright 1922, Moody Bible Institute of Chicago.

Gospel Hymns Nos. 1 to 6, Ira Sankey *et al.*, eds. (New York, 1894), from which the hymn on p. 76 is reproduced, is republished by Da Capo Press, Inc., New York.

The Memoirs of William Jennings Bryan, by himself and his wife Mary Baird Bryan (Philadelphia, 1925), from which the picture on p. 186 is taken, is republished by Haskell House Publisher, Ltd., New York.

Contents

Fundamentalism
and American Culture

Introduction

From its origins fundamentalism was primarily a religious movement. It was a movement among American "evangelical" Christians, people professing complete confidence in the Bible and preoccupied with the message of God's salvation of sinners through the death of Jesus Christ. Evangelicals were convinced that sincere acceptance of this "Gospel" message was the key to virtue in this life and to eternal life in heaven; its rejection meant following the broad path that ended with the tortures of hell. Unless we appreciate the immense implications of a deep religious commitment to such beliefs—implications for one's own life and for attitudes toward others—we cannot appreciate the dynamics of fundamentalist thought and action.

Yet to understand fundamentalism we must also see it as a distinct version of evangelical Christianity uniquely shaped by the circumstances of America in the early twentieth century. This book analyzes the impact of that cultural experience. It starts with the premise of the centrality of genuine religious faith and takes into account some continuities with other Christian traditions. The focus, however, is primarily on how individuals who were committed to typically American versions of evangelical Christianity responded to and were influenced by the social, intellectual, and religious crises of their time.

The fundamentalists' most alarming experience was that of finding themselves living in a culture that by the 1920s was openly turning away from God. "Christendom," remarked H. L. Mencken in 1924, "may be defined briefly as that part of the world in which, if any man stands up in public and solemnly swears that he is a Christian, all his auditors will laugh." The "irreligion of the modern world," concurred Walter Lippmann in his *Preface to Morals,* is ". . . radical to a degree for which there is, I think, no counterpart." "There remains no foundation in authority for ideas of right and wrong," said Joseph Wood Krutch in a somber requiem for Western Civilization. "Both our practical morality and our emotional lives are adjusted to a world that no longer exists."[1]

Fundamentalists shared with the discontended intellectuals of the 1920s, if little else, a sense of the profound spiritual and cultural crisis of the twentieth century.[2] Unlike their more disillusioned contemporaries, however, they had very definite ideas of where things had gone wrong. Modernism and the theory of evolution, they were convinced, had caused the catastrophe by undermining the Biblical foundations of American civilization. "Modern-

3

ism," President James M. Gray of Moody Bible Institute stated flatly, "is a revolt against the God of Christianity." It is a "foe of good government." "The evolutionary hypothesis," declared William Jennings Bryan in a similarly sweeping statement, "is the only thing that has seriously menaced religion since the birth of Christ; and it menaces . . . civilization as well as religion." Given the seriousness of these threats, the response demanded was clear. In the intellectual battle between true Christianity and the philosophical materialism of modern life, said J. Gresham Machen, "there can be no 'peace without victory'; one side or the other man must win."[3]

During this period of its national prominence in the 1920s, fundamentalism is best defined in terms of these concerns. Briefly, it was militantly antimodernist Protestant evangelicalism. Fundamentalists were evangelical Christians, close to the traditions of the dominant American revivalist establishment of the nineteenth century, who in the twentieth century militantly opposed both modernism in theology and the cultural changes that modernism endorsed. Militant opposition to modernism was what most clearly set off fundamentalism from a number of closely related traditions, such as evangelicalism, revivalism, pietism, the holiness movements, millenarianism, Reformed confessionalism, Baptist traditionalism, and other denominational orthodoxies. Fundamentalism was a "movement" in the sense of a tendency or development in Christian thought that gradually took on its own identity as a patchwork coalition of representatives of other movements. Although it developed a distinct life, identity, and eventually a subculture of its own, it never existed wholly independently of the older movements from which it grew. Fundamentalism was a loose, diverse, and changing federation of co-belligerents united by their fierce opposition to modernist attempts to bring Christianity into line with modern thought.[4]

Two types of interpretation of fundamentalism have prevailed to date. The most common has been to look on fundamentalism as essentially the extreme and agonized defense of a dying way of life. Opponents of fundamentalists proposed such a sociological explanation in the 1920s, and through the next generation fundamentalism was commonly regarded as a manifestation of cultural lag that time and education eventually would eliminate. But as it became apparent in recent decades that fundamentalism and its new evangelical offspring were by no means disappearing from American life, some later interpreters began to take more seriously the internal history of fundamentalism and its relation to other traditions.[5]

By far the most important manifestation of this shift was the interpretation of Ernest Sandeen, presented in its most complete form in 1970. Rejecting social explanations of fundamentalism, Sandeen found its roots in genuine doctrinal traditions. Basically, according to Sandeen, fundamentalism was the outgrowth of the "millenarian" movement that developed in late nineteenth-century America, especially through Bible institutes and conferences concerning the interpretation of Biblical prophecies. The movement's millenarian teachings, appearing in their most common form as "dispensational premillennialism," divided all of history into distinct eras or dispensations. The final dispensation would be the "millennium" or one-thousand-year personal reign of Christ on earth. According to Sandeen, these Bible teachers acquired from conservative Presbyterians at Princeton Theological Seminary the newly defined dogma that the Bible was "inerrant" in every detail. Millenarianism, however, was primary. This tradition, rather than the events of the 1920s, Sandeen argues, is crucial in understanding fundamentalism.[6]

Sandeen's thesis has much to recommend it and his impressive study remains valuable. He is certainly correct in supposing that millenarianism and Princeton theology are two of the important keys for understanding fundamentalism. Indeed, avowed "fundamentalists" today are almost all strict millenarians who also insist on Biblical inerrancy. Nevertheless, the meaning of "fundamentalism" has narrowed considerably since the 1920s. If one traces the roots of today's strictly separatist and dispensationalist "fundamentalism," Sandeen's central argument is seen to be basically correct.[7] Yet this approach fails to deal adequately with the larger phenomenon of the militantly anti-modernist evangelicalism of the 1920s, known at the time as "fundamentalism." This broader fundamentalism in turn had wider roots, cultural as well as theological[8] and organizational. It is true that the millenarians stood at the center of the fundamentalist coalition of the 1920s, and the development of their thought is crucial to understanding the broader fundamentalist movement. Yet the millenarians themselves were significantly affected by many other influences and traditions. In fact, these other influences were so strong that it is doubtful that premillennialism was really the organizing principle even in their own thought.

This book is concerned with the broader national movement and the influences that shaped it. It is about the movement that for a time in the 1920s created a national sensation with its attempts to purge the churches of modernism and the schools of Darwinism. This movement included William Jennings Bryan, J. Gresham Machen, and Billy Sunday, in addition to millenarian organizers such as William Bell Riley, Frank Norris, and John Roach Straton.[9] Thus in this study we are not only looking for the roots of the separatist and empire-building evangelists who call themselves "fundamentalists" today, but more importantly we are concerned with the background of the wider coalition of contemporary American evangelicals whose common identity is substantially grounded in the fundamentalist experience of an earlier era. The anti-modernism of the 1920s was a major factor in shaping much of subsequent twentieth-century American evangelicalism; though as the subsequent analysis should make clear, evangelicalism is an older tradition that has been shaped by many other factors.

This inquiry goes beyond both Sandeen and the older sociological interpretations. It views fundamentalism not as a temporary social aberration, but as a genuine religious movement or tendency with deep roots and intelligible beliefs. And it seeks to clarify the way in which this movement and these beliefs were conditioned by a unique and dramatic cultural experience.

This story begins just after the Civil War, when evangelical Protestantism was still the dominant religious force in American life.[10] While there were already signs of the impending demise of this unofficial religious establishment, confidence and unity prevailed. By the end of the 1870s, the beginnings of a major schism were apparent—a split typified by the diverging paths of two friends and associates in pre-Civil-War reform, Henry Ward Beecher and Jonathan Blanchard. More evident than this schism at the time, however, was the positive work of Dwight L. Moody, who built the new revivalist empire that was the base from which much of fundamentalism grew.

The second section of this book turns from accounts of prominent individuals to discussion of the emergence of the distinctive emphases that came to characterize fundamentalism. Among these, four are especially important—dispensational premillennialism, the holiness movement and its implications for social reform, efforts to defend the faith, and views of Christianity's relationship to culture. This section brings the story up to the beginning of World War I.

Before World War I, the emerging fundamentalist coalition was largely quiescent. Few could have predicted the explosion that followed. The war intensified hopes and fears, and totally upset existing balances in American culture. It brought out an aggressive and idealistic theological modernism. It also revealed that the reaction against evangelicalism, which had been proceeding quietly for half a century, was far more general than had been thought. Moreover, the war raised the question of the survival of civilization and morality.

In a postwar atmosphere of alarm, "fundamentalism" emerged as a distinct phenomenon. Its adherents moved on two fronts. Many fought against the onslaughts of liberalism within the major denominations. Meanwhile, William Jennings Bryan and other fundamentalists campaigned to ban the teaching of Darwinism in American schools. The ridicule heaped on Bryan at the Scopes trial in Tennessee in 1925 and his subsequent sudden death marked a turning point for the movement. It quickly lost its position as a nationally influential coalition. Yet as fundamentalists retreated from their notorious national campaigns, they were relocating and building a substantial subculture.

Three themes recur in this work. First, within fundamentalism we find a strikingly paradoxical tendency to identify sometimes with the "establishment" and sometimes with the "outsiders." Fundamentalism emerged from an era in which American evangelicalism was so influential that it was virtually a religious establishment; eventually, however, fundamentalism took on the role of a beleaguered minority with strong sectarian or separatist tendencies. During the development of fundamentalism its adherents wavered between these two opposing self-images. This tension reflected an ambivalence in their relationship to the major denominations. It also involved an ambivalence toward American culture which is especially apparent in fundamentalist attitudes toward patriotism and social reform. These fundamentalist attitudes cannot be understood in terms of a consistent ideology. They make sense only in terms of the establishment-or-outsider paradox. Here it will be seen that often premillennialism was not the decisive influence in forming fundamentalist attitudes.

The second major theme involves the relation of fundamentalism to the earlier American evangelical heritage. Revivalism and pietism were at the center of the traditions carried on by fundamentalism. Its individualism and its effort to return to the "Bible alone" came directly from the pietist and revivalist heritage. Holiness teachings, a major though generally overlooked component of fundamentalism, likewise grew out of this nineteenth-century revivalist heritage. Especially as expounded by D. L. Moody, a key transitional figure, these influences tended toward individualistic, culture-denying, soul-rescuing Christianity. Nevertheless, nineteenth-century American revivalism developed in the context of an older Puritan and Calvinist heritage to which it still had many ties. The Reformed traditions encouraged more positive attitudes toward intellect, the organized church, and the ideal of building a Christian civilization. Fundamentalist ambivalence about these subjects can be better understood if seen as reflecting not only immediate experience, but also the conflict between the pietist and the Calvinistic traditions.

The third major theme concerns the tension between trust and distrust of the intellect. This involves the strong ambivalence toward culture that provides this book with its recurring motif. During the 1920s, fundamentalists were often regarded as anti-scientific and anti-intellectual. This evaluation was accurate to the extent that most fundamentalists were unwilling to accept the principal assumptions and conclusions of recent science and philosophy. Indeed fundamentalists reflected many of the popular, sentimental, and sometimes anti-intellectual characteristics of the revivalist heritage. Nevertheless they stood in an intellectual tradition that had the highest regard for one understanding of true scientific method and proper rationality. In science they were steadfastly committed to the principles of the seventeenth-century philosopher Francis Bacon: careful observation and classification of facts. These principles were wedded to a "common sense" philosophy that affirmed the ability to apprehend the facts clearly, whether the facts of nature or the even more certain facts of Scripture. This philosophy, essentially the "Scottish Common Sense Realism" (see Chapter I) that had dominated mid-nineteenth-century America, was the basis of much of the unity in fundamentalist thought. These largely unspoken assumptions, as well as their faith in the Bible, separated the fundamentalists so entirely from most of the rest of twentieth-century thought that their ideas appear simply anomalous. Thus in the fifty years following the 1870s, the philosophical outlook that had graced America's finest academic institutions came to be generally regarded as merely bizarre.

In the late nineteenth century the evangelical heritage of Christian doctrines and ideals had been developing in some innovative and vigorous ways. Now it was tested by a confluence of severe cultural, religious, and intellectual crises. These and other factors transformed significant aspects of America's evangelicalism into a new phenomenon known as fundamentalism.

PART ONE
Before Fundamentalism

I. Evangelical America at the Brink of Crisis

In 1870 almost all American Protestants thought of America as a Christian nation. Although many Roman Catholics, sectarians, skeptics, and non-Christians had other views of the matter, Protestant evangelicals considered their faith to be the normative American creed. Viewed from their dominant perspective, the nineteenth century had been marked by successive advances of evangelicalism, the American nation, and hence the kingdom of God. Although many saw some unmistakably ominous portents, few expected evangelical progress to cease. The Civil War, widely interpreted as "a true Apocalyptic contest," had been the greatest test of American evangelical civilization. For many Northerners the victory confirmed, as one Presbyterian observer put it, that "we as individuals, and as a nation, are identified with that kingdom of God among men, which is righteousness, and peace, and joy in the Holy Ghost."[1] Mission enthusiasts foresaw similar advances worldwide. "The sublime idea of the conversion of the world to Christ," said Professor Samuel Harris of Yale in 1870, "has become so common as to cease to awaken wonder."[2]

The seemingly inexhaustible power of spiritual awakenings was foremost among the factors that generated such confidence. America, lacking many older institutions, had been substantially influenced by revivalism. The negative associations of revivals primarily with excess or with the frontier were only distant memories. Awakenings were now most respectable and even necessary signs of vitality in cities as much as in the countryside, among the educated as certainly as among the unlettered. The most immediate common memories were of the popular revivals that had swept through army camps, both Northern and Southern, but the outstanding model for renewal was the great revival of 1857–58. These awakenings, centered in the cities, grew out of noonday prayer meetings led by businessmen and bankers. Revival was not confined to the poor or the ignorant. Most college-educated Americans had attended schools where periodically intense spiritual outpourings were expected among the student body. "Revivalism" in 1870 suggested such names as Jonathan Edwards, Timothy Dwight, Lyman Beecher, and especially Charles Finney (whose career was near its end)—all with strong New England ties and all distinguished educators known by their title "President."

The examples set by these illustrious forebears, who had met the challenges of Enlightenment "infidelity" with spirituality and intellect, gave confidence for the new era. This confidence was the prevailing mood at the international meeting of the Evangelical Alliance in New York in 1873. The ideas expressed at this meeting provide a fair sample of the conventional evangelical wisdom of the day. "At critical times" and in the presence of "hosts of unbelief," in the words of a typical spokesman, "the spiritual interests of the nation have been saved by revivals." Skepticism might again be growing, yet "if still there are Pentecostal effusions, primitive Christianity survives . . . and will yet vindicate its reality and potency by a repetition of early victories."[3]

The evangelical commitment to social reform was a corollary of the inherited enthusiasm for revival. Reform was in a sense subordinate to revival in that it was usually considered to be effective only when it flowed from hearts transformed from self-love to love for others. "Christianity is a universal philanthropist," declared a British preacher at the Evangelical Alliance, in a line of thought with which his American listeners would not disagree.

> It trains the young; it feeds the hungry; it heals the sick. It rejoices in the increase of the elements of material civilization. But it maintains that all these agencies are subordinate. The divine method of human improvement begins in human hearts through evangelical truth, and it spreads from within outwardly till all is renewed.[4]

Yet social reform was not really a secondary consideration; at least it might not be dispensed with or substantially ignored. The assumption that Christianity was the only basis for a healthy civilization was basic to evangelical thinking—as essential as the belief that souls must be saved for the life to come. Virtue among the citizenry, as almost all political economists said, was the foundation of successful civilization, especially a republican civilization. Religion was the basis for true virtue; the purer the religion, the higher the morality. Christianity was the purest religion. The supposedly self-evident superiority of Western civilization and especially northern Europe was clearly due to the influence of Christianity and Protestantism in particular.[5]

Americans were proud of their own unique achievement since they had shown that the moral basis for national success could be maintained voluntarily without an officially established church. "In what sense can this country then be called a *Christian* country?" asked the Reverend Theodore Dwight Woolsey, retired president of Yale, in an address lauding separation of church and state. "In this sense certainly," he continued, "that the vast majority of the people believe in Christianity and the Gospel, that Christian influences are universal, that our civilization and intellectual culture are built on that foundation, and that the institutions are so adjusted as, in the opinion of almost all Christians, to furnish the best hope for spreading and carrying down to posterity our faith and our morality."[6]

The Northern victory in the Civil War had mixed effects on the reform impulse. On the one hand, the outcome seemed evidence of God's endorsement of the sacred character of the Union and the Constitution. Few outside Dixie questioned that. Moreover, the Republican Party, which in its reforming origins stood against Rum and Romanism as well as Rebellion, was in the ascendant. Yet there was a sense of excess in reform and a desire for stability. The slavery issue had been resolved only at immense cost and no other reform captured the popular imagination. A few, including the aged Finney, attempted to revive anti-Masonry. Others founded the Prohibition Party in 1869 and the Woman's Christian Temperance Union in 1874. Some spoke out for women's rights or for care of the freed slaves. Some worked for a Christian amendment to the Constitution. Others proposed campaigns against "worldly amusements." Most of the causes were old ones; almost all were motivated by the desire to ensure the stability of evangelical civilization.[7]

Perhaps the continuing interest in Sabbatarianism best illustrates this concern. The Puritan Sabbath was probably the most distinctive symbol of evangelical civilization in the English-speaking world, and remained a major reform issue where religious and social interests coincided. In view of the increasing complexity of modern life, affirmed the Congregational National Council in 1871, "the rest of the Sabbath is indispensable to the continuance of health, virtue and Christian principle in this nation."[8] Mark Hopkins, famed model of college teachers and presidents, held that God's law agreed with the interests of working people. Using the familiar terminology of the prevailing moral philosophy, Hopkins argued that people had a "right" to one day's rest because their God-endowed "moral constitution" was "preconformed" to the Sabbath rhythm.[9] While evangelicals agreed that "Sabbath desecration" had "reached alarming proportions," they remained convinced that "a proper recognition of the sanctity of the holy Sabbath is one of the chief cornerstones in the foundation of the Church and of our Christian civilization."[10]

The evangelical interest in Sabbatarianism and other causes involved genuine concern for the welfare of the laboring classes and the poor,[11] but their outlook was middle-class Victorian and their program to meet the challenges of the 1870s was essentially conservative. This was evident in the day devoted to "Christianity and Social Reform" at the 1873 Evangelical Alliance. "Christian Philanthropy," "the Care of the Sick," "Intemperance and its Suppression," "Crime and Criminals," "Industrial Schools . . . in the Prevention of Crime," and "the Labor Question" were on the agenda. Only the last of these dealt with a new American social problem and the advice given was that, although laborers had some legitimate complaints, the causes might be removed "gradually and safely, by wise and conservative legislation." Strikes "lead to ruin."[12]

American evangelicals enjoyed a remarkable consensus about the economic and moral laws that supported a sound economic system—that is, the prevailing free enterprise capitalism. College courses in "political economy," usually taught by college presidents, almost invariably inculcated the same principles. President M. B. Anderson of the University of Rochester told the Evangelical Alliance that the Bible and reason agreed "that the pursuit of wealth by legitimate processes is in entire harmony with morality and depends on it." The right to property and inheritance were sacred, but must be balanced by the law of benevolence, "the truest charity . . . which educates and trains the poor into the capacity to supply their own wants by their own labor and skill." Socialism stood in antithesis to these laws. "Socialism, that spectre which so haunts the European mind," said Anderson, is the creation of those "to whose minds the intelligent self-restraint born of an educated conscience is a stranger."[13]

Education, then, broadly conceived as education in Christian morality, stood next to preaching the Gospel itself as an answer to new industrial and urban problems.[14] At the time, it appeared that evangelicalism was still dominant in the American schools. Public schools used texts like *McGuffey's Readers,* which warned against hard drink, lauded the values of the Bible, the rewards of Sabbath keeping, and hard work, and above all stressed that virtue would be rewarded. The same lessons were taught in colleges; indeed, it was still true that the presidents of most colleges were ordained clergymen.[15] In the 1870s the revolutionary trend toward universities, elective courses, separation of the disciplines, and academic freedom (on the premise that there might be more than one variety of truth) was just beginning.[16] For Victorian evangelicals, orthodox piety and theological dogmatism,[17] combined with a classical curriculum, still provided the basis for an education that would sustain a stable civilization.

This old order correlated faith, learning, and morality with the welfare of civilization. Two premises were absolutely fundamental—that God's truth was a single unified order and that all persons of common sense were capable of knowing that truth. The implications of these assumptions were carefully worked out by the philosophical school known as Scottish Common Sense Realism. In 1870 Common Sense philosophy had been influential in America for a century, and for the past half-century it had been the dominant philosophy taught in American colleges. In spite of competition from various forms of Romantic Idealism, Common Sense Realism remained unquestionably *the* American philosophy.[18]

Common Sense philosophy was marvellously well suited to the prevailing ideals of American culture. This was not entirely accidental since the American nation and Scottish Realism both took shape in the mid-1700s. This philosophy was above all democratic or anti-elitist. Common Sense said that the human mind was so constructed that we can know the real world directly. Some philosophers, particularly those following John Locke, had made our knowledge seem more complicated by interposing "ideas" between us and the real world. These ideas, they said, were the immediate objects of our thought; hence we do not apprehend external things directly, but only through ideas of them in our minds. David Hume raised the question of how we can know that these ideas correspond to what is actually there. The answer of Thomas Reid, the principal formulator of the Scottish Common Sense philosophy, was akin to Samuel Johnson's kicking a rock to refute a similar theory proposed by Bishop Berkeley. Reid said that only philosophers would take this skeptical doctrine seriously with its absurd implications. Everyone in his senses believes such truths as the existence of the real world, cause and effect, and the continuity of the self. The ability to know such things was as natural as the ability to breathe air. If philosophers questioned such truths, so much the worse for philosophers. The common sense of mankind, whether of the man behind the plow or the man behind the desk, was the surest guide to truth. The democratic implications are obvious. In anti-elitist eighteenth-century America "common sense" became a revolutionary watchword. As Thomas Jefferson recognized, it provided one basis for a new democratic and republican order for the ages.[19]

Common Sense philosophy continued to appeal to Americans into the nineteenth century also because it provided a firm foundation for a scientific approach to reality. In a nation born during the Enlightenment, the reverence for science as the way to understand all aspects of reality was nearly unbounded. Evangelical Christians and liberal Enlightment figures alike assumed that the universe was governed by a rational system of laws guaranteed by an all-wise and benevolent creator. The function of science was to discover such laws, something like Newton's laws of physics, which were assumed to exist in all areas. By asserting that the external world was in fact just as it appeared to be, Common Sense provided a rock upon which to build this empirical structure.

At the same time, a great number of American thinkers, following the suggestion of Thomas Reid, believed that the inductive scientific method of seventeenth-century philosopher Francis Bacon was the one sure way to build on this common sense foundation. Bacon's name inspired in Americans an almost reverential respect for the certainty of the knowledge achieved by careful and objective observation of the facts known to common sense. Whether the subject was theology or geology, the scientist need only classify these certainties, avoiding speculative hypotheses.[20]

Common Sense and empiricism provided the new nation with a basis for establishing a national moral order. The evangelical educators had taken the lead in shaping the opinions of the nation. The Bible, of course, revealed the moral law; but the faculty of common sense, which agreed with Scripture, was a universal standard. According to Common Sense philosophy, one can intuitively know the first principles of morality as certainly as one can apprehend other essential aspects of reality. "God has created everything double: a world without us, and a correspondent world within us," said the eminent textbook author Francis Wayland in a representative Common

Sense formulation. "He has made light without, and the eye within; moral qualities in actions, and conscience to judge of them; and so in every other case." On the foundation of certain knowledge of first moral principles, one could through Baconian induction arrive at authoritative conclusions concerning moral, political, and economic laws. "An order of sequence once discovered in morals," Wayland affirmed, "is just as invariable as an order of sequence in physics."[21] On this basis, college presidents such as Hopkins, Anderson, or Wayland himself could with assurance point the way for Christian civilization.

The essentially optimistic view of human nature implicit in Common Sense philosophy appealed to the American temper.[22] Although there was still room for the Calvinist and evangelical dogma that all people were born sinners, the belief that all were endowed with the potential to know God's truth was more conspicuous. Strict Calvinists had maintained that the human mind was blinded in mankind's Fall from innocence; in the Common Sense version, the intellect seemed to suffer from a slight astigmatism only. Moreover, one of the first dictates of Common Sense philosophy was that individuals were moral agents capable of free choice. These premises—which were essential to the economic, political, and religious individualism so widespread in America—were at odds with traditional views of determinism and depravity. The strict Calvinists, however, had long been able to effect some sort of reconciliation between determinism and the experience of freedom and were not to be deterred from employing a philosophy that offered so much support in other areas.[23]

Most importantly, this Common Sense account of reality was considered to provide a sure base for the rational and scientific confirmation of the truths of the Bible and the Christian faith. The Bible, it was constantly asserted, was the highest and all-sufficient source of authority. Indeed in America the Bible was the primary source for many of the ideals that shaped the culture. The Protestant doctrine of the perspicuity of Scripture provided a further basis for the belief that the common person could readily understand Biblical teaching. Common Sense paralleled this doctrine with its insistence on the perspicuity of nature.[24] In an age that reverenced science, it was essential that this confidence in Scripture not be based on blind faith alone. God's truth was unified, so it was inevitable that science would confirm Scripture. Evangelical colleges still used the texts and arguments of Bishop Joseph Butler, *Analogy of Religion Natural and Revealed to the Constitution and Course of Nature* (1736), and William Paley, *Natural Theology* (1802), to demonstrate the truth of Christianity. No honest inquirer, the evangelical apologists asserted, if true to his own experience, could finally doubt the arguments when they were properly understood. Over and above the evidence of design in nature, there were simply too many parallels between the laws of civilization as discovered by impartial science and the teaching of the Bible to leave room for reasonable doubt. "Faith," said Mark

Hopkins, "—that is, the faith of the New Testament—is not simple belief. It is confidence in a person, and that confidence is never given except on rational grounds."[25]

The old order of American Protestantism was based on the interrelationship of faith, science, the Bible, morality, and civilization. It was about to crumble. In 1869 Oliver Wendell Holmes, Sr. (who moved in sophisticated Unitarim circles in Boston) predicted the impending catastrophe. The collapse would not be as dramatic, however, as that of Holmes's famous "one hoss shay." Too many vested interests of the churches and indeed of civilization itself, he observed privately, rested on evangelical "idolatry and bibliolatry" for these to be removed "all at once as the magnetic mountain drew the nails and bolts of Sinbad's ship. . . ." Churchmen could hardly be expected to admit the implications of the new views frankly. Yet Holmes was convinced that a vital part of the whole structure was about to be removed. The Bible could no longer stand up to scientific standards. Without that, little would remain that was distinctly evangelical. "The turth is staring the Christian world in the face, that the stories of the old Hebrew books cannot be taken as literal statements of fact."[26]

In the 1870s evangelicals frequently commented to each other on the seriousness of the new threats, though they did not share Holmes's conclusions. "Infidel bugles are sounding in front of us, Papal bugles are sounding behind us," declared Professor Roswell Hitchcock at the Evangelical Alliance in 1873. "It would be idle to say," he confessed, "that we are not alarmed."[27] "At no time," wrote W. A. Stearns, President of Amherst College, in a similar context, has Christianity "been assaulted with such variety and persistency of argument for its overthrow as during the hundred years just passed." Yet it seemed that whenever evangelical leaders voiced such concern they followed with declarations of confidence that those who had nearly driven out the skepticism, atheism, and even the Deism of the Enlightenment from American public life could still look to new victories. "Never since the crucifixion," Stearns continued, "has the religion of Christ, in its purest forms had a stronger hold on the popular heart than at this day."[28] This kind of assurance was unmistakably the prevailing note at the Evangelical Alliance. Unity, of course, said Alliance speakers, was necessary for continued advance, but by working together they could surely expect to "lift up among all people a victorious standard in the face of modern skepticism, rationalism, the claims of the Papacy, and every other false system."[29]

The seriousness of the danger of skepticism and rationalism was portrayed vividly to Americans by the delegates from continental Europe, where higher critical views of Scripture were already far advanced. The European evangelicals most frequently attacked the Biblical criticism of F. C. Baur and the Tübingen school in Germany and the radical questioning of the historicity of the Gospel accounts of the life of Jesus by D. F. Strauss in Germany and

J. E. Renan in France. A Dutch report on "The Religious Condition of Holland" referred to the exponents of higher criticism in his country as "our enemies" and a report on "Christian Life in Germany" deplored "the critical and speculative rationalism," but assured the Americans that "wherever it pronounces its doctrines, opposition is not wanting." Theodor Christlieb, also a German representative, spoke of concentrating on the defense of "the fundamentals of the faith," likening the doctrine of the supernatural redemption and atonement by Christ to a "fortress" or "citadel" surrounded by "its moat . . . the doctrine of the Holy Scripture."[30]

The American spokesmen, who at this time knew higher criticism chiefly as news from abroad, had not yet developed this fortress mentality. Rather they assessed their strength in remarkably chauvinistic and self-confident terms. Referring to the Great Awakening, which he viewed as the unifying spiritual force leading to the American Revolution, President William F. Warren of Boston University told the Evangelical Alliance that "toward the middle of the last century came the fullness of God's time for generating a new Christian nationality." America had seen various forms of infidelity, such as that of Thomas Jefferson, Thomas Cooper, and Thomas Paine, known as the "three doubting Thomases," and then more recently Transcendentalism, Owenist socialism, Spiritualism, and phrenology, but "none of them were of American origin." The old idea of American innocence versus European corruption still seemed plausible. "Thus all these threatening surges of Antichristian thought," Warren told the international audience, "have come to us from European seas; not one arose in our own hemisphere." Infidelity had never taken root in America, and Warren could confidently claim that "in all the ranks of American unbelievers the Christian apologist of learning and ability can nowhere find a foeman worthy of his steel."[31]

This lionhearted rhetoric, however, was contradicted by evidence of the beginnings of evangelical disarray over the question of Darwinism. A series of addresses on that subject in the "philosophical section" of the sessions on "Christianity and Its Antagonists" generated enough controversy to raise unscheduled debate from the floor at the 1873 meeting of the Alliance. This debate anticipated in microcosm the heated controversy that would soon break out among American evangelicals.

An attempt to reconcile Darwinism and the Bible, presented by the Reverend James McCosh, President of the College of New Jersey (Princeton), sparked the floor debate. McCosh's position was particularly important because he had an international reputation as a Scottish Common Sense philosopher. In 1868 he came from Scotland to Princeton and became America's greatest (indeed its last great) exponent of that philosophy. In line with the basic premises of Common Sense, McCosh insisted that it was impossible seriously to deny that there was a God who had created human beings. "Common-sense turns away from it. Philosophy declares that this would be an effect without a cause adequate to prove it." McCosh thought, however, that evolution and Christianity could be reconciled without violating this principle. Science and Scripture, he said, are parallel and mutually confirmatory revelations. "Both reveal order in the world; the one appointed by God; the other discovered by man." Evolution therefore does not pose a serious threat to faith. "Those who view development in the proper light see in it only a form or manifestation of law."[32]

McCosh had conceded too much for some. The Reverend George W. Weldon of London took the floor and declared that although "as Bishop Butler says, we do not know the whole of the case" and although the Bible was not designed to teach science, nevertheless the choice was clear. "If man is sprung from primeval matter, he can not be the man spoken of in Genesis." The two visions were irreconcilable. Another Englishman, a botanist, took the floor and declared that at least with respect to plants Darwin's theory was a good working hypothesis. He then demonstrated his Christian orthodoxy by reciting the headings of the Westminster Shorter Catechism. He did not believe literally, however, "'that God created all things out of nothing in the space of six days.'" This brought Charles Hodge of Princeton Theological Seminary, a venerable Presbyterian warrior, to his feet. The basic issue is a simple one, he said, in a summary of his classic formulation of the conservative position, which would be published in *What is Darwinism?* the following year. "Is development an intellectual process guided by God, or is it a blind process of unintelligible, unconscious force, which knows no end and adopts no means?" The supernaturalism of the Biblical view, Hodge was convinced, was utterly incompatible with the naturalism that he saw as essential to Darwin's position.

The debate continued as other papers were presented. A Princeton College professor produced elaborate charts showing parallels between the discoveries of science and the order of the six "days" of the first chapter of Genesis. He held, as did many conservative evangelicals, that in Hebrew "days" could refer to an indefinite period of time. A missionary from China volunteered that he had been studying comparative religions for twenty-five years and that all these religions showed remarkable parallels to Christianity. This fact, he said, should do much to "strengthen the scientific proof of the Scripture doctrine of the common origin of mankind."

Finally President Anderson of the University of Rochester offered to summarize the issue in a speech which the conference unanimously requested be published with the other Alliance documents. Anderson pointed out in answer to Hodge that the term "evolution" could be used in two different ways—either as God's method of development or as pure chance. Christians could accept only the former. Distinguishing his view from that of McCosh (and in terms that would be repeated by fundamentalists many years later) he said that evolution was not a "verified law," but an "unverified working hypothesis." This observation was based on the principles of "Baconian" science that still prevailed in much American evangelical and scientific thought. "Positive science," said Anderson, "claims to be conversant only with ascertained facts and verified laws." The demand to confine science to rigorous observation of facts and demonstration of laws precluded the acceptance of speculations as scientific conclusions. "Hypotheses, or guesses, are all but indispensable for the direction of research in scientific inquiry; but such hypotheses are not science."[33]

Almost all the basic lines of argument had been presented, but the issue was far from settled. The implications of Darwin's theory, particularly concerning impersonal natural process as opposed to divinely guided order, went far beyond biology. The new Biblical criticism which gave naturalistic historical explanations of cultural development was based on virtually the same assumptions. So was the new scientific social thought. The old scientific theology could not simply incorporate the conclusions of the new science into its body of beliefs. For over a century its proponents had reconciled themselves to the results of the first scientific revolution (associated with Bacon and Newton) by doing just that—adding new scientific discoveries to their beliefs and interpreting them as more evidence for the argument from design.[34] At least since Jonathan Edwards, American theologians had not challenged the fundamental assumption of scientific inquiry—that truth was reliably discovered by objective examination of the facts that nature presented. The Common Sense philosophy supported a version of just such an approach. Science had been allowed to operate on a naturalistic basis free from theological assumptions, except for the assumption that objective investigation of nature would confirm what was revealed in Scripture.[35]

When Darwinism brought about the second scientific revolution, evangelicals who had adopted this method of reconciling science and religion were faced with a dilemma. If they kept their commitment to autonomous scientific inquiry now, the very foundations of theistic and Christian belief seemed to be threatened. Moderates such as McCosh attempted to steer a middle course. For most educated American evangelicals, however, the commitment both to objective science and to religion was so strong, and the conflict so severe, that they were forced into one of two extreme positions. They could choose to say with Hodge that Darwinism was irreconcilable with Christianity—a new form of infidelity—and that it was speculative and hypothetical rather than truly scientific. The alternative solution was a redefinition of the relationship between science and religion. The basis for this redefinition was already well developed in the philosophical tradition of Kant and German Idealism and in the theological work of Friedrich Schleiermacher and Albrecht Ritschl. Religion would no longer be seen as dependent on historical or scientific fact susceptible of objective inquiry; religion had to do with the spiritual, with the heart, with religious experience, and with moral sense or moral action—areas not open to scientific investigation. Thus science could have its autonomy, and religion would be beyond its reach. Since mid-century some American evangelical theologians, especially in New England, had been moving in this direction under the influence of romanticism and Idealism. This solution also appealed to the strong sentiment and moralism of American Protestantism.

At the Evangelical Alliance meeting of 1873, the new direction was suggested by the most popular American preacher of the day, Henry Ward Beecher. Urging that American preaching should strive for such unassailable sentimental goals as "to inspire men with an idea of manhood," and to kindle the "nobility of a heart opened when God has touched it," the famed Brooklyn preacher had discovered a formula that would for many years allay the fears of respectable evangelical Americans concerning the new science and learning. "While we are taught," said Beecher, "by the scientists in truths that belong to the sensual nature, while we are taught by the economists of things that belong to the social nature, we need the Christian ministry to teach us those things which are invisible."[36]

II. The Paths Diverge

PROLOGUE: THE VICTORIAN SETTING

The people facing this crisis were "Victorians."[1] Their culture was dominated by a Protestant middle class which combined an at least formal reverence for their religious heritage with a deep concern for morality, respectability, and order. The leaders of this culture believed that they had a mission among the poor at home and among the heathen abroad (in the words of President McKinley) to "uplift and Christianize." The Victorians placed great value on both rationality and sentiment. Their era, characterized by the desire for order in society, was a technological one—an age of statistics, standardization, professionalism, specialization, and tremendous industrial expansion. It was an age of print, a medium well suited to preserving the interests of permanent order. Yet it was also an age of emotion and romantic sentiments. Victorians loved their orators, especially those who could make them weep.[2]

Change was rapid and doubtless often disconcerting. The social changes were the most dramatic. America was changing rapidly from a culture dominated by small towns and the countryside to one shaped by cities and suburbs. Waves of "uprooted" immigrants, together with rapid industrialization, created virtually insurmountable urban problems. Industrialization, with the drive for efficiency usually overcoming traditional moral restraints, created ethical, social, labor, and political problems beyond the capacities of traditional solutions. The characteristic response in America was neither panic nor rigid conservatism. The response might best be characterized as "innovative conservatism." Among the captains of religion as well as the captains of industry, creative leaders substantially altered aspects of the old order, but always with the stated goal of preserving its essence.

HENRY WARD BEECHER AND
A NEW AMERICAN THEOLOGY

In the 1870s New England still dominated the councils of American Protestantism. Almost every theologian or churchman of any standing had been born in New England, educated in New England, or himself taught in New England. Only the theological school at Princeton, the bastion of conservative or "Old School" Presbyterianism, could compete in reputation with the New England tradition. The Civil War left the Southern theologians, who had often stood close to Princeton, isolated and without national influence. At the same time, the war enhanced the already considerable New England prestige and cultural leadership. The "Yankee" war, with its extravagant worship of the Northern concept of the Union, encouraged continued reverence for the prophets of the New England religious establishment.

Henry Ward Beecher (1813–1887) was the heir to all the sentiment, enthusiasm, and veneration bestowed by Americans on this victorious and Victorian Yankee evangelical tradition. His father was Lyman Beecher, an early (moderate) evangelical exponent of anti-slavery and "New England theology." Henry Ward himself had championed abolition (though perhaps inconsistently). Indeed, as one of Harriet Beecher Stowe's several activist brothers, he could be said to be part of the first family of the Christian Northern cause. He was famous in his own right as a man of eloquence and high ideals. He was widely considered the best preacher of the age and was a front-runner for chief patriot; in his orations he skillfully equated Christian redemptive meaning with the spirit of the Union.[3] Even after 1874, when in a sensational trial he was accused of committing adultery with one of his parishioners (his defense was sustained by a divided jury), Beecher continued to be seen almost as a national saint. This veneration is a measure of the degree to which his message had captured the spirit of much of the popular Protestantism of the time.[4]

Henry Ward Beecher exemplified a progressive spirit, by the end of his career defined as "liberal." Theological "liberalism" at this early stage, it is important to note, lacked almost all the social emphases that it would take on in the twentieth century.[5] Like the older "liberalism" in Unitarian Boston, progressive religion appealed primarily to the prosperous middle class and tended to endorse its social elitism.[6] As William McLoughlin points out, Beecher's message was aimed at relieving the anxieties of his affluent Brooklyn suburbanite audience, who sensed a conflict between their new wealth and the stern Puritan morality in which they had been raised. Beecher, like all the popular preachers of the era, preached a gospel of virtuous wealth as a commendable moral example to the poor.[7] He also provided relief from traditional Calvinist theological anxieties with a gentle liberalism that gradually unfolded as his sensibilities developed along with those of his national audience.

Henry Ward Beecher was not a theologian. Although he was well informed, he claimed he "never read a book through"[8]—presumably with the exception of those he wrote. He was not altogether consistent as a thinker and, in Paul Carter's marvellous phrase, preached "charity at the price of clarity."[9] Much of his ambiguity, however, apparently was intentional. The aspects of his father's New England Calvinism that Henry Ward Beecher rejected were those based on "abstract truth."[10] The moral government of God, God's relationship to humans, and the nature of religious experience had all been reduced to clear propositions through Common Sense and Baconian analysis. Popular as these Enlightenment views remained in American theology, they were out of style in the more advanced "culture." The sophisticated literary and intellectual community in America revered the purely romantic ideals revealed in Nature (always capitalized): truths of the heart, sentiment, "imagination," and "sublimity."[11] The vogue of Transcendentalism among the literary elite and its continued attractiveness to the young provided a further impulse to bring evangelical religion into harmony with the standards of the best society.[12] Beecher was acutely aware of this cultural gap and struggled to bridge it both for himself and for his parishioners. In Beecher's only novel, *Norwood* (1867), the village champion of romanticism says to a New England cleric:

> A truth which does not admit of a logical statement seems to you a phantasy. You believe not upon any evidence of your spirit but upon the semi-material form which language and philosophical statements give to thought.[13]

Beecher's romanticism softened the implications of traditional doctrines without denying them altogether. Thus, for example, with respect to "Future Punishment," the subject of the most heated theological debates in the Civil War era, Beecher began an 1870 sermon with the assertion that the Bible "employs not the scientific reason, but imagination and the reason under it." Imagination, central to faith, discerns "clearly invisible truth in distinction from material and sensuous truth." The idea of eternal punishment for all who do not know Christ, accordingly, makes us "shiver and tremble with sensibility." Such sensibilities accounted for the move away from the "medieval literalization" of the doctrine. Nevertheless, Beecher did not shock his audience and deny this doctrine. "I must preach it," he says with apparent sincerity, even though "it makes me sick." It is a "great element of moral government." No one else, however, he hastens to add, need accept this view. "We are to be utterly tolerant of those who have adopted other theories; . . .

we are neither to disown them as Christians, nor to discipline them for believing as they do—the day has gone by when a man is to be disciplined for his honest belief. . . ."[14]

Beecher used romanticism in similar fashion in the service of science. By 1885 he was sufficiently freed from denominational inhibitions to publish *Evolution and Religion,* "which," says Frank Hugh Foster, the historian of New England liberalism, "was the first avowed and complete adoption of evolution in its full extent among our theologians."[15] Beecher characteristically mixed tradition with romanticism in his defense of the new. He spoke of "two revelations," suggesting the traditional distinction between the complementary and harmonious revelations in Scripture and nature. But the terms were romanticized. The revelation he placed alongside God's record in nature was not Scripture alone but the far broader "record of the unfolding of *man* and of the race under the inspiration of God's nature." The "sublime history of God as an engineer and architect and as a master-builder" could be seen in material creation. The "master builder" suggested traditional theistic evidences, yet "sublime" lifted them beyond scientific inquiry. Even with regard to evolution, there was no need to worry about the crucial question of human origins. "Whatever may have been the origin," Beecher insisted, "it does not change either the destiny or the moral grandeur of man as he stands in the full light of civilization today."[16]

Beecher saw the progress in science and morality as the coming of the Kingdom of God. Addressing his defense of evolution "to all those clergymen who are standing tremulous on the edge of fear in regard to the great advance that God is making today," he explicitly equated the Biblical injunction to "be sure to meet the Lord when he comes in the air" with willingness to see God's coming "when He is at work in natural laws, when He is living in philosophical atmospheres, when He is shining in great scientific disclosures, when He is teaching the human consciousness all around. . . ."[17]

Several tendencies of emerging American religious liberalism can be seen here. First, the progress of the Kingdom of God is identified with the progress of civilization, especially in science and morality. Second, morality has become the essence of religion and is indeed virtually equated with it. Third, the supernatural is no longer clearly separated from the natural, but rather manifests itself only in the natural.

Beecher's religion frankly interpreted God through human experiences. "The only part of the Divine nature that we can understand," he told Yale divinity students in 1871, "is that which corresponds to ourselves." If we are to further God's moral government, we must "comprehend that on which God's moral government itself stands, which is human nature." Beecher advocated a *"Life School"* of preaching which would "understand *men*" as opposed to creeds and traditions. Even Scripture should be subordinated to the authority of the modern age. The oaks of civilization, said Beecher, had evolved since Biblical times. Should we then "go back and talk about acorns?"[18]

It would be some time before the professional theologians caught up with Henry Ward Beecher. A popularizer who gloried in ambiguity and sentiment, he could move much more quickly than professional academics. Ambiguity and sentiment were difficult to try for heresy and, in any case, no ecclesiastical body had greater prestige than Beecher himself had. He could rise above church trials, as he did in the 1880s by simply leaving the Congregational Associations when there were rumors of charges against him. Professional theologians, on the other hand, were bound by their denominations and the theological schools that hired them and these in turn were usually committed to official creeds and vows to combat heresy. A great deal of caution and discretion was therefore necessary in order successfully to introduce the new views.

Thus the intellectual revolution was a relatively quiet one. Nonetheless, Frank Hugh Foster, who lived through and wrote about the era in which theological liberalism emerged in New England, indicated how rapid the transition could be. In his opinion, 1877 was the turning point. In that year there was among Congregationalists a minor flurry over future punishment. This controversy, like many that had preceded it, reflected efforts to tone down some of the harsh conclusions of Calvinism without abandoning its main assumptions. Yet it set off a change in the whole atmosphere within the next ten years. The most dramatic evidence of this change was the bloodless revolution at Andover Theological Seminary. Between 1879 and 1882, Edwards A. Park and two others of the "old faculty" at Andover retired, occasioning an almost immediate shift at the school toward the new liberal trends. By 1886 the new faculty had made enough departures to collect and publish a volume, *Progressive Orthodoxy*. The title itself reveals much about this early stage of liberalism. Their purpose clearly was to preserve the essentials of evangelicalism, not to destroy them. The "real issue," they said, "is between Christianity as a supernatural redemption and a mere naturalism." The actual doctrines they proposed, moreover, were Christocentric and in many respects orthodox. Yet a progressive principle was unmistakably present as well. Theology was no longer viewed as a fixed body of eternally valid truths. It was seen rather as an evolutionary development that should adjust to the standards and needs of modern culture.[19]

That the "New Theology" should spread so rapidly during the 1880s and 1890s into many strongholds of American Protestantism suggests that the walls of the old-style orthodoxy, so strong in appearance as late as the 1870s, had in fact restrained a flood of new views that had been gathering for some time. Gradual modifications in the content of the prevailing American theology together with inconspicuous shifts from Common Sense to Idealism had been feeding a rising tide of change. But the real waves came from abroad and by the time they hit America their full force had developed.

Three strong concussions were felt almost simultaneously—evolutionary naturalism, higher criticism of the Bible, and the newer Idealistic philosophy and theology. The first two did not immediately create a national theological crisis largely because the third seemed to provide a counterforce against the most destructive effects of the others.

The Idealism of the New Theology answered naturalism and higher criticism in two steps. One was by merging the supernatural with the natural, so that the supernatural was seen only through the natural. Simultaneously, however, Idealism posited a strong dualism between the material world, known through science and logic, and the spiritual world, known by intuition and sensitivity. As Newman Smyth, one of the earliest New England spokesmen for the New Theology, put it, there is an essential "dualism which exists in the constitution of nature. There are two kinds of force, two lines of law, two orders of development, two processes of evolution—body and mind, nature and spirit, earth and heaven." God, although seen everywhere, is spirit and thus beyond the reach of natural science. "The science of the senses may knock in vain for this truth to be opened to it, but the poet finds it revealed wherever he looks."[20]

As Henry Ward Beecher was already pointing out, such dualism (in addition to its apologetic value) could be made quite palatable to the Victorian religious disposition. First, while not challenging the sanctity of natural science, it appealed to a strain of moderate anti-intellectualism relying on religious experience, sentiment, and sublimity, as opposed to the seemingly cold rigor of the intellectualism of the old theology. Second, and probably more important, it had a clear moral application. New Testament texts that opposed "flesh" to "spirit" could be interpreted in terms of lower animality versus higher religious qualities. As Paul Carter asserts, Darwinism simply reinforced the idea of sin as connected to animality. Christian belief was the highest stage in human evolution, overcoming the original, lower, animal nature. "Every man falls when, by yielding to the enticements of his lower, animal nature, he descends from his vantage ground of moral consciousness to the earthiness out of which he had begun to emerge," wrote Beecher's spiritual successor, Lyman Abbott, in 1892. As Carter observes, this is not far from the popular YMCA hymn of the era, "Yield not to temptation. . . . Dark passions subdue."[21] The evangelical tradition had long been strong on the condemnation of the appetites of the flesh—with alcohol and sex seen as the chief temptations. In the pulpit, liberals could not easily be distinguished from conservatives on such practical points, and practical morality was often for American Protestants what mattered most. Phillips Brooks, Beecher's only clerical peer in eloquence and fame, summarized this main emphasis in a sermon which reconciled evolution, competitive individualism, and the ethics of Jesus. In answer to the question "What do you need?" he said simply, "Go and be moral. Go and be good."[22]

2. THE BLANCHARDS OF WHEATON:
FROM EVANGELICALISM TO FUNDAMENTALISM

Many years later, in the mid-1920s, Charles Blanchard, the aging president of Wheaton College in Illinois, reflected on his long experience in an era of remarkable change. He expounded some general principles that had guided him. "We are not required to explain the universe," he remarked near the beginning of the autobiography he would never complete, "but we are required to live in it according to the plan of God." Our duty, he advised, is "not to waste time in trying to find out *how* things come to be as they are, but to improve the time by seeking to live under present circumstances *as we ought.*"[23] In pointing to the moral imperative as the first principle in responding to the intellectual challenges of the era, Blanchard drew on an enduring theme in American evangelicalism. Indeed, it was also a major element in his own family history. Nearly a century earlier, in 1839, Blanchard's father, Jonathan, then a leading young spokesman for abolition, delivered the commencement address at the radical Oberlin College, where Charles G. Finney was president. Finney was noted for attacking academic institutions that "give young men intellectual strength, to the almost entire neglect of cultivating their moral feelings."[24] Jonathan Blanchard, like Finney, had great respect for learning directed toward moral ends. "The perfect state of society," he said, will approach "as knowledge and piety advance." Morality was the goal, "exterminating sin in all its burrows." "Society is perfect," his address concluded, "where what is right in theory exists in fact; where practice coincides with principle, and the law of God is the law of the land."[25]

There had been some shift of emphasis in the rigorous moral stance between the nineteenth century and the twentieth century Blanchard statements. Most notably, Jonathan Blanchard's proposals for reforming society were essentially optimistic. They were "postmillennial," assuming spiritual and cultural progress amounting to a millennium, after which Christ would return. Blanchard's son Charles had turned to premillennialism, seeing little hope for society before Christ returned to set up his kingdom. The gradual transitions of their respective moral views reflects an important continuity of fundamentalism with its evangelical heritage.

Jonathan Blanchard (1811–1892) was a product of the same tradition of New England evangelicalism that fostered theological liberalism. Born in New England, he attended Andover Seminary. In the mid-1830s, inspired by Theodore Dwight Weld, he became an anti-slavery lecturer—then a dangerous business. Unpopularity and physical threats only increased his conviction that the cause was morally right. In 1837 Blanchard moved to Cincinnati to complete his theological training at Lane Seminary, where Lyman Beecher was president. During the next eight years in Cincinnati, Blanchard became pastor of a sizable New School Presbyterian church (then closely allied with his native Congregationalism), helped found the anti-slavery Liberty Party, and was appointed a representative to the World's Peace Convention, held in London in 1843. During these years the Blanchards were close friends of the Beechers. Lyman Beecher preached at Jonathan Blanchard's ordination and a few days later both, together with Calvin Stowe, presided at the ordination of Lyman's talented son, Henry Ward.[26]

In 1845 Blanchard became president of Knox College in Galesburg, Illinois. He was typical of the old-time college presidents. He built the fledgling college into a flourishing institution. He was, however, notorious for his refusal to compromise on any moral point. His initial move to Galesburg was delayed three weeks when he had his family and all his possessions unloaded on the banks of the Mississippi rather than continue during a Sabbath a journey on a riverboat that was behind schedule because of bad weather. In Galesburg the apocryphal story circulated that he had stood in front of one of the first Sunday trains and told the engineer to go back to the roundhouse, upon which the engineer returned the sentiment, suggesting a warmer destination. Blanchard engaged in serious controversy with local Masons and liquor interests, whom he considered to be allied. His career at Galesburg ended in a conflict with some of the Presbyterian founders of Knox, in which another of Lyman Beecher's sons, Edward, was one of Blanchard's chief supporters. After refusing a number of similar positions, in 1860 Blanchard became president of The Illinois Institute in Wheaton, a college of Wesleyan background that turned to Blanchard for more Congregational support.[27]

Blanchard's policies at both Knox and Wheaton were based on the prevailing convictions about the necessary interrelationship of reason and morality. Right thinking led to right living. The task of education was therefore a moral one. "In the moral conflict of the world," he declared in his inaugural address at Knox, "institutions of learning are the forts."[28]

Blanchard's assumptions, grounded in Scottish Common Sense,[29] were that God had built into the universe a system of law, essentially moral law, and had created the minds of people so that reason and moral sense could apprehend that law. The millennium would occur when the inhabitants of a society recognized, and freely obeyed, this law. "'The kingdom of God,'" he said at Knox, "is simply: Christ ruling in and over rational creatures who are obeying him freely and from choice, under no constraint but that of life."[30] Opposing the way of the kingdom were vices, superstitions, and false religions. These morally, intellectually, or spiritually blinded one to true moral duty.[31]

In 1860 Jonathan Blanchard was still very much in the mainstream of American evangelicalism. With the end of the Civil War, however, that mainstream diverged into two distinct branches. While Henry Ward Beecher represented those who continued to adjust the religion to the tenor of the new age, Blanchard in the last thirty years of his life represented those who attempted to hold firm to standards drawn from the evangelicalism of the ante-bellum era.

Victory in the Civil War had virtually put out of business the old national coalition for reform which had united against slavery. Although the old reformers were feted, there was a sense of weariness with strenuous reform efforts. Jonathan Blanchard, however, was undaunted by the mood of the Gilded Age. With the slavery question settled, he simply turned to old business. The anti-Masonic movement had been a major reform and political movement before anti-slavery overshadowed it in the 1830s. Now it resumed its place at the top of Blanchard's list of crusades. Enlisting Charles Finney in the cause,[32] he followed the pattern that had led to anti-slavery's success. He founded the National Christian Association in 1868, sent out teams of lecturers, held regular conventions, and wrote constantly against secret societies in the *Christian Cynosure*. In 1880 Blanchard even ran for President for "The American Party," following the model of the old Liberty Party. The widespread opposition he encountered Blanchard took to be evidence of the similarities of the two causes.[33] At the point of small beginnings, high hopes, and strong opposition, however, the similarities between the two movements ceased.

Fighting Freemasonry was an unpopular business in the era after the Civil War. It meant attacking a powerful institution of strong loyalties, made up of many of the most influential business, political, and professional leaders in American society.[34] For Wheaton College it meant much opposition. During the last third of the century most other American colleges shed their controversial prophetic and reforming stances. Knox, for instance, had a Mason as president, had Greek-letter fraternities, and gradually dropped its tight religious restrictions. Wheaton, on the other hand, increasingly found its identity by fighting against the mainstream.[35]

These fights were simultaneously conservative and radical. Blanchard, who had by now been joined in his campaigns by his son Charles, believed that America was a "Christian nation" and worked for a Christian amendment to the Constitution.[36] Their concepts of Christian ideals, however, showed little regard for prevailing middle-class standards. The 1874 platform of the National Christian Association included recognition of Christianity in the United States Constitution, Sabbath and prohibition laws, outlawing secret lodges, preservation of the "civil equality secured to all American citizens by articles 13th, 14th, and 15th of our amended Constitution," international arbitration for peace, that "land and other monopolies be discountenanced," "justice to Indians," abolition of the Electoral Colleges, and election of President and Vice President by direct vote of the people.[37] While there was a note of hopefulness in presenting these programs, they were all issues whose time had not yet come, or had already passed.

The resulting perception that society was in rebellion against God involved a sense of theological as well as moral decline. The two always went together. *The Christian Cynosure,* accordingly, never hesitated to put truth before friendship and was in the forefront of those warning of doctrinal laxity among Congregationalists.[38] Henry Ward Beecher was a special target for attack. "I loved him as a brother," wrote Jonathan Blanchard. Now, however, he viewed Beecher as a full-fledged hypocrite. Ever since the days of anti-slavery and temperance campaigns, said Blanchard, Beecher had been ready to say one thing on one occasion and the opposite on the next. In 1872, two years before the Beecher scandal, Blanchard described the Brooklyn pastor as "a crafty leader of degeneracy and corruption," and asserted that "the American churches have drunk and are still drinking the poison of his teachings. . . ." "If Mr. Beecher's teachings are the gospel of Christ, what need had Christ to be crucified." When an Oberlin, Ohio, newspaper objected to his contentiousness, Blanchard responded by attacking Beecher in even stronger terms (". . . dealing out the love of Christ to sinners with the indiscriminate fondness of a successful prostitute who loves everybody who does not condemn her trade. . . ."), and also by attacking Beecher's illustrious sister, Harriet. Harriet, he said, was "sneering the doctrine of human depravity . . . out of good society . . . while she is holding up the worn garments of her Puritan ancestors till her readers see nothing but '*the holes in their coats*'. . . ." Henry Beecher did much the same thing. "When he is about to assail some fundamental truth, held and suffered for by the Puritans, he always begins by proclaiming himself their descendant." Beecher was "preaching Scripture like Satan, and, like Satan, defeating its practical intent." He and his sister had forgotten the lesson: "'Ye adulterers and adulteresses, know ye not that the friendship of the world is enmity with God?'"[39] Such language left little between the Blanchards and the Beechers of the old New England reforming alliance.[40] In fact, Blanchard was finding New England Congregationalists increasingly reluctant to support his efforts.

New patterns of alliance began to emerge, and were apparent by the end of the 1870s. The closest affinities of the Blanchards had always been with the revivalists who preached a fundamental gospel message of sin, conversion, and a holy life. With these tendencies, it was almost inevitable that the Blanchards would come into the orbit of Dwight L. Moody, who was then forging a new revivalism. Moody's immense success sparked new hopes for revitalizing the heritage. When the evangelist's first triumphant national tour brought him to Chicago in 1876, Jonathan Blanchard took part in the dedicatory services and continued thereafter to give him enthusiastic support in the *Christian Cynosure.*

Significantly, Blanchard even reprinted in the *Cynosure* Moody's sermons on the premillennial return of Christ and editorially emphasized the points on which postmillennialists and premillennialists could agree. Moody, he was pleased to observe, had "no definite theory drawn out in detail." Clearly Blanchard was softening his old postmillennial stance. In 1881 he attended Moody's annual Northfield conference; but when asked to present the post-millennial theory of Christ's coming to the predominantly premillennial group, the elderly social reformer declined, saying that he believed "both theories and neither."[41]

Jonathan Blanchard's son Charles, though deeply dedicated to preserving his father's views, completed Wheaton's transition into the new evangelical, and eventually fundamentalist, outlook. The alliance with the Moody forces was clearly the crucial step. During 1883 and 1884 Charles Blanchard, who had assumed the presidency of Wheaton in 1882, preached regularly in the "Moody" (Chicago Avenue) Church in Chicago. There he met Miss Emma Dryer who enlisted the educator's support in founding the Bible Training Institute that Moody himself soon made one of his enterprises. Most impor-tantly, Miss Dryer helped to convince Blanchard of the truth of dispensa-tional premillennialism,[42] a doctrine central to the emergence of the later fundamentalist movement. By the end of his career, Charles was a signifi-cant figure in the fundamentalist movement. In 1919 he drafted the doctrinal statement of the World's Christian Fundamentals Association and in 1925 arch-fundamentalist William Bell Riley delivered the eulogy at his funeral.

Charles Blanchard saw an essential continuity in his work which covered the era from Finney to Riley. The best evidence for this continuity was the continued presence of opposition to their stand for what was right. In his projected autobiography he recalled a conversation he had with Finney when Blanchard was still a young lecturer for the National Christian Associ-ation. Finney remarked that Blanchard must be experiencing much opposi-tion and recalled that there used to be much opposition at Oberlin also. "That is always true when you are doing good," the aging evangelist af-firmed. "Now we are really too popular. The world does not hate us any more. . . . You need not be worried when the world hates you." Blan-chard took the lesson to heart. Among his favorite texts, recalled from his anti-Masonic forays, were "Have no fellowship with the unfruitful works of darkness" and "Come out from among them and be separate."[43]

Yet the evils opposed had become increasingly circumscribed since the days when the Blanchards had worked for emancipation, peace, rights of Indians, and popular democracy. No longer was the goal to build a "perfect society;" at best it was to restrain evil until the Lord returned. Reviewing his own "labors for the purifying of human society," Charles Blanchard men-tioned in addition to education and anti-Masonry only his reform efforts against Sabbath-breaking, strong drink, and "narcotic poisons" (mainly tobacco).[44] Apparently he perceived these causes as the essentials of the "Puritan" heritage. Speaking in 1912 at the seventy-fifth anniversary of Knox College, and doubtless having in mind its lax moral course since his father had left, he declared of the founders of such institutions: "They were

Puritans. They knew that greed and pleasure loving never could construct a
glorious civilization. They did not play cards, nor go to dances, nor tolerate
liquor shops, nor attend theatres. . . . "[45] The abolition of selected sins of
the flesh was the principal moral concern remaining for those whose hopes
for a Christian America had been crushed by the changes in the modern
world.

Much had changed since the days of the alliance of Jonathan Blanchard
with the Beechers. One side of American evangelicalism was becoming a
movement of the disinherited. In 1915 Charles Blanchard wrote that the true
disciples of Christ usually would be found "in smaller, poorer churches."[46]
So also had the Blanchard ethical rigor subtly shifted away from efforts to
transform the culture toward symbols of separation from it. Jonathan Blanchard had been a Puritan exhorting America to become Zion; Charles was a
Puritan in an American Babylon.

III. D. L. Moody
and a New American Evangelism

"As he stood on the platform," wrote the Reverend Lyman Abbott in
praise of Dwight L. Moody, "he looked like a business man; he dressed like a
business man; he took the meeting in hand as a business man would. . . ."[1]
Abbot's comment, written shortly before Moody's death in 1899, points out
some characteristics of Moody's revivalism that since have sometimes been
obscured. Moody's evangelism had a degree of middle-class respectability
about it that was not always present in American revivalism. His methods
and his message sparked nothing like the fierce controversies that stalked his
immediate predecessor, Charles Finney, during Finney's early career. Neither did Moody's businessman style partake of the extravagant, theatrical,
acrobatic, and country-yokel touches of his immediate successor, Billy Sunday. Moody's meetings, although warmed by the informalities of Ira Sankey's hymnsings, were relatively decorous. Sentiment rather than sensation
characterized his messages. They contained (as the title of a collection of his
sermons advertised) "living truths for head and heart, illustrated by . . .
thrilling anecdotes and incidents, personal experiences, touching home
scenes, and stories of tender pathos."[2] His message, aside from the constant
stress on the necessity of conversion, was of the love of God. His theology,
although basically orthodox, was ambiguous to the point of seeming not to
be theology at all. Moody could thus maintain cordial relations with mem-

bers of both emerging parties in American Protestantism. As Lyman Abbott, Henry Ward Beecher's successor and a spokesman for the new theology, put it, "Not the least of the many services which Mr. Moody rendered to the age has been this practical demonstration that religion is more than theology, and that, based upon this principle, a true Christian catholicity is always possible."[3]

Moody's contribution to emerging fundamentalism was both large and complex. Moody was a progenitor of fundamentalism—it could even be argued that he was its principal progenitor. He believed in Biblical infallibility and premillennialism. He did as much as anyone in America to promote the forms of holiness teaching and the ethical emphases that were accepted by many fundamentalists. His closest associates had virtually all the traits of later fundamentalism, and many of them in fact participated directly in organizing the fundamentalist movement in the twentieth century. Yet Moody himself lacked the one trait that was essential to a "fundamentalist"—he was unalterably opposed to controversy. Moody was a pragmatic activist, determined that nothing should stand in the way of preaching the Gospel effectively. "Couldn't they [the critics] agree to a truce," he suggested in 1899, "and for ten years bring out no fresh views, just to let us get on with the practical work of the kingdom."[4] As best he could, he tried simply to avoid the new issues. While he disapproved of liberalism in the abstract, he cultivated friendships with influential liberals in the hope that peace would prevail.[5] "People are tired and sick of this awful controversy," he remarked in one of his last sermons. "I hope the motto of the ministers of this country will be, 'quit your fighting and go to work and preach the simple gospel.'"[6]

Although by the end of his career his popularity was fading, Moody's influence was broad and lasting. Scarcely a leader in American Protestantism in the next generation, it seemed, had not at some time been influenced by Moody.[7] He was a transitional figure in an age of rapid change, yet he helped to make some characteristics of that age lasting parts of the revivalist tradition. Perhaps as much as Henry Ward Beecher, although in quite different ways, he helped to fuse the spirit of middle-class Victorian America with evangelical Christianity.

MOODY AND HIS EMPIRE

Moody was a Horatio Alger figure—the honest and industrious boy from a New England village who went to the city to find fame and fortune.[8] Arriving in Boston at age seventeen in 1854, Moody's first evangelical interests were aroused through contacts with the YMCA, an organization that had recently originated in England for evangelism to young men in cities. Moody soon moved to Chicago where his religious fervor was intensified by the urban revivals of 1857–58. By 1860 he decided to give up a promising shoe business to devote himself full-time to YMCA work and to other Christian ministries in the city. He started his own Sunday school for poor and immigrant children and eventually (by 1864) organized the Illinois Street Church, a congregation with no denominational ties. In 1866 he became president of the Chicago YMCA and was a locally known evangelistic leader.

That the YMCA rather than any denomination should be Moody's main formal contact with the Christian community was indicative of an important tendency in American evangelicalism, greatly furthered by Moody himself. During the awakening of the first half of the century an "empire" of independent evangelical organizations had burgeoned to support home and foreign missions, publication and distribution of Bibles and Christian literature, Sunday schools, charities, and reforms of most of the notorious vices. Like the YMCA, many of these programs were imported from England. Also, like the YMCA, they were extra-ecclesiastical organizations, often with lay leadership, enlisting volunteers to support specific causes.

This system encouraged the personal empire-building which developed during Moody's time. Events in the business world of the Gilded Age paralleled this trend and likewise encouraged individual initiative and freedom from centralized regulation.[9] Moody himself followed such a pattern. His success soon took him beyond the YMCA and, although he cultivated cordial relations with all evangelical denominations, he had formal connections with none. Many of his associates followed a similar pattern. While most of them retained some formal denominational ties, their strongest allegiances were to a variety of specialized works: revival agencies, prophetic conferences, schools, publications, and local churches. These practices were perpetuated in later fundamentalism. Even where denominational concerns continued, the organizational dynamic of the movement was built around individual leaders and empires made up of agencies dedicated to specific causes. It was a religion structured according to the free enterprise system.

Moody's own rise to success was spectacular. His YMCA work gave him contacts in England, where he was invited to conduct some modestly conceived evangelistic services in 1873. Aided by Ira Sankey as song leader, Moody succeeded beyond all expectation. By the end of 1873 they had touched off something akin to a national revival in Scotland, making Moody and Sankey internationally renowned figures. During the next year they triumphantly toured the British Isles, returning to America in 1875 as national heroes. Americans were, of course, immensely impressed by the accomplishments of the American evangelistic innocents abroad. The religious leaders of virtually every American city clamored for their services.

Following his highly successful first round of campaigns in America, Moody turned to building structures that would widen and perpetuate his principal concern—evangelism. His methods reflected the influence of his earlier YMCA connections—the key to the future was to reach and train young people. In 1879 he founded a school for girls at his home base in Northfield, Massachusetts, followed in 1881 by the Mount Hermon School for boys. In 1886 he gave his support to Emma Dryer's new Bible training school in Chicago, which he designed for quick Christian training of laymen to meet the needs of urban evangelism. In addition, beginning in 1880, he made his home in Northfield the site for summer conferences—another of the popular new evangelical institutions. At Northfield a wide variety of Protestant leaders spoke, although Moody's personality and piety were always dominant. The most significant of the conferences was the inspiring international gathering of students in 1886 which led to the formation the next summer of the immensely influential Student Volunteer Movement, embodying the missionary enthusiasm of thousands of collegians in America and England for "the evangelization of the world in this generation."[10]

MOODY'S MESSAGE

The motto of the Student Volunteer Movement summarized exactly the controlling principle in Moody's own thought. Although Moody was not a frankly pragmatic analyst of the techniques of successful evangelism in the way Charles Finney had been, he often tested doctrines for their suitability to evangelism.[11] "His system of theology," explained an early interpreter, "is bounded by his work as an evangelist." Moody judged his sermons, said the interpreter, by whether they were "fit to convert sinners with." "By this rule of fitness he tests all the ideas which present themselves to his mind."[12]

This test kept Moody's message simple and positive. The "Three R's" adequately summarized his central doctrines: "Ruin by sin, Redemption by Christ, and Regeneration by the Holy Ghost."[13] Moody presented these themes in an attractively informal fashion, primarily through illustrations and anecdotes, often from Scripture. Although most of the Biblical and evangelistic aspects of his message were not new to revival audiences, the one feature that almost everyone noticed was that Moody emphasized the love of God. Moreover—a striking omission—he did not preach Hellfire and God's wrath. Although he never repudiated the doctrine of eternal punishment, his uneasiness with the subject was not far from that of the evangelical liberalism of Henry Ward Beecher. In Moody's case, it appears that he avoided distressing subjects largely because he sensed that because of the mood of the modern age they did not meet his pragmatic test. As he himself explained, "Terror never brought a man in yet."[14]

If Moody's theology was shaped by evangelistic concerns as adjusted to the spirit of the age, so also was his view of what it meant to be a Christian. The sins emphasized most in his preaching were a rather stereotyped set of notorious vices, thoroughly familiar to revivalist audiences. In a sermon on "Temptation"—to cite a particularly clear, and characteristic example—he denounced the "four great temptations that threaten us to-day": (1) the theater, (2) disregard of the Sabbath, (3) Sunday newspapers, and (4) atheistic teachings, including evolution.[15] Since Moody's sermons were filled with illustrations from Scripture, they did at times touch on a full range of sins, including subtle tendencies as well as notorious vices. He frequently attacked greed and avarice among businessmen, and would warn against putting "other gods" such as family, wealth, honor, or self, before the true God."[16] Jealousy, envy, self-seeking, irritability, peevishness, and snappishness were also among the sins against which a person should struggle.[17] Still, the themes that pervade his preaching on sin and on which he most often dwelt were drunkenness and selling liquor, Sabbath breaking (including boating, fishing, hunting, excursions, and using public transportation), "pandering the lusts of the body," sins of fallen women, "telling vile stories," theater attendance, "worldly amusements," and disrespect for parents, especially mothers whose hearts would be broken by their children's indulgence in the above vices.[18] These vices he described as evidences of loving "the world" or "worldly pleasures." "A line should be drawn," he said, "between the church and the world, and every Christian should get both feet out of the world."[19]

Equally important as Moody's preaching to the success of the revivals was the immensely popular singing of Ira Sankey, whose message reinforced Moody's both in sentimentality and content. Sankey's hymns used simple and touching contrasts between sinners lost, wandering, and beleagured in their sinfulness and the tender love of Christ. One of the most popular hymns "The Ninety and Nine," tells of the Saviour's love as he makes his blood-stained way through thickets, deserts, and thunder-riven mountains to retrieve one lost sheep. Jesus and home were often virtually equated—as in the similarly popular, and even more sentimental, "Where is my Boy to-night?", a mother's lament for the lost innocence of her wandering boy—a song that incidentally mentions nothing more explicitly Christian than the mother's "love and prayer." The famous "Hold the Fort for I am Coming," based on a Civil War incident, and appealing to less passive sentiments, suggested a similar contrast between a world almost hopelessly beset by sin and the power of Jesus to save.[20]

Wholly spiritualized allusions to the Civil War, together with temperance hymns (as "Where is my Boy tonight?") were, however, about as close as the Moody-Sankey revivals came to explicitly social or political questions. Moody, in fact, probably did as much as anyone to set the trend (which fit the national mood of the 1870s and 1880s) away from earlier nineteenth-century evangelical emphasis on the directly social dimensions of sin and holiness. This shift was quite intentional for Moody, who in his YMCA and city work had at first adopted the common evangelical idea that charity and evangelism should naturally go together. As he reportedly remarked in a frequently quoted statement,

> When I was at work for the City Relief Society before the fire I used to go to a poor sinner with the Bible in one hand and a loaf of bread in the other. . . . My idea was that I could open a poor man's heart by giving him a load of wood

or a ton of coal when the winter was coming on, but I soon found out that he wasn't any more interested in the Gospel on that account. Instead of thinking how he could come to Christ, he was thinking how long it would be before he got the load of wood. If I had the Bible in one hand and a loaf in the other the people always looked first at the loaf; and that was just the contrary of the order laid down in the Gospel.[21]

As the last sentence indicates, Moody dropped direct social involvement for the same reason that he avoided controversial theology—both threatened to distract from his primary concern for evangelism. In his mind it was certainly not a question of condoning a lack of compassion for the poor; rather he was convinced that the most compassionate possible care was for a person's eternal soul. Furthermore, evangelism was, according to his theology, the best way to meet social needs. Conversion inevitably led to personal responsibility and moral uplift, qualities which the conventional wisdom said the poor most often lacked. The emphasis on motherhood and domesticity in Moody's preaching was part of the widespread evangelical conviction that stability in the home was the key to the resolution of other social problems. Once wanderers came "home" and the poor acquired the sense of responsibility found in strong Christian families, poverty would cease.[22] So individual conversions would eventually bring social reform. The context of Moody's remark on his own change was the Biblical statement, "But seek ye first the kingdom of God, and his righteousness; and all these things shall be added unto you."[23]

Nothing in Moody's views on personal or social questions was out of the ordinary in the middle-class individualism of the day. Moody rose to fame in the heyday of American individualism and his thought is pervaded by its assumptions. The sins he stressed were personal sins, not involving victims besides oneself and members of one's family. The sinner stood alone before God. The Christian community provided emotional support, encouragement, and example;[24] but ultimately the decision to accept the message of salvation was, in the democratic American and Arminian tradition, essentially the decision of each individual, as was the decision to conquer sin. "Whatever the sin is," Moody exhorted in a typical statement, "make up your mind that you will gain victory over it."[25]

This last remark, however, also reflects one of two genuinely new directions in which Moody was helping to move the revivalist wing of American evangelicalism. After about 1870 Moody actively taught a new version of holiness doctrine which emphasized "victory" over sin. He also taught premillennialism. Influential new forms of each of these teachings were also promoted through closely related movements organized in America by some of Moody's closest friends and younger lieutenants, including Reuben Torrey, James M. Gray, C. I. Scofield, William J. Erdman, George Needham, A. C. Dixon, and A. J. Gordon.[26] These movements and these men, as we shall see, had a great deal to do with shaping fundamentalism. Of the two related movements, Moody was more directly involved with promoting the holiness teachings. Holiness was a central emphasis at his Northfield conferences and he published two books loosely presenting the new teachings.[27] With respect to premillennialism, a more divisive issue, he was careful to avoid the doctrinaire and partisan spirit of the movement. Although he preached regularly on the subject, and many of Sankey's hymns dealt generally with the theme, Moody never endorsed the details of the new dispensational version of premillennialism.[28]

Premillennialism did, however, give shape to the general outlook of the new evangelism Moody was promoting. He professed to be attracted to it because its pessimistic view of culture gave a strong impetus to evangelism.[29] So his most quoted statement, which summarized his philosophy of evangelism, appears in the context of his standard sermon on the return of Christ. "I look upon this world as a wrecked vessel," he said. "God has given me a lifeboat and said to me, 'Moody, save all you can.'"[30]

The view that "the world" would "grow worse and worse"[31] was an important departure from the dominant tradition of American evangelicalism that viewed God's redemptive work as manifested in the spiritual and moral progress of American society. The departure was by no means complete. The separation from the world that was demanded was not radically outward as in the Anabaptist tradition, but rather an inner separation marked by the outward signs of a life free from specific vices. Despite the hopeless corruption of the world, there was no demand to abandon most of the standards of the respectable American middle-class way of life. It was to these standards, in fact, that people were to be converted.

Moody was quite ambivalent toward American culture and its prospects. He never gave up, for instance, the nineteenth-century American evangelical hope that the republic of virtue could be saved by the revival. "Revival," he declared in 1899, in a statement that might just as well have come from Timothy Dwight or Lyman Beecher at the outset of the Second Great Awakening in 1801, "is the only hope for our republic, for I don't believe that a republican form of government can last without righteousness." Moody remained hopeful that American culture would not become increasingly worse. "I think it is getting very dark," he said in the same 1899 sermon,

> but don't think for a moment I am a pessimist. . . . Pentecost isn't over yet. The revival of '57 isn't over yet by a good deal. Some of the best men we have in our churches were brought out in '57. Why shouldn't we have now at the close of this old century a great shaking up and a mighty wave from heaven.[32]

*   *   *

Moody's central place in the heritage of fundamentalism suggests an important aspect of its character, shaped by a fondness neither for controversy nor for precise formulation of doctrine and the details of prophetic history. Fundamentalism was always a sub-species of the larger revivalist movement. As such it always involved an ambivalent attitude toward American culture, which evangelicalism had done much to shape. When the battles against modernism arose, fundamentalism always retained a tension between an exclusivist militancy and an irenic spirit concerned with holiness and saving souls. These latter elements in the tradition of Moody gave the movement its largest appeal. Yet when the organized and vocal core of militants attempted to speak for the hosts of true evangelicals and indeed even to lead them into battle, as in the 1920s, the ranks sometimes seemed to disperse. As for Moody, so probably for the majority of the sympathizers of the anti-modernist movement, evangelism and the next revival were always the chief aims.

PART TWO
The Shaping of a Coalition

This Age and the Millennium

IV. Prologue: The Paradox of Revivalist Fundamentalism

Fundamentalism was a mosaic of divergent and sometimes contradictory traditions and tendencies that could never be totally integrated. Sometimes its advocates were backward looking and reactionary, at other times they were imaginative innovators. On some occasions they appeared militant and divisive; on others they were warm and irenic. At times they seemed ready to forsake the whole world over a point of doctrine; at other times they appeared heedless of tradition in their zeal to win converts. Sometimes they were optimistic patriots; sometimes they were prophets shaking from their feet the dust of a doomed civilization.

Their attitudes toward intellect, ideas, and systems of ideas reflected this pervasive ambivalence. On the one hand, a major element in the movement, well developed in nineteenth-century revivalism, was the subordination of all other concerns—including concern for all but the simplest ideas—to soul-saving and practical Christianity. Dwight L. Moody stood in this camp. To Moody most formal ideas seemed divisive and hence all but the least controversial were to be avoided.[1] The stance of some of his closest associates, however, was strikingly different on this point. The differences came out clearly in a survey conducted in 1899 by *The Record of Christian Work*, a Moody publication. A number of prominent evangelists were asked, "What was the teaching of Christ regarding his disciples' attitude towards error, and towards those who held erroneous doctrines?" Reuben A. Torrey, one of Moody's best known lieutenants, responded with an unmistakable fundamentalist answer:

> Christ and His immediate disciples immediately attacked, exposed and denounced error. We are constantly told in our day that we ought not to attack error but simply teach the truth. This is the method of the coward and trimmer; it was not the method of Christ.

43

D. L. Moody's answer could hardly have been more directly opposed:

> Christ's teaching was always constructive. . . . His method of dealing with error was largely to ignore it, letting it melt away in the warm glow of the full intensity of truth expressed in love. . . . Let us hold truth, but by all means let us hold.it in love, and not with a theological club.[2]

Behind these two answers lay not only contrasting personalities but different basic assumptions, assumptions concerning the importance of ideas as such. Both approaches are important to an understanding of the resulting movement. Moody's approach showed one side of the revivalist heritage. Torrey, on the other hand, represented part of a major organizing force in fundamentalism that, far from rejecting intellect, assigned vast importance to ideas. This tendency is nowhere seen more clearly than in the commitment of such leaders as Torrey to dispensational premillenialism. Although the millenarian movement and the anti-modernist movement were by no means co-extensive, dispensationalism was nevertheless the most distinctive'intellectual product of emerging fundamentalism and is the best indicator of one side of its basic assumptions.

The contrast between Moody and his dispensationalist associates points toward a feature of later fundamentalism and helps to explain some characteristics that otherwise seem contradictory. Not only did the later movement involve an alliance between revivalists in the pietist tradition and denominational conservatives in the Calvinist tradition (especially as represented by Princeton theology), but within the revivalist wing itself there was a thoroughgoing amalgamation (much more than an alliance) of these two traditions—the pietist and the Calvinist. This amalgamation had been an important aspect of American revivalism since its origins in the Great Awakening. Seventeenth-century Puritanism had combined highly intellectual theology with intense piety.[3] The Awakening of the eighteenth century introduced into an essentially Calvinist context a new style of emotional intensity, personal commitment to Christ, and holy living inspired directly by German and Methodist pietism. In the unrestrained American environment this union spawned innumerable variations of Calvinist and Arminian theology multiplied by countless varieties of denominational and revivalist emphases. The Calvinists tended to stress intellect, the importance of right doctrine, the cognitive aspects of faith, and higher education. On the other hand, more pietistically and emotionally oriented groups, such as the Methodists, tended to shun intellectual rigor and to stress the practical and experiential aspects of faith. Yet many groups in America stressed both the intellectual and the experiential-practical aspects. Many Congregationalists and Presbyterians, especially those of the revivalist branches known in the nineteenth century as "New School," combined educational and doctrinal emphases with intense emotion. Jonathan Edwards was their model. Even "Old School" Presbyterians, including those at Princeton Seminary renowned for their doctrinal conservatism and severe intellectual demands, had a place for sentiment and some pietist leanings. The Baptists, who were less centralized and standardized, had some similar pro-revivalist intellectual leadership along with some distinctly non-intellectualistic elements.

The surge of revivalism associated with the rise of Charles Finney in the 1820s which developed in the "New School" tradition certainly did not forsake intellect, but it did create new channels for emphasis on emotion throughout American evangelicalism. Sandra Sizer in her analysis of the rise of the gospel song in nineteenth-century America has suggested that Finney's revivals marked the beginning of the attempt to build a new Christian community united by intense feeling. The focal point for this emphasis was the "social religious meeting," small groups gathered for prayer, Bible study, witnessing, and song. Witnessing, or testifying to one another about how God had transformed their lives, was an important way in which these communities built themselves up and provided emotional support. Finney added emphasis on such meetings to his more-or-less conventional mass-preaching services, but by the time of the remarkable businessmen's revival of 1857–58 the awakening itself originated in noon-hour prayer meetings which were just such "social religious meetings."[4] Every new evangelical movement of this entire era, through the rise of fundamentalism and including the holiness, pentecostal, and premillennial movements, had a base in some form of "social religious" gathering.

The revivals of Moody and Sanky, Sizer argues persuasively, in a sense applied the principles of the smaller group meetings on a massive scale. The use of a song leader, which Sankey made a lasting part of evangelism, was a conspicuous means of building emotional ties. The most common theme was the distress of sin, to be relieved by a passionate surrender to the incredible love of Jesus. Hymns that told stories of prodigals reclaimed and the like made the song itself a kind of witnessing. In contrast to eighteenth-century hymns like those in the influential collection of Isaac Watts, the focus of revivalist songs shifted from praise of the awful majesty of God and the magnitude of his grace revealed in Christ's atoning work, to the emotions of those who encounter the Gospel. Similarly, Moody's sermons virtually abandoned all pretense of following conventional forms of explicating a text, and were closer to "layman's exhortation" filled with touching anecdotes with an emotional impact comparable to that of personal testimony.[5]

Yet the emphasis on a community of feeling seen here is only half the picture, even if we look solely at the movement most closely associated with Moody. Nineteenth-century American evangelicalism involved a definite belief system as well as popular or rhetorical forms and strategies.[6] Fundamentalism, as such, was concerned primarily with preserving the belief system; yet its proponents were equally concerned with promoting the popular forms, organizations, and strategies that were an inextricable part of the movement. Moody concerned himself primarily with this practical, less ideological, and more pietistic side. Yet his lieutenants Torrey, Gray, Pierson, Gordon, Blanchard, Erdman, and Scofield added to that piety a strong interest in ideas. In the type of fundamentalism that grew out of their work, these two emphases, on piety and on correct belief, were fused. In this respect their movement showed characteristics that had been common to American Calvinist tradition since the first Great Awakening, indeed since the Puritans.

In fact the millenarian (or dispensational premillennial) movement had strong Calvinistic ties in its American origins. The movement's immediate progenitor was John Nelson Darby (1800–1882), who broke with the Church of Ireland and became the leader of the separatist Plymouth Brethren group. During his later career Darby spent a great deal of time proselytizing in North America. He found relatively little interest there in the new Brethren sect, but remarkable willingness to accept his views and methods of prophetic interpretation. This enthusiasm came largely from clergymen with strong Calvinistic views, principally Presbyterians and Baptists in the northern United States. The evident basis for this affinity was that in most respects Darby was himself an unrelenting Calvinist. His interpretation of the Bible and of history rested firmly on the massive pillar of divine sovereignty, placing as little value as possible on human ability.[7]

The organizers of the prophetic movement in America were predominantly Calvinists. In 1876 a group led by Nathaniel West, James H. Brookes, William J. Erdman, and Henry M. Parsons, all Presbyterians, together with Baptist A. J. Gordon, initiated what would become known during the next quarter-century as the annual Niagara Bible Conferences for prophetic study. To achieve wider publicity, virtually this same group in 1878 organized the first International Prophecy Conference, which became the model for similar conferences held every decade or so until the end of World War I. These early gatherings, which became the focal points for the prophetic side of their leaders' activities, were clearly Calvinistic. Presbyterians and Calvinist Baptists predominated,[8] while the number of Methodists was extremely small.[9]

A Calvinistic movement with a strong interest in complex details of prophetic interpretation might have seemed contrary to the prevailing trends of the day. Even to revivalist evangelicals like D. L. Moody, who accepted the outlines of premillennialism, this doctrinal rigor was unappealing. John Nelson Darby puzzled over how Moody could on the one hand accept the prophetic truths concerning God's sovereignty in history, and yet inconsistently allow room for a non-Calvinist view of human ability when it came to personal salvation.[10] But Moody was more American—or at least what is usually characterized as American. He preferred action to intellectual systems, and freedom to authoritarianism.

The more perplexing question is how Moody's lieutenants, as American as he and quite popular as evangelists and pastors, could succeed so well in this American climate in promoting the complex system of dispensationalism. In fact, it was in the United States that this view of things, although imported from England, really took root. Even a century later it continues to have immense appeal.[11] The question is just how this set of ideas and emphases fit into the American and evangelical worldviews in order to be accepted as widely as it was.[12] For a substantial number of Americans, or American evangelicals, something in their outlook was conducive to the authoritarian and ideological character of dispensationalism as well as to the sentiment and activism more usually associated with American revivalism.

The intimate relationship between these two sides of the emerging fundamentalist movement can be observed strikingly in Reuben A. Torrey (1856–1928). Torrey came closest to being Moody's successor, rising to prominence as a world-touring evangelist in the first decade of the twentieth century. Torrey was one of the principal architects of fundamentalist thought. For someone who aspired to popularity, Torrey seems to have been incongruously pompous. As William McLoughlin put it: "on the street he usually wore a high hat, and he always talked as though he had one on."[13] A Congregationalist and a graduate of Yale who had studied in Germany for a year, he was one of several leaders who represented the direct tie between fundamentalism and the New England tradition in which learning was so revered.[14] A sympathetic biographer described him as almost immune to emotional persuasion: "rather was he swayed by the logical element of cold reason."[15] Another admirer said he did "not remember his ever getting a laugh from any congregation."[16] Torrey characterized his own preaching style as "scholarly" and said that he thought of his approach as that "of a lawyer" before a jury.[17]

A counterpoint to this somewhat unpromising approach to mass evangelism (although it must be remembered that Charles Finney also described himself as a lawyer-like preacher) was Torrey's singing partner, Charles Alexander. "Charlie" who was less formal than Sankey, represented the religion of the heart to the same extent that Torrey's style suggested a religion of the mind. His role in the Torrey campaigns was "warming up the crowd" (for instance, with singing contests between the audience and the choir, or between the men and the women). McLoughlin described his methods as "the techniques of a master of ceremonies at a Rotary convention."[18]

Naturally these two complemented each other[19] with Alexander always the more popular, but Torrey (who in principle favored heart religion and talked a great deal about the Holy Spirit) providing the intellectual backbone. This relationship between heart and intellect almost always characterized the central individuals and groups in the emerging fundamentalist movement. At least seventy-five percent of fundamentalists' talk and writing was devoted to popular piety, simple Bible study, and soul winning—themes that one might associate with Moody, Sankey, or Alexander. The other twenty-five percent, however, gave the movement its distinctive character and distinguished it from the general revivalist trend of which it was a part. These distinguishing features need to be explained, especially some rather remarkable intellectual traits and assumptions. For understanding these and for understanding their relationship to American culture, the growth of dispensational premillennialism within the larger revivalist and anti-liberal movements offers some most intriguing clues.

V. Two Revisions of Millennialism

In 1909 William Newton Clarke, a leading liberal Baptist theologian, looking back over his career, recalled that during the 1870s American evangelicals had debated with unusual fervor the question of the return of Christ. "The premillennial and postmillennial views of the advent," he recollected, "were presented, elaborated, and defended, sometimes with conspicuous power."[1]

This debate concerning the "last times" was intimately related to a crisis in basic assumptions that was rending the Western Christian world during Clarke's lifetime. New patterns of thought demanded that intellectual inquiry focus on describing the natural forces that seemed to determine how change took place. No longer viewing knowledge as the fixed truths of special or natural revelation, human scientific inquiry now concentrated on speculative hypotheses that explained natural processes of development. In the shape of Darwinism and higher criticism, these assumptions led toward conclusions that seemed to threaten the foundations of traditional Christian belief. Even the highest ideals, truths of the heart, moral sentiments, and the religious experiences through which some Christians said God was known, were often viewed as largely the product of historical developments.

For many liberal Christians the only way to save Christianity at all was to affirm that God continued to reveal himself both in profound religious and moral experiences and in cultural processes as well. Despite naturalistic explanations of historical development, God could still be seen in the progress of humanity and civilization. Cultural advance revealed the kingdom of God. Thus the topic of the coming of the kingdom, so intensely discussed of the 1870s, involved not only the basic issue of the nature of Christianity, but also a wide set of questions concerning the proper relation between Christianity and modern civilization.

The question of Christianity and civilization was complicated. Mid-nineteenth-century Western culture was in the midst of a process of secularization—by which is meant a trend away from distinctly Christian influences.[2] The magnitude of the revolution was, as Martin Marty points out, "comparable to the Renaissance and the Enlightenment." Yet in America, as Marty also demonstrates, this upheaval produced little direct confrontation between the forces of faith and infidelity. Unlike many European countries, the United States experienced little virulent anticlericism and hostility to Christianity in the nineteenth century. The characteristic American response to secularization was to bless its manifestations—such as materialism, capitalism, and nationalism—with Christian symbolism.[3]

Postmillennialism, by far the prevalent view among American evangelicals between the Revolution and the Civil War, helped provide the framework for this approach to secularization. Articulated as a distinct view in early eighteenth-century England, postmillennialism was promoted in America during the Great Awakening, notably by Jonathan Edwards. According to the postmillennialists, the prophecies in the book of Revelation concerning the defeat of the anti-Christ (interpreted as the Pope and other leaders of false religions) were being fulfilled in the present era, and were clearing the way for a golden age. This "millennium" (the "one thousand years" of Revelation 20) would be the last epoch of the present historical era. During this time the Holy Spirit would be poured out and the Gospel spread around the world. Christ would return after this millennial age (hence "postmillennialism") and would bring history to an end.[4]

Postmillennialists typically were optimistic about the spiritual progress of the culture. They saw human history as reflecting an ongoing struggle between cosmic forces of God and Satan, each well represented by various earthly powers, but with the victory of righteousness ensured. In the early nineteenth century many American postmillennialists believed the defeat of the Satanic forces to be imminent. With the Papal and Islamic powers in an apparent state of decline, the more literal-minded concluded that the twelve hundred and sixty days (years) of the reign of anti-Christ (Revelation 11) would end around the 1860s. In any case American evangelical postmillennialists saw signs of the approach of the millennial age not only in the success of revivals and missions, but also in general cultural progress. The golden age would see the culmination of current reform efforts to end slavery, oppression, and war. Moreover, in this wonderful era science, technology, and learning would advance to undreamed of accomplishments.[5]

Americans were easily persuaded that their nation was destined to lead the way in such cultural advances. By the Revolution many evangelicals were already loudly proclaiming that the triumph of the American cause and of American principles was a sign of the kingdom.[6] The spiritual hope was thus partly secularized and nationalized as the American civil religion was born. At the same time, however, the American experiment and the continuing efforts for cultural reform and progress were to a degree Christianized. The idea of transforming the culture fit well with the Calvinist Puritan tradition, but the idea of "Christianizing" the culture never turned out to be as simple as supposed. In some areas—such as the campaign against slavery—evangelicals succeeded somewhat in transforming the culture by Christian standards. In other areas, just as certainly, the culture—with its materialism, capitalist competitiveness and nationalism—helped shaped American Christianity. Seemingly oblivious to this distinction at the time, evangelicals generally regarded almost any sort of progress as evidence of the advance of the kingdom.

After the Civil War the more liberal evangelicals, whose basic epistemological categories were profoundly altered by the new naturalism and historicism, began gradually to abandon the dramatically supernatural aspects of the postmillennial view of history. In particular they ceased to take seriously the idea that history was determined by a cosmic struggle between the armed forces of God and Satan and that these supernatural powers might directly intervene at any moment. William Newton Clarke found New Testament predictions of the early physical return of Christ to be the anomaly that decisively destroyed his belief in the total infallibility of the Bible.[7] In place of spectacularly supernatural concepts of the kingdom, Clarke saw it as "natural and normal." The kingdom was not future or otherworldly, but "here and now." It was not external, but an internal ethical and religious force based on the ideals of Jesus.[8]

Clarke's controversial contemporary, Arthur Cushman McGiffert of Union Theological Seminary in New York, similarly described the kingdom that Jesus preached. "The kingdom of God," said McGiffert, "was the burden of his preaching, not a kingdom lying in another world beyond the skies but established here and now." This kingdom meant "the control of the lives of men and of all their relationships one with another and of all the institutions in which those relationships find expression by the spirit of Jesus Christ who has shown us what God is and what he would have this world be."[9] Such sentiments were reiterated countless times in the half-century from 1880 to 1930.

While these liberals were not absolutely optimistic about cultural progress and recognized the continuing power of evil,[10] they did retain both the formal structure and the essential confidence of the older postmillennial view. They had, however, discarded many supernaturalistic features that lay beyond ordinary experience. They had also secularized it in that they moved the site of the kingdom to this world where its progress could be seen in the divinely inspired developments of everyday life. For such progressive thinkers, though they were still committed to many Biblical ideals, modern culture was becoming normative for understanding revelation; a generation earlier, evangelicals, though often much influenced by current cultural ideals, had regarded the Bible as the preeminent guide to understanding culture.

The new premillennialism, which like the new liberalism began to be widely accepted in America during the 1870s, was an almost completely antithetical response to the crisis in evangelical models.[11] Premillennialism, which had an ancient Christian lineage, provided a framework for answers to the critical questions of how truth is known and how Christianity relates to civilization. In America before the Civil War premillennialism of a traditional variety was an important minority position held by some mainline Protestant leaders. It did not differ greatly from the postmillennialism of the same era. Both saw history as controlled by a cosmic struggle, both allowed for interpreting some Biblical prophecies literally, and both thought that some prophecies about the time immediately preceding the millennium were already being fulfilled in current events. They disagreed primarily over whether Christ would come before or after the millennium. The premillennialists were prone to a more literal interpretation of Scripture and were less hopeful concerning progress. During the 1860s, premillennialism of this sort was rapidly rising in popularity.[12]

With this general model available, those who turned to the new dispensational premillennialism responded to the crisis of the post-Civil-War era by shoring up the places in the foundation of Christian belief that they considered most in danger of erosion. In the areas where liberalism appeared vague and ethereal, dispensational premillennialism was explicit and concrete. Dispensationalism certainly did not grow only in reaction to liberal theology. In the 1870s, liberalism was not yet a *cause célèbre* and dispensationalists had many other concerns. The intellectual and cultural issues that fostered liberalism were already present, however, and their impact on Protestantism in Germany was known and feared.[13] It is clear that the views of John Nelson Darby as accepted by the American adherents of the Niagara and International Prophecy conferences of the late nineteenth century, popularized by W. E. Blackstone's *Jesus is Coming* and systematized by James H. Brookes and then by his protégé C. I. Scofield,[14] opposed the liberal trends at almost every point.

These teachers held that the Bible was absolutely reliable and precise in matters of fact, that its meanings were plain, and that whenever possible it should be taken literally. They reached a central conclusion which was equally distant from that of their liberal contemporaries. Christ's kingdom, far from being realized in this age or in the natural development of humanity, lay wholly in the future, was totally supernatural in origin, and discontinuous with the history of this era. This was a point on which the new dispensational premillennialism differed from older forms of premillennialism. For the dispensationalists the prophecies concerning the kingdom referred wholly to the future. This present era, the "church age," therefore could not be dignified as a time of the advance of God's kingdom.

The key to understanding the whole dispensational system is a very ingenious and complex interpretation of a prophecy in Daniel 9 concerning
"seventy weeks" (see accompanying chart for the text of this crucial passage).
The seventy weeks (or seventy "sevens") is interpreted as meaning four
hundred ninety years. Four hundred eighty-three of these years (seven weeks
and sixty-two weeks) are thought to refer precisely to the period from the
rebuilding of Jerusalem recorded in Ezra and Nehemiah to the time of
Christ. The startling and ingenious aspect of the interpretation is that it
posits that these first sixty-nine weeks were not immediately followed by the
seventieth. Rather, it suggests that the entire church age (not clearly indicated in the Old Testament prophecies) intervenes between the sixty-ninth
and seventieth week.[15] This leaves a host of prophecies to be fulfilled in this
last brief seven-year time, which is the final period before Christ sets up the
millennial kingdom. These events, as elaborated in Daniel and Revelation,
will include the appearance of the "anti-Christ" or "false prophet," who will
likely be an ecclesiastical tyrant backed by the united apostate churches; the
corresponding emergence of a political leader, known in Revelation as "the
Beast," who will reunite ten nations that have grown out of the Roman
Empire (the ten toes in the vision of Nebuchadnezzar in Daniel 2) forming a
new Roman Empire ("Babylon" in Revelation); the return of the Jews in
unbelief to Palestine; the conversion of some of the Jews; their intense
persecution, especially by the great world leaders, during the final three and
one half years or "great tribulation;" the personal return of Christ with all the
saints forming an army that will engage and defeat the combined forces of
the Gentile world powers, the Beast, and the false prophet, at a place in the
Near East known as Armageddon. With this victory the millennial reign of
Christ at Jerusalem will commence.[16] These long-postponed seven years thus
allowed a time for the literal fulfillment of prophecies that dealt with the
restored nation of the Jews and not with the church. According to the view
that came to prevail (although the movement split internally over chronology)[17] the living true saints of the church would at the outset be rescued from
the turmoil of the seven years in the "secret rapture," by which they would be
taken out of the world to "meet Christ in the air."

The immediate implications of the idea that the four hundred ninety years
should be divided into a four-hundred-eighty-three-year section and a much
later seven-year period center on the church age that fills the intervening gap.
This current age or dispensation is sharply separated from all teachings of
Scripture having to do with the Jewish people, whether in the Old Testament
or in the age of the kingdom to come. Even Christ's ministry was set in the
era before the church age began. Thus his teachings in the Sermon on the
Mount and the Lord's Prayer proclaim righteousness on legal grounds
(being still part of the Jewish "dispensation of law") rather than on a doctrine of grace (which characterizes the church age or "dispensation of
grace").[18] The church age is thus a historical "parenthesis." The Old Testa-

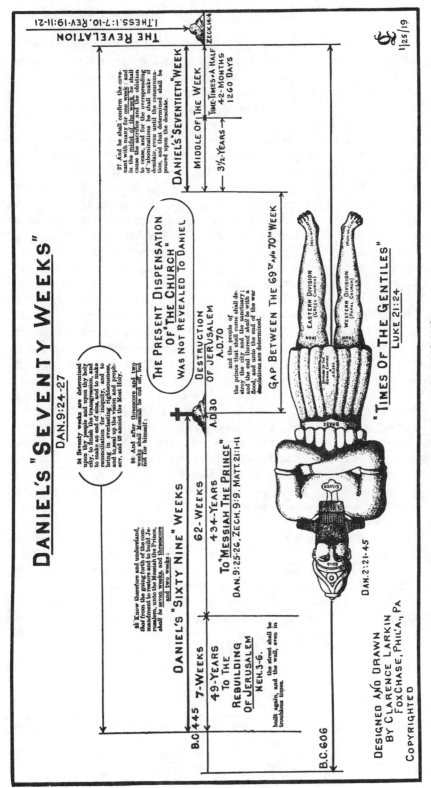

From *Dispensational Truth or God's Plan and Purpose in the Ages* (Philadelphia, 1920 [1918]).

ment hardly intimated its coming, the age having been rather a "mystery" revealed only with the Jews' rejection of Christ's kingdom. Unlike the postponed kingdom, which has a definite material and institutional structure, the interim church age of grace is a non-institutional age of the Holy Spirit. The true church is not the institutional church, which is worldly and steadily growing in apostasy. It is rather a faithful remnant of the spiritual who are "separate and holy" from the world.[19]

These then are the essentials of the dispensational premillennial system. "Dispensationalism" refers to the sharp separations of the various historical eras, or dispensations, recounted or predicted in the Bible. Dispensational interpreters, who divided history back to the beginning, usually found seven distinct eras. Details varied and are less significant than the system.[20] By no means all premillennialists associated with the prophetic movement and later fundamentalism were dispensationalists; yet the traits of the dispensationalism that were prevalent represent the main tendencies of the movement.

Ironically, the dispensationalists were responding to some of the very same problems in Biblical interpretation that were troubling theological liberals in the nineteenth century. If Biblical statements were taken at face value and subjected to scientific analysis, major anomalies seemed to appear. Among these were that many Old Testament prophecies did not seem to refer precisely to the church, that Jesus and his disciples seemed to expect his return and the establishment of the kingdom very shortly, and that much of the teaching of Jesus seemed to conflict with the theology of Paul. Liberals resolved such problems by greatly broadening the standards for interpreting Biblical language. Dispensationalists did the opposite. They held more strictly than ever to a literal interpretation but introduced a new historical scheme whose key was the interpretation of the church age as a parenthesis. Once the key step was accepted, the rest of Scripture could be fit into the scheme, and aspects that others viewed as inconsistencies could be explained as simply referring to different dispensations.

The underlying reasons for the growing acceptance of this new model for Biblical interpretation are not entirely clear. Two factors, which will be discussed in succeeding chapters, seem to have converged. One was a set of intellectual predispositions—characteristic of one type of nineteenth-century thought—to interpret Scripture in a literal way and to develop a distinctive view of history. The other was the secularization of the culture. With the rapid process of secularization throughout the nineteenth century, inevitably some people questioned the continued close identification of the church with the culture. In Great Britain the issue focused on the established church, so that John Nelson Darby's original impetus to find new principles of Biblical interpretation apparently was his need to explain the seeming corruptness of the establishment.[21] In America, later in the century, increasing secularization was more often perceived as the failure of postmillennial promises concerning the growth of the kingdom in this age. Non-Christian growth throughout the world appeared to be proceeding at a more rapid rate than was Christian advance. Whether such thoughts about the state of culture led to new ways of looking at Scripture, or whether the ways of looking at Scripture led to new ways of viewing the relationship of church and culture is not clear. Each factor, as well as the convergence of the two, however, can give us insight into the distinctive traits of the movement.

VI. Dispensationalism and the Baconian Ideal

Dispensationalist thought was characterized by a dual emphasis on the supernatural and the scientific. Supernaturalism was a conscious and conspicuous organizing principle. Underlying dispensationalist thought, however, was an almost equally important set of ideas concerning how to look at things scientifically.

At a major prophetic conference in 1895, Arthur T. Pierson, one of the leading representatives of the movement, summarized the basic philosophical assumptions of dispensational thought—and indeed much of the thought of the anti-modernist movement generally. Speaking of various systematic theologies that he considered artificial because they did not have the Second Coming at their center, he said: "I like Biblical theology that does not start with the superficial Aristotelian method of reason, that does not begin with an hypothesis, and then warp the facts and the philosophy to fit the crook of our dogma, but a Baconian system, which first gathers the teachings of the word of God, and then seeks to deduce some general law upon which the facts can be arranged."[1]

Whatever one might think of the accuracy of Pierson's claim to be a true representative of the method of the early seventeenth-century champion of the objective empirical method, his appeal to Francis Bacon sounded a note that still rang true to many American Protestants. At least throughout the first two thirds of the nineteenth century "Lord Bacon" was the preeminently revered philosopher for many Americans, especially those of the dominant evangelical colleges. This popularity of Bacon, in turn, was built on the strong support for the Baconian tradition in Scottish Common Sense Realism.[2]

Mid-nineteenth-century America is usually characterized, in literary history at least, by the full flowering of romanticism. Yet, especially among American college leaders, scientists, and theologians, transcendental and romantic trends had by no means successfully replaced commitment to empirical scientific analysis. Rather, the prestige that "the great Mr. Locke" had been given in eighteenth-century America was now challenged and surpassed not as much by Kant and Coleridge as by an even more rugged empiricist, Francis Bacon.[3] Romantic and empiricist interests were not mutually exclusive, of course. The most uninspired taxonomer could weep at the sentiments of Longfellow, or break into a doxology over evidence of God's design in nature. Evangelical professors who insisted on not going beyond the careful arrangement of the facts, could at the same time champion the popular romanticism and "religion of the heart" of the revivals.[4] Even Common Sense Realism, although surely a foundation for empiricism, was based ultimately on an appeal to pre-rational intuitions that left room for moral sentiments.

Nevertheless, when it came to identifying their philosophical stance, until after the Civil War American evangelicals overwhelmingly preferred the method of Francis Bacon to "metaphysical speculations." Common Sense philosophy affirmed their ability to know "the facts" directly. With the Scriptures at hand as a compendium of facts, there was no need to go further. They needed only to classify the facts, and follow wherever they might lead.[5] To return to Arthur Pierson's statement of this principle: "a Baconian system . . . first gathers the teachings of the word of God, and then seeks to deduce some general law upon which the facts can be arranged."

To whatever degree dispensationalists consciously considered themselves Baconians (it is rare to find reflections on philosophical first principles), this closely describes the assumptions of virtually all of them. They were absolutely convinced that all they were doing was taking the hard facts of Scripture, carefully arranging and classifying them, and thus discovering the clear patterns which Scripture revealed. The unusual firmness of the facts of Scripture was believed guaranteed by its supernatural inspiration. Dispensationalists acknowledged that Scripture possessed a human as well as a divine character and they consistently denied mechanical dictation theories of inspiration. But the supernatural element was so essential to their view of Scripture, and the natural so incidental, that their view would have been little different had they considered the authors of Scripture to be simply secretaries. Their language and metaphors sometimes betrayed this fact. James Brookes, for instance, spoke on one occasion of "the Holy Spirit in the last letter He dictated to the apostle Paul. . . ."[6] At a major Bible conference on "the Inspired Word," organized by millenarian leaders in 1887, William Hoyt, although he attacked a dictation theory, spoke nonetheless of the prophetic portions as a "photographically exact forecasting of the future. . . ." Using a term just coming into vogue, he said the Bible was in every detail "kept *inerrant*."[7]

"Inerrancy," which was to become a code word for much of the fundamentalist movement, had a scientific quality that was related to the view of truth as directly apprehended facts. It was vital to the dispensationalists that their information be not only absolutely reliable but also precise. They considered the term "inerrancy" to carry this implication. Statements found in Scripture would not deviate from the exact truth. The importance of this assumption for prophetic interpretation is obvious. Precise numbers of years had to be calculated and correlated with actual historical events. Nathaniel West, one of the leading American interpreters of prophecy, insisted that the four hundred eighty-three years must mean "'*exactly*' 483 literal years" and the one thousand years "exactly ten centuries" on the grounds that these figures were ordained of God in the same way as were the laws of nature described by Newtonian physics.

> All are established, firm as the ordinances of the heavens, and the dominion of the Sun and the Moon, by whose motions they are measured, and whose offspring they are. Science, the boast of modern times, has nothing more fixed, nothing more exact.

Likewise, West said, the "Law of the Seven"—a rule he applied to all sorts of things from the Sabbath to the four hundred ninety prophetic years and the seven dispensations—"is as much a literal law of God in Chronology governed by Sun, Moon and Stars, as are the laws of motion and gravitation, in Astronomy, which Kepler and Newton discovered. . . ."[8] Thus the millenarian's view of Scripture was, in effect, modeled after the Newtonian view of the physical universe. Created by God, it was a perfect self-contained unity governed by exact laws which could be discovered by careful analysis and classification.

This view of Scripture is implicit in their apologetics. Often they used a variation on the argument from design with Scripture rather than nature providing the evidence. Arthur T. Pierson, who was active in the formulation and defense of the millenarians' view of Scripture and had organized the 1887 conference on the Bible, also had produced a work significantly entitled, "*Many Infallible Proofs*." In this he maintained that if one approached Scripture "in a truly impartial and scientific spirit," all honest doubt would be cured. "Nothing," he said, "is to be accepted unless based on good evidence. . . ." He asserted with utter confidence that the facts of Scripture would speak for themselves: "if there is one candid doubter living who has faithfully studied the Bible and the evidences of Christianity, he has not yet been found." The reason why Mohammedans and Roman Catholics did not avow true Christianity was that for them it was considered a crime to read the Bible. "The consequence of searching the Scriptures would be the ruin of false faiths."[9]

When Scripture was looked upon as the compellingly perfect design of God, every detail was significant. Hence, even though the Bible was not intended to teach science, God had guided even the poetic language so as to anticipate scientific discoveries. Pierson, in addition to the standard evidences for Scriptural accuracy, pointed out some more unusual cases. Job, for instance, anticipated the modern discovery of the vibrations of light (morning and evening "sing"—both sound and light make vibrations) and the weight of air ("To assign to the wind its weight"). Solomon anticipated some of the basic operations of the human body. "Or ever the silver cord is loosed" referred to spinal marrow; "or the golden bowl be broken" suggested the basin that holds the brain; "or the pitcher be broken at the fountain" meant the lungs; and "or the wheel broken at the cistern" referred to the heart as a wheel circulating blood. "Longfellow or Tennyson," he hazarded, "might covet" the language used by Job "to describe refraction."[10]

In this view Scripture was an encyclopedic puzzle. It was a dictionary of facts that had been progressively revealed in various historical circumstances and literary genres and still needed to be sorted out and arranged.[11] Pierson went further than most in his anti-allegorical efforts to turn poetry into science. He also strayed from the characteristic dispensationalist claim to stick to plain meanings. Such extremes illustrate the general view of Scrip-

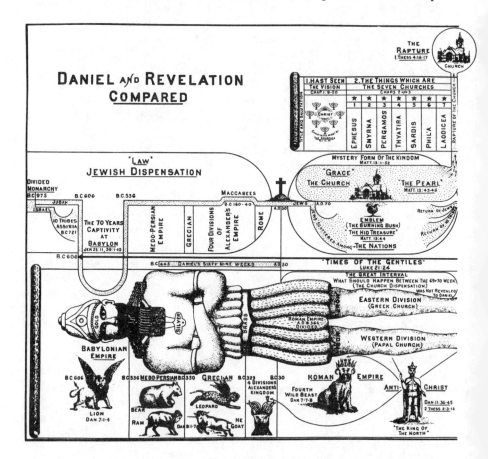

ture as a precisely designed unified production of God in which no clue was too small to be used in the search for hard facts.

The role of the interpreter, according to the same Baconian assumptions, was not to impose hypotheses or theories, but to reach conclusions on the basis of careful classification and generalization alone. The disposition to divide and classify everything is one of the most striking and characteristic traits of dispensationalism. C. I. Scofield, the great systematizer of the movement, epitomized this tendency. In "*Rightly Dividing the Word of Truth*," an authoritative summary of his views, Scofield interpreted the phrase of his title from the King James Bible to mean that "The Word of Truth, then, has right divisions . . . *so any study* of that Word which ignores those divisions must be in large measure profitless and confusing."[12] The work sketched out a series of distinctions: "The Jew, the Gentile, and the Church of God," "The Seven Dispensations," "The Two Advents," "The Two Resurrections," and "Law and Grace." Regarding the last distinction (to take an example that became a source of conflict with other Calvinists who insisted on the pri-

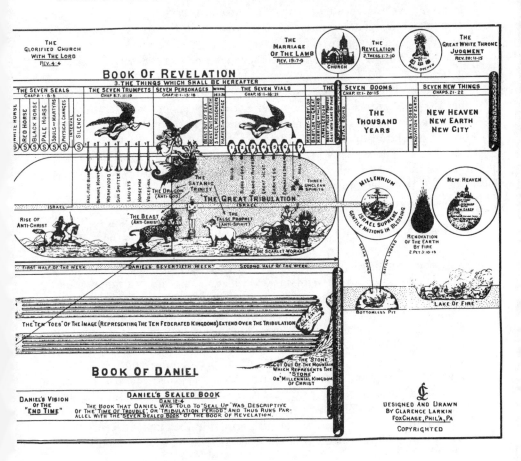

macy of grace in all ages) Scofield said characteristically, "It is . . . of vital moment to observe that Scripture never, in *any* dispensation, *mingles* these two principles."[13] Distinctions were also made on the basis of seemingly small variations in Biblical language. So, for instance, Scofield placed great weight on the distinction between "the kingdom of God" and "the kingdom of heaven" and on the differences among *in, with,* and *upon* as used with reference to the Holy Ghost.[14]

Dispensationalist leaders regarded these methods of dividing and classifying as the only scientific ones. Scofield, for example, contrasted his work to previous "unscientific systems."[15] Similarly, Reuben Torrey regarded ideas basically as things to be sorted out and arranged. One of his major works, *What the Bible Teaches* (1898), is an incredibly dry five-hundred-page compilation of thousands of Biblical "propositions" supported by proof texts. The closest analogy would be to an encyclopedia or dictionary. Torrey explicitly defended this utter lack of style or elegance. "Beauty and impressiveness," he said in the preface, "must always yield to precision and clearness." As usual, his model was the scientist. Torrey depicted his work as "simply an attempt at a careful unbiased, systematic, thorough-going, *inductive* study and statement of Bible truth. . . . The methods of modern science are applied to Bible study—thorough analysis followed by careful synthesis."[16]

Induction had to start with the hard facts, and dispensationalists insisted that the only proper way to interpret Scripture was in "the literal sense," unless the text or the context absolutely demanded otherwise.[17] All dispensational interpreters agreed on this. Prophecies must mean exactly what they said ("Israel" must mean the Jews, never the church). Prophetic numbers referred to exact periods of time. Predictions would come true as real events, although the Bible might use images to describe them—as "The Beast" of Revelation 19 for the earth's last and worst political tyrant.[18]

These literalistic conclusions reflected the accentuation of an attitude toward the Bible that had been strong in America since the days of the Puritans. The Puritans too had assumed that Biblical interpretation was an exact science with precise conclusions. "There is only one meaning for every place in Scripture," wrote William Ames, a contemporary of Francis Bacon and one of the great Puritan expositors. "Otherwise the meaning of Scripture would not only be unclear and uncertain, but there would be no meaning at all—for anything which does not mean one thing surely means nothing."[19] The Puritans accordingly attempted to keep to the plain meaning of Scripture, developing a "plain style" of preaching as opposed to the flourishes of Anglican rhetoric. Nineteenth-century American dispensationalists moved in a similar direction. Their method of presenting their views was the "Bible reading," a plain exposition of the words of the text, as opposed to the flowery orations of such princes of the pulpit as Henry Ward Beecher or Phillips Brooks.[20] Like the Puritans,[21] the dispensationalists were strongly oriented toward the printed word, eschewing the mysterious in both exposition and worship. They assumed a literate audience who could follow the exposition of the text and also study it on their own. Personal devotions *meant* Bible study, combined with prayer.

Such emphasis on the printed word is sometimes viewed as socially conservative and elitist[22] and in the emerging fundamentalist movement seems oddly yoked with the revivalist orientation toward the spoken word which had parallel populist and radical overtones. There is no explaining this paradox except to observe that it is in conformity with such recurrent conflicts in fundamentalism as that of head and heart religion or that of being simultaneously the religious establishment and cultural outsiders. All of these tensions were inherited from the American revivalist-evangelical-Puritan tradition which was an amalgamation of traditions and not always internally consistent. The strong concern for the exact meaning of the printed word, however, is one of the principal things that distinguish fundamentalism from other less intellectual forms of American revivalism or from the more experientially oriented holiness tradition or—most populist, sectarian, and vocally oriented of all—pentecostalism.

Nevertheless, the prophetic teachers regarded their approach as a popular one. The literalistic approach, they maintained, was simply that of common sense. Since it was based on laws of language and meaning which were common to all people, the method was especially appropriate for the "common man." "Appeal to the common sense of any stranger . . . ," said the Reverend Stephen H. Tyng, Jr., of New York, host of the first International Prophetic Conference in 1878. Common sense, he said, would prove that "a literal rendering is always to be given in the reading of Scripture, unless the context makes it absurd."[23] "I insist," said Professor Jerry Lummis (of Lawrence College, Wisconsin) in an address at the 1886 Conference, "that the New Testament statements conform to the laws of language as truly as do those of Xenophon." We should expect no "mystical" language with "secret or hidden meaning." Rather, said Lummis, the prophetic teachings of Christ "are just as easily apprehended by the common sense of the common people as are His teachings in respect to duty."[24] "In ninety-nine out of a hundred cases," concurred Reuben Torrey, "the meaning that the plain man gets out of the Bible is the correct one."[25]

The belief that the facts and laws they were dealing with were matters of plain common sense was basic to the dynamics of the movement. Although fundamentalists emphasized that it was scientific, they never regarded their scheme of Biblical interpretation as esoteric. Esoteric, complicated, mystical, allegorical, and other fantastical interpretations were the characteristic productions of theology professors, especially Germans.[26] Their own scheme was by contrast presented as simple and straightforward interpretation of fact according to plain laws available to common sense and the common man. Fundamentalism did not develop in seminaries, but in Bible conferences, Bible schools, and, perhaps most importantly, on the personal level of small Bible-study groups where the prophetic truths could be made plain.

The structures of the movement harmonized with its ideology. Rather than developing a hierarchical order from the top down, it first grew from a network of inter-personal and inter-institutional relationships,[27] as the informal summer Bible conference demonstrates. The vacation setting put everyone on almost the same level and social amenities gave way to the higher spiritual purpose. Yet in the context of common sense informality and equality, a new hierarchy readily emerged. The structure was at least analogous to the ideology. As in the Baconian view of reality one began with particular facts and built from them conclusions of universal validity, so out of the network of seemingly egalitarian relationships among Bible teachers and students effective evangelistic leaders emerged to build authoritarian empires.

Not everyone associated with the networks of Bible teachers, Bible institutes, Bible conferences, and evangelists precisely fit the ideological mold of dispensationalism and thoroughgoing Baconianism. Dwight L. Moody was an outstanding exception. A whole spectrum of opinions separated him and his dispensationalist associates. Yet, while there was not complete uniformity of belief, the intellectual predispositions associated with dispensationalism gave fundamentalism its characteristic hue.

VII. History, Society, and the Church

HISTORY

More explicitly articulated than their Baconianism (which they simply regarded as self-evident common sense), the dispensationalists' other distinct intellectual predisposition was a strong inclination toward the supernatural. "Heightened supernaturalism"[1] appeared everywhere in dispensationalist thought. Their view of the supernatural origins of Scripture rendered the human element negligible. They stood firm against any erosion of traditional doctrinal emphasis on the miraculous, especially in fundamental teachings about the birth, work, death, and resurrection of Christ. Their view of his dramatic second coming fit this pattern. The great conflict preceding the millennium would be a terrible confrontation between the hosts of Christ and the minions of Satan. This coming conflict, moreover, would mark the culmination of a fierce struggle that dominated all of history. Accordingly,

Christians must view themselves as caught between two powers, Christ and Satan.[2]

Clearly, this view of history is anti-humanist and anti-developmental. Natural developments in which humans are the key agents play little if any role. Rather, humans participate in a larger cosmic struggle, the details of which have been planned and often revealed in advance. Change takes place almost solely through dramatic divine intervention, which transforms each era into the next. Each dispensation of history, says Scofield, represents "some change in God's method of dealing with mankind," involving "a new test of the natural man." Mankind invariably fails these tests, and God ends each dispensation with judgment and introduces a wholly new era.[3] All history is thus ordered by abstract principles of testing with God as the primary agent of change.

There is, however, room in God's plan for some development within each dispensation. The church in particular is declining in the present era from its original purity, while the whole civilization is also becoming increasingly corrupt. This view provides a negative parallel to secular concepts of progress. The very same evidence that the secular humanist might take as an indication of progress, the dispensationalist would regard as a sure sign of accelerating retrogression.

They drew opposite conclusions from the evidence and in essential first principles the dispensationalists' view of history was strikingly different from most other nineteenth- and twentieth-century views. A modern historian would perhaps feel that dispensationalists were not dealing with history at all. Modern historiography assumes that human and natural forces shape the course of history and its basic model is something like a biological concept of development. Dispensationalists, on the other hand, start with the assumption that supernatural forces shape history. Their model is the ongoing warfare between God and Satan. The data that each group considers relevant to historical explanation are so different that even basic communication would be difficult or impossible.[4] These totally opposed views of history lay at the heart of the conflict and misunderstanding between theological liberals and their fundamentalist opponents. The liberal party came increasingly to view history in the sense of natural development as the key to understanding all reality, including Scripture. Fundamentalists, on the other hand, insisted more and more that the supernatural account of things in Scripture was the key to understanding anything about natural reality, including history.

The dispensationalist view seems less eccentric if placed in the context of the whole development of Western historiography. The conflict between God and Satan and the centrality of Scripture for understanding the past had long been basic to Western historical thought. Even in nineteenth-century America, widely held views of history, influenced by postmillennial theology, were often dominated by such categories. Certainly any Christian

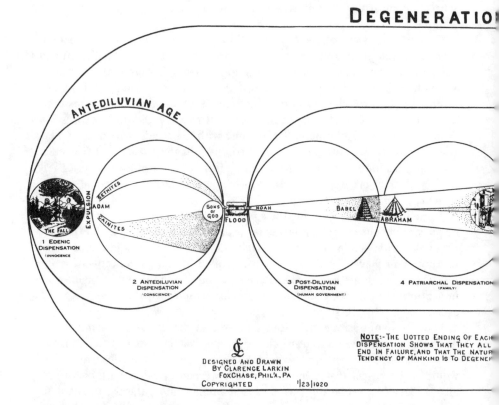

DEGENERATIO[N]

ANTEDILUVIAN AGE

1 EDENIC DISPENSATION
(INNOCENCE)

EXPULSION
ADAM
SETHITES
CAINITES
THE FALL

SONS OF GOD
NOAH
FLOOD

BABEL
ABRAHAM

2 ANTEDILUVIAN DISPENSATION
(CONSCIENCE)

3 POST-DILUVIAN DISPENSATION
(HUMAN GOVERNMENT)

4 PATRIARCHAL DISPENSATION
(FAMILY)

NOTE:- THE DOTTED ENDING OF EACH DISPENSATION SHOWS THAT THEY ALL END IN FAILURE, AND THAT THE NATUR[AL] TENDENCY OF MANKIND IS TO DEGENER[ATE]

DESIGNED AND DRAWN BY CLARENCE LARKIN FOXCHASE, PHIL'A, PA COPYRIGHTED 1|23|1920

interpreter of history from Augustine to Edwards would easily have understood the dispensationalists' approach. What he might have found puzzling would not be the supernaturalism but the peculiar system of classification of historical eras.[5]

Despite its overall similarities to older Christian views of history, dispensationalism has a number of peculiarities that identify it as a product of nineteenth-century thought. These have to do especially with its explanation of how dramatic historical change takes place, a common preoccupation of the thought of the era. In the prevailing naturalistic explanations of change the principal model was development through conflict. This is apparent in the work of the two most influential theorists of mid-century, Darwin and Marx. Marxism in fact has some formal similarities to the nearly contemporary development of dispensationalism. History is divided into distinct periods, each dominated by a prevailing principle or characteristic. Each age ends in failure, conflict, judgment on those who rule, and the violent introduction of a wholly new era. History thus proceeds in dramatic steps toward a final age of peace. The crucial difference is that in the Marxist scheme the scientific approach to history assumes that the laws of change are governed

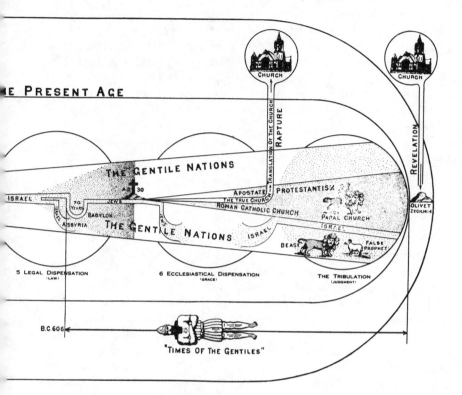

by wholly natural factors of human behavior; in dispensationalism science discovers revealed principles of supernatural laws that have guided historical change.

The most nearly parallel theory, however, was geological catastrophism. This interpretation of the growing evidence of the earth's great age constituted a major strand in both English and American scientific thought during the first half of the nineteenth century. After mid-century it was still very prominent in America as a way of reconciling science and religion. Pious catastrophists, including some leading figures in American natural science, explained the various layers of flora and fauna as the result of successive epochs of geological history, each providentially brought to end by a catastrophe that led to a new age.[6] Thus the indisputable evidence of dramatic change from epoch to epoch could be accounted for, with the hand of God kept decisively in the picture.

Dispensationalists did the same thing with Biblical history. Each epoch ended with a catastrophe: the dispensation of "Innocence" ended with the Fall, that of "Conscience" with the Flood; "Human Government" was disrupted at Babel; "Promise" ended in captivity in Egypt; "Law" ended with the rejection of Christ; "Grace" with the tribulation; and even the millennium ended with Satan "loosed a little season."[7]Although geological and Biblical catastrophism seemed to develop independently, they did overlap concerning the Flood, which both agreed was the end of a distinct era. Curiously, many dispensationalists introduced an additional version of geological catastrophism into their interpretations of Genesis 1. They argued that between Genesis 1:1 ("In the beginning God created the heaven and the earth") and Genesis 1:2 ("And the earth was without form and void"), "the earth had undegone a cataclysmic change as the result of divine judgment." This "catastrophe," occurring in an era of undetermined length, could account for a great deal of scientific data concerning the age and changed character of the earth.[8]

SOCIETY

The area where dispensationalists were perhaps most out of step with the rest of nineteenth-century thinking was in their view of contemporary history, which had little or no room for social or political progress. When they spoke on this question, dispensational premillennialists were characteristically pessimistic. Baptist Bible teacher A. J. Frost, for instance, addressed the 1886 International Prophecy Conference with the thesis that the world's moral condition was steadily "growing worse and worse." Frost cited statistics embellished with rhetorical flourishes that revealed dramatic increases in both England and America of murder, suicide, theft, indecent assault, drunkenness, and divorce. "And yet," he said, "Christian men in all our religious denominations are boasting of the moral and religious progress of the age, whereas the two foremost Christian nations on the globe are every day sinking lower and lower in immorality and crime. . . ." The condition of the cities, said Frost, was particularly alarming. These were "becoming plague-spots of moral and political leprosy, the hotbeds of lawlessness and crime. . . ." Politically, the signs of the times were especially ominous in the "seething, surging, rioting masses of the dangerous classes of the ground tier" and the "armies marching and countermarching with banners on which are emblazoned dynamite, anarchism, communism, nihilism." The end was near.[9]

Such rhetoric aside, dispensationalists as a group never fully developed or carefully articulated their political views. Rather their opinions seemed to reflect the conventional slogans of the day. Much of what they said on this subject was highly stylized and could have been summarized under such headings as "Rum, Romanism, and Rebellion," which played a notorious role in the election of 1884, when a supporter of the Republican James G. Blaine attributed these interests to the Democrats. The following summer, Joshua Denovan told the Niagara Conference that the American system was "very much in the grasp of millionaires and rings of monopoly, of Rome and Rum." In this instance Denovan balanced the ticket by substituting for "Rebellion" another familiar millenarian theme—luxury and ostentation.[10]

Clearly the dispensationalists were not much interested in social or political questions as such, except as they bore on spiritual history. Their disillusionment was not so much with politics itself as with the postmillennial claims that Christianity in this age would rescue civilization. The idea of a "Christian civilization" was often a particular target of their scorn. The Pope in Rome was the preeminent example of this pretense and always fair game for Protestant Americans. So A. J. Gordon described him as "gnawing the bone of infallibility, which he acquired in 1870, and clutching for that other bone of temporal sovereignty which he lost the very same year. . . ."[11] But the more radical millenarians were turning such rhetoric toward the Protestant "Christian" world itself. Nathaniel West, one of the leading millennial interpreters of the day, elaborated on this theme. "Gigantic is the misconception," he proclaimed, "to dream that God has given the Church, unable to reform herself, to build the Christian State up to a Kingdom of Christ, or to reform the world." The better names in the Word of God for the "Christian-State" were "Babylon the Great" or "Mother Harlot." Temperance and peace, for example, were two of the leading nineteenth-century reform movements supposed to advance the kingdom throughout Christendom. Now, observed West:

> In its most Christian portion, the United States, it spends the sum of $900,000,000 per annum, for *whiskey* alone, chief staple in the national revenue, while on the breast of Europe today, no less than 28,000,000 of woman-born, enrolled and armed to the teeth, stand ready to imbrue their hands in each other's blood;— officered, led, inspired, and paid by the *"Christian State."*[12]

The decline of civilization was inevitable. First of all, as Nathaniel West explained it, there was "the law of deterioration in the march of empires." This law applied to every dispensation. More precisely, the present age would end with the revival of the Roman Empire and the rule of the Beast, the last Roman emperor, in alliance with the "False Prophet," the last ecclesiastical tyrant.[13]

Such views hardly fit with the idea of progress that characterized European and American thought throughout the nineteenth century. The rapid spread of premillennial thought must have reflected some disillusionment with the progress of civilization. No doubt social pessimism contributed to the growth of the dispensationalist movement in post-Civil-War America during the Gilded Age. The war clearly had not introduced a golden age of the reign of righteousness as some had predicted. Moreover, the progression from General Washington to General Grant hardly suggested the coming of a millennium. Indeed, one could argue that the last quarter of the nineteenth century was "a period probably as tension-ridden as any other quarter of a century in our history. . . ."[14] Despite much optimism and continued talk of progress, there still was much cause for pessimism as well. So premillennialists' rejection of the idea of progress did not leave them alone in this era of Mark Twain and Henry Adams, when secular commentators frequently predicted a social cataclysm.[15]

Yet it would misrepresent the nature of the growing interest in premillennialism in America to characterize it basically as a reaction to social and political conditions. Such factors were indeed present and for some persons important. But when these issues were discussed, as they were with some regularity in prophetic literature, they almost invariably appeared on back pages after the Biblical studies and were presented only as secondary points of confirmation of prophecy. Most tellingly, as will become apparent in the later discussion of their view of Christianity and culture, dispensationalists were not all of one mind in their opinion of American society. Some utterly condemned it; others were ambivalent.

THE CHURCH

In dispensationalists' occasional remarks on the subject, the reason most frequently given for their views, aside from the sheer logic of the Biblical exposition, was that the poor prospects for the worldwide advance of the church convinced them of the impossibility of postmillennial claims. Even though the missionary movement was at its height, the simple facts were that the non-Christian population of the world was growing faster than the number of converts. Furthermore, even in so-called Christian lands the unconverted population was vastly greater than the number of converts. Half of Christendom was in the grip of Popish superstition, and the rest, if the condition of cities and the statistics on vice were an indication, was losing ground faster than any evangelistic effort could make up for. William E. Blackstone, whose book *Jesus is Coming* did much to popularize the movement, supplied charts for the 1886 International Prophecy Conference to illustrate that even if one counted all the merely nominal Protestants as part of the truly Christian population the total was less than the growth of the heathen and Mohammedan population in the last century. All the converts gained by missionaries added together made up only the tiniest fraction of the non-Western world. A. J. Frost made a similar point:

> A ship recently sailed from Boston to the Congo region of Africa. It had on board one hundred thousand gallons of rum and one missionary. How long will it take such a Christendom as we have described to convert the world?[16]

Premillennialists were enthusiastic about mission efforts because one of the signs of the end was that the Gospel would have been preached to all nations. Yet they scoffed at the idea that the heathen nations would soon be converted.[17]

At the 1914 Prophetic Bible Conference, pessimism about the spread of

DIAGRAM EXHIBITING THE
ACTUAL AND RELATIVE NUMBER OF MANKIND
CLASSIFIED ACCORDING TO THEIR RELIGION.

Each square represents 1,000,000 souls.

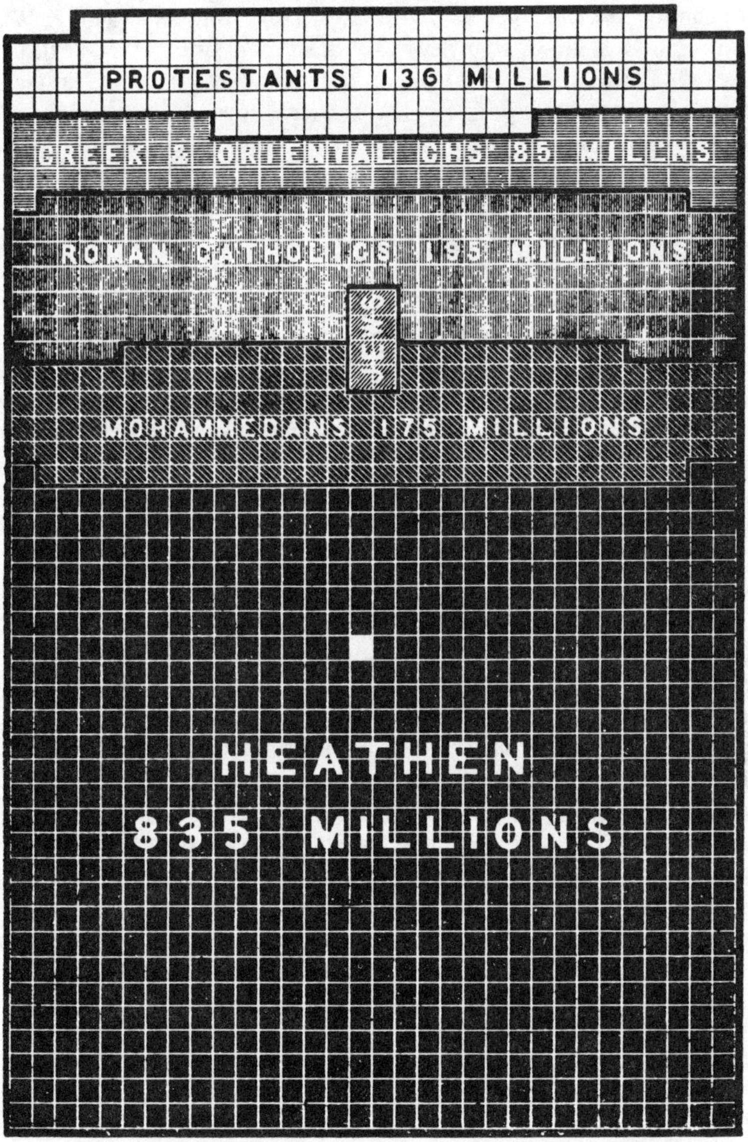

PROTESTANTS 136 MILLIONS

GREEK & ORIENTAL CHS 85 MILLIONS

ROMAN CATHOLICS 195 MILLIONS

JEWS

MOHAMMEDANS 175 MILLIONS

HEATHEN
835 MILLIONS

The one white square in the black indicates converts from Heathenism.
In 100 years the heathen and Mohammedan population has increased 200,000,000.

From *Prophetic Studies of the International Prophetic Conference (Chicago, November, 1886)*, (Chicago, 1887), p. 204.

Christianity still seemed to be the primary factor (outside of the Bible itself) supporting the premillennial as opposed to the postmillennial view. That conference included a panel of six of its leaders speaking on the theme "How I Became a Premillennialist." All six panelists mentioned the influence of such prominent Bible teachers as Brookes, Blackstone, Scofield, J. Wilbur Chapman, and William B. Riley. They also mentioned other key factors. Charles G. Trumbull, editor of the *Sunday School Times* and leading promoter of holiness teaching concerning "the victorious life," related premillennialism to that theme. A Jewish convert considered especially important his orthodox Jewish expectation of the Messiah. Another was impressed by the observation that there were no premillennialists among the higher critics who questioned Scripture. The remaining three each mentioned a disillusionment with the postmillennial expectation that the world would soon be converted.[18]

During this era American premillennialists seem to have been more disillusioned about the prospects for missions than about the present state of the churches in America. Although believing that the apostate church was the "Great Whore of Babylon," very few American millenarians prior to World War I seem to have considered their own denominations in this category. In any case, few actually separated from their churches. John Nelson Darby was puzzled by this when he first brought his teaching to America. Many Americans were interested in his approach to prophetic studies, yet few took seriously the Brethren teaching of the "ruin of the church."[19]

The reason for this lack of concern was no doubt related to American evangelicals' characteristic lack of strong views about the nature and authority of the church. Lacking direct experience with such doctrines, they had not formed a distinct concept of the church against which they might react. This general absence in America of a clear theory on the church reflected organizational structures that had developed more for reasons of circumstance than of ideology.[20] Instead of "churches" (in the sense of the official organized religion of a territory) or "sects" (in the sense of separated groups of true converted believers), America had "denominations," which were sometimes churchly, sometimes sectarian, and usually both. The denominations were the product of a combination of European churchly traditions, ethnic loyalties, pietism, sectarianism, and American free enterprise. Often a denomination would advertise itself as the true church and speak in its own councils as if it were. At the same time the denominational system was really based on the premise that the true church could be denominated in many ways. Moreover, denominational structures were usually loose enough that revivals, reforms, Bible conferences, and schools could be promoted by members outside of denominational control. Hence the system allowed room for a practical sectarianism which often left denominational ties weak or nominal.

The dispensationalist theory of the inevitable decline of the church did, however, provide a rationale that would eventually support the move of many fundamentalists toward formal independence. But most people did not act on the implications of this view until their own experience demanded it. As long as the denominational model was tolerable for practical affairs, they were willing to live with considerable tension between theory and practice. When the old model broke down, however (not until the 1920s), the dispensationalist view of the church was available to account for the phenomenon and to provide a rationale for new structures.

Dispensationalist views were themselves a force in precipitating the eventual crisis. The theory of the inevitable demise of the church encouraged an alertness to the signs of decay in American denominations. In 1886 A. J. Frost, in his litany of the ills of the church and the world, identified the doctrinal issues that would become the focus of later fundamentalist attacks. "A thousand pulpits," he proclaimed, "are drifting from the doctrine of inspiration, the deity of Christ, the vicarious atonement, the resurrection of the body, and the eternal retribution."[21] Similarly, during this era James H. Brookes's influential journal *The Truth* carefully noted each new trend away from the truth, cheering on the conservatives in every ecclesiastical conflict. In the 1890s during the last years of Brookes's career, he not only continued his slashing attacks on such notorious advocates of new views as Charles A. Briggs or Lyman Abbott, but also assailed even such revered American religious institutions as the YMCA (for tolerating evolutionists) and Christian Endeavor (for adopting a "New Decalogue" concerned with good citizenship rather than leading people to Christ).[22] These increased efforts to combat Protestant apostasy seldom led to actual ecclesiastical separation.[23] Rather, most critics were content to point out that the wheat and the tares had to grow together, and saw themselves (as W. E. Blackstone put it) as part of a spiritual "church within, or among the churches" which was the true "church militant."[24]

An important reason that most American dispensationalists did not consider separation from their denominations a necessary consequence of their belief, was that they thought of religion primarily in terms of individuals rather than institutions. The important spiritual unit was the individual. The church existed as a body of sanctified individuals united by commitment to Christ and secondarily as a network of *ad hoc* spiritual organizations. The institutional church hence had no particular status. Separation, at least at this time, could be regarded as an individual question rather than an institutional one. The true Christian was one separated from sin and worldliness. Therefore, dispensational and premillennial teachings were not at this time central to a definition of the Christian's relationship to the world, culture, and the churches. More immediately relevant was the question of how an individual was to live a spiritually separated and victorious life.[25]

Holiness

VIII. The Victorious Life

"Indeed, within the last twenty years," C. I. Scofield observed in 1899, "more has been written and said upon the doctrine of the Holy Spirit than in the preceding eighteen hundred years."[1] Scofield's estimate, which appeared in his own work on the Spirit, was not implausible.[2] During the preceding decades the movements known in the twentieth century as "Holiness," "Pentecostal," and "fundamentalist" had been taking shape and each had a common origin in the resurgence of interest in the Holy Spirit that was sweeping American evangelicalism. While Pentecostalism did not emerge as a self-consciously distinct entity until the famous outbursts inspired by Charles F. Parham at the beginning of 1901, many of its doctrines and expectations had already been shaped by the surge of theories about the Holy Spirit to which Scofield referred.[3] Most of these speculations, like those of Parham himself, developed in the vigorous "Holiness"[4] movement that emerged during the last third of the century, basically out of Methodism. Less well known is the fact that many writers of holiness works were evangelists and Bible teachers like Scofield who had Calvinist leanings.[5] Indeed, almost all of Moody's lieutenants associated with the rise of dispensationalism wrote works on the Holy Spirit. While their views on the exact nature of the outpouring of the Holy Spirit differed somewhat from those of their Methodistic allies, in 1899 they still saw themselves as in the same spiritual camp. Even more than dispensationalism, their stress on the work of the Holy Spirit seems to have shaped their distinctive outlook at this time.[6]

The dispensationalist and holiness teachings held by the more Calvinistic evangelists and Bible teachers were closely connected. The holiness teachings of nineteenth-century American evangelicalism were built upon the idea that the present era was the age of the outpouring of the Holy Spirit which had begun on or near the time of the first Pentecost as recorded in the book of Acts. Dispensationalism's central teaching—that the church age was the unique age of the Spirit—stressed the same thing. The holiness teachings, which, as we shall see shortly, had roots in earlier nineteenth-century American revivalism as well as in Wesley's Methodism, seem in fact to have prepared the way for the acceptance of dispensationalism.

The campaigns and conferences organized by the associates of Moody to promote these two new doctrines were often kept distinct.[7] Holiness teachings apparently were considered less divisive and more practical than dispensationalism. The chief practical use of dispensationalism was to inspire and intensify the all-important missions effort.[8] It further provided rationale for understanding the demise of the institutional church, an issue that became increasingly important as the campaign against modernism grew in the early twentieth century. In the meantime, however, holiness teachings had a wider range of practical uses. As will be seen, the new doctrines of the Holy Spirit emphasized a profound personal experience of consecration, a filling with Spiritual power, and a dedication to arduous Christian service. Especially when the movement was in its more positive stages, prior to World War I, experience and practice were its primary concerns.

These emphases did not conflict with the intellectual and calculating Baconianism of the evangelists any more than the message of Moody and Sankey conflicted with that of Torrey or Scofield. Evangelists of the latter sort were simply combining two complementary methods of defending authentic Christianity. American evangelicals, lacking a high view of the church or of tradition, could appeal to either or both of two bases of authority for their faith: personal experience and the Bible. The Wesleyan or Methodist tradition, which in the nineteenth century influenced almost all of American revivalism, stressed personal experience verified by the witness of words and works. Such testimony did not have to conflict with defense of the authority of the Bible grounded in reason and science. While Methodist Holiness advocates and later Pentecostals took the objective authority of Scripture for granted and accentuated the experiential, dispensationalist holiness teachers tried to emphasize both.

Connecting the Methodist Holiness tradition with the Reformed holiness doctrine was a complex web of interactions going back at least to the eighteenth century and John Wesley's work on "Christian Perfection." Wesley, who was much concerned with morality, noted that Scripture commanded one to "be perfect." He was convinced that this state must therefore be obtainable. He proposed a resolution to the obvious difficulties by limiting the definition of sin. "Nothing is sin, strictly speaking," he said, "but a voluntary transgression of a known law of God." This definition emphasized, in a spirit that later in America would suit the modern democratic age, the concept of sin as a voluntary act of will.[9] Moreover, according to Wesley, believers could by God's grace be freed not only from particular sinful acts, but also from the disease of sinful motives and the "power" of sin. This state he called "entire sanctification." It usually involved both a growth in grace and a dramatic experience. The condition of "perfection" or having "perfect love" had to be maintained at all times and was one from which the Christian might fall.[10]

This teaching conflicted sharply with the Reformed and Puritan concepts of Christian life that had prevailed in colonial America. Although the Puritans and their Presbyterian brethren intensely sought holiness, they did so with the assurance that the progress of the pilgrim would be marked by obstacles and failures. Perfection would never be attained in this life. Rather, the Christian's life was one of constant and intense struggle, involving every aspect of his or her nature. In this struggle a person's naturally sinful and corrupt condition (which remained even if increasingly weakened and mortified) fought against the new regenerated heart which through the Spirit of Christ grew in true holiness. The Christian's life was a warfare, with many setbacks that taught humility and dependence of God's grace.[11]

These two opposed views clashed at first and were then synthesized during the evangelical revivals of the first half of the nineteenth century in America. Charles Finney brought the two views together and by 1840 was introducing something very similar to the Methodist holiness teaching into Reformed circles. Finney and his associates, notably Asa Mahan, developed the Oberlin Theology, a qualified version of perfectionism. Even more than Wesley thay emphasized the role of the will, founding their case on Yale theologian Nathaniel Taylor's argument, based in turn on Common Sense philosophy, that nothing is either sinful or righteous unless it be a free act of will.[12] The regenerate person, Finney and Mahan said, is not commanded to perform acts beyond his capacity. He must have the ability to choose the good in every instance of responsible choice. To choose correctly, however, a special work of the Holy Spirit, beyond mere regeneration, must completely overwhelm his will. Given this special work, defined so as to affirm both human free agency and complete dependence on God's gracious power, "entire sanctification is attainable in this life."[13]

During the thirty years from 1840 to 1870 American evangelicalism was revolutionized by outbursts of similar holiness teaching across a broad denominational front. Parallel to Finney's influence among the Reformed was Phoebe Palmer's among Methodists. An inspiring Bible teacher, Mrs. Palmer promoted holiness renewal through "Tuesday Meetings" in New York City from 1837 until her death in 1874. Such gatherings, large and small, for Bible study, prayer, song, and personal testimony, provided the base for widespread growth of evangelical teaching with holiness emphasis.[14] More specifically, Phoebe Palmer's work led to the foundation in 1867 of the influential National Camp Meeting Association for the Promotion of Holiness, out of which the separatistic Holiness movement soon grew. The hallmark of the teachings of Palmer and most later advocates of this "Methodistic" wing of the holiness movement was a dramatic second blessing attained by an act of consecration described as placing "all on the altar." The act of faith was crucial. "If you have faith to be sanctified, you are sanctified."[15] The result was present purification, being saved now from all sin. By the end of the century this experience was widely described (in terminology so important to the subsequent Pentecostal secessions) as "The Baptism of the Holy Ghost." In the meantime, numerous denominations had been formed embodying the radical demands of the varieties of Holiness teachings. The Wesleyan Methodists and the Free Methodists were founded before the Civil War. In 1865 Willaim Booth established the "Christian Mission" in East London, which by 1880 had become the Salvation Army and was expanding to America. The Church of God (Anderson, Indiana) was founded in 1880 and the Christian and Missionary Alliance in 1887, both teaching Holiness doctrines. Various smaller groups, mostly growing out of the Camp Meeting movement, split off from the Methodist churches, eventually forming into groups such as the Nazarenes and the Pilgrim Holiness Church.[16]

Meanwhile evangelicals in the Reformed tradition continued to be affected by this general holiness revolution. The seemingly spontaneous city revivals of 1858 grew out of this base, resulting in small gatherings for prayer marked by holiness teachings. The next year William E. Boardman, a Presbyterian clergyman, published *The Christian Higher Life*. Boardman's work was soon supplemented by that of Hannah Whitall Smith and her husband Robert Pearsall Smith, converts of the 1858 revival, who also became Presbyterians. The Smiths promoted holiness teaching in America and then in England, with their greatest success in Hannah's *The Christian's Secret to the Happy Life* (1875). These writers emphasized two dramatically experienced acts of faith. The first (justification) involved cleansing from the guilt of sin; the second (sanctification), which brought the higher life and happiness, involved cleansing from sin's power and "victory over sin and inward rest of soul."[17]

Oberlin perfectionism was also modified by these new trends as well as contributing to them. In 1870 Asa Mahan published *The Baptism of the Holy Spirit*, which title suggests the important shift from earlier Christocentric themes to an emphasis on the outpourings of the Holy Spirit such as took place at the first Christian Pentecost. Sometime after the Christian's conversion, said Mahan, "'the Holy Ghost comes upon,' 'falls upon,' and is 'poured out upon him,' and thus 'endues him with power from on high' for his life mission and work."[18]

By 1870, holiness teachings of one sort or another seemed to be everywhere in American revivalist Protestantism. Their pervasiveness is suggested by the tremendous popularity of such new gospel song writers as Fanny J. Crosby, her English counterpart Frances R. Havergal, Philip P. Bliss, and a number of less well-known figures, all of whom rhapsodized about holiness and consecration. Their hymns, especially those by women, were filled with themes of total surrender and being overwhelmed by the love of Jesus and

No. 48. Oh, to be Nothing.

"Neither is he that planteth anything, neither he that watereth."—1 Cor. 3: 7.

GEORGIANA M. TAYLOR, 1869. R. GEO. HALLS. Arr. by P. P. BLISS.

Very slow.

1. Oh, to be nothing, noth-ing, On-ly to lie at His feet,

CHO. Oh, to be nothing, noth-ing, On-ly to lie at His feet,

FINE.

A broken and emptied ves-sel, For the Mas-ter's use made meet.

A broken and emptied ves-sel, For the Mas-ter's use made meet.

Emptied that He might fill me As forth to His ser-vice I go;

D. C. CHORUS.

Broken, that so un-hin-dered, His life through me might flow.

2 Oh, to be nothing, nothing,
  Only as led by His hand;
A messenger at His gateway,
  Only waiting for His command,
Only an instrument ready
  His praises to sound at His will,
Willing, should He not require me,
  In silence to wait on Him still. *Cho.*

3 Oh, to be nothing, nothing,
  Painful the humbling may be,
Yet low in the dust I'd lay me
  That the world might my Saviour see
Rather be nothing, nothing,
  To Him let our voices be raised,
He is the Fountain of blessing,
  He only is meet to be praised. *Cho.*

From *Gospel Hymns Nos. 1 to 6*, Ira Sankey *et al.*, eds. (New York, 1894).

the cleansing tide of his Spirit. "Oh to be Nothing," "None of Self and All of Thee," "Dying with Jesus," and "Take Me as I Am" were popular and typical titles. "Take my life and let it be Consecrated, Lord to Thee," wrote Havergal. "Take my will and make it Thine, It shall be no longer mine; Take my heart, it is Thine own, It shall be Thy royal throne." The power for Christian service was seen as the result of total consecration to Christ, and the imagery was often passionate and passive.[19] A common image (as in the second verse of "Oh to be Nothing") was that of an instrument, like the aeolian harp so popular in the romantic poetry of the time, on which the Saviour plays.

These romantic, sentimentalized, and often imprecise holiness teachings underwent one further modification before assuming the form they most often took when associated with American fundamentalism. This development involved a curious transatlantic exchange, with British elements added in the process. In 1873, while in England during the time of the early Moody campaigns, Pearsall and Hannah Smith and William Boardman organized a series of meetings for Bible study and the promotion of holiness. These grew into larger conferences the next year, settling permanently at the scenic Lake-District site of Keswick in 1875. Asa Mahan, Boardman, and Pearsall Smith were among the speakers at these early meetings. The most influential British founders of the movement seem to have been quite careful to avoid the charge of teaching perfectionism, an accusation that had some plausibility considering the American company they were keeping. This tension was heightened when in 1875, just before the first meeting at Keswick itself, Pearsall Smith, up to then the principal attraction, was found to have been involved in an "indiscretion" in a hotel room with a young woman student of higher spirituality. While his failing seems to have been suggestive, rather than active, his associates judged that his behavior did not comport well with his status as a leading teacher of holiness. Suddenly he dropped—or was pushed—from public life.[20]

The resulting gap was almost immediately filled by H. W. Webb-Peploe, a distinguished and impressive Church of England clergyman, who dominated the Keswick movement, as it became known, for almost fifty years and did a great deal to define the Keswick teaching. Especially important was Webb-Peploe's firm opposition to Methodist-type perfectionism. He and his fellow representatives of the Keswick position objected to the recent Wesleyan views which taught the eradication of sinful nature in this life. Such illusions, said Keswick teachers, would lead to trust in self rather than in Christ. Their view was rather that we should recognize that everything we do in this life is tainted by sin arising from the original corruption of our natures.[21]

While rejecting as too strong the Wesleyan view of the *eradication* of one's sinful nature, the Keswick teachers rejected as too weak the more traditional view that one's sinful nature was simply *suppressed* by Christ's righteousness. This view, they felt, would encourage a life not only of constant conflict with sin, but also of defeat by sin, and even tolerance of it as normal. They came to call their own view *counteraction*.[22] What they had in mind is best described by a favored analogy. Our sinful nature is like an uninflated balloon with a cart (the weight of sin) attached. Christ fills the balloon and the resulting buoyancy overcomes the natural gravity of our sin. While Christ fills our lives we do not have a *tendency* to sin, yet we still are *liable* to sin. Were we to let Christ out of our lives, sin would immediately take over. Hence the state of holiness must be constantly maintained and renewed.[23] So rather than using Methodistic-Holiness terms such as "the Baptism of the Holy Spirit" or "second blessing," most Keswick teachers spoke of repeated emptyings by consecration and "fillings" with the Holy Spirit, or the "Spirit of Jesus."[24]

In this way the Keswick teachers could offer a doctrine that in practice had many of the same implications as the more Wesleyan Holiness teachings, but in theory avoided the claim, so offensive to those with Calvinist leanings, of ever being totally without sin. In effect, the promise was that as long as Christ dwelt in the heart a Christian could be free from committing any known sin. There was therefore no excuse for tolerating any known vice, appetite, or sinful habit.

The rest of Keswick teaching follows from these concepts of sin and counteracting grace. There are two stages of Christian experience: that of the "carnal Christian," and that of the "spiritual."[25] To move from the lower to the higher state takes a definite act of faith or "consecration," the prerequisite to being filled with the Spirit. This consecration means an "absolute surrender," almost always described by the Biblical term "yielding." Self is dethroned, God is enthroned. This sanctification is a process, but one that begins with a distinct crisis experience. It is analogous to man struggling in the water (lost sinner) who grasps hold of a rowboat (regeneration), climbs aboard and rests in the boat itself (sanctification). Then he is in a position to rescue other struggling men (service).[26] Missions and witnessing were the principal manifestations of such service and every Keswick conference concluded by emphasizing these themes.

The return of the holiness teachings to America after the mid-1870s, now modified into their Keswick form, was (as with almost everything evangelical during the era) related to the work of D. L. Moody. In 1871 Moody had himself undergone an intense second experience. Reuben Torrey said later that Moody told him that this experience of the filling of the Spirit was so overwhelming that Moody "had to ask God to withhold His hand, lest he die on the very spot for joy."[27] Keswick teachings originated in England while Moody was there and resembled his own work with respect to avoidance of doctrinal controversy[28] and stress instead on practical piety and service. Sankey's hymns often stressed the popular themes of consecration.[29] Although Moody did not follow Keswick terminology precisely, he taught very similar views and made them central in his work. The Northfield conferences especially resembled the Keswick gatherings.[30] Meetings for "consecration" in which Moody urged participants "to yield themselves wholly to God" were regular features of these conferences.[31] "Get full of the Holy Spirit" was the way Moody urged students to take the necessary first step in getting ready to go to the mission field.[32] Reuben Torrey, for whom the work of the Holy Spirit was also a consuming interest, reported that early in his career Moody had urged him, "Now, Torrey, be sure and preach on the baptism with the Holy Ghost."[33] To all appearances Torrey followed this advice throughout his long career, preaching his sermon "The Baptism with the Holy Spirit" (which differed from the Keswick emphasis on "filling" mainly in terminology)[34] almost everywhere he went.

By 1890 a definite movement or sub-movement with emphasis on the Holy Spirit was taking shape among the evangelists and Bible teachers associated with Moody. As with the other sub-movements, conferences provided a basic structure. Northfield, of course, was already a strong base of operations. In addition, in 1890 in Baltimore the first major public conference on the Holy Spirit was held. A. C. Dixon, its organizer, noted that it fit in with the major conferences on prophecy and in defense of Biblical inspiration recently held. Much of the personnel overlapped with that of the prophetic conferences. The emphasis of the speakers was on the importance for present believers to receive the Holy Spirit as described in Acts 2. At least one hundred of the ministers present "requested prayer for the fulness of the Holy Ghost."[35] At the time the organizers apparently thought of themselves as part of the general holiness revival, and this conference was not devoted to any one fully developed doctrine of the Holy Spirit. During the next few years, however, more explicit Keswick teachings emerged within the group, especially after the appearances of several notable British Keswick speakers at Northfield.[36]

The aspect of Keswick teaching which aroused the greatest enthusiasm among Moody's *aides-de-camp* was the practical concept of "power for service." This phrase became a favorite of Moody's and seems to have been adopted by nearly all his lieutenants. "Victory," "peace," and "resting in the Lord" were also important aspects of Keswick teachings, but among the Americans at least the main emphasis was on service. These concerns harked back to the activism of Finney, Mahan, and other precursors of Keswick who had stressed the importance of "power," especially for witnessing. A. J. Gordon, in the 1880s one of the leading champions in the Moody circle of the work of the Holy Spirit, said much the same thing.[37] C. I. Scofield, who eventually more or less canonized Keswick teachings in his *Reference Bible*, stated in 1899 (Torrey used almost the same words) that being filled with the Spirit was "indispensable" before a Christian "should be willing to perform the slightest act in the service of Christ."[38]

The emphasis on practical results was especially prominent in the Holy Spirit conference of 1890 and its sequel, held in Brooklyn in 1894. At the first conference A. C. Dixon employed a common analogy with electricity and the power of the dynamo. "God's power is like the Niagara current," said Dixon. "Faith is the connecting wire between the battery of God's power and the hearts of men."[39] The age demanded action, not contemplation. Unlike the holiness movement of the Civil War era, this newer Reformed holiness movement was male-dominated and masculinity was equated with power and action.[40] A century of evangelical activism had provided channels for such action. Speakers at both conferences stressed that the church had many good programs, but not enough real power behind them. They envisioned a wide-spread application of the renewed power. Especially at the 1894 conference the speakers emphasized the importance of the Spirit's power for service in a host of evangelical activities—missions, evangelism, Sunday-school work, young peoples' work, church administration, city evangelism, institutional churches, and rescue missions.[41]

IX. The Social Dimensions of Holiness

Dispensationalist and Keswick teachings were two sides of the same movement; yet it is important to bear in mind that the movement had more than two sides. Arthur T. Pierson, prominent in both sub-movements, made this clear in *Forward Movements of the Last Half Century,* his end-of-century review of evangelical progress. Pierson gave special prominence to the holiness revival, especially of the Keswick variety, and ended with a brief account of premillennialism. But in between he devoted hundreds of pages to a wide variety of "philanthropic, missionary and spiritual movements" including rescue missions, city evangelization, orphanage work, student and young peoples' movements, women's work, Bible schools, missions of all kinds, evangelism among the specially needy, efforts for church unity, medical missions, "divine healing," and increased prayer and spiritual life.[1] In 1900 the offensive against liberalism was not yet noted as a distinct movement by Pierson. When it did arise, the anti-liberal movement was part of these developments, to which it gave for a time a new "fundamentalist" direction. In the meantime, the holiness emphasis seems to have been the most basic, providing the dynamic for almost every other aspect of the movement.

The "power for service" of this holiness teaching meant first of all verbal evangelism; yet in the 1890s it often meant social work among the poor as well. This was evident at the 1894 conference held in Brooklyn on "The Holy Spirit in Life and Service." The principal emphasis was not on social concerns, but they were certainly an integral part of the evangelical program.

S. H. Hadley of the Water Street Mission of New York (one of two who spoke briefly on rescue work) stressed, in opposition to the common theory that only the "worthy poor" deserved aid, the importance of "the relief of the unworthy poor." "If you have worthy poor," he suggested, "keep them your-selves." Only one in five hundred of those coming to missions such as his would be interested in anything more than "to beat me out of a night's lodging or a ten-cent piece." Yet in the twenty-two years since Jerry McAu-ley had founded the mission, thousands of men and women had been rescued from drunkenness or prostitution.[2]

In a more representative way, Baptist pastor Cortland Myers of Brooklyn summarized the prevailing opinions on the role of charity in the movement. "The church of Christ," he said, "is not a benevolent institution nor a social institution, but an institution for one purpose—winning lost souls to Christ and being instrumental in redeeming the world." Nevertheless, the "practi-cal side of Christianity," although "secondary" to this supreme purpose, was essential. Referring specifically to city evangelization, Myers said that preach-ing without practical charity would be empty as in the legend of St. Patrick who for three days only preached while St. Bridget truly proclaimed the Gospel through acts of charity. "Bridget was nearer to the spirit of her master," said Myers, "than Patrick."[3]

In fact in the years from 1870–1890, before the rise of the Social Gospel, holiness-minded evangelicals had their Bridgets as well as their Patricks and had assumed leadership in American Protestant work among the poor. It is worthy of note that in the 1890s Reuben Torrey was president of "The International Christian Workers Association." This organization, founded in 1886, was designated by Aaron Abell, in his study of Protestant social work in the late nineteenth century, "the most important" of the era's Prot-estant social service organizations.[4] A. J. Gordon and J. M. Gray served on the board of this agency. From reports of the activities of its various Chris-tian workers, there can be no doubt that the overriding interest of this organization was evangelism. It is also clear that they rejected Moody's dictum that one should not carry a loaf of bread in one hand and a Bible in the other lest someone think only of the bread and ignore the word. Booker T. Washington (who a year later made a special trip from Boston to Atlanta to make a five-minute speech to a predominantly white audience of Christian Workers) told the Christian Workers convention in 1892 that he had "been drawn to this convention mostly, if I understand its object correctly, because it seeks not only to save the soul but the body as well."[5] Addressing the same convention, D. H. Warner, a Washington, D.C., banker, agreed. "Religion is a practical thing," he observed, "when it walks down into the lowest dives of our land and takes those who have been buried in sin and wickedness, and lifts them up, cleanses them and sets to work to uplift the rest of human-ity. . . . Is not religion a practical thing that can induce people from all walks of life to consecrate their services to the bettering of mankind."[6]

Historians who have studied this social consecration in nineteenth-century America have most often found it to be related to the holiness tradition. Timothy L. Smith, in his pioneering work on the subject, sees a relationship between the evangelical compassion for the poor and the mid-century holiness teachings of Finney and the Oberlin theology, W. E. Boardman, and the Methodist Holiness movement associated with Phoebe Palmer. Smith also connects this impulse with the time's optimistic postmillennial hope of reforming society in preparation for the return of Christ.[7]

Yet the postmillennialists were certainly not the only innovators in Christian social work. Two of the most prominent Episcopal clergymen of the day, Stephen H. Tyng, Sr. and Jr., were active in organizing the premillennial movement in America. Tyng, Jr. organized the first American Bible and Prophecy Conference at New York's Holy Trinity Episcopal Church in 1878. The Tyngs had been premillennialists for many years.[8] They were also among the nation's most notable pastors in implementing local evangelical social action. Tyng, Sr. was the chief promoter of the American Female Guardian Society and Home for the Friendless in New York City, which by 1868 maintained six industrial schools as well as other services. His son was probably the leading Protestant of the 1860s and 1870s involved in the organization of local churches into effective social service agencies. Appealing to the ideal of restoring the standards of the early church and to the need to meet new social problems, Tyng effectively enlisted the various talents of his congregation to aid the poor. According to Aaron Abell, Holy Trinity Church became "one of the great mission churches of America" and its members "were valued chiefly for their ability to influence the indifferent, the destitute, and the outcast." In the same year that Holy Trinity was hosting the first of the major prophetic conferences, the church was endowed with an annual income for "'support of undenominational, evangelistic and humanitarian work among the poor of New York City.'"[9]

Premillennial teachings alone hardly account for such concern; these social works grew out of the general revivalist enthusiasm of the period and usually had some direct connection with holiness teaching. The Tyngs had been among the leading preachers of the revival of 1858. Although they held a traditional Reformation view of sanctification (that vestiges of a sinful nature remain in the Christian), they nonetheless spoke of total personal humility which, together with the indwelling of Christ, resulted in "the certain control of that inner life, 'that overcometh the world' and 'doth not commit sin.'"[10] Timothy Smith characterizes Tyng, Sr.'s evangelicalism as "nearly perfectionist."[11]

Whether or not the premillennial evangelists of the post-Civil-War era had yet adopted specific holiness doctrines, the stress on the sanctifying work of Christ in the believer's life provided a strong moral impulse to complement the zeal for the salvation of souls. The "institutional church," of which the younger Stephen Tyng's was an early model, by the end of the century provided one of the principal ways in which Protestants could combine evangelism with social work and community service. Bethany Presbyterian Church, in Philadelphia, sponsored by John Wanamaker, was a leading example of such work, providing (in addition to preaching) a day nursery, kindergartens, diet kitchens, an employment bureau, a workingmen's club, a dispensary, and a college. Bethany's two leading pastors during the 1880s and 1890s were outstanding holiness and premillennialist spokesmen,[12] A. T. Pierson and Wilbur Chapman. For the Baptists in the same city Russell Conwell built an even more impressive service-oriented empire around his church. Although Conwell was finding acres of diamonds for himself by preaching a gospel of wealth, the other side of his work involved establishing Samaritan Hospital and Temple College and organizing hundreds of workers to provide athletic, literary, and benevolent services of all sorts for the surrounding community.[13]

In Boston, another Baptist, A. J. Gordon, one of the most highly respected premillennial pastors of the day and a leading holiness teacher, expanded his church to include similar programs, although not on so grand a scale. Encouraged by Moody's revival in Boston in 1877 to undertake work among drunkards, Gordon instituted the Industrial Temporary Home. On the premise that it was futile to preach to those who had empty stomachs, the Home sought jobs as well as providing food and lodging. As was true of many who engaged in such rescue work at that time, the Boston pastor did not hesitate to seek to use the state for social betterment. Prohibition was widely considered the most effective way of attacking urban problems at their root, and after the Civil War it seemed natural for evangelical social reformers to place renewed emphasis on this cause. In this respect Gordon resembled a fellow New Englander, Jonathan Blanchard. After the war Gordon allied himself in prohibition work with the old-time anti-slavery reformer, Wendell Phillips. In 1884 Gordon helped to promote the new Prohibition Party, which continued to be his principal political interest until his death in 1895. Like Phillips and Blanchard, he also championed the legal recognition of the rights of women.[14]

These ministries were a part of the wider holiness revival. Torrey emphasized that the "one great secret of success" in rescue and related works was the common experience of "the Baptism of the Holy Ghost."[15] Moody's associates, such as Gordon, Torrey, Dixon, Pierson, and Chapman, were finding many successful allies in the new independent Holiness groups that emphasized vigorous work among the poor. Gordon, in fact, helped to inspire A. B. Simpson, who in the 1880s founded the Christian and Missionary Alliance, designed especially to bring the Gospel to the urban poor.[16] The Salvation Army, imported from England at about the same time, had a similar ministry to the outcasts of society.[17] During the 1880s these organizations founded scores of rescue missions, homes for fallen women, and relief programs, worked among immigrants, and sought or provided jobs for countless numbers of poor people. Preaching the Gospel was always their central aim, but social and evangelistic work went hand in hand. Uplifting the sinner, as well as saving his soul, was high among their priorities.[18]

Evangelicals with more moderate Keswick-type holiness views applauded these efforts and clearly considered them and their own work as part of one movement. J. Wilbur Chapman in his holiness work, *Received Ye the Holy Ghost?* (1894), concluded with impressive accounts of the accomplishments of spirit-filled Christians who sacrificed the comforts of life to work in the midst of the appalling conditions of the urban poor. He lauded the great rescue workers of the day, S. H. Hadley and Emma Whittemore, who moved in his own circles, and climaxed the volume with the example of "Mrs. Booth, the mother of the Salvation Army, one of the grandest women God has ever called into his service." Catherine Booth had done so much because she was filled with the Holy Ghost. "That is always the secret of POWER."[19] A. T. Pierson, in his end-of-century survey, although criticizing the Army on a number of counts, nonetheless lauded its "hundred-fold methods" for uplifting, saving, and transforming men and women as "having proved effective beyond anything of the sort."[20]

By this time the most vigorous Protestant efforts to reach the poor were not confined to the various holiness-oriented groups. By the 1890s some liberal Protestants were beginning to move toward less evangelistically oriented reform efforts and found a more decidedly social "Social Gospel."

Yet probably as indicative of the prevailing spirit after 1890 were the broadly based efforts of some theologically conservative evangelicals to meet social needs. Of these the most impressive were those sponsored by the popular non-denominational weekly journal, *The Christian Herald.* Founded in 1878, the magazine was originally called *The Christian Herald and Signs of the Times* and was (as the name implied) largely a premillennialist organ, featuring such contributors as A. J. Gordon, A. T. Pierson, Samuel Kellogg, and England's Charles Spurgeon.[21] By 1890 the weekly enjoyed a respectable circulation of about thirty thousand. During the next twenty years, under the leadership of Louis Klopsch, a New York businessman, the journal became one of the nation's leading agencies of relief work, distributing nearly three and a half million dollars for famine relief, overseas orphanages, its own Bowery mission, and a summer home for tenement children. In this same period, with these causes as its central focus, the Christian Herald increased its circulation by almost ten times, reaching about a quarter of a million by 1910.[22] This growth meant broadening the base. Premillennialism was dropped and there was no apparent emphasis on holiness teachings. Leaders of the Bible institute movement occasionally contributed on other subjects, however, and judged the magazine to be theologically safe.[23]

Despite its theological conservatism and its continued championing of a number of exclusively evangelistic efforts, by 1910 the *Christian Herald* had become distinctly progressive in politics. It endorsed labor unions, worked for legislation concerning women's and children's labor, advocated better treatment of immigrants and blacks, and waged an unceasing campaign for world peace.[24] These efforts were part of a large evangelistically oriented conservative Protestant movement that continued to enjoy some sense of unity. This movement had many sides. Dispensationalism and holiness were two; social concern was another. At some time all these were intimately associated.

There was a tendency among the premillennialist holiness Bible teachers, expressed by Moody, to see the world as a "wrecked vessel," implying that one should concentrate on saving souls and stay away from social issues except for what could be reached by preaching conversion and repentance. Most evangelical preachers, furthermore, along with their businessmen supporters and most of their contemporaries, viewed the cause and cure of poverty as related directly to the initiative of the individual. The present account stresses the degree of involvement in social concerns but does not intend to deny the more prominent evangelical endorsement and confirmation of the prevailing values of middle-class America. The intention is to correct the impression that revivalist evangelicals of this era were overwhelmingly complacent and inactive on social questions. In fact, many of the same evangelist associates of Moody who took the lead in preaching dispensationalism and holiness also led in preserving the tradition of evangelical social work. Though they were dedicated first to saving souls, greatly occupied with personal piety, and held pessimistic social views, their record of Christian social service, in an era when social reform was not popular, was as impressive as that of almost any group in the country.

X. "The Great Reversal"

The evangelicals' interest in social concerns, which lasted into the early years of the twentieth century, has been something of a puzzle to historians of fundamentalism. The chief question is the rather dramatic disappearance of this interest—or at least its severe curtailment—by the 1920s. In recent years many evangelical interpreters have commented on this "Great Reversal" in evangelical social views, although they have not always been clear on precisely what was lost.[1] Non-evangelical interpreters have tended to see a less sudden transition. Some have seemed to discount late nineteenth-century evangelical social efforts because they were motivated primarily by desire to "save souls."[2] Others have concluded that, at least since the Civil War, an emphasis on the "private" implications of the Gospel has almost invariably been a feature of the revivalist tradition, especially the premillennialist wing. This private Christianity, looking toward the next world and individual salvation, was contrasted with the "public party" of the Social Gospel of the early twentieth century, which was associated exclusively with the theologically liberal wing of the church.[3]

In order to clarify matters, and to distinguish two quite distinct stages of the "Great Reversal," it is important to note first that social concern may emphasize one or both of the following: (1) political means to promote the welfare of society, especially of the poor and the oppressed, and (2) reliance on private charity to meet such needs. Although before the Civil War many evangelicals displayed neither type of social concern, many others emphasized both. The ensuing transition came in two stages. From 1865 to about 1900 interest in political action diminished, though it did not disappear, among revivalist evangelicals. As we have just seen, however, the revivalist evangelicalism of this era still included vigorous champions of social concern, especially in the form of private charity. The lessening of political concern, then, did not in itself signify a "Great Reversal" in social concern, even though it shifted the focus and prepared the way for what followed. The "Great Reversal" took place from about 1900 to about 1930, when all progressive social concern, whether political or private, became suspect among revivalist evangelicals and was relegated to a very minor role.

The preparatory stage, from 1865 to 1900, can be described in a number of ways. Using the terms broadly we may call it a transition from a basically "Calvinistic" tradition, which saw politics as a significant means to advance the kingdom, to a "pietistic" view of political action as no more than a means to restrain evil.[4] This change can be seen as a move from Old Testament to New Testament models for understanding politics. It corresponds also, as is often noted, to the change from postmillennial to premillennial views of the relation of the kingdom to the present social and political order. In America it was also related to the rise of the holiness movement.

From the time of the Puritans until about the middle of the nineteenth century, American evangelicalism was dominated by a Calvinistic vision of a Christian culture. Old Testament Israel, a nation committed to God's law, was the model for political institutions. Hence the Christian ideal was to introduce God's kingdom—a New Israel—not only in the lives of the regenerate elect, but also by means of civil laws that would both restrain evil and comprehensively transform culture according to God's will. Charles Finney expressed this ideal when he declared that "the Christian church was designed to make aggressive movements in every direction—to lift up her voice and put forth her energies against iniquity in high and low places—to reform individuals, communities, and government, and never rest until the kingdom . . . shall be given to the people . . . —until every form of iniquity shall be driven from the earth." Jonathan Blanchard similarly spoke of "a perfect state of society," meaning that "the Law of God is the Law of the Land."[5]

Holiness teaching spread from the pietist Methodist tradition into the culturally influential Calvinist camp of American evangelicalism within the context of these assumptions concerning the role of God's law for people and society. At first the Reformed teachers of holiness simply fused the two ideals. Both Charles Finney and Asa Mahan, for instance, when they first defined Oberlin "perfectionism" in the late 1830s, described the standards for "holiness" in terms of God's law revealed in the Old Testament covenant. "Whatever the old covenant, or moral law, *requires of* the creature," wrote Mahan in a typical statement, "the new covenant . . . *promises to* the believer."[6] Such formulations, echoing and amplifying themes sounded by the Puritans, did not abrogate the Old Testament law, but kept it functioning as a most important guide.

This stress on the law had definite political implications. Finney included a section on "Human Government" in his *Systematic Theology*. A government's aim should be to promote holiness or "the great law of benevolence." Toward this goal of benevolence "or universal good-willing," Christians "are bound to exert their influence to secure a legislation that is in accordance with the law of God." Finney did not allow that such political activity would divert from saving souls. On the contrary, he insisted that "the promotion of public and private order and happiness is one of the indispensable means of doing good and saving souls."[7]

The growing emphasis on the role of the Holy Spirit, however, almost demanded some sort of dispensationalism that would draw a clear line between the Old Testament dispensation of law and the New Testament dispensation of the Holy Spirit. In 1839, Charles Finney was already declaring that the day of Pentecost marked "the commencement of a new dispensation," in which the new covenant replaced the old.[8] The distinction between the two covenants was not new, but the central place given to Pentecost and the Holy Spirit soon pushed interpretation in a new direction. In the new dispensation those who had received the anointing with the power of the Holy Spirit were radically different from professing Christians who were still in bondage to the law. Moreover, the freeing and empowering work of the Spirit was known experientially, not by laboriously conforming to codes of law and order. Accordingly, in the thirty years after Finney and Mahan first adopted their holiness views, the place of the law was drastically reduced in the writings of Reformed advocates of holiness. After 1870, when they spoke of the dispensation begun at Pentecost, they stressed the personal experience of being filled by the Spirit and the resulting positive personal power for service. By this time it was rare to find holiness teachers of any sort stressing the Old Testament law as the secret to a happy Christian life. The mood of the revivalist evangelicalism of the day was suggested by Philip Bliss's verse, "Free from the law, oh happy condition. . . ."[9]

The Spirit-oriented holiness teaching, spreading quickly in this period, encouraged a clear distinction between law and Spirit, Old Testament and New Testament, and seems to have been a major factor paving the way for the acceptance of a more definite dispensationalism in the later nineteenth century. By the 1870s when the dispensationalist movement began to take hold in America, holiness teachers already commonly spoke of "the Dispensation of the SPIRIT."[10] This and similar phrases became commonplace within the premillennial movement,[11] with the age of the Spirit sharply separated from the age of law. C. I. Scofield in his classic formulation called these two dispensations "Law" and "Grace." He did not make Pentecost itself the turning point but he did argue that the special characteristic of the age of grace was the presence of the Holy Spirit in every believer and the necessity for repeated "fillings" with the Spirit.[12]

The contrast between the present New Testament age of the Spirit and the previous Old Testament age of law did involve a shift toward a more "private" view of Christianity. The Holy Spirit worked in the hearts of individuals and was known primarily through personal experience. Social action, still an important concern, was more in the province of private agencies. The kingdom was no longer viewed as a kingdom of laws; hence civil law would not help its advance. The transition from postmillennial to premillennial views was the most explicit expression of this change. Politics became much less important.

Few premillennial-holiness evangelists, however, carried the implications of their position to the conclusion—more often found in the Anabaptist tradition—that since Satan ruled this age and its governments, Christians should avoid all political action, even voting.[13] Far more characteristic was a position—typical of the pietist tradition—that saw governments as ordained by God to restrain evil, so that politics in this respect was a means to do good. What they gave up—at least in theory—was the Calvinist-Puritan Old Testament covenantal view of the identity of the people of God with the advance of a religious-political kingdom. Even this idea was not abandoned totally or consistently. Sabbath legislation—despite its Old Testament origins and intention to promote both Christianity and human welfare—continued to be an interest of many. Likewise, prohibition, which was both an attack on a demonic vice and a progressive reform for improving civic life, received support from almost all evangelical quarters.

In any case, at the turn of the century, even while many premillennial-holiness leaders continued to urge private charity, they were also ready, at least on occasion, to urge quite progressive political reform. A. C. Dixon encouraged Christians to promote, and even organize, political parties "for the carrying forward of any great reform." He based his argument simply on the duty to "Do good to all men."[14] Similarly, Charles Blanchard, although a convert to premillennial and holiness views, had not yet abandoned—as he eventually would—progressive reform ideals, or even the idea of "Christian civilization," inherited from his father. "Christian men should lead," he urged in 1897, in fighting such injustices as unequal taxation, benefits to favored railroads and other corporations, delays in justice in the courts, justice denied to the poor because of excessive legal expenses, and pardons for corrupt officials while poor immigrants served out jail terms. "If Christian ministers and members will not take pains to perform their civil duties," asked Blanchard, "how are we to expect those others will?"[15]

More consistently pietistic and premillennial, yet just as progressive, was the position taken by James M. Gray in a sermon preached around 1900. Gray's case is particularly striking, since later, when he served as President of Moody Bible Institute, his political views became rigidly conservative.[16] In 1900 he explained that he was "not expecting the millennium to be brought about by moral and political reforms." Moreover, he warned that Christians should not allow their money to go "into the pockets of peculators, and boodlers, and loafers and incompetents who feed at the public crib." Nevertheless he saw many areas where Christians could use the government to fulfill their social duties toward their neighbors. What is involved, he asked, in my duty to love my neighbor? "I shall feed him if he is hungry, clothe him if naked, visit him if sick, and especially seek to win his soul if lost." Christians should not hesitate to use other means to show this love, even to the unbeliever. "Is it consistent with the spirit and the mind of Christ that we shall have no interest to ameliorate their material and physical condition, or make it better than it is because they are not following with us?"

Gray's answer was unmistakably progressive:

> There are crowded tenements in our cities where hundreds of souls are herded together through greed of grasping landlords under conditions inferior to those of the cattle in the stockyards; in some of these tenements are sweat-shops where clothing is made at starvation wages and disease bred and scattered wherever their products go; there are dram-shops, brothels and gambling dens open in multiplying variety for the allurement of our young men and women; if our newspapers are to be believed, law is defied continually by municipal and state officers to the demoralization of both public and private standards of right and wrong; Sunday is desecrated; and life is imperiled by the iniquity of those in authority, when it is in the power of the members of the Christian church[17] in almost every community to overawe and remove that official iniquity as Christ Himself drove the traders and money-changers from the temple.[18]

Gray went on specifically to recommend breaking up the American Ice Trust, reputedly in unholy alliance with Tammany Hall. Because the Trust raised ice prices "during the terrible heat of the early part of this summer, it was practically impossible for the suffering and dying poor to alleviate their miseries. . . ." He also endorsed the standard causes of the prohibition movement, the banning of gambling, and Sabbath legislation, as other important ways of helping the poor. He even went so far as to cite very favorably the example of Glasgow, where the gas, telephone, and transportation systems were owned by the government and the government was run by Christians. But even if we should work for such good, he cautioned, we must not expect any more than to limit the reign of evil until Christ returns. The rallying cry of Christians in public life should be, "Hold the fort, I'm coming."

We return then to the question of the "Great Reversal," or what happened to evangelical social concerns. Clearly the earlier stage, the shift from a more Calvinistic to a more pietistic view of politics after the Civil War, was not in itself sufficient to eliminate a sometimes strong emphasis on social aspects of the Gospel. Neither premillennialism nor holiness teachings, both associated with this earlier stage, were sufficient causes either. In fact the holiness views seem to have provided an important impulse for continuing social concerns. Some evangelists, Moody in particular, did use the priority of evangelism, together with premillennialism, as an excuse to avoid saying much on social issues.[19] Most of his constituency was apparently Republican and conservative,[20] as were most Protestants at that time. Yet in 1900 strong social concerns were still commonly expressed by some of Moody's prominent admirers, both through evangelistically oriented private charity and by advocacy of some political means aimed at the public good.

The "Great Reversal" (although not as great at the popular levels as sometimes suggested) appears really to date from the second stage, which extended from 1900 to 1930, when social concerns dramatically disappeared or were at least subordinated to others. Though it carries us ahead of our story, we may look briefly at this time period. During this second period the members of the group in question, associated with the Bible institute movement, did not generally alter their theories on premillennialism or holiness. Neither did they abandon politics or become entirely "private" in their outlook. If anything, as will be seen, after World War I they showed increased interest in relating Christianity to the welfare of the entire society, as the anti-evolution campaign and growing anti-communism demonstrated.[21] Sometimes they did use premillennialism or personal holiness to argue that Christians should not become much involved in work for the public welfare. Moreover, they abandoned the view of Finney and the other mid-nineteenth-century moral philosophers that the kingdom would be positively advanced by good laws. This helped to prevent them from developing any positive or progressive political views of their own. In fact, however, they applied their reservations regarding political action quite selectively, disregarding them when they themselves became concerned with a public issue.

It seems then that the basic causes of the "Great Reversal" must be broader than simply the rise of the new dispensationalist or holiness views. At times these theories certainly augmented trends toward more private Christianity. When the occasion arose, these doctrines were readily available to provide rationales for rejecting social reform. So they were contributing causes of the "reversal." Other factors, however, seem to have determined which aspects of social action and reform were avoided.

Social factors contributed to the transformation also; but clear evidence for most of these is lacking or very difficult to assess. From the time of Moody through the fundamentalist controversies of the 1920s, the constituency of these revivalist evangelical movements appears to have been the predominantly white, aspiring middle class of Protestant heritage. Often they had, like Moody himself, grown up in rural communities and moved to cities.[22] No doubt the tensions inherent in this experience increased with the accelerating urbanization and pluralization of the nation during this whole period.[23] These tensions, however, were doubtless mixed with so many others for those who responded to the Gospel that the weight of the social factors, while no doubt of great importance, is impossible to measure. World War I, more than any other general social experience, intensified conservative reaction of every sort.[24] Yet even such social factors do not fully account for the fundamentalists' rejection or endorsement of social causes. Too many non-fundamentalists, including some liberal and moderate Protestants,[25] had similar social experiences for these alone to offer an adequate explanation.

The factor crucial to understanding the "Great Reversal," and especially in explaining its timing and exact shape, is the fundamentalist reaction to the liberal Social Gospel after 1900. Until about 1920 the rise of the Social Gospel and the decline of revivalist social concerns correlate very closely. By the time of World War I, "social Christianity" was becoming thoroughly identified with liberalism and was viewed with great suspicion by many conservative evangelicals. The Federal Council of Churches tried to maintain some unity in 1912 by instituting a commission on evangelism to counterbalance its well-known social activism. By this time the balance was precarious, and the issue of evangelism as opposed to social service was widely debated.[26] World War I exacerbated the growing conflict. When fundamentalists began using their heavy artillery against liberal theology, the Social Gospel was among the prime targets. In the barrage against the Social Gospel it was perhaps inevitable that the vestiges of their own progressive social attitudes would also become casualties.[27]

To understand the fundamentalists' strong reaction against anything that even looked like the Social Gospel, it is necessary to distinguish the liberal Social Gospel from the kinds of evangelical social concern that we have been discussing. It was absolutely essential to the earlier evangelical support of public or private social programs that they be understood as complementary outgrowths of the regenerating work of Christ which saved souls for all eternity. The evangelicals' theological stance theoretically in no way should have been threatened by a commitment to social action per se. The necessary first step in the Christian's life was repentance for sin and total dependence on God's grace. Good works should follow. The only question was what form these should take—individual or public, private or political.

The Social Gospel, however, put almost all the weight on the second half of the equation. Following the lead of philosophical pragmatism, proponents of the Social Gospel held that the only test of truth was action. "Religious morality," said Walter Rauschenbusch, is "the only thing God cares about."[28] The implication was that theological doctrine and affirmation of faith in Christ and his deeds were irrelevant, except as an inspiration to moral action, more specifically social action. The Social Gospel, at least in its classic form as represented by Rauschenbusch, did not deny outright the validity of specific beliefs, but took the pragmatist position that we cannot know anything about their validity until we see what they do.[29] In sharp contrast, conservative evangelicals held that truth could be known directly and not only by a pragmatic test. Moreover, in their view God cared as much about our beliefs as about our actions, although the two were never seen as entirely separable.

The threat that conservative evangelicals perceived in the Social Gospel was not that it endorsed social concern—evangelicals themselves often made similar endorsements. It was rather that the Social Gospel emphasized social concern in an exclusivistic way which seemed to undercut the relevance of the message of eternal salvation through trust in Christ's atoning work. In the nineteenth century some revivalists, and some confessionally oriented conservatives, had already warned against putting too much emphasis on social concerns. Now, however, the question was not simply one of balance. Traditional Christian belief seemed to be at stake. The Social Gospel was presented, or was thought to be presented, as equivalent to the Gospel itself.

Those evangelicals and conservatives who had warned that social interests would inevitably undermine concern for right belief and salvation of souls, now appeared to have confirmation for their claim. Prominent exponents of the Social Gospel were specifically contrasting their own social views with the old individualist soul-saving evangelicalism. Furthermore, the liberal and Social Gospel emphasis on the kingdom of God as realized in the progress of civilization was readily contrasted with premillennialist eschatological hopes. The dichotomy between the Social Gospel and the revivalist Gospel became difficult to ignore. As the attacks on liberalism heated up, the position that one could have *both* revivalism and social action became increasingly cumbersome to defend.[30] In any case this attempt at balance declined in proportion to the increase of strident anti-modernism.[31]

By the 1920s the one really unifying factor in fundamentalist political and social thought was the overwhelming predominance of political conservatism. Whether they spoke as pietists who would use government merely to restrain evil, or as Calvinists preserving Christian civilization, or even when they sounded like radical Anabaptists opposing all Christian involvement in politics, they were (with few exceptions) anti-liberal. In part this was simply part of the wider social expression of middle-class desire for normalcy. But among fundamentalists these tendencies were reinforced by the close relationship between the Social Gospel and the progressive movement in politics. Rejecting the one seemed to demand rejecting the other.

Throughout the eighteenth and nineteenth centuries, revivalist Protestants in America reflected fairly closely the patterns and shifts of the political thought of the times, often providing their own Christian versions of prevailing trends. Sometime around 1900 this parallel development was interrupted. To employ a psychological analogy, it was as though a series of shocks had arrested an aspect of personality development. The shocks were religious, intellectual, and social, sharpened by the disruption of World War I. The result was almost as if the positive aspects of the progressive political era had not only been rejected but even obliterated from memory. To continue the analogy, fundamentalists emerged from the experience not so much without social or political views as fixated on a set of views that had been characteristic of middle-class Americans in the last years before the crisis occurred. Their social views were frozen at a point that had been the prevailing American political opinion around 1890, save that the fundamentalists of the 1920s had forgotten the degree to which their predecessors—and even they themselves—had earlier espoused rather progressive social concerns.[32]

XI. Holiness and Fundamentalism

The death of D. L. Moody in 1899 and the end of the nineteenth century coincided with the beginnings of serious fragmentation within the evangelical revivalist movement. The dispensationalist movement began to break apart over the issue of whether the secret rapture would remove believers from earth before or after the "tribulation" of the end times. Although contact among the leaders of the two camps continued (with the Scofield-Gaebelein pretribulationists dominant), the controversy brought the demise of the important Niagara Bible Conference in 1901 and a cessation of the "international" prophetic conferences from 1901 to 1914.[1]

Of greater consequence was the revolution in the Methodistic Holiness wing of revivalism. In 1901 Charles F. Parham carried the prevalent "Pentecostal" insistence on "Baptism of the Holy Spirit" (as described in Acts 2) to the conclusion that tongues should still be the sign of a Pentecostal experience. Parham's student, W. J. Seymour, popularized this new Pentecostalism beginning in 1906 at the Azusa Street revival in Los Angeles, after which this movement grew into its own many varieties.

Significantly, the first major split within Pentecostalism reflected differences concerning holiness among the late-nineteenth-century revivalists. The original Pentecostal teachers, Parham and Seymour, taught a Methodistic Holiness view of a "second blessing" of entire sanctification in which the sinful nature was eradicated. This, they said, was followed by a third blessing, "Baptism of the Spirit," accompanied by tongues. By 1910, however, a significant group had developed within Pentecostalism who did not have Methodistic backgrounds. These taught a view resembling the Reformed teaching that sanctification was a continuing process rather than a distinct experience. They also held that the Baptism of the Spirit resulted not in perfect holiness, but rather (in a phrase reflecting Keswick influence) "enduement for service." This "Baptistic" or "Keswick" Pentecostal teaching led to the formation of the Assemblies of God and was also the basis for Aimee Semple McPherson's International Church of the Four Square Gospel, founded in the 1920s. These groups, like most Pentecostals, shared many traits with fundamentalists that reflected their common origins in the revivalism of the Moody era.[2]

In the meantime revivalist evangelicals who did not seek the gift of tongues were embarrassed by the emergence of these cousins in Christ. During the early decades of the century they were at pains to disclaim any ties.[3] The favor, however, was not returned, as the Pentecostals were quite willing to claim antecedents in the earlier revivalism. Reuben Torrey who (unlike most Keswick teachers) had emphasized a definite experience based on Acts 2, "the Baptism with the Holy Spirit," was a favorite theologian of Pentecostals and has even been referred to as "a kind of John the Baptist figure for later international Pentecostalism."[4] A. J. Gordon and A. B. Simpson had been champions of divine and miraculous healings. Gordon had even argued that just as the gift of healing should continue past the Apostolic age, so perhaps should the gift of tongues.[5] Dispensationalism, which fit so well with the Pentecostal and holiness ideas of the "Age of the Spirit," easily gained acceptance in the new Pentecostal movement, even though the Scofield-type dispensationalists maintained that tongues ceased with the Apostles.[6] Despite close resemblances of Pentecostals to "fundamentalists,"[7] Pentecostals were only tangentially part of the fundamentalism of the 1920s. Pentecostals often identified themselves as "fundamentalists," read fundamentalist literature, and adopted anti-Modernist and anti-evolution rhetoric; yet other fundamentalists seldom welcomed them as allies or called them into their councils. The influence, then, was largely in only one direction, from fundamentalism to pentecostalism.[8] One reason was Pentecostals' prior separation from the major denominations. Another was the fundamentalists' antagonism. The family ties were nonetheless strong enough that adherents of the two traditions could reestablish some contacts in later twentieth-century evangelicalism.[9]

At the turn of the century, however, the prior controversy between Methodistic Holiness and Keswick teachers was the principal internal issue dividing the exponents of resurgent revivalism that had grown in the Moody era. Until the 1890s almost all of those who were rediscovering the work of the Holy Spirit had viewed each other as allies. Keswick teachers, A. B. Simpson, the Salvation Army, and the Holiness Camp Meeting movement all gave each other approving nods and borrowed methods and emphases. During the 1880s and 1890s, however, most of these movements with the exception of Keswick were forming independent denominations, which forced them to define their differences. Soon these differences became matters for dispute and by about 1900 these disputes were becoming noticeably sharp.

A particularly dramatic illustration of this phenomenon can be found in the writings of A. M. Hills, an evangelist and leading writer of the Nazarene movement which had then recently separated from Methodism. Hills had been a classmate of Reuben Torrey at Yale and had preached his ordination sermon. Hills had studied holiness doctrine at Oberlin and been helped in his search for the Holy Spirit by the writings of Torrey and Keswick teacher F. B. Meyer.[10] In his exposition of Holiness teaching, *Holiness and Power* (1897), although he presented a Methodistic view, he supported his positions with numerous appeals to Keswick authors including Torrey, Gordon, Chapman, Meyer, and Pierson.[11] About this same time he was invited, in another display of cordiality, to the Bible Institute of Chicago (Moody), where Torrey then presided. There, he recounted later, he had not been around for twenty-four hours before it was being whispered, "He is an eradicationist!" Within two days, said Hills, a "callow youth" sitting near him at the table said in a very loud voice for all to hear, "The doctrine of the eradication of the carnal nature by the Holy Spirit is one of the most damnable heresies that ever cursed the Christian Chruch." The "uneducated young man," Hills surmised, was parroting what was taught in the Bible Institute's classrooms. Moody himself, Hills had heard it reported, had mocked and belittled those who claimed entire sanctification. As further evidence of the break, Hills noted that in 1901 he attended a ten-day Holiness convention in Chicago, which neither Torrey nor anyone else from Moody Bible Institute had bothered to attend.[12] For his part, Hills in 1902 published his response, *Pentecost Rejected,* which included a long attack on Keswick holiness teaching as having virtually no doctrine of holiness at all.[13]

By 1910 the controversy was heating up on all sides. Hills published two works, one entitled *The Tongues Movement,* condemning those who had perverted the meaning of Pentecost, and the other, *Scriptural Holiness and Keswick Teaching Compared,* whose title explains its theme.[14] As is common in family feuds, the ill feeling among recently estranged kin were as intense as toward the liberals whose errors were more patent. As H. A. Baldwin, a Free Methodist pastor, put it in 1911, "Keswickism" was "one of the most dangerous enemies of the experience of holiness. . . ."[15]

By this time the artillery fire was flying in both directions. In 1912 H. A. Ironside (who later became the pastor of Moody Church in Chicago) published the most famous attack on the separatist Holiness movements, *Holiness, The False and the True.* Ironside agreed with Hills that tongues-speaking Pentecostalism was an aberration, but at that point similarity ended. According to Ironside, who had been reared in the Salvation Army, such "absurd delusions" as tongues were the natural results of the impossible

Holiness demands for perfection. Moreover, Ironside charged, "as to down-right wickedness and uncleanness, I regret to have to record that sins of a positively immoral character are, I fear, far more frequently met within holiness churches and missions, and Salvation Army bands, than the out-sider would think possible." This condition combined with the pressure to claim perfection, said Ironside, was strewing the world with spiritual ship-wrecks. "The ex-Salvation Army," he claimed, "was many times larger than the original organization."[16]

Despite such acrimony among the champions of various forms of Chris-tian holiness, all the branches of the movement prospered during the first two decades of the century. Keswick teachings appear to have flourished most among the middle-class clientele inside established denominations, while separatist Holiness groups and Pentecostalism in particular appealed more to the socially and economically disinherited.[17] Keswick teachings were somewhat less radical than those of the other groups, and it seems probable that there is a correlation between the radicalism of a view of sanctification and the social class to which it will appeal. So traditional Reformed teach-ings—rather moderate on sanctification—have had a socially more respecta-ble base than any of the holiness views. Similarly, Protestant liberalism, with a strong ethical emphasis but a non-radical concept of personal sanctifica-tion, had the most affluent social base.[18]

The Keswick teachings, already growing in popularity, received their most important boost in America in 1910 with the conversion to the movement of Charles G. Trumbull, editor of the respectable and popular weekly, the *Sunday School Times*. Trumbull used his influence to familiarize American Protestants with the teaching of "the victorious life." He also helped to formally organize the movement, initiating in 1913 an "American Keswick" conference, which settled permanently at Keswick, New Jersey, in 1923. That same year Robert McQuilkin, Trumbull's associate, founded Columbia Bible School, an important center for promoting Keswick views.[19] Trumbull himself soon after his conversion became a protégé of C. I. Scofield. Eventu-ally he wrote a biography of Scofield in which Trumbull and his teacher are pictured together as "Paul and Timothy," suggesting the close connection between the dispensational and Keswick movements.

At the American Keswick conferences, true to the English model, the emphasis was almost entirely on personal experiences of joy, peace, and "victory," with the practical results seen in enhanced devotional life and zeal for missions.[20] In contrast to earlier holiness movements in America, this seems to have lacked almost entirely a social message. For Trumbull this was a matter of principle. Writing around 1914 about Sunday schools for *The Fundamentals,* Trumbull argued that social service programs were particu-larly dangerous. They included many things "Christian in spirit," but put fruit ahead of roots. Trumbull pointed to the popular Billy Sunday as a proper model. Sunday said little about social service in the current progres-

Dr. Scofield and Mr. Trumbull in a special session of the Southfield Bible Conference, Crescent City, Florida. Friends call this "Paul and Timothy."

From Charles Gallaudet Trumbull, *The Life Story of C. I. Scofield* (New York, 1920).

sive sense, but his evangelism, said Trumbull, "lifts society as the usual social service program can never do."[21] Similarly, in response to criticism that the Keswick conferences had "no real objective outside of oneself and a personal experience," Trumbull's reply was that no one would make such a charge if he had seen the zeal for foreign missions shown at the conferences.[22]

The early decades of the twentieth century were perhaps the years of greatest enthusiasm for foreign missions and in this area Keswick's record was indeed strong. J. Hudson Taylor (1832–1905), a Britisher who founded the China Inland Mission in 1865, had become deeply committed to Keswick views.[23] The China Inland Mission became a model for independent and self-sacrificing missionary work as well as a source for much of the later fundamentalist agitation against liberalism in the mission fields. The Student Volunteer Movement, originating out of Moody's Northfield conference, also had close Keswick ties. Many impressive young men of the era responded to these teachings by consecrating their lives to missionary service.[24]

Missionary and evangelistic efforts were the chief positive forces holding together a wide coalition of revivalist and conservative evangelicals. Premillennialists, who held that the preaching of the Gospel to all nations was a sign of the end time (Matthew 24:14), had every bit as much enthusiasm for the evangelization of the world as did the most optimistic postmillennialists, who still ardently hoped and prayed for the conversion of the world in their generation.[25] All agreed that an extraordinary work of the Holy Spirit would be necessary for any success in world mission efforts. The most immediate cause for hope was the spectacular Welsh revival, which began in 1904 and soon claimed some one hundred thousand converts. Keswick influences, as well as Calvinism, were strong in this awakening which was seen as a great outpouring of the Holy Spirit. In the years immediately following, sparks from the Welsh awakening seemed to kindle flames of revival around the world.[26] Prayer, which was of inestimable importance for the entire evangelical movement, focused on pleas for the continuation of such divine work.

Keswick ideas were so well suited to these positive aspects of the American evangelicalism of the day that they seem to have met with little opposition from those with more traditional views of sanctification. Even *The Presbyterian,* the conservative guardian of Reformed tradition, in 1917 gave high praise to a Keswick conference held at Princeton. The editors emphasized the similarities, rather than the differences, between the new and the traditional teachings. They found sanctification and "surrender" a welcome alternative to the social ethics of liberalism.[27]

When the Keswick conferences came to Princeton, from 1916 to 1918, they were entering the lair of the aging lion of strict Presbyterian orthodoxy, Benjamin Breckinridge Warfield of Princeton Theological Seminary. Unlike most of his contemporaries, Warfield was not in the least distracted by the popularity, success, or practical results of a doctrine. True to the Princeton tradition, he spotted a major doctrinal innovation and pounced. During the next several years, in a series of sharp and condescending criticisms, Warfield attempted to tear apart once and for all innovative holiness teachings of every sort.

The essence of Warfield's criticism was, as he put it in a review of a work by young Lewis Sperry Chafer, that the Keswick teacher was plagued by "two inconsistent systems of religion struggling together in his mind." One was Calvinist, so that he and his "coterie" (one of Warfield's favorite words) of evangelists and Bible teachers often spoke of God's grace doing all; but behind this Calvinist exterior lurked the spectres of Pelagius, Arminius, and Wesley, all of whom made God's gracious working subject to human determination. The resulting synthesis, Warfield said, was "at once curiously pretentious and curiously shallow."[28]

Warfield found the popular writings of Charles Trumbull expeciàlly culpable on the score of shallowness. Trumbull often used the slogan, "Let go and let God." This Trumbull explained in terms of "Christ within us" who would control our lives so long as we did not resist him. This formula, said Warfield, made God wait for our act of faith (a common Calvinist objection to most modern evangelism). So Christ was supposedly let in and out of peoples' lives like steam or electricity turned on or off. This view led to an unresolvable dilemma, said Warfield. Once Christ had taken over our lives, who made the decision if we fell into sin? It could not be Christ. Neither could it be our old nature—which was counteracted by the filling with Christ's Spirit. It must be an independent agent within us—our free will— that operates apart from both our old and new natures. So, said Warfield, Mr. Trumbull is guilty of a "bathos of inconsequence" when he asserts that Christ has "constituted Himself my very being (save only my power to resist Him) my body, mind, soul and spirit." If this were the case, Warfield queried sarcastically, why did we have victory only over *known* sins? "There is indeed one dogma," he concluded, "which takes precedence in Mr. Trumbull's mind to the dogma of 'Christ in us.' This is the dogma of the inalienable ability of the human will to do at any time and under any circumstances precisely what in its unmotivated caprice it chances to turn to."[29]

W. H. Griffith Thomas, a rather distinguished English scholar who taught in Toronto, and one of the few of the "coterie" of evangelists and Bible teachers for whom Warfield indicated any respect, replied at length. Thomas defended the essentially Augustinian character of the Keswick position. He admitted that he found more truth to the idea of "freedom of the will" and "more power in Methodism than Calvinists usually would admit." While chiding Warfield for his polemical tone, Thomas had a barb of his own to thrust at the Princeton theology's most sensitive spot. Warfield's writings, he said, manifest "the absence of any recognition of the fact that the Movement he criticizes and condemns expresses a spiritual experience and not merely a theological theory."[30]

This debate, unlike those that separated advocates of various Holiness and Pentecostal doctrines from each other, remained for the time being a quarrel between allies. By 1919 the controversy with modernism had pre-empted all other concerns and conservatives of all sorts within major denominations were trying, despite their differences, to close ranks.

Warfield's critique pointed out some of the characteristic traits of the Bible institute movement and the direction in which much of revivalist evangelicalism in America had been moving for at least a century. The Puritans in early America dwelt on the sovereignty of God's grace and the inability of sinful individuals to influence God's will. Jonathan Edwards, for example, when he analyzed religious experience made clear that the "divine and supernatural light" that a Christian perceived was not contingent on the agency of a free human will, but on the prior gracious work of the Holy Spirit who granted the ability to see and respond to that light.[31] After Edwards's time revivalist theology in America moved steadily toward emphasizing the human side of religious experience. This tendency was manifested in various ways of positing the free and decisive character of the human free will. Free will was virtually an American dogma; indeed it was practically an unassailable article of faith for most of Western culture. It was also a concept that was a great aid to evangelism, which seemed most effective when based clearly on

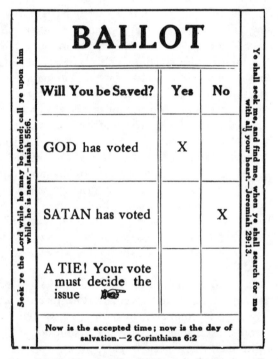

Strict Calvinists objected to emphases on free will in revivalist theology. Tract printed by the [Moody] Bible Institute Colportage Association (Chicago, n. d.).

personal "decision." Even Keswick's tradition, which was clearly stressing supernatural grace when it spoke of the "filling with the Spirit," "Christ dwelling in you," and "let go and let God," still reserved (as Warfield pointed out) a key place for the free individual. It also tended to shift the emphasis toward the emotional aspect of the individual's decisions. The experience had to be dramatic and recountable. The best evidence for Christianity ultimately was the saved individual who could "witness" to what God had done. Hence intense prayer and witnessing stood high on lists of fruits of the Spirit.

    Keswick's teaching played at least two important roles complementary to dispensational premillennialism in the Bible institute movement.[32] First, it provided an important subjective confirmation of the faith to stand alongside more objective arguments from the Bible and common sense. Secondly, while premillennialism involved abandonment of the optimistic estimate of the conquering power of the Holy Spirit throughout society, Keswick promised personal "victory." Although one might not expect to see the millennium in this age, in one's own life there was hope for a spiritual outpouring which would result in an era of personal victory, peace, and practical service. The light of optimism, then, still prevailed in the American evangelical outlook—only it now shone on the individual rather than on the culture.

During the years just before World War I, when Keswick and other holiness teachings flourished, the personal piety, optimism, and activism that characterized these movements might well have been taken for the overwhelmingly dominant traits of conservative American Protestantism generally. Yet while these things were prominent and probably helped delay some outbreaks of controversy, they were accompanied by other intellectual and theological characteristics that fostered contentiousness. This was especially true of evangelicals in the more-or-less Calvinistic traditions, where most of the doctrinal militancy against modernism appeared. These two tendencies— the personal, practical, and irenic on the one hand, and the eager to engage in controversy on the other—sometimes worked at cross-purposes. Both tendencies, however, could be found in the same individual. As A. C. Dixon put it at (of all places) an ecumenical missions conference in 1900, "Above all things I love peace, but next to peace I love a fight, and I believe the next best thing to peace is a theological fight."[33]

The Defense of the Faith

XII. Tremors of Controversy

Both dispensationalism and holiness teachings developed into significant movements in the context of a troubled culture that had always thought of itself as Christian and was now rapidly becoming secularized. As in every age, evidence of moral decline was readily at hand; in the decades spanning the turn of the century the spectre of teeming cities, the immorality and irresponsibility associated with urban poverty, the disruptiveness of industrialization, and the strangeness of non-Protestant immigrants gave particular credence to suspicion that this might be the end of an era—the Christian era.

Although not fully explainable in terms of their social causes, dispensationalism and holiness teachings were partially a response to cultural conditions. Neither of these movements was co-extensive with fundamentalism. Yet each contributed important elements to the emerging fundamentalist outlook. What made them part of fundamentalism as such was the direct and explicit reaction against one aspect of the apparent secularization—the rise of theological liberalism.

In almost every major American denomination, sometime between the late 1870s and World War I, serious disagreements broke out between conservatives and liberals. In these struggles the traditionalists were not necessarily fundamentalists in any strict sense. They were first of all denominational conservatives who had their own distinct traditions and characters. Some, like the traditionalists among the Disciples of Christ, were regarded as a part of the fundamentalist movement largely because their aims were parallel and in certain of their attacks they had common opponents. What made others more fundamentalist was their combination of militant anti-modernism with participation in a larger movement that, despite its mix of separable elements, possessed some degree of conscious unity. The active cooperation of denominational traditionalists with the theologically innovative dispensationalists and holiness advocates in the battle against modernism was particularly important in shaping a distinct fundamentalism. These traditionalists were found mostly among Baptists and Presbyterians. B. B. Warfield is a striking example. Warfield apparently despised the newer holiness teachings and certainly disdained dispensationalism. His own position was Old School Presbyterian traditionalism. Yet he cooperated with the larger fundamentalist movement, even with dispensationalist and holiness teachers, and in fact made an important contribution to fundamentalism, as did the Old School Presbyterian tradition generally.

The issues debated so intensely in the denominations usually centered on the authority of Scripture, its scientific accuracy, or the supernatural elements in Christ's person and work. There were also parallel and closely related disputes over denominations' distinctive doctrines or traditions— strict Calvinism among Presbyterians, immersion among Baptists and Disciples of Christ. Almost every major denomination struggled with some such issue, although some denominations avoided at least temporarily any dramatic disruption.

In the South the debates were in most cases short-lived, because dissent was simply not tolerated. As early as the first half of the nineteenth century, advanced theological views had usually been associated with advanced social views and abolition. Southern theology already had a strong conservative bent. The War Between the States simply intensified Southern determination to resist change. Hence there was a strong anti-modernist impulse in Southern religion well before modernism became a distinct movement in America. This theological conservatism, often combined with the warm revivalist evangelicalism inherited from the early nineteenth century,[1] created in Southern religion many characteristics that resembled later fundamentalism. Until the 1920s, however, Southern revivalist conservatism and Northern fundamentalism developed more or less independently, although in parallel ways. The principal direct connection between the two movements was that several important fundamentalist leaders came from the South.[2] When in the twentieth century fundamentalism became a distinct entity, Southerners with a long history of revivalist conservatism eventually flocked to the movement.

An early sign that sparks of liberalism would quickly be snuffed out in the Southern atmosphere came in 1878 when Alexander Winchell was forced by the Southern Methodist denomination out of his position at Vanderbilt for holding questionable views on Genesis. In the following year Crawford H. Toy's resignation from the Southern Baptist Seminary at Louisville had similar causes.[3] The Toy case was followed some years later by that of his friend, William H. Whitsitt, who had the indiscretion to publicize historical research showing that baptism by immersion had not continued as an unbroken tradition since apostolic times. The Landmark Baptists, an especially rigid traditionalist group, speaking through the vitriolic *Western Recorder* of Tennessee, led the fight that forced Whitsitt's resignation as president of the Southern Baptist Seminary.[4]

Among Southern Presbyterians serious scholarly discussion of the issues was similarly brought to a quick end with the dismissal of James Woodrow, uncle of Woodrow Wilson, from Columbia Theological Seminary for his claim that evolution was compatible with the teachings of Scripture.[5] In the South, but not in the North, evolution was already a chief symbol of heresy. Southern thought had been shaped by Puritan, Scottish philosophical, and Baconian influences, which together encouraged an enormous reverence for Scripture as a source of hard fact, as opposed to speculative hypotheses such as those of Darwin.[6]

In the North, by contrast, the cultural forces for change which fanned the new religious ideals were so strong that stamping out the spark in one place could not prevent a general conflagration. Many of the major Northern denominations suffered through painful heresy trials. Even conservative victories turned out to be largely illusory. Liberalism continued to grow almost as though the trials had never taken place. Among the Congregationalists, from the time of the flurry over future punishment in 1877[7] through the 1880s, conservatives were temporarily successful in their efforts to restrain liberalism. At Andover Seminary, where the move toward the New Theology centered, they even managed to have Professor Egbert C. Smyth removed from the faculty for a time. Yet by the 1890s the issues were settled in favor of the progressives and conservativism was defunct as an ecclesiastical force.[8] Among Northern Methodists, the emphasis on the experiential religion of the heart and its practical moral consequences was congenial to a rapid development of liberal theology during the last fifteen years of the nineteenth century. Conservatives made some counter-efforts in the early twentieth century and charged Boston University theologians Hinkley G. Mitchell and Borden P. Bowne, two leading advocates of a personalistic theology, with holding lax views of Scripture. Bowne was acquitted, but Mitchell was dismissed from his post. In 1908, however, in connection with appeals of the Mitchell case, the General Conference effectively ended such trials of professors.[9] The Protestant Episcopal Church had a similar isolated case in 1906 when the Reverend Algernon Sidney Crapsey was convicted for denying the Virgin Birth. In general, however, the Episcopal tradition of toleration for diversity prevailed.[10]

The Northern Baptist and Northern Presbyterian controversies had the most to do with the development of interdenominational fundamentalism.[11] The Baptists, who had much greater local autonomy, developed much greater diversity, with all the major parties—denominational traditionalists, dispensational premillennialists, and avowed liberals—well represented within the same denomination. In America, the Baptists had long been a coalition of diverse elements. On the one hand they had a confessional Calvinist tradition; yet at the same time they had a strong emphasis on doctrinal freedom. Calvinism was strong in the seventeenth-century Puritan origins of the American movement and also in the important eighteenth-century separation of New England Baptists from Congregationalism after the Great

Awakening. Baptists, however, had an individualistic view of the church as a voluntary association of individuals who had experienced conversion. The Calvinist confessionalism was qualified by opposition to ecclesiastical centralization and vigorous affirmation of the individual right to theological freedom. Moreover, the emphasis on conversion in the pietist camp and especially in nineteenth-century frontier revivalism reinforced Arminian doctrines which emphasized human freedom of choice and were, as much as Calvinism, a venerable part of the diverse Baptist heritage.

In this relatively open atmosphere Biblical criticism and liberal theological tendencies appeared early among Baptists in the Northern United States and soon flourished as in no other evangelical denomination, except perhaps the Congregationalist. By the 1870s three positions on Scripture were already perceptible. Some scholars, under German influences, rejected the infallibility of Scripture in favor of subjective experiential verification of the truth of Christianity; most still assumed that the Bible was infallible in doctrine and without error in detail; others stood in a middle position. During the next decades militant conservatives won two isolated victories, removing Ezra P. Gould from Newton Theological Seminary in 1882 and Nathaniel Schmidt from Colgate in 1896. Nevertheless, they could not begin to hold back the liberal enthusiasm which swept over all of the Northern Baptist seminaries regardless of the degree of their earlier orthodox opposition. By 1900 liberals were well represented everywhere and by World War I strict conservatives had almost disappeared from the older seminaries.[12] Moreover, under the leadership of President William Rainey Harper, the (Baptist) Divinity School at the University of Chicago became after the 1890s the leading American center for aggressive theological liberalism, including on its faculty such outstanding "modernists" as Shailer Mathews, George Burman Foster, Gerald Birney Smith, and Shirley Jackson Case.[13] At Colgate Theological Seminary William Newton Clarke, whose views on the kingdom we have already encountered, was another outstanding voice for Baptist liberalism. Perhaps most important was the combination of pragmatic liberal theology with the new "Social Gospel" in the work of Walter Rauschenbusch at Rochester Theological Seminary. Rauschenbusch developed the liberal idea of the kingdom into an optimistic social theology that explicitly opposed the individualistic and otherworldly emphases often associated with revivalist evangelicalism.

Most striking in these Baptist developments is the degree of tolerance and room for open discussion that most representatives of both liberal and conservative views showed toward each other. During the decades spanning the turn of the century the "Baptist Congress" provided a forum in which both sides vigorously represented their views. During the same period most Baptist seminaries still included both conservatives and liberals. Even in the midst of the ongoing debates, the various traditional segments of Northern Baptists strengthened their ties by the formation in 1907 of the Northern

Baptist Convention. Yet the new Convention included explosive new elements that could easily trigger a chain reaction. In 1897 one astute observer predicted that "old and new will wage a war of extermination, and neither will live to gain the satisfaction of having destroyed the other."[14] The explosion was delayed, however, and ten years later a similar analyst did not find the outlook so clear. "Two parties are in process of formation in the denomination . . . ," said Professor H. C. Vedder. "At times there are symptoms that their opposition may break out into an open warfare; at times a peaceful issue seems not only hopeful, but certain."[15]

In part this hope must simply have reflected the enthusiastic optimism and activism of the evangelicalism of the age. These years were, as Gaius Glann Atkins in retrospect described them, "the Age of Crusades." They were filled with "a superabundance of zeal, a sufficiency of good causes, unusual moral idealism, excessive confidence in mass movements and leaders with rare gifts of popular appeal."[16] Although they had deep-seated ideological differences, most American Protestants were not first of all ideological in orientation. So, in spite of the ongoing debates, they were uniting on the home front, as the formation of the Federal Council of Churches in 1908 best attests. Looking abroad, the fires of revival could be seen around the world[17] and certainly the rank and file of American Protestants saw no conflict between revivalism and the essence of Christianity. Considering the advance of missions, the nineteenth seemed Protestantism's greatest century and many a judicious observer supposed that the new century might be greater still. The clouds of emerging controversy, however real and ominous, were in most of America hardly noticed in the midst of the bright halos of surrounding light of evangelical idealism. "On the whole," recalled Atkins, "the ten or fifteen years before the war were, controversially, a kind of Truce of God."[18]

There was another reason why this was a time of peace even within a group with as much diversity as the Baptists. Although the issues were well aired and strenuously debated in the seminaries and among the denomination's leadership, they were not well known on a popular level. Albert H. Newman, probably the leading Baptist historian of the time, in 1905 provided an unusually clear analysis of the current status of the theological debates. Newman identified three major parties among Baptists in America. At one extreme were the liberals with their dazzlingly impressive academic strength. On the other extreme were the premillennialists, whom Newman characterized as "intensely anti-rationalistic," uncompromising concerning Scripture, tending to equate higher criticism with the Devil, and working through independent agencies and Bible institutes. In the middle was a moderate conservative party, "still in the vast majority" and controlling most of the working forces of the denomination. Despite these major divisions, the debates inspired no large-scale public interest. "Even in New England and the Middle States," Newman estimated, "not one Baptist member in ten is conscious of any important change in theology or departure from the old

Baptist orthodoxy." For the Western and Southeastern states his estimate was not one in twenty; for the Southwest, not one in a hundred. Newman, who himself apparently considered such ignorance compatible with invincibility, concluded that the denomination "never possessed so many advantages and never encountered so few obstacles to progress." "'Things are getting better,'" he said, "and not worse."[19]

The moderate character of the dominant conservative party, standing between the two aggressive new movements on the extremes, was one reason for optimism. Although some Baptist conservatives insisted on the inerrancy of Scripture in detail,[20] this position was far from being a test of Baptist orthodoxy. The leading conservative Baptist theologian of the time, Augustus H. Strong, president of Rochester Theological Seminary, had a concept of truth that reflected the influence of some of the same philosophical trends that were shaping theological liberalism. While holding a high view of Biblical authority, Strong's starting point was that truth was not doctrinal or propositional, but rather "the truth is a personal Being, and that Christ himself is the Truth." Strong attributed the intellectual difficulties in the church to a view of truth that was too abstract and literal. People mistakenly supposed that the perfection attributed to the deity could be attributed equally to statements about Christ made by the church, the ministry, the Bible, or a creed. "A large part of the unbelief of the present day," he said, "has been caused by the unwarranted identification of these symbols and manifestations with Christ himself. Neither the church nor ministry, Bible or creed, is perfect. To discover imperfection in them is to prove that they are not in themselves divine."[21]

Strong rejected very explicitly the idea of Scripture as inerrant and in his influential *Systematic Theology* eventually dropped language that might even suggest such a conclusion.[22] Statements similar to Strong's could readily be found elsewhere among Baptist conservatives. Robert Stuart MacArthur, pastor of Calvary Baptist Church in New York City (which became a fundamentalist center under his successor, John Roach Straton), in 1899 strongly defended traditional Christianity while maintaining that "A true doctrine of inspiration may admit mistakes, or at least the possibility of mistakes, in history and biographical statements, while it denies error in matters of faith and morals. . . ."[23] Even Curtis Lee Laws, editor of the conservative *Watchman-Examiner* (and in 1920 inventor of the word "fundamentalist" to describe this Baptist party), did not insist on inerrancy, emphasizing the "experimental" verification of the Bible's truth rather than its value as scientific statement. Like the dispensationalists and (as will be seen shortly) the Princeton theologians, Laws viewed the objective character of Biblical truth as analogous to the laws of physics. Like the Princetonians, he viewed Biblical truth as known by common sense. "The infallibility of the Bible is the infallibility of common sense, and of the experimental triumph within us." Yet, as this last phrase suggests, the truth of Scripture known by

on the part of the ministry. Contrariwise, Presbyterians from the New England and English Puritan traditions, who also helped form the church in America, insisted that the creed should be interpreted with more latitude. This debate, although sometimes subsiding, continued right into the twentieth century. The broader New England and more "American" party became associated with revivalism which, especially in the New School movement of the first two thirds of the nineteenth century, brought with it demands for a more flexible version of Calvinism. The Scotch-Irish Old School party, strongest in Pennsylvania, at Princeton Seminary, and in the South, although including a warmly pietistic strain, continued to put doctrine first. It insisted that the Westminster standards represented as closely as was humanly possible the system of doctrine contained in Scripture.

In connection with such traditions, Old School Presbyterians had preserved a distinctive view of truth. They tended to view truth in its purest form as precisely stated propositions. This applied not only to the *Confession,* but also to the infallible Scriptures that the *Confession* summarized. In either case truth was a stable entity, not historically relative, best expressed in written language that, at least potentially, would convey one message in all times and places.

This view of things was particularly compatible with the Scottish Common Sense philosophy. No doubt it was not coincidental that this philosophy developed in Scotland where Presbyterianism was strong. Certainly in America some of its most ardent and persistent supporters, especially of the Scotch-Irish party, were those who emphasized the importance of traditional Reformation dogmatic statements.

These affinities were reinforced by direct connections. Just before the American Revolution, Princeton College secured as president an outstanding Scottish clergyman and educator, John Witherspoon, who made the college the center for Scottish Realism in America. By 1812 when the Presbyterian Church established its own seminary at Princeton, Scottish Realism was likewise what the faculty taught. It would be difficult to exaggerate its influence on Princeton theology in the nineteenth century.[3]

Many Americans during the first half of the century employed the Common Sense categories, but at Princeton the appeal had especially to do with their conscious preservation of the classic Protestant emphasis on *scriptura sola.* Combating Roman Catholic apologists, the defenders of the Reformation in the sixteenth and seventeenth centuries had to stress the sufficiency of Scripture as the only rule of faith and practice. This position implied a corollary, "the perspicuity of Scripture." If, as the Protestants argued against the Catholics, neither the church nor tradition was essential to understanding the Biblical message, then it was necessary to claim that even simple Christians could understand the essential message of the Bible on their own. "The Scriptures are so perspicuous in things pertaining to salvation," affirmed Francis Turretin, the seventeenth-century theologian whose Latin text was used at Princeton, "that they can be understood by believers without the external help of an oral tradition or ecclesiastical authority."[4] This meant that in interpretation of the essentials of Scripture the common sense perceptions of the common man could be relied upon. "The Bible is a plain book," said Charles Hodge. "It is intelligible by the people. And they have the right and are bound to read and interpret it for themselves; so that their faith may rest on the testimony of the Scriptures, and not that of the Church."[5]

At Princeton, as well as in much of the rest of nineteenth-century Protestant America, the idea that a person of simple common sense could rightly understand Scripture was grounded in the more general affirmation of the Scottish philosophy that in essentials the common sense of mankind could be relied upon. "That man is capable of real knowledge to a certain degree," Archibald Alexander told the first students at Princeton Seminary in 1812, "all must admit. . . ." Any assertion to the contrary was self-contradictory. "The fact is," Alexander continued,

> that we are so constituted by our nature that we are under the necessity of believing many propositions. By no reasoning, or voluntary effort, can a man cease to believe that he exists, that he perceives, that he feels pleasure and pain, that other beings exist, etc."[6]

Any sane and unbiased person of common sense could and must perceive the same things.

Here and in other Common Sense statements we find the affirmation that basic truths are much the same for all persons in all times and places. This assumption is crucial to an understanding of the view of Christianity at Princeton and in fundamentalism generally. At nineteenth-century Princeton, unlike the situation among most later fundamentalists, the underlying philosophical basis for this assumption was frequently articulated in opposition to the currents of the day that threatened to erode it. The formidable *Princeton Review,* long under the editorship of Charles Hodge, repeatedly presented detailed and laudatory expositions of the Common Sense position.[7] Sir William Hamilton, the leading nineteenth-century proponent of the Scottish system, recieved especially glowing praise. He was a "matchless genius," the "Socrates" of his age, "like a pure intelligence." His philosophy was "the one perennial philosophy of common sense . . . the only true philosophy." It was "the consummation of that of Bacon." Among other things, the reviewer asserted, "He seems, in no degree, under the influence of what is called the historical development of human intelligence."[8]

Such eternal truth, whether revealed in Scripture or in nature, was best refined by the scientific method. Baconianism appeared everywhere in the writings of the Princetonians,[9] just as it did among American scientists of the era.[10] The Princeton theologians saw themselves as champions of "impartiality" in the careful examination of the facts, as opposed to "metaphysical and philosophical speculations" such as those of German Biblical critics.[11] Following the precepts of Baconianism, the Princetonians described the proper function of science as "taxonomical," or the gathering and classifying of facts. While dispensationalists used this method to classify the historical data in Scripture, Princeton theologians applied it more traditionally to the task of arranging theological statements. They often drew an analogy between theology and the hard sciences. As Charles Hodge said in introducing his *Systematic Theology:*

> If natural science be concerned with the facts and laws of nature, theology is concerned with the facts and the principles of the Bible. If the object of the one be to arrange and systematize the facts of the external world, and to ascertain the laws by which they are determined; the object of the other is to systematize the facts of the Bible, and ascertain the principles or general truths which those facts involve.[12]

Using the analogy to natural science, Hodge considered truth adequately supported only when it was based on the exact apprehensions of intellect, and not on indefinable feelings. In answer to Friedrich Schleiermacher, who argued that true religion was grounded on feelings, Hodge insisted that "intellectual apprehension produces feelings, and not feeling intellectual apprehension."[13] Although certainly not opposing religious feelings per se[14] Hodge attacked all the trends of his day which based knowledge of Christian truth on such experiences. When Christianity becomes, as the Germans said, "the life of the soul," then, said Hodge, "the word of God is made of none effect." If "the beautiful solo of Dr. Bushnell," should "seduce us from cleaving to the letter of Scripture, by telling us the Bible was but a picture or a poem," then the cause of the true faith would ultimately be lost. When, however, Professor Edwards A. Park of Andover proposed at mid-century that the theology of feeling should be seen in opposition to the theology of intellect, Hodge insisted that the two were inseparable and that Park's views were "not the language of the heart, but of a head made light by too much theorizing."[15]

Genuine religious experience, Hodge was convinced, grew only out of right ideas; right ideas, in turn, could only be expressed in words. Hodge developed this point in relation to the doctrine of the inspiration of Scripture, which was an increasingly embattled position in the Princeton line of defense as the century wore on. Writing in 1857, Hodge observed that some interpreters suggested that "inspiration" applied to the thoughts of the sacred writers, but not to their exact words. To Hodge this was sheer nonsense. "No man can have a wordless thought, any more than there can be a formless flower," he said. "By a law of our present constitution, we think in words, and as far as our consciousness goes, it is as impossible to infuse thoughts into the mind without words, as it is to bring men into the world without bodies." The purpose of inspiration was to communicate a "record of truth." For such a record "accuracy of statement" and an "infallible correctness of the report were essential." These would not be assured if the selection of words were left to humans, whose memories were faulty. Although the method of inspiration was not merely mechanical dictation, the Holy Spirit could guarantee the accuracy of the reports only by inspiring the authors to select correct words.[16]

This view of Scripture, which had been taught by Archibald Alexander at the seminary's inception,[17] received its classic expression in 1881 when Archibald Alexander Hodge and the young B. B. Warfield published their famous defense of the "inerrancy" of Scripture. This they took to be "the great Catholic doctrine of Biblical Inspiration, i.e., that the Scriptures not only contain, but ARE THE WORD OF GOD, and hence that all their elements and all their affirmations are absolutely errorless, and binding the faith and obedience of men." Following the elder Hodge closely, they insisted that the inspiration must extend to the words. "Infallible thought must be definite thought, and definite thought implies words." The result was "the truth to fact of every statement in the Scripture."[18]

This view of truth as an externally stable entity placed tremendous weight on the *written* word. If truth were the same for all ages, and if truth was apparent primarily in objective facts, then the written word was the surest means permanently and precisely to display this truth. Religious experiences, rituals, traditions, even unrecorded words spoken by God or Jesus, as essential as all of these were, nonetheless were transitory. Unassisted, none could guarantee that sure facts would be objectively apprehended in all ages. "The Bible is to the theologian," said Charles Hodge in his *Systematic Theology,* "what nature is to the man. It is his store-house of facts. . . ."[19] At Princeton it was an article of faith that God would provide nothing less than wholly accurate facts, whether large or small. Common Sense philosophy assured that throughout the ages people could discover the same truths in the unchanging storehouse of Scripture.

Another important element in this view of Scripture was tied to the Common Sense tradition. Common Sense philosophy, in contrast to most philosophy since Descartes and Locke, held that the immediate objects of our perceptions were not *ideas* of the external world, but (as the *Princeton Review* put it) "we are directly conscious of the external objects themselves." The same principle applied to memory; what we remember is not the *idea* of a past event, but the past event itself. So, for example, we do not remember the *idea* of Rome (which is in the present) but Rome itself, which is in the past. For such knowledge of the past, we must furthermore rely on the testimony of honest witnesses, else we could not know the past at all, which would be contrary to common sense.[20]

This view that the past could be known directly through reliable testimony meant that Scripture was not regarded as representing the *points of view* of its authors respecting the past, but it was rather an infallible representation of the past itself. This distinction was intimately connected with the demand at Princeton that Scripture be accepted as without error, even in historical detail. Increasingly, modern thought suggested that the point of view of the observer stood between the facts and his report of the facts. This would suggest that even the most honest and authoritative accounts of the past would be altered in detail by the observer's point of view. At Princeton, however, the ideal for truth was an objective statement of fact in which the subjective element was eliminated almost completely. In their view, Scripture did just that. Although they did not deny the human element, divine guidance was thought to produce accounts where the warp from point of view had been virtually eliminated.

The whole Princeton view of truth was based on the assumption that truth is known by apprehending directly what is "out there" in the external world, not a function of human mental activity. The mind discovers objective truth, which is much the same for all people all ages.

Yet, if truth is so objective and common sense so reliable, how does one account for the wide prevalence of error? This was the great obstacle to the whole Common Sense philosophy and the rock against which in the nineteenth century it repeatedly foundered, until all but its most stubborn exponents were dislodged. How is it that there are so many rational and upright people of good will who refuse to see the truth which consists of objective facts that are as plain as day? As the nineteenth century wore on, Americans were confronted with a bewildering diversity of ethnic and religious groups, and the Anglo-Saxon Protestant religious and moral consensus was breaking down. Questions concerning why others did not see the truth became increasingly acute. The Princeton and fundamentalist Common Sense explanations of why individuals accepted error has, of course, a great deal to do with understanding the fundamentalist reaction to modern ideas.

The Common Sense view of truth and error stood in a relationship to the prevailing modern views that was closely analogous to the relationship between Ptolemaic and Copernican accounts of the universe, and the difficulties in relating one view to the other were just as insuperable. As in the Ptolemaic astronomy the earth was regarded as a fixed point with the heavenly bodies all revolving around it, so in the Common Sense view of knowledge there was one body of fixed truth that could be known objectively, while around it revolved all sorts of errors, speculations, prejudices, and subjective opinions. Most other modern schemes of thought have tended toward the view that all observers, like all bodies in the Copernican universe, are (as it were) in motion—caught in historical processes. Rather than seeing truth as objectively existing at one fixed point, they have viewed knowledge as at least to a considerable degree relative to a person's time and point of view.[21]

For B. B. Warfield, the greatest champion of the Princeton cause, during the critical period of the shipwreck and breaking apart of the Common Sense consensus in America, between the Civil War and World War I, accounting for the immense growth of error from a Common Sense position was a crucial concern. Like his predecessors, Warfield emphasized that faith must be grounded in right reason. Although the Holy Spirit was the agent for a change of heart, "how can even a prepared heart respond, when there are no 'reasons' to draw out its actions?" Reason is as necessary to faith, said Warfield, as light is to photography. Warfield indeed wrote as though he had unbounded confidence in the apologetic power of the rational appeal to people of common sense. In a remarkable passage written in 1903, he pulled out all the stops in urging the powers of reason to advance Christianity:

> It is the distinction of Christianity that it has come into the world clothed with the mission to *reason* its way to its dominion. Other religions may appeal to the sword, or seek some other way to propagate themselves. Christianity makes its appeal to right reason, and stands out among all religions, therefore, as distinctively "the Apologetic religion." It is solely by reasoning that it has come thus far on its way to its kingship. And it is solely by reasoning that it will put all its enemies under its feet.[22]

With this opinion of the power of unaided reason in demonstrating the truth of Christianity, it was essential to Warfield's position to maintain that intellectually the believer and the non-believer stood on common ground. This common-ground approach eliminated from Warfield's apologetics the use of a venerable line of explanation for the failures of reason. In the traditions of Augustine, Calvin, and Jonathan Edwards the Fall was often regarded as having so blinded the human intellect that natural knowledge of God had been suppressed and therefore no one could have true understanding without receiving the eyes of faith. A version of this approach had recently been revived by conservative Calvinists in the Netherlands, including Herman Bavinck and Abraham Kuyper. Reflecting Continental philosophical trends, these theologians postulated an antithesis between Christian thought, the first principles of which recognized God's sovereignty over all creation, and *non*-Christian thought which was predicated on human autonomy. Just as the premises concerning the most basic aspects of reality were opposed, said Bavinck and Kuyper, so also would be the conclusions that Christians and non-Christians would reach concerning reality. Warfield, although he had some close contacts with these Dutch Calvinists, was utterly mystified by this approach to apologetics which he described as "a standing matter of surprise." True to the demands of Common Sense, Warfield saw the effects of the Fall on human consciousness as pervasive but quite limited. "The science of sinful man is thus a substantive part of the abstract science produced by the ideal subject, the general human consciousness, though a less valuable part than it would be without sin."[23]

How then, if Christian and non-Christian reason are essentially part of one human consciousness, does one explain the undeniable fact that human inquiry so often leads to totally wrong conclusions. Among traditional explanations were moral error,[24] faulty reasoning, speculative hypotheses, metaphysical fancies, and the prejudices of unbelief or false religions. It was disturbing, however, in the latter decades of the nineteenth century to find that scientists who had been reared as Christians, morally upright, and certainly reasonable, were abandoning the faith as a consequence of their scientific studies. Warfield was particularly concerned with the case of Charles Darwin. Part of the explanation of Darwin's rejection of Christianity, he observed, was that he placed too much weight on speculation and hypothesis so that he developed an "invincible prejudice" or "predilection for his theory of the origin of species." In addition, Warfield saw a more basic issue, which he feared might be a widespread problem in the scientific community. Concentrating so intensely on their narrow scientific investigations, they were losing their capacity to deal with spiritual, moral, or ethical matters. "We can only account for Mr. Darwin's failure to accept the guidance of his inextinguishable conviction here," concluded Warfield, "by recognizing that his absorption in a single line of investigation and inference had so atrophied his mind in other directions that he had ceased to be a trustworthy judge of evidence."[25]

Early in the twentieth century Warfield confronted the manifestation of this same problem in the growing rejection of the miraculous, not only by scientists, but even among theologians. In this case he saw a bias in their first principles. "Mere unreasonable dogmatism" prejudiced the opponents of miracles. The solution, however, was not to set one worldview or set of premises against another as competing hypotheses. Rather it was the Baconian method of setting a body of facts, objectively knowable by unbiased and dispassionate observers against the eccentric and prejudiced biases of all competing worldviews. "In other words," Warfield concluded triumphantly, "are the facts that are to be permitted to occur in the universe to be determined by our precedently conceived world-view or is our world-view to be determined by a due consideration of all the facts that occur in the universe?"[26]

With the most influential conservative element in the Presbyterian church holding this view of the utter perspicuity of truth[27] and Scripture, it is hardly surprising that the controversies in that denomination were more protracted and severe than elsewhere. If one takes into account that fundamentalist and conservative reactions to liberalism were often just what they claimed to be, reactions against major modifications of traditional Christianity, then these Presbyterian conservatives were the most consistently clear in identifying the central changes that had taken place. At the same time, their peculiar views of Scripture and of truth involved them in equally heated debates over much narrower issues, such as the inerrancy of Scripture or revision of the *Westminster Confession of Faith*. The broad and narrow versions of the issues, accordingly, were easily confused on both sides.

The Presbyterian furor reached its peak in the 1890s. Early in the decade moderately liberal leaders attempted a revision of the Confession of Faith, which was defeated in 1893.[28] In the meantime conservatives counterattacked by bringing in succession formal action against three of the most famous of the progressive seminary professors, Charles A. Briggs, Henry Preserved Smith, and Arthur Cushman McGiffert. By the end of the decade all three had left the Presbyterian church as a result of these actions. Union Theological Seminary in New York severed its ties with the denomination in 1892 in response to the General Assembly's actions against Professor Briggs. Although some broad issues of departure from Calvinist orthodoxy were involved, in each case the specific allegations concerned the narrow issue of inerrancy. On several occasions during the decade the General Assembly declared that the doctrine of inerrancy was a fundamental teaching of the church.[29]

As in other denominations, something of a truce seemed to prevail during most of the first two decades of the twentieth century; yet conservative Presbyterians were using the time to retrench themselves in the positions they had committed themselves to and successfully defended during the intense battles of the 1890s. This defensive strategy had an important bearing on the larger fundamentalist movement. For one thing it seemed to establish a precedent for the successful restraint of liberalism by formal ecclesiastical action. For another, it helped to characterize the movement as committed to defending a few fundamentals of faith. This latter effect, which was ironic in view of the elaborate confessionalism of conservative Presbyterians, apparently was not entirely intended. In 1910 the Presbyterian General Assembly, in response to some questions raised about the orthodoxy of some of the graduates of Union Theological Seminary, adopted a five-point declaration of "essential" doctrines. Summarized, these points were: (1) the inerrancy of Scripture, (2) the Virgin Birth of Christ, (3) his substitutionary atonement, (4) his bodily resurrection, and (5) the authenticity of the miracles. These five points (which included both the narrow issue of inerrancy and some of the broad issues concerning the supernatural in Christianity) were not intended to be a creed or a definitive statement. Yet in the 1920s they became the "famous five points" that were the last rallying position before the spectacular collapse of the conservative party. Moreover, because of parallels to various other fundamentalist short creeds (and an historian's error), they became the basis of what (with premillennialism substituted for the authenticity of the miracles) were long known as the "five points of fundamentalism."[30]

As the issues broadened in the decades of relative peace at the beginning of the century, so apparently did conservative Presbyterians' willingness to cooperate with others who had a strict view of Scripture and were adamant against compromise on the essential supernatural elements in Christianity. With these increasingly important criteria in mind, the dispensationalist and

Keswick Bible teachers, with whom the Princeton party had many disagreements, looked more and more like worthwhile allies. The conservative wing of the Presbyterian church, of which Princeton was only the leading edge, already included some prominent leaders from the more evangelistically oriented movement. Although Princeton and the interdenominational Bible teachers' movement developed their views of Scripture and of the essential importance of the supernatural for independent reasons, they had much in common philosophically, and therefore spoke the same language and defended the faith in similar fashion.[31]

The emergence of this alliance is most clearly perceptible in the foundation in 1903 of the Bible League of North America. This organization, with its journal, *The Bible Student and Teacher,* was initially dedicated to semi-popular scholarly defense of the faith. It had the leadership predominantly of prominent conservative professors at Northern and Southern Presbyterian seminaries. Soon, however, dispensationalists became active in the movement, regular contributors to the journal (on non-dispensationalist themes), and board members.[32] By 1913 board membership of the journal had been expanded well beyond the alliance of conservative Presbyterians and dispensationalists, with the editorship in the hands of a Methodist. The journal's name was changed to the *Bible Champion,* which signalled a more militant and popular stance. This anti-modernist coalition had one principal goal— "to maintain the historic faith of the Church in the divine inspiration and authority of the Bible as the Word of God."[33] The outlines of a broad fundamentalist alliance were emerging.

XIV. *The Fundamentals*

The Fundamentals was conceived by a Southern California oil millionaire and edited by Bible teachers and evangelists. Published in twelve paperback volumes from 1910 to 1915, it was meant to be a great "Testimony to the Truth" and even something of a scholarly *tour de force.* Lyman Stewart, the chief promoter and financial backer, described the prospective authors as "the best and most loyal Bible teachers in the world." He had a businessman's confidence that the product would "doubtless be the masterpieces of the writers."[1] Stewart hired as his first editor A. C. Dixon, a well-known evangelist and author, then pastor of Moody Church in Chicago. He had greatly impressed Stewart with a sermon attacking "one of those infidel professors in Chicago."[2] Dixon and two successors, Louis Meyer (a Jewish-Christian evangelist) and Reuben Torrey, assembled a rather formidable array of conservative American and British scholars, as well as a number of popular writers.[3] Lyman Stewart, with the aid of his brother and partner Milton, set out to ensure that the truth would not languish because of unavailability. They financed free distribution to every pastor, missionary, theological professor, theological student, YMCA and YWCA secretary, college professor, Sunday school superintendent, and religious editor in the English-speaking world, and sent out some three million individual volumes in all.[4]

The public response, however, was not as great as must have been hoped. Although the publishers reported many individual positive responses,[5] neither theological journals nor popular religious periodicals seemed to take more than passing notice.[6]

The Fundamentals, however, had a long-term effect of greater importance than its immediate impact or the lack thereof. It became a symbolic point of reference for identifying a "fundamentalist" movement. When in 1920 the term "fundamentalist" was coined, it called to mind the broad united front of the kind of opposition to modernism that characterized these widely known, if little studied, volumes. In retrospect, the volumes retain some usefulness in tracing the outlines of the emerging movement. They represent the movement at a moderate and transitional stage before it was reshaped and pushed to extremes by the intense heat of controversy.

At the center of the interdenominational expression of the anti-modernist movement were the evangelists and Bible teachers of the dispensational and Keswick movements; in *The Fundamentals,* however, they showed remarkable restraint in promoting the more controversial aspects of their views. Keswick teachings appeared rather extensively in the volumes, but these were not as yet cause for much dispute, at least not in the generally Reformed camp that made up the coalition. Dispensationalism and premillennialism, which were controversial, were almost entirely absent.[7] Clearly an effort was being made to build and maintain alliances. Only about half of the authors selected were from the Bible teachers' group. In order to establish a respectable and self-consciously conservative coalition against modernism, premillennial teachings were best kept in the background.

In the meantime, however, the same group of Bible teachers and evangelists who promoted *The Fundamentals* were moving on other fronts to promote their own distinctive dispensationalist views. Backed by Stewart money they founded the Bible Institute of Los Angeles in 1908. In the same year they also managed re-publication and massive free distribution of William E. Blackstone's *Jesus Is Coming.* Probably most important, in 1909 there came the publication, by Oxford University Press, of the *Scofield Reference Bible.*[8]

In *The Fundamentals* the movement's interests were focused on a broad defense of the faith. Perhaps one third of the articles defended Scripture, typically with an attack on the foibles of higher criticism. Another third dealt with traditional theological questions—apologetics, the nature and work of each of the persons of the Trinity, the doctrines of sin and salvation. The remaining articles are more difficult to classify. Each of the first five volumes, which were otherwise heavy on higher criticism and doctrine, concluded with personal testimony. Five other volumes (VII–XI) ended with polemics against modern "isms," Russellism, Mormonism, Eddyism, Modern Spiritualism, and Romanism—indicating, as is evident in most conservative publications of the era, that the alarm caused by breakdown of the evangelical consensus extended beyond the menace of Protestant liberalism. Beginning with Volume VII there was a decided shift toward more popular topics. Volume XII, devoted to evangelism and missions, was intended as the capstone of the enterprise.[9] Despite the interest in the defense of the faith that was giving the movement new shape, it was still close to the days of D. L. Moody, and its preeminent concern remained that of reaching lost souls.

Thus the practical essays and personal testimonies in *The Fundamentals* display an overwhelming emphasis on soul-saving, personal experience, and individual prayer, with very little attention to specific ethical issues, either personal or social. Political causes—even prohibition—were studiously avoided. Sabbath observance was urged, but not as a political issue. A few writers alluded to the dangers of communism and anarchy, but the one essay on socialism was remarkably moderate. The church should stay out of politics, it stated, but genuine Christian profession was compatible with personal advocacy of socialism.[10] Charles Trumbull warned against too much "social service" at the expense of creating "victorious soul-winners." But missionary leader Robert Speer, another Keswick advocate, stressed that the salvation of souls would help to free the world "from want and disease and injustice and inequality and impurity and lust and hopelessness and fear."[11] The coalition agreed that the church's mission was not political, but as yet it did not seem to see itself as especially divided from its liberal brethren over social questions.

The crucial issue seems rather to have been perceived as that of the authority of God in Scripture in relation to the authority of modern science, particularly science in the form of higher criticism of Scripture itself. Despite the variety of nationalities and backgrounds of the contributors, in essay after essay the central argument on this point was, with few exceptions, virtually the same. True science and historical criticism were to be much applauded. The "Scientific and Historical method," said Baptist professor J. J. Reeve, is "irresistible" to the scholarly mind. "The scientific spirit which gave rise to it is one of the noblest instincts in the intellectual life of man."[12] "What is called 'higher' criticism," agreed W. H. Griffith Thomas, "is not only a legitimate but a necessary method for all Christians, for by its use we are able to discover the facts and the form of the Old Testament Scriptures." Thomas adamantly opposed, however, the "illegitimate, unscientific and unhistorical use" of this method.[13]

The thing that separated true scientific criticism from the illegitimate and false, most commentators agreed, was that the "true criticism enters upon its inquiries with an open mind"[14] while the false is controlled by speculative hypotheses. Canon Dyson Hague of London, Ontario, whose essay was chosen to lead the series when a four-volume edition was issued in 1917, clearly sounded the themes which echoed through the volumes. "For hypothesis-weaving and speculation," he remarked, "the German theological professor is unsurpassed." Appealing to the Anglo-Saxon tradition associated with Bacon and Newton, Hague observed that "in philosophical and scientific enquiries . . . no regard whatever should be paid to the conjectures or hypotheses of thinkers . . ." for "the great Newton himself" had said, "'Non fingo hypotheses': I do not frame hypotheses."[15]

These principles were the foundation stones for Reuben Torrey's defense of Christianity, which he said was established on the basis of "historically proven fact." Claiming to "assume absolutely nothing," Torrey argued that "true science does not start with an *a priori* hypothesis that certain things are impossible, but simply examines the evidence to find out what has actually occurred."[16]

The central unproven, unprovable, and wholly unscientific hypothesis or prejudice, everyone agreed, was the prejudice against the supernatural and the miraculous.[17] While much specific evidence was marshalled to demonstrate the integrity of Scripture and the conjectural nature of the higher critical theories,[18] the arguments always returned to this basic point. Without an *a priori* rejection of the miraculous, Scripture would always prove compatible with the highest standards of science and rationality.

These champions of science and rationality did not strictly confine their defense of the Christian fundamentals to reason alone. A number, while acknowledging the value of true science, emphasized its limits with respect to knowing God.[19] Occasionally, this approach was carried to an anti-intellectualistic conclusion. Philip Mauro, a fiery New York lawyer converted to a radical dispensationalist version of Christianity, was clearly an advocate of rationality; yet he unequivocally condemned all "philosophy," which he defined as "the occupation of attempting to devise, by the exercises of human reason, an explanation of the universe."[20] The approach taken in an essay by B. B. Warfield was more typical. Warfield was certainly second to none as a champion of the rational defense of Christianity. Yet he carefully balanced his appeals to objective evidence with the subjective witness of the Holy Spirit. "The supreme proof," he concluded, "to every Christian of the deity of his Lord is then his own inner experience of the transforming power of his Lord upon the heart and life." This approach was thoroughly consistent with Common Sense philosophy, which grounded its first principles not in elaborate philosophical arguments but in the sense of mankind. So, said Warfield, the experience of the transforming power of the Lord is known by the Christian as surely as "he who feels the present warmth of the sun knows the sun exists."[21]

On questions of the degree to which objective evidence was essential for proving Christianity there was still some room for variety within the conservative camp. Robert Speer, for example, defended the deity of Christ almost entirely on the grounds of the evidence of the doctrine's practical benefits.[22] More explicitly, President E. Y. Mullins of Baptist Theological Seminary in Louisville, Kentucky, based the proof of Christianity almost exclusively on the experiential and the practical. Noting that this approach gave Christianity a point of contact with the new philosophy of Pragmatism, Mullins argued that "Christian experience transfers the whole problem of Christian evidences to the sphere of the practical life."[23] Mullins's position genuinely mediated between the old theology and the new philosophy and so had something in common with the more liberal reliance on the experiential and the practical. The inclusion of his work in *The Fundamentals,* together with a number of other mediating essays,[24] shows that the trenches were not yet deeply dug for the coming fundamentalist battle. Later, in the heat of the 1920s, mediating positions such as Mullins's would be no-man's-land.[25]

One line along which the dispensationalists at least were already well entrenched by 1910 was Biblical inerrancy. Departing from their usual practice, on this issue the editors chose only authors from their own camp. They did not have to turn to the Princeton theologians to find a strong defense of the complete inerrancy of Scripture. In fact their own emphasis on the supernatural character of the Bible was so strong that, despite their frequent protestations to the contrary, they tended to drift toward the dictation theory. Even James M. Gray, while mentioning the element of human personality in writing Scripture, immediately gives an illustration of a stenographer who changed a "now" into a "not" to show how every detail must be controlled by the original author. So by "miraculous control" the Bible was an "absolute transcript" of God's mind.[26] The Reverend George S. Bishop similarly spoke with no qualification of the "dictated inspiration" of the entire Bible and even referred to it as "a Book dropped out of heaven."[27]

In remarkable contrast, and indicative of the mediating positions still allowed within the emerging coalition, battle lines were not yet firmly fixed against every sort of biological evolutionism. Although one essayist, "An Occupant of the Pew," writing on "Evolutionism in the Pulpit," suggested that all evolutionism was of the Devil,[28] two of the men selected to write on this topic, James Orr of Scotland[29] and George Frederick Wright of Oberlin College, were well known to allow that limited forms of evolution might have been used by God in creation. Each argued strongly against Darwinian claims that evolution could explain the origins of life or the uniqueness of humans. Each allowed, however (as was common among conservative evangelicals in the later nineteenth century), that the "days" of creation might have been very long, allowing the possibility of some evolutionary development. Such limited evolutionism, said Wright, certainly did not exclude God's creative work. "If anything is to be *evolved* in an orderly manner from the resident forces of primordial matter it must first have been *involved* through the creative act of the Divine Being."[30]

The selection of the aging George F. Wright to write the most detailed analysis of biological evolution for *The Fundamentals* is a sidelight on the many-sided character of this early fundamentalism. Wright was a product of the old intellectually sophisticated New England Calvinism. During the 1870s he was the protégé of the foremost Congregationalist defender of theistic evolution, Asa Gray, and was even the target of conservative attacks. Wright never changed his mediating position, however, while the scientific community soon abandoned the attempt to defend both science and Scripture. Consequently, by 1910 Wright was clearly in the conservative camp,[31] even though later fundamentalist standards he would have been a suspect moderate.

Wright edited the *Bibliotheca Sacra,* one of the most respected American theological journals, originally designed in the early nineteenth century for the defense of New England orthodoxy. Under Wright's editorship, *Bibliotheca Sacra* stood with the emerging fundamentalist movement. After some uncertain years following Wright's death in 1921 the jounal completed its odyssey, falling into the hands of the important new dispensationalist theological seminary in Dallas, Texas. There it remained as an at least symbolic link between militant fundamentalism and the former days of the scholarly New England battles for the faith.[32] The moderation of Wright, as that of *The Fundamentals*, was clearly transitional in a movement that had not yet found any firm identity.

Christianity and Culture

XV. Four Views *circa* 1910

In retrospect, we can see that the decade preceding America's entry into the Great War was the end of an era for the American evangelical establishment. Throughout the nineteenth century there had seemed to be reasonable hope for establishing the foundations of something like a "Christian America." With the knowledge of what has happened since, it is apparent that this ideal was illusory and that the evangelical consensus itself was already irreparably damaged. The impasse that was to come could only dimly be perceived in the early twentieth century in the context of a long past of evangelical advance and a vigorous present. Competing denominationalists, liberals and conservatives, individualists and social reformers, confessionalists and primitivists .had long worked together in many of the same interdenominational agencies, published in the same journals, prayed for the same mission causes, and shared many of the same hopes.[1] There were indeed many sectarians and immigrant groups on the fringes which had little to do with the central evangelical movement. Yet the majority of Protestants who did identify with it had long since learned to live with some differences and cooperate in working for many common goals.

The new conservative coalition against liberalism was part of this establishment. It belonged to the mainstream and, as *The Fundamentals* project shows, aspired to bring about a consensus of religious thought in America. At the same time it was becoming more and more a voice of dissent, sometimes sounding a sectarian or anti-intellectual note.

If this emerging anti-modernist movement was in any sense a distinct entity, it was torn by internal disagreements and tensions. These differences could have a number of explanations, including incompatible denominational or doctrinal traditions. It may be more illuminating, however, to look at these divisions in the context of the spectrum of opinion on an issue central to the present inquiry—the relation of Christianity to American culture. Should the movement attempt to reshape the culture and its churches from within or rather condemn them and separate itself from them? On this

124

central practical question, as the four representative types in this chapter illustrate, there was no consensus. Basic differences and internal tensions were temporarily obscured in the movement by the anti-modernist agitation of the 1920s. Yet the lines of fissure were always present so that fragmentations were likely whenever it attempted positive programs.

1. THIS AGE CONDEMNED:
   THE PREMILLENNIAL EXTREME

At one end of the spectrum was a small group of dispensationalist spokesmen who pushed the cultural pessimism of premillennialism to its logical extreme. The controversial Arno C. Gaebelein, editor of *Our Hope*, promoted this position aggressively, as did Isaac M. Haldeman, a vigorous writer and pastor of the First Baptist Church of New York City. In *The Fundamentals* this position was represented by several essays by New York lawyer Philip Mauro.

Not surprisingly, the favorite topic of these rigorous dispensationalists was "the signs of the times." Gaebelein ran a regular feature in *Our Hope*, "Current Events and Signs of the Times—in the Light of the Word of God." In 1910, I. M. Haldeman completed the most comprehensive dispensationalist volume to date on *The Signs of the Times,* which quickly ran through several editions. Haldeman's signs, which were essentially the same as Gaebelein's and Mauro's, may be taken as fair sample of this prophetic worldview in the pre-World War I era.[2]

With one exception (the rise of the Jewish people in world leadership and the Zionist movement) the signs that the end was near could be seen in the grim evidence that civilization had failed. Haldeman and others, of course, could cite the usual assortment of famines, earthquakes, and pestilence; but they also could find considerable evidence, if not for wars, at least for rumors of wars. The "so-called 'Christian nations,'" said Haldeman noting recent armament statistics, are better prepared than ever "to blow out each other's brains."[3] Meanwhile the new wealth of entrepreneurs fulfilled Biblical prophecies of "heaping treasure together" and wanton displays of luxury as marks of the end of the age. The growth of commerical ties among European cities together with their shipping and railroad ties to the Near East represented the literal revival of Babylon.[4] And multimillionaire directors of trusts signalled the end times: "grasping after more, never content, and determined to rule, their wealth is a minister to corruption, an inspiration to official dishonesty, and a menace to the peace and comfort of society."[5]

Such rhetoric was most certainly not in any way connected with progressive reformism. Reform was in fact, according to Haldeman, Satan's way of lulling the world into ignoring the immensity of the crisis. If the Devil would lead the twentieth century "into a drunken orgy of sin and shame and outbreaking vice" as he had in the French Revolution, the reaction would ultimately result in a religious revival. On the contrary, "the Devil would be glad to see prohibition successful. Nothing would please him more than to be able to shut up every saloon and every house of shame."[6]

Haldeman, moreover, associated most reforms with the growing menace of socialism, which in turn he seemed to equate with anarchy. In any case reform reminded him of prophecies of the spread of "lawlessness." Most alarming was the appearance of reform and socialist sentiments even within the churches. Jesus Christ was no reformer, he argued, since he did not raise his voice against slavery or war. Furthermore Jesus rebuked Judas for his suggestion to give to the poor. Judas was "the only Socialist among professed Christians of whom the New Testament gives us record." Trying to save the world by socialism, said Haldeman, was like cleaning and decorating the staterooms of a sinking ship.[7]

Democracy fared little better. It, too, like socialist "lawlessness," was included in prophetic utterance. In Nebuchadnezzar's dream of the colossus, which was generally considered to represent four world empires ending with Rome, the feet and toes were iron mixed with clay. According to the dispensationalists, the ten toes represented the ten European nations whose federation (leagues of nations were already rumored) would be the final restoration of the Roman Empire. These nations were increasingly turning to constitutional or "mixed" democracies, and this was just what the mixture of iron and clay in the dream prophesied. Thus democracy was a symptom of weakness. Haldeman even went so far as to identify it with the socialist menace. The banner of democracy, he said, "is becoming more and more each day, the red flag, the symbol of socialism and the rule of man."[8]

Science and technology likewise were among the deceptively attractive human achievements that the Bible prophesied as signs of the end. The Bible spoke of the "increase of knowledge, the running to and fro" in the last days, which now could be seen to mean "rapid transit and rapid flight—the multiplications of human inventions." Science was impotent. The really important mysteries of life—such as the origin of life, and of motion, the mysteries of consciousness, thought, and the will—were "great riddles which laugh in the face of the most accomplished science." Science could not explain the "why" of even the simplest things. "Two and two do make four and that is all you know or can know about it," said Haldeman in an appeal to common sense. "There is not a scientist in the world can tell why. And yet this science dares to talk about the unreason of miracles. This is the thing that demands an entrance into our pulpits."[9]

The pulpits were indeed a major concern. Not only was there the continuing menace of Rome, but also the confusions of the cults, which fit the predictions of the coming of "many false teachers" who "repudiate sound doctrine." Even in Protestant churches, colleges, and universities, fundamental doctrines such as the resurrection of the body were "laughed out of court." As an alternative to true doctrine, modern theologians found the spirit of Christ in the culture around them, in every person who is good and honest and brave-hearted, in every work of art, in the telegraph and telephone, in education, and in social reform. Calling self-development "the Spirit of Christ," said Haldeman, is "nothing less than evolution under a taking name." It is "the old doctrine of Cain come to town again; it is offering the fruits of the earth, man bringing out the best things in his own life and evolving God'ward."[10]

In contrast, Christ's plan rejected the present world and age. Christ himself had not chosen to live in the world during this era. Rather, he was preparing a heavenly destiny for his people, the church. "All this settles the relation of the church to the present age." The church should not be concerned with the present culture. "The outlook of the church . . . is not on this age but on one to come." Christ has promised "to come and take the church out of this world."[11]

Even Haldeman did not go as far as he might in working out the ecclesiastical implications of this radically anti-worldly position. He did not call for ecclesiastical separation, and he himself remained in the Northern Baptist Convention.[12] A. C. Gaebelein, on the other hand, was one of the few of the prophetic leaders who did at this time interpret the radical doctrine of separation from the world as demanding separation from the worldly church. "*God's greatest call is separation*," he told the Prophetic Bible Conference of 1914. Gaebelein himself had separated from the Methodist apostasy in 1899 and demanded that others follow:

> How dare you support men and institutions who deny your Lord? How dare you keep fellowship with the enemies of the cross of Christ?
>
> Oh, listen to His call! Who is on the Lord's side? *If He tarry a little while longer you will find that you must either follow this solemn call of God or go along with the apostasy.*[13]

In 1914 Gaebelein was a leader with few followers. A half-generation later, when the fundamentalist battles to save the denominations had been lost, such separation would be for many a badge of orthodox fundamentalism. In the meantime, few were willing to see true Christianity as so radically opposed both to the culture and to its respectable churches.

2. THE CENTRAL TENSION

William B. Riley, just beginning to emerge as one of the chief architects of fundamentalism, was more typical. Riley also spoke on "The Significant Signs of the Times" at the 1914 conference. Riley mentioned essentially the same signs as Haldeman and Gaebelein, but without the attacks on democracy and socialism, and his mood was distinctly optimistic:

> There are those who say that the battle has gone against us. I confess I do not
> belong to that company. My own ministry keeps me from any pessimism in that
> regard.

As pastor of a flourishing Baptist church in downtown Minneapolis, Riley's
conclusion was not to separate, but to "'Strengthen the things that remain.'"[14]

Riley, rather than Gaebelein, was suited to be the leading spokesman for the
emerging movement, because he better represented the tensions of this multi-
faceted phenomenon. Like a number of the leading premillennialists, Riley's
background combined revivalism and a pietistic version of social reform.
Institutionally, one of the strengths of this combination had been the building of vigorous urban ministries. In Minneapolis early in the century Riley
had spoken strongly and clearly for social reform. Christians, he said, were
called by God to the cities. They should see in the cities not only their sin, but
also their suffering, and attempt to eliminate both. Christians, Riley affirmed, should side with the poor against the rich, even with honest labor
against capital. They should work for democracy, elect reformers to civic
office, and fight to eliminate all civic vices, especially liquor. "*The Church of
God*," he emphasized, "*is especially charged with civic reform!*" While this
did not mean that the church should seek political control as had the Roman
Catholic Church or Calvin in Geneva, it did mean that "when the Church is
regarded as the body of God-fearing, righteous-living men, then, it ought to
be in politics, and as a powerful influence, before which the saloon, and all
evil accessories, should be made afraid and in the face of which sins should
be made ashamed."[15]

Such affirmations were becoming rare among revivalist evangelicals and
increasingly so after about 1910. Yet the fact that such views had remained
acceptable in a movement known for its premillennialism is important.
Although the new dispensational premillennialism was the chief *distinguishing* trait of one side of the movement, it was not even for them the overwhelming controlling interest.[16] Evangelism came first. This evangelistic
commitment was shaped by an older set of ideals and assumptions which
characterized the pietistic American evangelical revivalism in the era around
the Civil War. This older tradition was in many respects culturally optimistic
and reformist. When premillennialism was added on, this tradition was by
no means obliterated. Rather the two were fused together in spite of the
basic tension between them.

The character of this ill-defined middle position is clearer when viewed in
the context of the emerging movement's most characteristic and increasingly
important institution, the Bible institute. Since dispensationalists lacked any
clear view of the organized church above the local level, the Bible institutes
played a major role in giving them some unity. They arose in response to the
demands of urban ministries and the desire to train lay leaders for evangelism. They also served as centers for training for foreign missions—always a
prominent concern. A wide variety of local evangelistic agencies, local con-

gregations, Bible conferences, publications, and independent national agencies for missions and other types of evangelism was informally united by common ties to various Bible institutes. The first of these institutes—A. B. Simpson's Nyack Missionary College—was founded in 1882, and by 1910 nearly a score of such schools had been founded by evangelists and successful pastors in major cities around the country. Of these, Moody Bible Institute was preeminent, not only because of its connection with the late evangelist, but also because of the leadership of two of the outstanding spokesmen for the movement, Reuben A. Torrey, first superintendent (from 1889 to 1908), and James M. Gray, who served from 1904 to 1934, first as dean and later as president.[17]

The extent to which evangelistic zeal overrode all else and consequently displaced interest in other types of cultural contacts is evident from surveying the *Institute Tie*, MBI's monthly publication, during its first year (1907–1908) as a national journal. Economics and politics merit only occasional reference and then usually as the source of homilies for Christian witnesses. With respect to the financial panic of 1907, for example, the editors, Gray and Torrey, noted that the national leaders did not know either the causes or the solution—and posed an analogous question: "What if we know not the cause of spiritual unrest and its remedy?" Those who fail to vote were poor patriots. The moral: Christians who did not witness were far worse. And A. T. Mahan's defense of naval maneuvers in peace time as necessary for war preparedness reminded the editors that Christian young folk should always keep themselves well prepared through attending evangelistic meetings and Bible institutes. In short, evangelism overshadowed everything else.[18]

These apolitical tendencies were reinforced by premillennialism, which could be used to side-step controversial political issues. "It was a disappointment to all," observed editors Gray and Torrey in 1907, "to learn that the Hague Conference, recently held, is barren of results so far as permanent measures of peace are concerned." But this, they said, was not surprising "to those familiar with the prophetic scriptures," since they know that peace must wait for the coming of the Prince of Peace. Moreover, in the event that future peace efforts should appear more successful, students of prophecy should know also that "it is quite possible that Satan can counterfeit a millennium in the days of the anti-Christ, for there is a kind of peace which force can procure; but it will be a lull before the awful storm."[19] All eventualities were covered by this analysis; in effect it said that Christian workers need not concern themselves with such questions, or even, it seems, with reading the newspapers—except of course in order to find illustrations for use in evangelism or Bible study.

This was the attitude also of Moody Bible Institute toward intellectual culture. The curriculum of the Institute was confined to Bible study, missions, and practical work.[20] Torrey and Gray were frequently asked whether the Christian student and worker should be (as John Wesley had put it) "a man of one book." This statement, it seemed to them, went too far. Yet their qualifications suggested something less than a total endorsement of the disinterested study of the Western intellectual tradition. One should read "intelligently and widely as time permits, giving the Bible first place always and reading other books through it, that is making all his other reading furnish information and illustration with which to better understand the Bible himself and to help others to understand it." This was preferable to reading only the Bible because "the more one knows, the more resources has he at his command with which to get in touch with people and to lead them to the goal."[21]

Although these remarks suggest an anti-cultural bias, it is important to emphasize again that even such statements as these did not amount to a repudiation of intellect or reason. In fact, at Moody Bible Institute, the same editorial page that carried the reflections on "a man of one book" noted and agreed with recent remarks of Woodrow Wilson, then president of Princeton, to the effect that people were not willing enough to think and that contemporary preaching was "too easy." The Moody monthly advocated more doctrinal preaching and suggested that another Jonathan Edwards was needed. Both Torrey and Gray were known to distrust excessive emotion, and the editorial suggested that more intellectual content in contemporary preaching would help to remove it not only from the political and sociological arenas, but also from the "amusement competition."

This last remark was doubtless directed at Billy Sunday, whose star was then rising in the Midwest, aided to no small extent by his talent for bringing the techniques of vaudeville to revivalism. With respect to the importance of intellect and precise statement, Sunday was at the opposite pole from the teachers at Moody Bible Institute. Certainly Sunday did not look like the next Jonathan Edwards. At his ordination examination for the Presbyterian ministry in 1903, his characteristic response to questions on theology and history was "That's too deep for me," or "I'll have to pass that up." "I don't know any more about theology," he once said with some accuracy, "than a jack-rabbit knows about ping-pong, but I'm on my way to glory."[22]

The more decorous conservatives who were concerned that liberalism would turn religion into morality and abandon true doctrine, were often appalled by Sunday's methods, as well as by his slipshod and often Pelagian teaching. In 1907, *The Watchman,* a conservative Baptist mouthpiece, said Sunday's preaching "outrages every accepted canon of religious worhsip."[23] Apparently Reuben Torrey agreed, at least privately, advising A. P. Fitt, Moody's son-in-law, not to let Sunday speak at the Institute because of his sensational evangelistic techniques.[24]

The difference was partly one of style. The early Moody Bible Institute was wedded to the style of Victorian culture. Torrey and other evangelists preached in cutaway coats and wing collars. Sunday, who did at first assume such airs in imitation of his early mentor, J. Wilbur Chapman, soon gained a reputation for abandoning clerical dignity by preaching in his shirt sleeves.[25] At the Institute, by contrast, at the height of the summer of 1908, James M. Gray sent a stiff note to the faculty warning against *sitting in their offices* during the Chicago heat without coats and vests. Gray found such conduct "unusual" as well as detrimental to the "students who need our example of conventionality."[26]

It was difficult, however, to argue with success. By 1913 Sunday was an immensely successful national figure and in the next several years outdistanced even D. L. Moody himself in numbers of conversions claimed.[27] Conservatives, whether Baptist,[28] Presbyterian,[29] or of the Bible institute sort, came to support his efforts almost unanimously. The Moody Bible Institute itself was filled with students eager to imitate Billy Sunday, sporting such nicknames as "Bob," "Bud," "Cyclone," "Gypsy," and "Joe."[30] Nevertheless, the Victorian style of the movement did not disappear entirely.[31]

As their concern for intellect and convention indicates, these premillennialist leaders had by no means abandoned the world at every point. James Gray, in struggling with separation from the world, acknowledged that "we cannot absolutely separate ourselves from its society, its literature, its politics, its commerce, but we can separate ourselves from its methods, its spirits, and its aims."[32]

Even in the area of social reform, which was perhaps the most obvious practical test of the degree to which the culture and its welfare was considered a proper Christian concern, the Institute's interest had not abated entirely—at least in principle. Although there is nothing like the degree of advocacy of social concern apparent earlier, nevertheless, when the occasion arose, Gray and Torrey were still true to their old affirmations. Gray compared his reasons for opposing the liquor traffic, gambling, white slavery, political graft, and other forms of social injustice to the reasons he would kick a dangerous banana peel off the sidewalk.[33] The metaphor is revealing. Protecting society from evil was still good for its own sake; yet one did not find such opportunities every day nor go out of one's way to seek them. All the same this indicated a greater concern for the physical needs of society than that expressed by more radically anti-worldly premillennial brethren. Thus, while Arno Gaebelein found the "Social Creed of the Churches" which was adopted by the Federal Council of Churches in 1908 unacceptable, the editors of the Moody *Institute Tie* considered it "a most righteous and reasonable appeal on behalf of laboring man which we should like to forward to the utmost of our ability."[34]

Even politics could on occasion be viewed with favor by these sometimes optimistic premillennialists. Listing "hopeful signs" for the year at the outset of 1908, the Moody editors of course first mentioned that "Revival is in the air." Not so typically, however, they added two other causes for hope. The prohibition movement was spreading nationally, and, in politics generally, "ethical revival is in the air." "No matter who receives plurality in November," Gray and Torrey observed in reference to growing demands for progressive reform, "we shall have a chief magistrate believing in cleaner government."[35]

3. WILLIAM JENNINGS BRYAN:
CHRISTIAN CIVILIZATION PRESERVED

William Jennings Bryan—who did not receive the majority in November of 1908 and hence had plenty of time to pursue his religious interests—represents in his attitude toward culture a third segment of the conservative evangelical movement. Despite his political prominence (he remained the leader of the Democratic Party until 1912 and was then Woodrow Wilson's Secretary of State until 1915), Bryan maintained even before his last election defeat that he was "more interested in religion than in government" because "the most important things in life lie outside the realm of government. . . ."[36] Bryan's religious interests, however, resembled his political ones. In both areas he dwelt on moral reform. During the first two decades of the century he spoke widely on the Chautauqua and religious circuits, urging the importance of the Bible and religion for civilization and in particular campaigning vigorously for prohibition and peace.[37]

Bryan represented the culturally dominant evangelical coalition which took shape in the first half of the nineteenth century. In it, the ideals of Christian piety went together with the ideals of the progressing and democratic American nation. These Christian and American ideals were revealed not only in the Bible but also in divine law available to all persons of common sense. Bryan's interest in peace and hope for universal harmony were part of an optimistic strain in the evangelical heritage that had suffered somewhat since the Civil War. Bryan's assumptions also included the more generally accepted faith in divine law and in the destiny of the United States to guide the world morally, as well as "a persistent faith in the essential goodness of Man who would respond immediately and wholeheartedly to the truth once he was made to see it and understand it."[38]

Any of a number of stock speeches on religious subjects would serve to exemplify Bryan's outlook, but a little known address entitled "The Old-Time Religion," delivered at the Winona Bible Conference in the summer of 1911, provides a particularly clear indication of his attitude toward the impending religious crisis. The setting, perhaps as much as the speaker and his subject, shows us the character of the respectable evangelicalism in what turned out to be its twilight days. The extended summer Bible conference, with a series of famous speakers as the main attraction, had become one of the principal means of evangelical expression and was still in its heyday. Like almost everything else of the time that was non-denominational and evangelical, it bore the strong impression of D. L. Moody. Moody had suggested to Winona's founder, the late evangelist J. Wilbur Chapman, that he establish a counterpart to the Northfield conferences at the Indiana resort. Although in 1911 the current director reminded the audience of the "Fundamental Principles upon which Winona was founded and for which it had ever stood, 'Faith in the inspiration of the Scriptures and belief in the deity of Christ,'" these are rather vague and inclusive terms. The divisive aspects of the Moody-Chapman heritage, including premillennialism, were not mentioned.[39]

The coalition represented at Winona in 1911 was broad. It was, in fact, not greatly different from that attending the Evangelical Alliance meeting of 1873. Although some of the conference Bible studies were laced with attacks on higher critics, in other areas more progressive tendencies predominated. Several speakers, including William H. Roberts, the first president of the Federal Council of Churches, affirmed the virtues of church union and the end of doctrinal exclusiveness. One of these speakers, a Presbyterian, observed that when he had heard his fellow Presbyterian Billy Sunday preach a sermon packed with Arminian theology, he had responded, "Good! The walls are breaking down." The present generation, he suggested, had a better understanding of the purposes of God than did John Calvin.[40] In the social sphere, advocates attacked the "liquor traffic" and "the white slave trade," appealed for more "industrial work" projects for Negroes, presented a plan (from the National Reform Association) to "thoroughly Christianize America" by making Bible teaching in the public schools both legal and mandatory, and championed international peace, to which an entire day was devoted.[41]

The Christianity of William Jennings Bryan and that of the Winona conference were much the same. They each combined a commitment to preserve traditional Christianity (rather broadly interpreted) with a willingness to cooperate with those who differed and an emphasis upon the practical and the social.[42] These were typical of most of the conservative evangelicalism of the day. They found wide expression in the popular press, as exemplified by the *Christian Herald,* as well as in denominational journals. The most ambitious such expression was the new "Men and Religion Forward Movement," a vigorous interdenominational campaign to mobilize laymen in a massive concerted effort in 1911–1912 to advance both evangelism and social action.[43]

Bryan's remarks on "The Old-Time Religion" were received with enthusiasm and frequent applause at Winona. Bryan indicated that he had picked his topic in reply to sermons claiming that Christianity should change to suit the conditions of the day. Bryan maintained the opposite: ". . . it is better to raise the temperature than to change the thermometer." Those who would change Christianity rather than the culture, said Bryan, were infected with the materialist philosophy that had for nineteen centuries challenged the spiritual religion of the Bible. The church, said "The Great Commoner," was healthy when it was poor; "but in the abundance of our wealth, we have surrounded ourselves with material comforts until the care of the body has absorbed our thought and the saving of the soul has become a secondary matter." Material advances might indeed be construed as progress in many areas, but the associated materialist philosophies of the modern world had nothing to offer to the soul of man.

To illustrate this point Bryan, whose quest for a dramatic settlement would eventually undo him, proposed a hypothetical contest. The idea, which he said had occurred to him only a few weeks before, would be comparable to a contest between Elijah and the prophets of Baal. It would be a "Bible test." On the one side would be those who believed the Bible to be inspired by God. On the other side would be atheists and materialists who said it was the work of man and outdated by modern progress. The challenge: "Let the atheists and the materialists produce a better Bible than ours, if they can." Let them "use to the full every instrumentality that is employed in modern civilization, let them embody the results of their best intelligence in a book and offer it to the world. . . . Have they the confidence that the Prophets of Baal had in their God?"

Bryan's defense of Christianity was essentially pragmatic, resting on his concept of civilization. True, he reiterated (to the most fervent applause) the basic doctrines of the old-time religion: God the Creator, the Bible as his Word, the divinity of Christ, and his saving work. Nevertheless, Bryan, himself a Presbyterian, admitted that he never had had time to study the doctrinal differences between Baptists, Methodists, and his own denomination. He added that his standard answer to those who asked him if he could explain everything in the Bible was that "if we will try to live up to that which we can understand, we will be kept so busy doing good that we will not have time to worry about the things that we do not understand. [Applause]" Bryan thus abandoned, in the spirit of popular American pragmatism, not only the fine points of theology but also any attempt to present a theoretical defense of Christianity and relied on the evidence of practical results in individuals and in nations. As is apparent in his challenge to the prophets of the modern Baal, he believed that the evidence of Christianity's beneficial effects on civilization was decisive. Speaking of his travels abroad, the future Secretary of State declared that he had found "that in the countries where other religions and philosophies prevail, except where they have borrowed from Christianity, they have made no progress in 1500 or 2000 years." Conversely, he was sure that "Christian civilization is the greatest that the world has ever known because it rests on a conception of life that makes life one unending progress toward higher things, with no limit to human advancement or development." In the light of this exalted view of the practical effects of Christianity on culture, it is easy to understand Bryan's passion in later years when he found that in America the two had become separated.[44]

Bryan's view of Christianity and culture was far more popular than any other conservative position and had been common in the revivalist tradition.

Despite some important differences, Bryan's position was not so very far from that of Billy Sunday, who had in fact moved to Winona Lake to have a permanent residence near the conferences.[45] The most obvious difference is that Billy Sunday was a premillennialist, whereas Bryan's basic optimism about the progress of the kingdom in American culture amounted to a very vague sort of postmillennialism. Sunday's premillennialism was not, however, related to the rest of his beliefs in any consistent way, so that it could hardly be said to be a determining trait. He mixed a simple do-it-yourself (with God's grace) Gospel message with the traditional American moral virtues of decency, patriotism, manliness, thrift, sobriety, piety, and hard work.[46] His interest in doctrine and denominational differences was even slighter than Bryan's. Like "The Great Commoner," Sunday always emphasized the use of Christianity to improve society. During the first part of his career he built a reputation as an advocate of progressive civic reform. By the eve of World War I, this interest had narrowed down to an attack on liquor, and he was capitalizing, in a way that Bryan never would, on the fear of too much liberal "social service." Yet his concern for the welfare of the nation did remain and was more than adequately demonstrated by his wartime patriotism. Premillennialism and suspicions of worldliness did not dim in the least his conviction that America represented Christian civilization—an ideal for which he, like Bryan, would make a desperate last stand in the 1920s.[47]

4. TRANSFORMING CULTURE BY THE WORD

Presbyterians Bryan and Sunday represent the more "American" side of that denominational tradition—a broad, somewhat tolerant, not highly doctrinal, moralistic, patriotic, and often optimistic version of evangelical Protestantism. These attitudes could be found in all the major American denominations of the era. They were the ideals of the evangelical consensus of the first half of the nineteenth century, although some of these attitudes could be traced back directly to the Puritan ideals for building a Christian culture. It is possible to distinguish conservatives within the mainstream American evangelical tradition from more strictly denominational conservatives.[48] Within a group as diverse as the Baptists, however, such lines cannot be clearly drawn. Most conservative Baptists had a strong commitment to preserve their special denominational heritage. While patriotic, almost all held dogmatically to the ideal of "separation of church and state." In other respects they seem to have had conventional American evangelical attitudes. A range of unexceptional opinion concerning the relationship of Christianity to culture was found among Baptist conservatives,[49] so that it is difficult to pin down a distinctive conservative Baptist position on the subject.

Among the Presbyterians, by contrast, the lines had been drawn more sharply by a mid-nineteenth-century schism between an "American" revivalist and activist "New School" and a traditionalist-confessionalist and doctrinaire "Old School." After the reunion of the two parties in 1869 the Old School position was preserved most carefully at Princeton Theological Seminary. On the other hand, the New School party of the nineteenth century helped to open the door for the growth of Presbyterian liberalism. At the same time, however, a conservative version of the New School tradition of activist revivalism and patriotic social reform was carried into the fundamentalist era by such leaders as Bryan and Sunday.[50]

These two traditions held in common the conviction that Christianity had an important mission to civilization. They differed on what was most important in accomplishing such a goal. The Old School tradition emphasized three points whose origins antedated the heyday of nineteenth-century American evangelicalism. One was a pessimistic assessment of most of culture and its achievements, with an emphasis on the pervasive effects of the Fall on the human race. Second was a view of the separation of church and state which had grown out of the Scottish controversies. Although Christians as individuals and groups might band together for moral and political efforts, the church as such should scrupulously stay clear of any involvement or even pronouncement on affairs of state. Third, the primary contribution of Christianity to culture was the fostering of right belief, as contained in the creeds. Moral action was important, but it always must proceed from true faith, for which right doctrine was necessary.

In principle, the twentieth-century heirs of the Old School tradition were interested in the welfare of civilization. Unlike the premillennialists, they expected to see signs of the kingdom in this age. One of the strongest manifestations of this concern appeared in the outright postmillennialism of B. B. Warfield. In contrast to his personal view of sanctification, Warfield held that in this age "Christ Jesus came forth not to war merely but to victory." Although he doubted that evil would be entirely eliminated, he thought that a spiritual "golden age" of the church lay ahead, in which the whole world would be won to Christ before his return.[51] Warfield who, as we have seen, expected Christianity "to *reason* its way to its dominion," interpreted the apocalytpic Biblical prophecies of warfare as pertaining to the battles and victories of the truth declared. Taking the "hint" of Revelation 19 that the sword of victory proceeds *out of the mouth* of the Conqueror, he concluded that "the conquest is wrought by the spoken word—in short, by the preaching of the Gospel." In this conquest, the moral evil of the world will be subdued.[52]

Although some, like Warfield, were sure that truth and reason would be victorious in the long run, other conservative twentieth-century Presbyterians had a less fully developed view of the progress of the kingdom and were more affected by the crisis of the civilization than by hopes for this age. When formulating the famous five Presbyterian "fundamentals" of 1910, the framers included in the preamble an elaborate litany of crisis. "It is an age of doubt . . . ," they said:

> Laxity in matters of moral opinion had been followed by laxity in matters of moral obligation. It is an age of impatience and restraint. The spirit of licence and lawlessness is abroad. Authority in Church and State alike is decadent because its defiance has so often been unchecked. The decline in the elements of essential religion is followed by a groveling and growing superstition that shames alike our sanity, our faith and our civilization.[53]

This period saw the rise to prominence of a brilliant New Testament scholar at Princeton Seminary, J. Gresham Machen, who eventually assumed Warfield's mantle as chief intellectual spokesman for conservative Presbyterians. Machen, who had a more limited view of the development of the kingdom in this age than did Warfield,[54] was at this early stage of his career intensely interested in the crisis of the culture in which he found himself. Having studied at Johns Hopkins, Marburg, and Göttingen, as well as at Princeton, Machen struggled to preserve both his inherited Presbyterian faith and his intellectual integrity in a world in which the leading intellectuals, and even many theologians, ridiculed traditionalist Christianity.[55]

In 1912, speaking at the opening session of Princeton Seminary, Machen addressed himself to the question of "culture and Christianity." Viewing the situation as "desperate" although not hopeless, he affirmed with "little hesitation" that the tremendous crisis of the church "lies chiefly in the intellectual sphere." Those who emphasize practical work such as evangelism, missions, and "relieving the misery of man" were engaged in activities of great importance, he conceded, but their gains would be temporary, if not founded on a solid intellectual base. What they failed to realize was the extent to which indifference or hostility to the Gospel was "due to the intellectual atmosphere in which men are living." In the long run, then, the key to the battle to win men to Christ was in the universities. "What is to-day matter of academic speculation," Machen proclaimed, "begins tomorrow to move armies and pull down empires."

Machen considered disastrous each of the two major ways in which Christians were responding to this crisis. The more dangerous was that of the liberals who said that "Christianity may be subordinated to culture." In Machen's view, this resulted in a counterfeit Christianity. Many evangelicals, on the other hand, seemed to seek to destroy, or at least to ignore, culture in order to maintain a pure Christianity. Machen declared this in some respects better than the liberal attitude but nevertheless illogical, unbiblical, and impossible to maintain. Since the cultural crisis was rooted in the intellectual crisis, an attempt to bypass culture and intellect, the arts and sciences, would simply make the situation worse. "The Church," he said, "is perishing to-day through the lack of thinking, not through an excess of it."

Machen's solution was the consecration of culture. "Instead of destroying the arts and sciences and being indifferent to them," he said, "let us cultivate them with all the enthusiasm of the veriest humanist, but at the same time consecrate them to the service of our God." Christianity, he declared, in reference to the great missionary impulse of the day, "must pervade not merely all nations, but also all human thought." Hence, "instead of obliterating the distinction between the Kingdom and the world, or on the other hand, withdrawing from the world into a sort of modernized intellectual monasticism, let us go forth joyfully, enthusiastically to make the world subject to God."[56]

This was the Reformed tradition, which, as Machen expressed it, saw the consecration of all culture to the service of God as both a religious obligation and a long-range practical necessity. The fact of the matter was, however, that conservative Reformed scholars were finding it increasingly difficult to remain Renaissance Christian humanists. Although they might, as Machen did, chart a broad course across civilization, the track they usually had to follow was of narrow gauge. This was certainly the case for Machen himself. Although he attempted to remain broad-minded and humane, he soon found himself increasingly caught up in peculiarly Presbyterian struggles that eventually forced him into a virtually sectarian position.

In the context of the growing warfare against modernism, Machen also found himself with a peculiar set of allies, including Gray, Bryan, and Sunday. Thus, despite his ambition to penetrate the academic centers of the culture, he more often found himself invited to places like the Winona Bible Conference. There Machen, who was raised in a dignified tradition of educated Southern aristocracy, was appalled by the "rough house" element. "Practically every lecture, on whatever subject," he wrote in 1915, "was begun by the singing of some of the popular jingles, often accompanied by the blowing of enormous horns or other weird instruments of music."[57] Nevertheless, Machen often returned to Winona. Likewise, when Billy Sunday spoke at Princeton in 1915, Machen defended him against sophisticate critics at the university. [58] Later, during the 1920s, James Gray even intimated on a couple of occasions that Machen should be his successor at Moody Bible Institute,[59] and about the same time admirers of Bryan embarrassed Machen somewhat by publicly offering him the presidency of "Bryan Memorial University" at Dayton, Tennessee.[60]

The affinity which grew out of fighting a common enemy tended to obscure essential differences within the movement concerning the task of Christianity within the world. All were militantly committed to an essentially supernatural, Biblically based, traditional faith. All, no doubt, were profoundly alarmed by the cultural crisis, especially after World War I when its dimensions became clear, and all no doubt felt personally uprooted by it. Yet there was no single social understanding common to the movement.

PART THREE
The Crucial Years: 1917–1925

XVI. World War I, Premillennialism, and American Fundamentalism: 1917–1918

Between 1917 and the early 1920s American conservative evangelicals underwent a dramatic transformation. In 1917 they were still part of the evangelical coalition that had been dominant in America for a century. Some theological conservatives, premillennialists, and revivalists were often warning against the modern tendencies of their liberal, postmillennial, or Social Gospel opponents; but all of these groups operated within the same denominations and interdenominational agencies, and at times still cooperated.[1] Occasionally the anti-liberals became rather strident, but the relative moderation of *The Fundamentals* was more characteristic of the conservative tone of the time. After 1920 conservative evangelical councils were dominated by "fundamentalists" engaged in holy warfare to drive the scourge of modernism out of church and culture.

Two factors help to explain this remarkable shift from moderation to militancy. One is that more aggressive and radical forms of theological liberalism had developed. Fundamentalists themselves occasionally explained the phenomenon thus, and their claim had some basis. Clearly, however, fundamentalism was more than a reaction to theological change. After 1920 fundamentalism became conspicuously associated with a major component of social and political alarm—most evident in the effort to save American civilization from the dangers of evolutionism. This perception of cultural crisis, in turn, appears to have created a greater sense of theological urgency. Thus, fundamentalist theological militancy appears intimately related to a second factor, the American social experience connected with World War I.

The most important clue to understanding the impact of the war on fundamentalism is the lack of a distinctive social or political stance in the emerging anti-modernist movement before World War I. Although a variety of traditions was represented, most of the movement's leaders in fact expressed relatively little interest in political or social issues. Most retained to some degree the idea that the strength of the American Republic was rooted in Christian principles, and they encouraged legislation for select causes.[2] Yet for a variety of reasons they had scruples against deep political involvement.

So while on the whole their tendencies were politically conservative, no particular position or interest characterized the movement.

The initial reactions of the proto-fundamentalists to World War I confirm this point. Almost as wide a variety of responses appeared among these adamantly conservative Protestants as in any group in America. Some were patriots or super-patriots; others were opposed to all wars. Still others displayed only moderate patriotism, expressly qualified by first allegiance to God.

One has only to look at the two most popular individuals connected with fundamentalism to see something of the pre-war variety of opinion. William Jennings Bryan, although not a typical fundamentalist in either his political activism or his brand of politics, distinguished himself in 1915 by resigning as Wilson's Secretary of State rather than take steps that might lead to war. A peace advocate rather than a pacifist, he reluctantly but dutifully supported the war after it was declared in April, 1917. Yet throughout the war he avoided the rabid anti-German hysteria that had possessed most Americans by 1918.[3]

Billy Sunday, on the other hand, competed with George M. Cohan[4] and Teddy Roosevelt for the position of most extravagant patriot. Although Sunday had little interest in the war until the United States joined it, he soon concluded that zeal for the Gospel and patriotic enthusiasm should go hand in hand. It apparently did not strain his principles (which included premillennialism and opposition to the "social gospel") to conclude in 1917 that "Christianity and Patriotism are synonymous terms and hell and traitors are synonymous."[5] As the war effort accelerated he used the rhetoric of Christian nativism to fan the fires of anti-German furor and was famous for sermons that ended with his jumping on the pulpit waving the flag. "If you turn hell upside down," he said, "you will find 'Made in Germany' stamped on the bottom."[6] Praying before the House of Representatives in 1918 he advised God that the Germans were a "great pack of wolfish Huns whose fangs drip with blood and gore."[7]

Between Bryan and Sunday were many conservative Protestants whose degree of patriotism does not seem to have been much different from that of the American public generally. For example, the conservative Baptist journal The Watchman-Examiner avoided commenting on the war for a long time before March 1917. The Baptist tendency to avoid politics may account for this. When the editor, Curtis Lee Laws, broke the silence in March 1917, he defended "pacifists" (meaning peace advocates) but said "pacifists are not 'peace-at-any-price' men." With Woodrow Wilson he agreed "we must prepare for war, however much we hate it."[8] During the war, although the magazine's support was unquestionable, it was not extravagant in the context of the excesses of the day.[9]

The conservative Presbyterian weekly The Presbyterian, by way of contrast, possibly because of its postmillennial leanings, emphasized the importance of religion and morality for civilization and had few scruples about war. Government was ordained to wield the sword, which was the only way to keep the peace. War would cease only at the coming of Christ, meaning apparently "when the world is evangelized." In the meantime, "The conflict is one between Jehovah and Prince of Darkness. Right and wrong cannot compromise."[10]

During the war conservative Baptists and conservative Presbyterians, together with virtually all Americans, became far more politically oriented, and by late 1918 their journals were filled with vigorous commentaries on the war. Aside from this important politicization, however, there was nothing especially remarkable in the development of their wartime views. At the end of the war their position, although more ostentatiously patriotic, was nevertheless consistent with their prewar attitudes.

The premillennialists, however, were not only politicized by the war, but for some the war experience involved a remarkable change in their view of the nation. This development is so dramatic, and the premillennialists played such a central role in organizing fundamentalism immediately after the war, that a close look at their wartime views is most helpful for understanding the relationship between fundamentalism and its cultural context.

Premillennialism taught that no trust should be put in kings or governments and that no government would be specially blessed by God until the coming of the King who would personally lead in defeating the forces of Satan. Although opinions varied, many premillennialists of the radically anti-worldly type followed the logic of this teaching to a pacifist conclusion. The dispensationalist journal *Our Hope,* for instance, was out-and-out pacifist at the beginning of the war. Its reasoning, however, was not that of Bryan or the humanitarians who opposed war because they favored peace. Rather, this thoroughly anti-political attitude consistently emphasized the hopelessness of all efforts to solve the world's problems through political efforts, whether pacifist or military. Bryan, they thought, was chasing illusions. Referring in 1913 to his proposal for a world court of arbitration, editor Arno C. Gaebelein said that such was typical of "man's plans during 'man's day.'" "'Peace and safety' is what the world and apostate Christendom wants to hear." "Sudden judgment," Gaebelein prophesied, "will someday bring the terrible awakening."[11]

When this prediction was in a sense fulfilled by the catastrophic European events of the next year, *Our Hope* took little interest, except to say that the war was a sure sign the end times were close. The conflict was important, however, in that it provided some more pieces to be fit into the prophetic puzzle. Gaebelein was intrigued by the question of whether German ambitions for empire might represent the beginning of the predicted re-forming of the Roman Empire. A thoroughgoing literalist, Gaebelein thought not, since Prussia and the greater part of present-day Germany had never been within the boundaries of the original Roman Empire.[12] The most revealing of the speculations concerning the combatants was *Our Hope's* prediction in 1916 concerning Russia, then part of the allied powers toward which the

United States was leaning. It "is known to every close student of prophetic portions of the Bible," Gaebelein affirmed, "that this power of the North will play a prominent and to herself fatal part during the predicted end of this age."[13] The apparent confirmation of this prediction in the Boleshevik Revolution of the next year, combined with preexisting prejudice against socialism, resulted eventually for Gaebelein, as we shall see, in a fierce anti-communist partisanship.

When the United States entered the war in the spring of 1917, Gaebelein was still intent on his neutralist, "signs of the times" and "I told you so" course. "It has doubtless awakened rudely from their dreams many who had not conceived that such a war was possible," he wrote in July. The Dictator and the Anti-Christ, he added, should be expected shortly. As to premillennialist service in the war, *Our Hope* published as late as September 1917 a thorough exposition of the question "Should a Christian Go to War?" in which the answer was clearly "No." Quoting the passages that advocated peace in the New Testament (and dismissing more easily than did most American Protestants any relevance of examples of divinely ordained warfare from the Old Testament dispensation), the author said, "The very question well-nigh answers itself." Christians should separate themselves from the world, should not enter politics nor vote, and should not "set to 'improve the world.'" On the other hand, they must obey the powers that be when governmental commands do not go against God's word, and they must pray for their government (which in any case is more effective than fighting). So the answer was that Christians must serve, but without fighting. "There are lines of duties as clerical, ambulance service on the field of battle, ministering to the wounded and dying in the hospitals—ministering *Christ*, as we minister to the body."[14]

While *Our Hope* continued into 1917 to confine itself to reading the signs of the times, *The King's Business,* then the leading premillennial journal, was more typical of the tension in the movement between other-worldly prophecy and genuine concern for the political direction of this world. *The King's Business* was in a sense a continuation of the work of *The Fundamentals,* having been recommended as such in the concluding number of that series The journal was published by the Bible Institute of Los Angeles, which at that time prospered with the Stewart brothers' oil money under the leadership of Reuben Torrey.[15]

During the two years preceding America's entry into the war its editors firmly and repeatedly announced their total opposition to the war. "At the present time," they said in a typical statement, "all other interests seem sacrificed to the monstrous war god."[16] Warfare was inevitable (prophecy made it clear that this war would not be the last), yet it was still terribly wrong. Indeed, the lead editorials of August 1915 could have been taken from the pages of the most sentimental liberal-pacifist journal. There is 'neither Greek nor Jew,' . . . English, German, or American," said the editors; hence "we must never forget we are brethren, and we must show our love for one another in every way possible." This sentiment is especially poignant in the face of the editors' note that they have lost a fine Christian friend on the Lusitania; still they steadfastly maintain that "'Vengeance' belongs to God, not to us. . . . Our part is to feed our hungry enemy (Rom. XII:20) and to 'overcome evil with good.'"[17] These high sentiments could, moreover, be translated into political action. The editors advised in the spring of 1916 that Teddy Roosevelt should be opposed because a vote for TR would be a vote for war.[18] In remarkable contrast to later fundamentalist opposition to unholy alliances, The King's Business in 1916 was willing to quote Bertrand Russell at length on the anti-war issue and to reprint an entire peace sermon by liberal Protestant spokesman Henry Sloan Coffin.[19]

The European war, by widespread testimony, sharpened interest in pro-phetic teachings even outside the usual perimeters of the premillennial camp. A remarkable example of this is found in the socially active, theologically conservative Christian Herald. When the European war broke out in 1914, peace became the overwhelming preoccupation of The Christian Herald; in contrast to The King's Business, however, this interest was framed in post-millennial terms which identified the progress of humanity with the advance of the kingdom. "World-wide philanthropy, international friendship, arbi-tration, popular education and advance in scientific hygiene, even the regula-tion of trusts," the editors had said on the eve of the war, "must all be included among the ideals toward which we have been reaching of late years." But there is another, they added, "—remote, illusive, but finer than all else—the vision of world-peace."[20] During the period prior to America's entry into the war in April of 1917, The Christian Herald continued to advocate peace. In the meantime, however, the editor, George Sandison, apparently altered his eschatology drastically. By January 1917 he stated that "we are living in a time of prophetic fulfillment, though just now how far that fulfillment may reach no man knows. . . ." "No one," he went on, "on this side of the Atlantic . . . occupies so high a position" in this field of prophetic interpretation as James M. Gray of Moody Bible Institute. Recent articles by Gray had "been widely read and universally appreciated" and now a new series, "The Mountain Peaks of Prophecy," was "certain of a still larger audience."[21] For the next three years until the end of Sandison's editorship, The Christian Herald was (as it had been at its inception) a predominantly premillennial journal.[22]

The dramatic wartime increase in interest in premillennialism created alarm among liberals[23] and precipitated what may be the strangest episode in the development of fundamentalism. Beginning in 1917, for several years the theologians at the University of Chicago Divinity School led a fierce assault on premillennial teaching. These attacks, directed largely against their cross-town rival, Moody Bible Institute, were the first stage of the intense fundamentalist-modernist conflicts. In retrospect it seems utterly bizarre that one of the liberals' main accusations during the war was that premillennialism bred a lack of patriotism and hence was a threat to the national security.

Whether the Chicago polemics were motivated primarily by theological or nationalist zeal is difficult to say. The question is probably unanswerable because to the modernists at Chicago the progress of Christianity and the progress of culture were so intimately bound together that the two were always considered together. "Modernism," in fact, meant first of all the adaptation of religious ideas to modern culture. So when the modernists affirmed the immanence of God, they characteristically meant that God is revealed in cultural development. The corollary was that human society is moving toward realization of the kingdom of God.[24] These principles, and especially this last, represented (as we have seen) new versions of postmillennialism; the spiritual progress of the kingdom could be seen in the progress of culture, especially democratic cultures in Europe and America.

World War I was a tremendous challenge to this faith in the progress of both culture and kingdom. European culture, for all its faults, had generally been viewed—together with its American offspring—as the best hope for the world. Now it seemed bent on destroying itself. When America was drawn into the war, liberal Protestants—like their conservative brethren—were divided. A fair number had at least some reservations about America's entry into the war and some of these continued simply to see the issue as war versus universal peace. Many others, however, viewed the war as a struggle for democratic civilization (and hence, in the long run, peace) against autocracy. Those who took this view were subject to the extreme and extravagant enthusiasm that swept the American people generally. For these modernists a war to ensure the safety of democracy and to end war, exactly fit the logic of their hopes for the kingdom.[25]

At the Divinity School of the University of Chicago patriotism seemed unrestrained, especially in its treatment of premillennialism. Shailer Mathews, Dean of the Divinity School, launched the attack in 1917 in a widely distributed pamphlet, "Will Jesus Come Again?" castigating premillennialism on theological, Biblical, and historical grounds.[26] Shirley Jackson Case, Professor of Early Church History, soon followed suit with a more extensive study, *The Millennial Hope: A Phase of War Time Thinking,* published in January of 1918. As the title implied, Case explained millennialism—in fact tried to dismiss it—on historicist grounds, showing how such thinking often became popular in times of crisis. He also noted, by way of introduction, that the current upsurge of premillennialism was especially dangerous, as it "strikes at the very heart of all democratic ideals" by denying human responsibility for the reform and betterment of society.[27]

Case told the press that his motive for publishing was his growing concern about the spread of premillennial ideas, about which the Divinity School received "many communications" every week. Case was convinced that the immediate cause of the millennialists' rise was a sinister conspiracy. "Two-thousand dollars a week is being spent to spread the doctrine," he told reporters. "Where the money comes from is unknown, but there is a strong suspicion *that it emanates from German sources. In my belief the fund would be a profitable field for governmental investigation.*"[28]

These sensational charges were not offhand or unrepresentative remarks, but were just what they now seem to be—outright expressions of wartime paranoia. This becomes clear from a survey of Shailer Mathew's journal, *The Biblical World.* In 1918 this scholarly publication might just as well have been called *The Biblical War,* filled as it was with the idealism of the crusade. On the home front the premillennialists were the chief enemy. During 1918 and 1919 most issues of the journal contained at least one major feature attacking premillennialism.[29] The editor even seemed willing to use unfounded charges and innuendo in order to cast the premillennialists in the worst light. An essay in May 1918 was prefaced by a reproduction of a letter from a Liberty Loan speaker who complained that premillennial evangelists were undermining enthusiasm for the war. The writer suggested that perhaps this movement, like the I. W. W., was financed by German money. The letter, said the editor, speaks for itself.[30]

Shirley Jackson Case repeated these accusations and added some of his own in the most hysterical attack of the series, "The Premillennial Menace," published in June. "The principles of premillennialism," he said, "lend themselves to the purposes of I. W. W. propaganda. . . . When one regards the present world as irremediably bad, it is only a short step to the typical I. W. W. tirade against existing institutions." But the burden of his message was that premillennialism threatened both the American war cause and the fundamental premise of modernist theology. "The American nation," said Case, "is engaged in a gigantic effort to make the world safe for democracy." Hence, "it would be almost traitorous negligence to ignore the detrimental character of premillennial propaganda." This posed an inestimable danger to both religion and culture because, "In the name of religion we are told that the world cannot appreciably be improved by human efforts." Mathews prefaced this contribution with similarly extreme remarks about the dangers of premillennialism to both religion and patriotism, adding (in an apparent effort to associate evangelical premillennialists with Russellites) a newspaper report "that several of the leaders of one of these movements have been found guilty of disloyal utterances and sentenced to imprisonment."[31]

Such acrimony indicated the extent to which the war fanned the smoldering coals of theological debate. For premillennialists and other doctrinal militants, of course, it did not take much provocation to unleash fierce controversy. The liberals had been traditionally the party of peace, tolerance and comprehensiveness. During and immediately after the war, however, liberals seemed openly ready to seek a showdown. The *Christian Century,* for instance, was as active as *The Biblical World* in attacking the premillennialists, running a twenty-one article series on the subject during the war.[32]

The premillennialists uniformly responded by denying any disloyalty and be reiterating their case for the Biblical source of their views; yet the liberal attacks had also opened the way for an important line of counterattack. The liberals had insinuated that premillennialism might be tainted by German gold. *The King's Business* responded: "While the charge that the money for premillennial propaganda 'emanates from German sources' is ridiculous, the charge that the destructive criticism that rules in Chicago University 'emanates from German sources' is undeniable."[33] This quickly became one of the most effective and widely-repeated accusations among opponents of liberal theology. Probably the most forceful statement of this idea came from W. H. Griffith Thomas, British premillennial scholar and Professor of Old Testament at Wycliffe College in Toronto since 1910. A loyal citizen of the British Empire, Thomas had been decrying the evil connection between German theology and German militarism since early in the European war.[34] In a particularly vitriolic essay written just as the war was ending, he dealt with the subject of "German Moral Abnormality." After ten pages of atrocity anecdotes (which by then were commonplace in American propaganda) he spent another half-dozen pages quoting patriotic sentiments taken from German sermons. He pointed out the self-evident incredibility of these sentiments in the light of the atrocities. How could one explain "these (let us put it mildly) aberrations"? Corrupt German Biblical scholarship was at the root of the astounding moral collapse of German civilization.[35]

The radical dispensationalist journal *Our Hope* likewise attributed German militarism directly to German theology. "Every word of this is true," remarked Arno C. Gaebelein in reference to a suggestion that if the churches in other countries had "'entered the conflict against German rationalism fifty years ago, as loyalty to Christ demanded, this most destructive and hideous of wars could never have occurred.'" This observation had important implications for the home front as well. "'The new theology has led Germany into barbarism, and it will lead any nation into the same demoralization.'"[36] The conservatives at Princeton Seminary, who had long been lonely voices in warning against the dangers of German "rationalism," saw a similar meaning in the demise-of-civilization motif. William B. Greene, at the seminary opening in the fall of 1918, described "the Present Crisis in Ethics," particularly as evinced in Germany's conduct of the war, as related to (among other things) rationalism, evolutionary naturalism, and the philosophy of Nietzsche.[37] Premillennialist Howard W. Kellogg stressed these same themes in a less restrained address given at the Bible Institute of Los Angeles during the same summer. "Loud are the cries against German Kultur . . . ," he declaimed. "Let this now be identified with Evolution, and the truth begins to be told." The truth, he suggested, was that this philosophy was responsible for "a monster plotting world domination, the wreck of civilization and the destruction of Christianity itself."[38]

These ideas, and the cultural crisis that bred them, revolutionized fundamentalism. More precisely, they created it (although certainly not *ex nihilo*) in its classic form. Until World War I various components of the movement were present, yet collectively they were not sufficient to constitute a full-fledged "fundamentalist" movement. The cultural issue suddenly gave the movement a new dimension, as well as a greater sense of urgency. During the 1920s the point was constantly reiterated that the argument between fundamentalists and modernists was not merely a theological debate (theological debate would not have created much fervor among Americans). The contention was that the whole moral course of civilization was involved. Evolution became a symbol. Without the new cultural dimension it is unlikely that the debate over Darwinism could have been revived in the spectacular way it was or that fundamentalism itself would have gained wide support. Americans had just fought a war that could be justified only as a war between civilization and barbarism. German barbarism could be explained as the result of an evolutionary "might is right" superman philosophy.[39] The argument was clear—the same thing could happen in America.

This insight transformed the premillennialist movement in a dramatic way. Before World War I many premillennialists had stayed aloof from cultural concerns and all were skeptical of any plans concerned merely with the future of civilization. By the end of the war their strongest line of attack on modernism committed them to a position which put forward the survival of civilization as a principal concern. This position accentuated the long-standing paradox in the thinking of American premillennialists. As premillennialists they had to say that there was no hope for culture, but at the same time they were traditional American evangelicals who urged a return to Christian principles as the only cultural hope.[40]

The latter emphasis, which had been largely (though never entirely) suppressed among premillennialists, re-emerged in full strength during the summer of 1918. This transformation of a group that had included many pacifists can be understood only in view of the extreme pressure of propaganda and public opinion toward patriotic excess. Liberals and conservatives alike found the force of popular sentiment irresistible. Even that staunch journal of peace, *The Christian Herald,* had by 1918 (though at the same time temporarily embracing premillennialism) succumbed to the characteristic American patriotism of that year, going so far as to praise Lutheran schools for giving up the teaching of German.[41]

Some of the most adamant premillennial advocates of political non-involvement likewise succumbed. *Our Hope* provides the most striking example. It should be recalled that this ardently premillennialist journal had shown little interest in the war prior to American involvement and in September of 1917 had answered "no" to the question "should a Christian go to war?" By April 1918 the war was becoming a godly cause. Citing the American government's claim that this was a defensive war provoked by a scheming, dishonest Germany, *Our Hope* concluded: "These are unanswerable arguments. There is an element of righteousness which any right thinking man cannot fail to see and which is, we believe, in harmony with the righteous government of God."[42] By July the wartime rhetoric and call to arms was fully developed. Wrote Arnold Gaebelein:

> If we had not done so the German warships would probably be bombarding our coast by this time and the hellish program of murder, pillage, and rapine would soon be carried out on our soil. . . . And now it is the solemn duty of everyone to do all and to give all in this cause and stand by the government, so the hosts of evil may be speedily defeated.[43]

James M. Gray and his *Christian Workers Magazine* of Moody Bible Institute did not have to travel as far to arrive at the same patriotic destination. In 1917 Gray attempted to maintain a balanced position and had published articles on both sides of the question whether Christians might participate in war. He himself favored dutiful support of the war on the grounds that magistrates were ordained by God.[44] He insisted, however, that Christians' attitude toward the Germans should be "malice toward none."[45] But with the revelations in the spring of 1918 concerning German war aims and alleged atrocities Gray also came to see America's war effort as a totally righteous cause:

> Hitherto we have felt it to be the Christian's duty to serve his government in this conflict even to the taking up of arms, but now this secondary obligation, strong as it is, fades out of sight in the thought of our responsibility to God as the executioners of His avenging justice."[46]

The King's Business, which of all the standard premillennial journals had campaigned most vigorously against military preparedness, had a more difficult struggle with the war issue; but in 1918 it too came to the same conclusion. In 1917 the California-based journal had warned against the disastrous and demoralizing effects of war, and urged Christians to "love our enemies," even if they were Germans.[47] By early 1918, however, the editors were beginning to believe that the Kaiser's capacity for evil rivaled that of the most notorious precursors of the anti-Christ, and that he might even be in some sort of league with both the Pope and the Mohammedans.[48] By May 1918 they got to the point of relating the Kaiser directly to the devil. Ignoring the traditional premillenial condemnation of the Constantinian ideal of church and state united in Christian culture against the infidels, *The King's Business* quoted with unqualified approval:

> "The Kaiser boldly threw down the gage of battle—infidel Germany against the believing world—Kultur against Christianity—the Gospel of Hate against

the Gospel of Love. Thus is Satan personified—'Myself and God.' . . . Never did Crusader lift battle-ax in holier war against the Saracen than is waged by our soldiers of the cross against the German."[49]

The editors of *The King's Business* used a traditional Puritan and evangelical theme to justify this apparent reversal of their views. During 1917 the editors had made the point (useful for evangelism) that no nation was righteous and none could receive God's blessing without repentance.[50] In 1918 this principle provided an opportunity to abandon, more or less gracefully, earlier misgivings about the war. Woodrow Wilson called for a day of prayer and fasting on Decoration Day, May 30, 1918. The editors saw this as America's only hope.[51] Americans responded to this call, the editors believed, in a most laudable fashion. Now the editors were convinced that they had simply been wrong about the demoralizing effects of war. The war had brought out courage and dedication that they had never thought possible.[52] But the key had been repentance. In a Thanksgiving editorial written before the war ended, *The King's Business* attributed the success of the American war effort primarily to the Decoration Day of prayer and fasting:

> This day was very widely observed, far more widely and earnestly we admit than we thought it would be, and God heard the prayers that went up on that day, heard them in a way that has made the whole world wonder.

In fact the day of fasting had coincided remarkably with the beginning of the effective American contribution to the war (Château-Thierry was June 4) and the dramatic reversal of the German offensive. So now these premillennialists sounded as convinced as mid-nineteenth-century evangelicals that God was on the side of America. "God has done wonderful things for this nation."[53]

Only at the official prophetic gatherings was the tradition of staying clear of politics still in evidence. Thus, at the two major prophetic conferences held in 1918, patriotic themes were kept in the background. Instead, the most engrossing political topic was the capture of Jerusalem by the British General Allenby. To a student of prophecy this was immensely more important than anything else that the allies did, since it cleared the path for the fulfillment of the predicted return of the Jews to Palestine.[54]

Significantly, however, the one speaker at either of these conferences to consider at any length the more general social and political questions was William B. Riley. Riley, as we have seen, exemplified the primary tension in premillennial cultural attitudes. Since early in his career he had been wrestling with the political implications of social issues. During his long Minneapolis pastorate, begun in 1897, he championed some progressive reforms and defended the right of ministers to deal with "secular" subjects. He also had been a vocal opponent of the Spanish American War. But when World War I broke out, he defended it on the basis of the Christian's "dual citizenship." Americans should be loyal both to the "heavenlies" and to the United States, the latter loyalty entailing an obligation to defend civilization against barbarism.[55]

Nevertheless, at the Philadelphia Prophecy Conference of 1918, even though Riley had two sons in the war he still was able to qualify the implications of patriotism. He spoke eloquently for charity toward the poor, but he warned that the self-sacrifice and heroism of the war should not create any illusions concerning human nature or any hopes for salvation of society without Christ. Similarly, while clearly supporting the American cause, he warned against allowing patriotism to revive unqualified confidence in American idealism. "'Make the world safe for democracy,'" he said, is a sentiment with which "we have no controversy." "But," he immediately added, "who will rise, and when will he come to *make democracy safe for the world?*" Only "the blood of the Son of God" could change human nature sufficiently for that. Preachers should not allow "the modern voices to lead them to substitute democracy for a divinely appointed plan of divine REDEMPTION. . . ."

Although pointing to modern tendencies that might be dangerously strengthened by the war, Riley, along with other premillennialists, saw in the war a central lesson about the welfare of society. For the past fifty years the trend had been toward the exaltation of man. Darwinism, not simply as a biological theory, but as a progressive evolutionary philosophy, was the best evidence of this trend. German "Kultur," where the doctrine of evolution had bred the twin evils of modernism and militarism, showed the inevitable result of such doctrines.[56] Riley, it seems, had long been searching for a way in which to show how Christianity involved concern for society as well as for individuals.[57] Now the war focused and clarified the issues and showed where the battle to save American civilization must be met.

World War I saw the rise of William B. Riley to leadership in the fundamentalist movement—a fact doubtless related to his ability to articulate the urgency of the cultural crisis. In 1919 he was the chief organizer of the World's Christian Fundamentals Association, the principal organization of the premillennial wing of the fundamentalist movement. Unlike any of the premillennialist organizations immediately preceding it, this new fundamentalist body expressed strong concern for the condition of American society. As in conservative-evangelical anti-German war-time rhetoric, evolution and modernism were tied together and seen as a cultural as well as a specifically religious threat. Out of these concerns, to which anti-communism was soon added, fundamentalist super-patriotism began to grow.[58] Thus a movement that had characteristically claimed that loyalty was not owed to kings and nations, and had been sufficiently apolitical in 1917 to be suspected of disloyalty, became sufficiently patriotic to make the defense of Christian civilization in America one of its major goals.

The war brought closer together individuals who held a variety of opinions on the proper relationship of Christianity and culture. Both radical and moderate premillennialists now gave greater importance to the preservation of civilization. American evangelicals, typified by Bryan, had always given Christian civilization top priority, and now they believed it to be gravely threatened. Postmillennialist confessional conservatives, represented by Princeton or by *The Presbyterian,* tempered their hope for civilization with Calvinist views of innate human depravity.[59] Important points of disagreement remained and would continue to surface. Now, however, all had a shared interest in the cultural question and all regarded the state of American civilization with a mixture of hopeful loyalty and increasing alarm.

XVII. Fundamentalism and the Cultural Crisis: 1919–1920

An overwhelming atmosphere of crisis gripped America during the immediately postwar period. The year 1919 especially was characterized by a series of real as well as imagined terrors. The disruption caused by massive demobilization and postwar economic adjustments was compounded by a number of acrimonious labor disputes and strikes and by a series of terrorist bombings. There was alarm over rapidly deteriorating moral standards and a deep suspicion of foreign influence. The immediate reaction was to focus on the sinister implications of the strikes and terrorism and to rechannel the enormous emotional force of wartime patriotism against a different foreign enemy—Bolshevism. In this "Red Scare," a real but limited threat excited near hysteria.[1] Clearly it was part of the general psychological disorientation of the nation. Americans had been whipped into a frenzy of wartime enthusiasm. Abruptly the war ended, leaving behind a directionless belligerence which sought a new outlet. It seemed as though the people needed an enemy, one that could account for the disruptions on the home front.[2]

The continued ambivalence of most premillennialists in this highly charged atmosphere of national crisis is well suggested by the two accompanying cartoons, which first appeared in *The King's Business* during the summer of 1919. The first, on the cover of the July issue, while intimating an ideal of Christian civilization, points only toward a future hope. The other, from the preceding issue[3] is aimed at more immediate solutions to social problems.[4]

These reactions to the widely proclaimed Bolshevik threat were not unusual in the atmosphere of acute paranoia which prevailed throughout the country in the summer of 1919, and do not necessarily indicate that premillennialism had become politicized by this time.[5] But the tension between the

Cover of July 1919 *King's Business*

deep disturbance awakened by cultural trends and the attempt to continue to respond only in the realm of prophecy and evangelism was more acute than ever. This is evident in the *Christian Worker's Magazine* of July 1919, in which editor James M. Gray identified the pressure to join the League of Nations as "the third greatest crisis" in the nation's history. Gray averred that to join the League would be to commit "national suicide," and urged his readers to send for the literature of Henry Watterson's "League for the Preservation of American Independence," which portrayed the League as incompatible with the "fundamentals of American independence." Yet, having yielded thus far to the desire to save the nation, Gray clearly was embarrassed and attempted to disclaim that he was suggesting anything more than prayer. "We have no position to maintain and are not taking sides," said Gray, "for this is a political more than a religious question, but we are urging our readers to reflect, . . . and above all to pray that the God of nations . . . may rule . . . that no harm may come to our nation and that His will may be done in the world."[6] By the time of the national election the next year, Gray dropped even this pretense of neutrality. He made it clear that both for reasons of national welfare (it would lead to war) and because of prophetic warnings (the league probably was condemned as the latter-day revival of the Roman Empire) Christians should do all they would to oppose the League.[7]

From *The King's Business,* June 1919, p. 588

WILL THIS FENCE HOLD THEM BACK?

Ironically, the premillennial publication that reacted most strongly to the threat of Bolshevism was the radical anti-cultural journal *Our Hope,* in which the war seemed to have created a heightened political consciousness. Although the editor, Arno C. Gaebelein, stuck to the sign-of-the-times format, his alarm about the political situation was clearly immediate and very real. For Gaebelein the pieces of the prophetic puzzle had suddenly fallen into place with the dramatic fulfillment of a prophecy. In 1916, before the Revolution, he had predicted that Russia (the "great power of the North") would "play a prominent and to herself fatal part during the predicted end of this age. . . ."[8] Now the Bolshevik Revolution made it clear what that role would be. In the "danger of Bolshevism," the bombings and attempted bombings of 1919, he now could see clearly that "The Beast Lifts the Head in Our Land." The government had been naïve and lax with respect to radicalism, and Americans should now expect not less but more lawlessness as "the full power of the god of this age—Satan—" is revealed.[9] On the same subject a year later, he pictured Americans as confronted with a life or death choice between civilization and communism. "*We are going through a reconstruction period,*" he said, ". . . and either we are coming out of it as a family of nations in which rich and poor alike will have been chastened, and in which each citizen will accord to his fellowman the same rights and privileges that he wants for himself, or the reconstruction period will expire by *giving birth to a World Communist Internationale,* in which our civilization and religion will be totally destroyed!!!"[10]

A sense of doom was created by apparent confirmations of premillennial pessimism in the daily news, and heightened by growing dismay about the moral condition of the nation. Premillennialists shared with many conservative Americans the conviction that the moral foundations of the nation were rapidly crumbling. Statistics documented the rise in crime rates.[11] Many Americans now flaunted the vicious habits often condemned by evangelical preachers. Young men and even women were openly smoking—*The King's Business* spoke of "The Yellow Peril of America."[12] It was particularly galling that churches accepted such changes. Methodist church choirs, for instance, allowed young women to display "brazen bared knees." "Who is responsible for this change of custom from the bended knee . . . ?" queried *The King's Business.* Dancing, once an abomination to Methodists, was now allowed even in their churches.[13]

All of these various postwar phenomena could easily be seen as related to one another. In November 1919 the Reverend Oliver W. Van Osdel, a prominent premillennialist pastor in Michigan, did just that in a sermon on the signs of the times. Van Osdel decried everything from such classic sins as selfishness, covetousness, and greed, to the League of Nations, the celebration of the anniversary of the Armistice by public dancing in the streets, and gymnasiums and moving pictures in the churches. In an impressionistic way

CLEVELAND MOFFETT'S IDEAL CHURCH

From *The King's Business,* May 1919, p. 396.

he summed up a fairly typical reaction to the complexity of the events and their relationships:

> Sometimes people ask what are the objections to dancing and theaters and card playing and such things; they say these are not to be severely condemned; but you will notice that the people who indulge in these worldly things are always loose in doctrine . . . the two go together, and when you find people indulging in worldliness they become loose in doctrine, then apostasy easily creeps in, the union of Christendom becomes possible and probably will be united through corrupt doctrine under one head, the Pope of Rome.[14]

One indication that many premillennialists were shifting their emphasis— away from just evangelizing, praying, and waiting for the end time, toward more intense concern with retarding degenerative trends—was the role they played in the formation of the first explicitly fundamentalist organization. In the summer of 1918, under the guidance of William B. Riley, a number of the leaders in the Bible school and prophetic conference movement conceived the idea of the World's Christian Fundamentals Association.[15] The first conference of the new agency was held in May 1919. It differed from earlier prophecy conferences primarily in the wider range of topics discussed. There was a program of well-worn Bible school lectures in defense of the faith and featuring some premillennialism. More important, a tone of urgency prevailed at the 1919 meetings. "The Great Apostasy was spreading like a plague throughout Christendom," declared the conference organizers. "Thousands of false teachers, many of them occupying high ecclesiastical positions, are bringing in damnable heresies, even denying the Lord that bought them, and bring upon themselves swift destruction." The Bible "was wounded in the house of its friends;" cardinal doctrines "were rejected as archaic and effete; false science had created many false apostles of Christ; indeed they were seeing that 'Satan himself is transformed into an angel of light.'" Yet, said the promoters, there was a "widespread revival— not a revival in the sense of great ingatherings resulting from evangelistic effort, but a revival of interest in and hunger for the Word of God." Indeed, the premillennial leaders had some reason for this hope, which was part of the crusading mood of the moment. The WCFA meeting in Philadelphia was reportedly attended by six thousand people and was only one of a series of conferences held in various cities in 1919.[16] Whereas a few years earlier the vast publication campaign of *The Fundamentals* had produced little perceptible effect, now the Fundamentals conference was the spark that helped to generate a nationwide movement.[17]

While for most premillennialists it was a departure to direct intense energy toward the organization of a counterattack on the degenerative trends in churches and culture, among the Presbyterian conservatives the cultural crisis of 1917-1920 served only to intensify existing concerns and efforts. Of the groups with a major role in the formation of classic fundamentalism, the Presbyterians had the most highly developed view of the connection between religion and culture. They had long linked the progress of truth to the progress of morality and civilization and the connection between theological decline and the demise of civilization was one with which they were quite familiar. The urgency of this concern had already been expressed in the alarmist preamble to the "five points" of 1910. With respect to organizing against modernism, Presbyterian conservatives were already in the field in 1919—indeed their representatives had been battling one or another sort of infidelity in America for close to two hundred years.

The unsettling years 1919 and 1920, however, served to accentuate the cultural dimension of the crisis for the doctrinaire Presbyterians and to bring out expressions of the same concerns felt in other circles. Writing early in 1920, David S. Kennedy, editor of the popular voice of Presbyterian militancy,

The Presbyterian, reiterated and summarized his own recent analysis of "The American Crisis." His statement, stressing the moral implications of this crisis, epitomizes the view of the nation that was coming to prevail throughout the conservative evangelical community:

> It must be remembered that America was born of moral progenitors and founded on an eternally moral foundation. Her ancestors were Christian of a high order, purified by fire, and washed in blood. Her foundation is the Bible, the infallible Word of God. The decalogue written by the finger of God is her perfect guide in her religious and social life. There has been some weakening of this moral standard in the thought and life of America. This is the result of an age of luxury within and freedom from conflict from without. There is but one remedy: the nation must return to her standard of the Word of God. She must believe, love and live her Bible. This will require the counteraction of that German destructive criticism which has found its way into the religious and moral thought of our people as the conception and propaganda of the *Reds* have found their way with poisoning and overthrowing influence into their civil and industrial life. The Bible and the God of the Bible is our only hope. America is narrowed to a choice. She must restore the Bible to its historic place in the family, the day school, the college and university, the church and Sabbath-school, and thus through daily life and thought revive and build up her moral life and faith, or else she might collapse and fail the world in this crucial age. . . .[18]

One result of the rapid spread of this type of thinking among conservative Protestants was the formal organization of an anti-modernist protest in the Northern Baptist Convention. This was the actual occasion of the invention of the term "fundamentalist." Curtis Lee Laws, editor of a prominent Baptist paper, *The Watchman Examiner,* coined the word, and defined "fundamentalists" as those ready "to do battle royal for the Fundamentals."[19] He and 154 other signatories called for a "General Conference on Fundamentals" to precede the yearly meeting of the Northern Baptists. They expressed "increasing alarm" over "the havoc which rationalism is working" in the churches, which were also affected by "a widespread and growing worldliness."[20]

As the term "fundamentalist" suggests, Laws's primary concern, as well as of the organizers of parallel fundamentalist movements at the time, was doctrinal. This point is worth emphasizing, because it might be supposed that fundamentalism was *primarily* a response to social and political conditions. It was not. First of all it was what its proponents most often said it was—a response to the spread of what was perceived as false doctrine.[21] After the war these suspect teachings were presented more widely, openly, and aggressively, reflecting a new openness and enthusiasm generated by a changed social setting. It is true that the crusading spirit of the war, together with the urgency of cultural alarm that followed, contributed to the intensity of the fundamentalist reaction. It also served to provide, as has been pointed out, a new cultural dimension to the movement. Nevertheless, these observations, although important, should not obscure the fact that for the fundamentalists the fundamental issues were theological.

Theology, however, did impinge upon other areas of the national culture—perhaps most observably in the schools and colleges. Most American colleges had been established by evangelical Protestants, and even the public schools had been dominated by Protestant ideas. In the half century since the Civil War, the schools had generally experienced a revolutionary secularization. Accordingly, those who were now organizing strategy for dealing with the religious dimensions of the cultural crisis saw the schools as an important arena for battle. William B. Riley in 1918 founded a paper entitled *Christian Fundamentals in School and Church,* which gave priority to the school issue. Here was a religious issue for which it was easy to rally support. Qualms about political involvement and establishments of religion could easily be forgotten when speaking about the schools. *The King's Business,* for example, which often printed remarks like "there is no such thing as Christian Civilization in any nation on earth today," could with respect to the education issue observe that in the public schools the Devil was dispensing "a Satanic poison that threatens the very foundations of the Republic," and made a plea for an all-out campaign to "MAKE THE COUNTRY SAFE FOR CHILDREN.[22]

At the pre-convention conference of conservative Northern Baptists in 1920, the school issue was the primary focus in planning for action at the Convention itself.[23] J. C. Massee, president of the new fundamentalist group (who had spoken also at the 1919 premillennialist WCFA Conference), warned against false teachers in Baptist colleges and seminaries. Massee declared that, even if an institution be nine-tenths sound, if it permitted *any* false teachings, "it remains unsafe until it has purged itself of that source of pernicious percolating poison." The schools, he said, were strongly affected by the general "drift away from the ancient landmarks" (a key phrase referring to strict Baptist principles), by "modernism in theology," "rationalism in philosophy," and "materialism in life." These could no longer be regarded as merely disturbing and were now dangerous and destructive. Massee's call for action was vivid, even if his imagery is laid on with a heavy hand:

> If we would save them, we must cease now to let Philistine teachers plow with our educational heifer, lest our denominational Samson, stripped of the goodly garments of his faith and virtue, fall under the witchery of a scholastic Delilah, and be permanently shorn of his strength, blinded as to his spiritual eyes, and bound to the unspeakable service of godless and mocking masters.[24]

Most of the speakers at the Baptist conference concentrated on questions of fundamental doctrines and/or strictly ecclesiastical issues. Another premillennialist, A. C. Dixon, must take credit for explicitly extending their concerns to the whole of American civilization. The logical necessity for this extension had already been established by wartime rhetoric. Dixon, former editor of *The Fundamentals,* and recently returned from serving in Spurgeon's former church in London, now clearly articulated the connections among the school issue, the future of civilization, and theological decline, with particular emphasis on the role of evolution. Evolution was not only a clear question of naturalism versus supernaturalism, theory versus fact, it was a part of "the conflict of the ages, darkness versus light, Cain vs. Abel, autocracy vs. civilized democracy." Greek philosophers, descended from Cain, had first developed evolutionary theory between 700 and 300 B.C. Darwin had added to this the idea of survival of the fittest, which Dixon described as giving "the strong and fit the scientific right to destroy the weak and the unfit." In Germany Nietzsche expanded this doctrine, and together with the German attacks on the Bible as the proper basis for civilization, this led inevitably to the barbaric German atrocities of World War I. By contrast, American civilization was founded on the Bible, Plymouth Rock, separation of church and state (a Baptist shibboleth), democracy and freedom, and the principles of Abraham Lincoln. Americans always stood with the weak and the oppressed against the oppressors. They had freed the slaves, "delivered little Cuba from her strong oppressor," and come to the rescue of Britain and her allies in the World War, "defending the weak against the aggression of the strong." America had won the victory of prohibition "over the oppressive powers of the drink traffic." Here Dixon, although a premillennialist, harked back to postmillennial visions of a democratic America leading the world to the triumph of righteousness. The agenda for the next evangelical crusade was an attack on the anti-democratic, "might is right," Bible-denying philosophy of evolution.[25]

The sense of social crisis also brought to the fore a new type of fundamental leader, the moral reformer. William B. Riley's rise to the leadership of the movement is, as has been already mentioned, evidence of this trend. The subsequent emergence of William Jennings Bryan as a prominent spokesman for fundamentalism fits the same pattern. It was in keeping with the direction the movement was taking that a politician should come to represent it.[26] In fact, the optimistic Bryan could really add little—beside the prestige of his support—to the combination of patriotism, evangelism, and Biblicism already articulated by a premillennialist such as A. C. Dixon. The fusion of these traditions suggests, however, that fundamentalism represented a new combination of revivalist, conservative, and premillennial traditions, united in an effort to bind together once again the many frayed strands of evangelical America.

Although the career of Frank Norris of Texas could be used to illustrate this same point,[27] John Roach Straton of New York City perhaps comes closest to the "ideal type" of the fundamentalist moral reformer. Straton came to Calvary Baptist Church in New York in the spring of 1918. He was a Southerner, rather well educated, who had held several other major city pastorates. In his early career he was an ardent champion of both moral and social reform, attacking not only notorious vices such as prostitution and the use of alcohol, but also advocating some more progressive causes, such as women's and children's labor reform, wage reform, fair housing, and prison reform.[28] During this period, although he preached a traditional Gospel of salvation, he was not a premillennialist in any significant sense and often sounded more like a postmillennialist believer in progress.[29]

Soon after his arrival in New York, the two major characteristics of his later career appeared: his social message became focused almost entirely on notorious vices,[30] and he emerged as a prominent card-carrying premillennial fundamentalist. His social program is evident in his nationally published sermon of the summer of 1918, "Will New York Be Destroyed if it Does not Repent?" in which he attacked the vice, gluttony, gaming, and indecency of New York's hotels and cabarets, comparing the city with Nineveh, Babylon, Sodom, Gomorrah, and (drawing upon more recent history) San Francisco before the earthquake. Although Straton pictured New York as facing an impending doom, there was still no trace of premillennial prophecy in his message. Rather, he suggested that "the destiny of the human race for hundreds of years to come is in the balance."[31] Despite the lack of explicit premillennialism in his prophetic preaching of 1918, by 1919 Straton had identified himself with premillennial fundamentalism and was in fact a speaker at the first WCFA conference.[32]

Premillennialism seems not to have dampened Straton's zeal to expose and eradicate the immorality of his time. The most sensational period in his career, in fact, commenced in the spring of 1920 with a highly publicized raid and exposé of vice in the Times Square area. During the succeeding years Straton supplied the New York newspapers with a steady stream of sensational attacks on vice, including everything from Sabbath desecration to ballroom dancing and prize fighting. Such attacks helped to tie fundamentalism to the popular idea of the Puritan tradition as morally repressive. One observer described Straton as "like Oliver Cromwell in a nightclub, or Bishop Asbury at the Saratoga races."[33] Straton's own view of the situation is caught in the title of his two most sensational books: "The Menace of Immorality in Church and State" (1920) and "Fighting the Devil in Modern Babylon" (1929).

Despite this latter title, Straton never quite made up his mind whether the United States was Babylon or the New Israel. Perhaps he thought of New York City as Babylon in the midst of Israel. At any rate, despite his non-stop prophecies of doom, he always remained a full-fledged patriot. Indicating that "the deadliest danger now confronting America is the union of irreligion and political radicalism," he declared:

Can anyone doubt that God has lodged with us in this free land the ark of the covenant of humanity's hopes? So surely as God led forth ancient Israel for a unique and glorious mission, so does he seem to have raised up Christian America for such an hour as this.[34]

Straton's impetus for his fierce attacks on the dance, theaters, and other worldly amusements seems to have been a sense that Christian America was losing touch with its foundation in Biblical teaching. The Bible, he said, in the context of a typical attack on dancing, "is the foundation of all that is decent and right in our civilization."[35] Thus it was consistent for Straton to identify himself with the central fundamentalist cause—the defense of the fundamental doctrines of the faith.[36] For Straton, whether attacking vice or debating modernists, the key issue was the same—the all-importance of Scripture. Frequently he made the accusation that attacks on the Bible would lead to lawlessness and ultimately to the total demise of civilization. At this point the theological aspect of fundamentalism merged with its con-

From *The King's Business,* July 1922, p. 642.

cern for the social and moral welfare of the nation. The battle for the Bible was a battle for civilization.

By the end of 1920 most Americans had recovered from the most extreme manifestations of crisis mentality and were set on course for a return to "normalcy." Fundamentalists too were committed to a return to the *status quo ante bellum,* but they wished to revive an evangelical theological consensus that had in fact been gone for at least a generation. Such a quest for normalcy could hardly be satisfied by a vote for Harding. Moreover, while the postwar sense of crisis was apparently only a temporary disruption for most Americans, for fundamentalists it was the beginning of a crusade. They began to organize precisely at the time of the crisis in 1919 and 1920, and as a result they institutionalized and preserved important parts of the outlook of that era of intense feeling and opinion.

XVIII. The Fundamentalist Offensive on Two Fronts: 1920-1921

Between 1920 and 1925 fundamentalism took shape as a movement distinct from its antecedents and representing more than just the sum of the sub-movements that supported it. It flourished on two fronts. In the major denominations fundamentalists battled against those who denied, or would tolerate denials of, the fundamentals of the traditional faith. In American culture as a whole they fought to stop the teaching of evolution in the public schools. By the early summer of 1925 fundamentalists appeared to be on the verge of winning major victories that would legislate reversals of long-developing trends away from evangelical orthodoxy in both churches and culture. Yet as the movement came closer to effecting such a revolution, the main body of its adherents hesitated to follow those radicals who would tolerate no compromise. During the following year the mood of the country swung sharply away from the uncompromising radicals, and their movement was left in a shambles. From 1920 to 1925 fundamentalism was a broad and nationally influential coalition of conservatives, but after 1925 it was composed of less flexible and more isolated minorities often retreating into separatism, where they could regroup their considerable forces.

The issues that shaped fundamentalism during this critical five-year period were most fully developed in ecclesiastical debates, although these cannot be separated from the context of the anti-evolution movement. Fundamentalism took definite form especially in the conflicts within the Northern Baptist and Northern Presbyterian (Presbyterian Church in the U.S.A.) denominations. These became centers of the anti-modernist movement because in each of these denominations advanced and aggressive modernism was faced by a conservative counter-force of comparable strength. In other denominations, either the liberals had already gained virtually complete freedom (as among the Congregationalists) or the conservatives were so overwhelmingly dominant (as among Southern Baptists and Southern Presbyterians) that there was no possibility of protracted controversy.

By World War I there were strong liberal and conservative parties within the Northern Baptist Convention, and among the conservatives there was also a prominent dispensational premillennialist element. In fact, the prophecy movement in America, which initially had been dominated by Presbyterians, was now (to judge by denominational affiliations of Bible teachers) predominantly Baptist.[1] The preservation of active Baptist affiliations was natural. The Presbyterians had some intellectual affinities to dispensationalism, but the Baptists had a broader set of interests in common with the prophetic movement. The Baptist movements themselves had formed in reaction against ecclesiastical establishments. Thus, like the dispensationalists, their traditions emphasized individual salvation, the right of conscience against ecclesiastical authority and the local congregation against centralized power, separation of church and state, and the New Testament in preference to the Old.

The dispensationalists prodded other Baptist conservatives into taking a strong stand against liberalism. In fact the original Baptist fundamentalist movement was not predominantly dispensationalist and its leadership included spokesmen for the larger element of non-dispensational conservatives. In January of 1917 Curtis Lee Laws, editor of the conservative *Watchman-Examiner,* began a series of editorials sharply contrasting "Old and New Theologies."[2] In the same year Augustus H. Strong, the leading conservative Baptist theologian of the day and recently retired president of Rochester Theological Seminary, completed writing *A Tour of the Missions,* a scathing denunciation of liberalism at home and abroad. Neither Laws nor Strong was a dispensationalist, and neither was especially narrow-minded or intolerant. Indeed, neither argued for the inerrancy of Scripture.[3] Laws admitted that the new theology was "based on a sounder religious psychology" than was the old and that the old was burdened with some outdated forms. The most important point he made, however, was that the two theologies contained "irreconcilable differences."[4] President Strong's final disillusionment with the new theology was dramatic and unexpected. Strong, whose seminary at Rochester had included Walter Rauschenbusch among its faculty, had spent much of his long career attempting to reconcile the assumptions of modern theology and criticism with traditional Baptist belief.[5] Now his tour of the mission fields startled him into the conviction that

the Baptists were "losing our faith in the Bible." "The unbelief in our seminary teaching," he said, "is like a blinding mist which is slowly settling down
upon our churches, and is gradually abolishing, not only all definite views of
Christian doctrine, but also all conviction of duty to 'contend earnestly for
the faith' of our fathers." Strong felt that this unbelief was connected with
desire for unity with other denominations, and he judged it not simply a
lapse in Baptist principles but the "far more radical evil" of apostasy from
Christ.[6]

The increasingly aggressive and ambitious character of interdenominational Protestant liberalism in the immediate postwar years aggravated such
concerns. In 1918 and 1919, journals such as *The Biblical World* and the
weekly *Christian Century* not only kept up a constant barrage of arguments
against premillennialism, but they also repeatedly asserted that they sought
the eradication of the defective forms of Christianity associated with conservatism. In the spring of 1919, for example, *The Christian Century*—whose
controversialist propensities had originated in battles among the Disciples of
Christ—ran an advertisement offering $100 for the best serial story "dealing
with the conditions of modern church life, especially the embarrassment and
evils of denominationalism, revivalism, traditional theology, etc., and making a constructive contribution to the modern way of thinking about religion."[7]

The spirit of interdenominational solidarity fostered by the war had raised
new hopes for cooperation and eventual unity of the denominations on a
broad liberal basis. Among Baptists efforts in this direction involved attempts to increase denominational centralization, which added to conservatives' alarm concerning the overall trend (although conservatives were not
themselves adverse to using centralized power when it furthered their own
cause). The idealistic Interchurch World Movement was most immediately
disturbing. Initiated just after the war, this was a colossal effort both to raise
money and to coordinate Protestant benevolence and missions. As its opponents pointed out, the Interchurch World Movement was American Protestantism's version of the League of Nations[8] and, indeed, although the plan
generated some enthusiasm in 1919, by 1920 the opposition was as strong as
that against the League. Early in the summer of 1920, the Interchurch collapsed, partly because of a lack of outside financial support, but also significantly because effective campaigns of the conservative opposition had seriously hurt internal support both from Northern Baptists and from Northern
Presbyterians.[9] Similarly, a proposal to unite America's Protestant churches
which was put forward with great enthusiasm in 1919 was by 1920 left in
ruins by popular resistance in various denominations.[10]

These events provided the ecclesiastical context for the organization of
Baptist fundamentalism as a denominational movement in the "war against
rationalism." At the pre-convention conference in 1920 the Baptist fundamentalists had emphasized the danger of false teaching in the Baptist schools.

At the subsequent meeting of the Northern Baptist Convention the new fundamentalist party succeeded to the extent of having a committee (including the president of the fundamentalist group, J. C. Massee)[11] appointed to conduct a formal investigation of the suspect institutions.

In 1921 the "Fundamentalist Fellowship," as it now became known, held another pre-convention conference and prepared to urge its views on the denomination as a whole. One of the major problems that would eventually ruin the movement was already disturbingly apparent. The Northern Baptist Convention was designed to promote positive practical cooperation, not to act as a court. Ultimately its power was derived from the Baptist constituency. Although expressing disapproval of some of the teachings that Massee and others had documented, the report of the committee investigating the schools (which the Convention accepted) pointed out there was nothing the Convention could do.[12] In anticipation of such a result, the pre-convention group in 1921 had searched for a way to regulate the teachings in the denomination. One possibility within the genuine American Baptist tradition (which included two quite opposite heritages on this point) was to adopt a creed. In preparation for such a move, in 1921 the Fundamentalist Fellowship, demonstrating an inclination toward centralized regulation, prepared a creed that incorporated elements of the Philadelphia and New Hampshire Confessions with other broad statements of Baptist principles. They postponed proposing this creed to the Convention itself for one year. Meanwhile, the conservative party took another tack, which they hoped would bring them to the same destination. A contributor offered nearly two million dollars to Baptist missions on the condition that the funds not be used in aid of anyone not subscribing to orthodox beliefs. The proposed test of orthodoxy was similar to the five fundamentals that the Presbyterian General Assembly had first adopted in 1910 and then reaffirmed in 1916.[13]

Mission work was a crucial factor in the emergence of fundamentalism as an organized movement, and long remained one of the most hotly debated issues in both the Baptist and Presbyterian denominations. Conservatism was strong in the mission field and so was dispensational premillennialism. As we have seen, missions had been a positive force for creating a sense of unity among revivalists and other conservative evangelicals. American Southerners were also well represented in foreign missions and so these Southern conservatives were drawn into fundamentalist militancy. The formation of the Bible Union of China in 1920 was especially significant. Dispensationalists and Southern Presbyterians (who as a rule were not dispensationalists) were particularly active in this organization.[14] On the mission field the implications of liberalism were obvious, practical and urgent. Here the suggestion of the more extreme liberals that God revealed himself in non-Christian cultures had profound implications for missionary programs. In Africa or Asia these implications were naturally far more obvious than in nominally Christian middle-class America. The conservatives believed the issue at stake was nothing less than the salvation of souls—and this was unquestionably foremost of all evangelical concerns. On this question feelings were deep and often unalterable. Conservative missionaries, such as those of the Bible Union, were quick to impress on any who would listen (as A. H. Strong already had) the dangers of the liberal teachings which were dampening evangelical zeal and thus allowing precious souls to go to perdition.

The mission field thus played a substantial role in making fundamentalism an interdenominational movement. In 1921, while the Baptist fundamentalists debated mission policy, similar concerns brought conservative Presbyterians into the distinctly fundamentalist phase of their controversies. The Presbyterian combatants, especially as represented by *The Presbyterian* of Philadelphia, had already assimilated the idea of the antithesis of true Christianity and modernism.[15] The furor over missions simply gave them a new point on which to press the issue. The debate started early in 1921 when dispensationalist W. H. Griffith Thomas returned from a visit to China, where he had ties with the Bible Union, and reported to a group of Philadelphia Presbyterians that liberalism was rife among Northern Presbyterian missionaries. The accusation created a minor sensation and several attempts were made to get the 1921 General Assembly to start an investigation. The issue was temporarily put aside; two conservatives, Robert E. Speer and Charles R. Erdman, both contributors to *The Fundamentals,* assured the Convention of the fidelity of the Presbyterian missionaries.[16] Erdman was a professor at Princeton Seminary and a well-known premillennialist. His appearance as a spokesman for tolerance was significant for the course the disputes would take in the next years.

In mid-1921 it was not yet apparent that fundamentalism would become a major national movement. Its critics still assumed, with some reason, that it was really the premillennial movement in disguise. So *The Christian Century,* in its first full-length attack on fundamentalism as such, declared that "the cult of fundamentalism with its verbal inspiration and infallibility, is chiliasm or adventism with a new name."[17] *The Baptist,* the official organ of the Northern Baptist Convention, went so far as to announce editorially in July 1921 that "Fundamentalism is Dead." This was a case of mistaken identity. *The Baptist* argued that the creed drawn up by the pre-convention group contained no precise statement on either infallibility of Scripture or the premillennial return of Christ. Hence, "Fundamentalism (using the term in its settled, technical sense, as designating the interdenominational movement to disseminate a certain group of theological ideas and to force a division in the churches along the line of these ideas) was definitely rejected."[18]

This made Curtis Lee Laws furious. He had helped to draw up the moderate creed, and the definition that *The Baptist* used would have separated him from the movement that he himself had named. Perhaps he was the more furious because the issue was a sensitive one among the Baptist fundamentalists themselves. A rift was developing between those who subscribed to

Laws's brand of Baptist fundamentalism and the supporters of William Bell Riley's World's Christian Fundamentals Association, which did indeed include inerrancy and premillennialism in their association's creed.[19] "*The Baptist* well knows," retorted the editor of the *Watchman-Examiner,* "that our Baptist Fundamentals movement has never had any connection whatever with the interdenominational movement." Within the Baptist denomination, Laws maintained, "aggressive conservatives—conservatives who feel that it is their duty to contend for the faith—have, by common consent, been called 'fundamentalists.'"[20]

While the definition used by *The Baptist* did point out the most obvious single element of the new "fundamentalism," Curtis Lee Laws captured the essence of the common attitude and motive that gave the diverse groups cohesiveness as a distinct movement. Fundamentalism was a loose interdenominational coalition of "aggressive conservatives—conservatives who feel that it is their duty to contend for the faith." This definition embraced the main concerns of the fundamentalist premillennialists, conservative Baptists, Presbyterian traditionalists, and the scattered militants in other denominations, who were beginning to develop a sense of common identity.

During the next year, as the battles in the churches intensified, fundamentalists began to move on a new front, following the standard of anti-evolution into battle to save the Bible and Bible civilization. As we have seen, this issue was already a leading fundamentalist concern. Late in 1920, it suddenly leapt into new prominence when William Jennings Bryan championed the cause. With prohibition and the women's question seemingly resolved for the time being, Bryan adopted anti-evolution as his latest crusade and gave the cause wide publicity.[21]

Bryan's reasoning on the subject echoed notes already sounded by other fundamentalist spokesmen. Although he alluded to the superiority of faith over science ("It is better to trust the Rock of Ages, than to know the age of the rocks . . ."), his principal point was that Scripture was in fact scientific whereas Darwinism was not. "Science," he affirmed in the best Baconian manner, "is classified knowledge; it is the explanation of facts." Darwinism was "guesses strung together," "a mere hypothesis." He cited the alarming effects of Darwinism on religion, morality, and civilization. Not only did it "destroy the faith of Christians," it "laid the foundation for the bloodiest war in history" by committing German culture to the philosophy of Nietzsche, a philosophy of materialism and brutal competition. Although it might be true that "*some* believers in Darwinism retained their belief in Christianity," so also, said Bryan, "some survive smallpox." The urgent need to extirpate this brutal atheistic materialism from American schools could hardly be overemphasized.[22]

Most of the conservatives in the denominations joined the outcry against the evils of evolution,[23] but Darwinism never became a major issue in the church controversies themselves. Anti-evolution usually did not appear on lists of fundamental doctrines to be used as tests of orthodoxy. Rather, those who promoted this aspect of the movement most fervently were the most militant premillennialists, including A. C. Dixon, William B. Riley, John Roach Straton, and J. Frank Norris of Texas.[24] In 1921 Riley was already organizing rallies in Kentucky, where Bryan also appeared on behalf of anti-evolution legislation.[25] Over the next two years anti-evolution became more and more the principal passion of interdenominational fundamentalists, and the WCFA repeatedly tried to enlist Bryan as its leader, despite his refusal to endorse its supposedly essential doctrine, dispensational premillennialism.[26]

The meteoric rise of the anti-evolution issue—which was closely connected with the World War I notion of saving civilization from German theology and its superman philosophy—was swiftly transforming the character of the fundamentalist movement, particularly its premillennialist branch, which found that a social and political question was now virtually its first concern.[27] This transformation was involved with an immense surge in popularity; the anti-evolution movement was becoming a national fad. Both the premillennial movement and denominational fundamentalism had been confined mostly to Northern states, but anti-evolution swept through the South and found new constituencies in rural areas everywhere. Many people with little or no interest in fundamentalism's doctrinal concerns were drawn into the campaign to keep Darwinism out of America's schools.[28] Those premillennialist leaders who had adopted the cause of anti-evolution experienced a radical metamorphosis within the space of a few years. Having gained the attention of the increasingly influential mass media, they seemed to have found the key to the success they had long been seeking. The more clearly they realized that there was a mass audience for the message of the social danger of evolution, the more central this social message became. Several years before, they had been drifting toward becoming a sectarian group, outsiders, and perhaps slightly un-American. Suddenly they appeared in a new guise, prophets at the center of a national movement for reform.

XIX. Would the Liberals Be Driven from the Denominations? 1922–1923

Sentiment for the fundamentalist program of recovering lost national foundations was growing rapidly, and the fundamentalists were in the optimal position to push their demand for faithfulness to the Bible in the denominations. In those denominations where there were large parties on each side, schism was widely feared. Everyone concerned seemed to envision the fundamentalists driving the liberals out of these denominations. Although in retrospect the obstacles to such an outcome are obvious, they were not all apparent in the spring of 1922, as the Baptist fundamentalists were laying plans to press their seeming advantage.

Thus, on May 21, 1922, as the Baptist Convention was approaching, the popular liberal Baptist preacher, Harry Emerson Fosdick, launched the liberal counteroffensive with a sermon entitled. "Shall the Fundamentalists Win?" This sermon so exactly captured the liberal sentiments of the moment that it received wide publicity, appearing in at least three journals as well as in a widely distributed pamphlet.[1] Unlike the authors of some other liberal attacks who tried to dismiss fundamentalism by associating it with one or another form of extremism,[2] Fosdick showed himself well-informed on the nature of the movement. Fundamentalists, he said, were especially intolerant conservatives. They were strongest in the Baptist and Presbyterian denominations. Their fundamental doctrinal tests were (1) special miracles such as the Virgin Birth (2) the inerrancy of Scripture (which Fosdick took to involve something like stenographic dictation), (3) the "special theory" of substitutionary atonement, and (4) the second coming of Christ to set up a millennial kingdom (a point which Fosdick persisted in identifying with all fundamentalism).[3] On all but the third of these points, Fosdick contrasted in some detail the fundamentalist position with that of other "multitudes of reverent Christians" who saw natural historical processes as God's way of doing things. He also mentioned in passing fundamentalist efforts to exclude "teaching modern biology" in public schools, a subject on which he had just debated with Bryan in the *New York Times*.[4] But his central concern was for the churches. Repeatedly he emphasized that the fundamentalist goal was to force those with other views out of the churches. The central theme of his message was the urgent need for tolerance on both sides.[5]

The fears that Fosdick entertained were somewhat allayed at the 1922 meeting of the Northern Baptist Convention because of the inability of the fundamentalists to settle on a coherent strategy. Most Baptist fundamentalists agreed that they should establish some sort of creedal test of orthodoxy within the denomination, but moderates such as Curtis Lee Laws, J. C. Massee, and Frank M. Goodchild, saw this move as demanding careful preparation and in 1921 had delayed presenting their new creedal proposal. Fundamentalist indecision was still apparent at the 1922 Convention. William B. Riley, however, forced the issue on everyone by proposing the adoption of one of the traditional Baptist creeds, the New Hampshire Confession. The opponents of fundamentalism totally outmaneuvered Riley. In a shrewd countermove, Cornelius Woelfkin, a liberal pastor from New York City, offered as a substitute, "That the New Testament is the all-sufficient ground of our faith and practice, and we need no other statement." Here was an appeal to a more sacred and seemingly more fundamental Baptist tradition than any creed. After heated debate Woelfkin's proposal was adopted 1,264 to 637.[6]

This dramatic reversal for Baptist fundamentalism, at the very moment when it should have been reaching the height of its power, split the movement irreparably. Apparently each of the conservative parties blamed the strategy of the other for the defeat. Protesting the moderation of the leadership associated with Laws, militants followed Riley in the formation of the Baptist Bible Union. This new agency was very close in both character and personnel to the WCFA, except that the Baptist group did not officially prescribe premillennialism (because of difficulties this would have created for some Southern and Canadian Baptists).[7] Presumably in counter-reaction, the more moderate Baptist fundamentalists became even more cautious in succeeding years, and in subsequent disputes stressed the necessity of working within the Convention structures to retain whatever influence they could. They thus became the first of many once-militant fundamentalist groups to drop some of their militancy when faced with the stark alternative of a bitter and devastating battle that would surely lead to schism and leave a denomination in ruins.[8]

Despite the Baptist disarray, fundamentalism was advancing elsewhere. At almost the same moment that the Baptist fundamentalist drive was stalled, Presbyterian conservatives entered the conflict in full force. By early 1922 the smallest spark would have sufficed for the fundamentalist furor to renew the raging controversy in the Presbyterian Church in the U.S.A. The kindling temperature of conservative Presbyterians had always been low. No mere spark, Harry Emerson Fosdick's sermon, although addressed primarily to the Baptist situation, hit the Presbyterian Chruch like a bombshell. The Baptist Fosdick was by special arrangement the associate pastor of the First Presbyterian Church of New York, where he preached his famous sermon. The conservatives, centered in Philadelphia, had long been appalled by loose practices common in the New York Presbytery. Since the early twentieth century they had been complaining that the New York Presbytery did not demand orthodoxy of its ministerial candidates, and such complaints had led to the declaration of fundamentals by the General Assembly in 1910 and 1916.

From William Jennings Bryan, *Seven Questions in Dispute* (New York, 1924).

Fosdick himself had been a particular target for conservative attacks for some time.[9] His sermon, together with the implication (not directly stated) that he agreed fully with the liberal views that he described, seemed to be the clearest case of open heresy in a hundred years.

Clarence E. Macartney, pastor of the Arch Street Presbyterian Church in Philadelphia, and like Fosdick one of the famed preachers of the day, led the conservative attack. To "Shall the Fundamentalists Win?" Macartney replied with "Shall Unbelief Win?" in which he showed how Fosdick's naturalistic alternatives to "fundamentalism" diverged from traditional Christianity. When leaders such as Fosdick were "blasting at the Rock of Ages," it was certainly time to "*contend* for the faith."[10] Macartney himself led the drive for a dramatic conservative victory in the Presbyterian denomination. Under his guidance the Presbytery of Philadelphia petitioned the General Assembly to condemn the teachings expressed in Fosdick's sermon and to instruct the Presbytery of New York to see that further preaching from the First Church conformed to orthodox Presbyterian standards. This proposal became the focal point of intense campaigns of charges and countercharges during the months preceding the General Assembly of 1923.[11]

In the first full-fledged test of strength the two sides proved to be closely matched. Militant conservatives (now often referred to as "fundamentalists") offered William Jennings Bryan as their candidate for moderator. Bryan, maintaining the record of his political heyday, missed election by a narrow margin. This defeat probably signaled only a reluctance of some militants to dwell on the evolution question.[12] On the main issue of the Assembly, however, Macartney and Bryan were successful in leading the condemnation of the New York Presbytery's laxness regarding Fosdick, and the Assembly instructed the Presbytery to report its corrective actions to the 1924 meeting. As part of the same action, the 1923 Assembly reaffirmed, by a vote of 439 to 359, the five-point doctrinal declaration of 1910 and 1916.

During the year that followed, the Presbyterian controversy approached its peak of intensity. The intellectual position of fundamentalist forces seemed greatly strengthened when Princeton's impressive New Testament scholar, J. Gresham Machen, turned his attention almost fulltime to the controversy, with the publication of *Christianity and Liberalism* in 1923. Friends as well as many foes of the movement acknowledged the strength of Machen's arguments and that he defined the central issue for all fundamentalists with great clarity. Although Machen maintained cordial relations with many premillennialists and revivalists, he was not typical of fundamentalists in a number of ways (the best known was his opposition to prohibition),[13] and was sometimes uncomfortable with the title of the movement for which he was a leading spokesman. Yet on the main issue at stake Machen would entertain no compromise and welcomed any allies who would share his stand. "The great redemptive religion which has always been known as Christianity," he declared in the opening of *Christianity and Liberalism,* "is battling against a totally diverse type of religious belief, which is only the more destructive of the Christian faith because it makes use of traditional Christian terminology." Liberalism, said Machen, was vulnerable to criticism on two basic grounds. First, it was "un-Christian" and, second, it was "unscientific." The latter point Machen did not develop at length in *Christianity and Liberalism.* He did, however, summarize briefly his views on this subject, that Christianity was a religion based on facts, and that these facts were open to scientific investigation. Liberalism, on the other hand, was based on "appeals to man's will" and on an "indefinite type of religious aspiration." Hoping to preserve Christianity by adjusting it to the dictates of modern scientific culture, the liberals had separated it from the realm of fact and the scientific. Machen believed that they grossly overestimated the merits of modern scientific civilization. Machen, a rugged individualist and politically an active conservative, saw the drive toward uniformity in modern culture, especially in the reign of the "experts" over American schools, as threatening to turn the nation into "one huge 'Main Street.'"[14]

His major objection to liberalism was that it was simply un-Christian. The human religious aspirations that liberals rescued from the jaws of modern science were not Christian at all. They amounted to paganism. If Christianity was not based on the fact that Christ died to save sinners and rose again, then the New Testament made no sense and the religion that remained was mere faith in humanity. "If a condition could be conceived in which all the preaching of the Church should be controlled by the liberalism which in many quarters has already become preponderant, then, we believe, Christianity would at last have perished from the earth and the gospel would have sounded forth for the last time." To Machen the solution seemed clear. Liberals should be forced out of Christian churches. "A separation between the two parties in the Church," he declared, "is the crying need of the hour."[15]

At this point, it appeared that the logic of fundamentalism, as the Presbyterians had formulated the issue, might prevail. The liberals, said one writer in the *Christian Century* in August 1923, had simply been outmaneuvered. In choosing the word "fundamentalism," he felt, they had adopted a "nearly irresistible rallying-cry," which would appeal to the man in the street, who liked the idea of getting back to essentials. "The Fundamentalists have succeeded in giving the liberal and intelligent leaders of the church the appearance of renegades who are sniping the church from the ramparts."[16]

Even the secular liberal press, the natural ally of the liberal churchmen, was defecting. Within two weeks of the end of 1923 both the *Nation* and the *New Republic* published essays arguing that the fundamentalists had logic on their side when they invited the modernists to leave their denominations. The fundamentalists, these formidable political journals each observed, were not denying the rights of the modernists to think as they pleased. They were only claiming that if the modernists wanted to think thoughts which contradicted the creeds that denominations had always affirmed, then it would be only gentlemanly to withdraw and found denominations on some other basis.[17]

Almost simultaneously the leading voice of liberal Protestantism, the *Christian Century,* conceded that the issue was not a peripheral one raised by extremists, but involved the essential character of the Christian religion. "Two worlds have crashed," said *Century* editor Charles Clayton Morrison, "the world of tradition and the world of modernism. One is scholastic, static, authoritarian, individualistic; the other is vital, dynamic, free and social." Arguments such as Machen's, he admitted, were on this point correct. In fact there were "two religions" and the clash between them was "as profound and as grim as that between Christianity and Confucianism."[18]

XX. The Offensive Stalled and Breaking Apart: 1924–1925

Although the liberals now conceded that the issue of fundamentalism versus modernism was a most serious one, they were a long way from conceding defeat. During 1924 both press and public were eager for any contribution to the ongoing spectacle of clergymen at each other's throats. H. L. Mencken suggested building special stadia for these entertainments.[1] In the spring of 1924 in New York City Charles Francis Potter, a Unitarian, debated John Roach Straton in a highly publicized series that added plausibility to such popular characterizations of the disputes. Certainly the liberals were not willing to let the fundamentalist charges go uncontested, and in 1924 a striking number of liberal spokesmen brought out strong defenses of their views.[2]

Probably the most influential of such statements was *The Faith of Modernism* by Shailer Mathews, Dean of the University of Chicago Divinity School. While not presented as such, Mathews's book was clearly meant to answer Machen's *Christianity and Liberalism*. The antagonist throughout was a "confessional or dogmatic Christian" who held views closely resembling those of the Princeton professor.[3] Although liberalism itself was too broad to have one standard view, Mathews's answer to Machen displays many characteristics of the movement at its height.

"*The use of scientific, historical, and social method in understanding and applying evangelical Christianity to the needs of living persons,*" said Mathews, "*is Modernism.*" When Mathews said that Christianity was scientific and empirical he had something vastly different in mind from what Machen meant when he said the same thing. The basic premise underlying all of Mathews's thought, as well as much of the scientific thought of the day, was that ideas and beliefs are not mirrors of external reality but products of the mind shaped by natural evolutionary and cultural developments. Thus religion was not based on static or standardized objective knowledge of God, but rather could best be understood as a social or historical development. Christians had faith that God indeed was acting in history, but they knew of him only through human religious experience which changed as society changed.

In Mathews's view, human religious experience provided the data for the scientific study of religion. The Bible, accordingly, was not a source of facts or true propositions about God, but "a trustworthy record of a developing experience of God which nourishes our faith." Similarly, the doctrines of the church were the products of group religious experience. Christianity "Is the *concrete religious life of a continuous ongoing group rather than the various doctrines in which that life found expression.*" The goal of the modernist, therefore, was "to carry on this process of an ever growing experience of God."[4]

Since the scientific study of religious faith concluded that faith was always the product of human social circumstances and needs, Mathews saw the current conflict as a clash of "two social minds." The doctrines taught in the confessions of the church which Machen and the Presbyterian controversialists made so much of were simply the products of the faith of another era. So, said Mathews, "if Christianity is essentially only what the seventeenth century thought it, a theological system inherited from the past, the charge that Modernism is un-Christian is logically sound."[5]

Mathews, however, had a different test for Christianity. Christianity was not doctrine, but life. *"It is a moral and spiritual movement, born of the experiences of God known through Jesus Christ as Savior."* Hence the true test was a pragmatic one. "The Modernist Christian believes the Christian religion will help man meet social as well as individual needs."[6] The needs of modern society, which after all is where God is found today, should therefore properly set the agenda for Christians. The principle that God was immanent and revealing himself in the modern world, was at the heart of the modernist impulse.

Mathews insisted that this understanding of religion as experience and practical morality was indeed Christianity. "Humanity," he said clearly,

> is not good enough. It must be transformed, regenerated. But if democracy and science alone are not sufficient where is the power for such a change? We confidently reply, in Christianity.

"Modernists," he added, "as a class are evangelical Christians. That is, they accept Jesus Christ as a revelation of a Savior God." It was God in Christ in whom Christian salvation was revealed, "not in a man made into a God." For the modern Christian, therefore, Christ was the focal point of the revelation of God's answer to the needs of society. The answer was above all a moral and a practical one. It brought "a full moral life" which was impossible without God. Ultimately it introduced "goodwill" which, "though never fully realized, is of the nature of God, and is the law of progress, the foundation upon which human society can safely be built. . . ."[7]

Despite such able defenses of the modernist position, there was no chance that this view of Christianity would gain official endorsements from the Baptist and Presbyterian denominations. The contending parties were so entirely opposed, both in premises and conclusions, that no compromise was viable. Simple communication, in fact, was virtually impossible, even between two such able representatives of the extreme positions as Machen and Mathews.

By this time liberalism was being assailed in a number of denominations. When fundamentalism became a national sensation, conservative denominational movements with their own traditions and backgrounds temporarily joined in the fundamentalist fray. Some of them had only a tangential relationship to the rest of fundamentalism. Among the Disciples of Christ, for instance, although the controversy was as intense as among the Presbyterians or Baptists, their conservative party had a unique set of interests. They shared with the main body of fundamentalists a strong opposition to liberalism, especially the liberalism represented by the former journal of the Disciples, *The Christian Century*. The controversy focused, however, on preserving strict Disciples traditions, particularly Baptism by immersion. This exclusivism separated the Disciples conservatives from other fundamentalists, even though both groups recognized some mutual affinities. By the 1920s the conservative Disciples "Restoration Movement" had been battling liberals strenuously for a decade and a half. In 1924 at the height of the other denominational controversies, the conservatives established the Christian Restoration Association which seriously threatened to split the denomination. Although a formal schism was averted, within a few years separatism had led to the virtual independence of the liberal and conservative factions within a loose denominational structure.[8]

The fracas in the Protestant Episcopal Church was even less directly relevant to the main development of fundamentalism. But in 1924 and 1925 an Episcopalian *cause célèbre* generated enormous publicity. Apparently encouraged by the wave of anti-modernist sentiment, conservative Episcopalians attempted to use the ecclesiastical machinery against the new doctrines. In November 1923 the House of Bishops issued a Pastoral Letter defending the traditional understanding of the Virgin Birth, the bodily resurrection of Jesus and other affirmations of the Apostles' Creed as a prerequisite for ordination to the Episcopal priesthood. During 1924 a number of heresy trials were threatened or pending, and in 1925 one of these culminated in the expulsion from the ministry of retired Bishop William M. Brown, a theological and social radical. The conservatives in this controversy were led by Bishop William T. Manning, who, although adamantly opposed to liberalism was a strict fundamentalist neither in his opposition to evolution nor in his view of Scripture.[9]

The Methodist Church in the North did include some full-fledged fundamentalists. Methodists had been prominent in the work of the Bible League of North America, and the dispensationalist prophecy conference movement always included a few Methodist representatives. At the height of the fundamentalist disputes in other denominations, Methodist conservatives, led by Harold P. Sloan, pushed to restrict liberalism, especially in denominational publications. Yet Methodism was too little oriented toward strict doctrinal definitions for its fundamentalists to grow to large numbers or to have much impact.[10] In the South, although Methodism had produced at least one major fundamentalist leader in evangelist Bob Jones, Sr., who founded his own college in 1926, conservative efforts in the denomination in the 1920s were even more scattered than in the North.[11]

In the South generally, religious conservatism was directly tied to cultural conservatism in ways that differed from the North. The preservation of evangelical religion went hand-in-hand with the preservation of the Southern way of life.[12] Their Northern counterparts had experienced the secularization of a society once dominated by evangelical thought. In the South, however, evangelicalism was still a virtually unchallenged establishment. Southerners had made stringent efforts to keep their religion intact since the Civil War, as evidenced by the late nineteenth-century prosecutions of several professors for heresy.

Up until the 1920s fundamentalism developed its distinct character mostly in the North.[13] Then its rise to prominence and early successes in the 1920s exerted an immediate appeal on many Southerners. The Northern controversies reawakened Southern conservatives to the dangers of modernism—a term most Southerners since 1865 instinctively opposed. Southerners in the Southern Baptist Convention and the Southern Presbyterian Church (the Presbyterian Church in the U.S.), quickly adopted moderate declarations of loyalty to the fundamental doctrines of the faith. Evolutionism had long symbolized to the South the inroads of liberal culture. It was now the focus of concurrent controversies over public education, and was especially feared by Southern conservatives. For the most part Southerners retained their own religious style and identity, but some were beginning to find in Northern fundamentalists an identifiable group of outsiders who might be trusted. Even the most moderate liberalism, on the other hand, while present in Southern churches, was widely viewed with suspicion.[14]

The closest parallels to the major Northern controversies were not in the Southern United States, but in Canada. Protestant groups in Canada had many contacts with those in the States, and the transdenominational impact of both liberalism and fundamentalism was felt simultaneously in both countries. On the other hand, Canadian Protestants also had a distinct British heritage. In the States, church union efforts collapsed after World War I, but in Canada they led to the formation of the United Church of Canada in 1925. The strongest opposition to this Methodist, Presbyterian, and Congregational union came from Presbyterian conservatives, who kept about a third of their denomination out of the union.

Direct carry-overs from the United States controversies were found among Canadian Baptists. T. T. Shields of Toronto, although not a dispensationalist, was one of the most militant leaders of the Baptist Bible Union. During the early 1920s in the Baptist Convention of Ontario and Quebec, Shields kept up a steady, well supported and vitriolic attack on modernism at McMaster University. The issue was not settled until 1926 when a Convention majority managed to censure Shields, precipitating his break away to the Union of

Regular Baptists of Ontario and Quebec in 1927. In the same year, Baptists in Western Canada, where dispensationalist influences were stronger, experienced a similar schism. As in the States, fundamentalist influences in Canada were not confined to major denominations, but could be found in Holiness groups such as the Salvation Army, and in smaller immigrant denominations.[15]

In 1924 and 1925, however, the principal theaters of action were the large Baptist and Presbyterian denominations in the Northern United States, where liberalism was under such heavy assault that it could not even win by direct frontal attack. Mathews and others attempted to persuade the denominations that modernism was a legitimate and superior form of Christianity. A far more effective counterattack, however, was the appeal to the strong American tradition of tolerance. In most American churches this ideal, at least in theory, was regarded as almost sacred. Liberals could cite this tradition as they attempted to gain support in the Northern denominations from large middle parties not firmly committed. Thus began to break up the fundamentalist coalitions. Under strong pressure to disown the fundamentalists' avowed position of intolerance, many conservatives fell back. Only the most militant held to the logic that, if modernism was not eliminated, the churches must be divided.

This was the most effective countermove of the antifundamentalist forces in the Presbyterian Church. In reaction against the 1923 decisions that condemned Fosdick and reaffirmed the "five points," a group of ministers worked for several months following the General Assembly to draw up a public protest. In January 1924 they issued the "Auburn Affirmation" for which they secured some thirteen hundred signatures by the time of the 1924 Assembly. This protest asserted, on constitutional grounds that had been upheld by progressive parties since 1729, that Presbyterian ministers had some liberty in interpreting the Westminister Confession of Faith, the church's official statement of Biblical teaching. Furthermore, the protest emphasized that the five-point declaration was both extra-constitutional and extra-Biblical. The insistence on the inerrancy of Scripture, they said, went beyond both the Confession and the Bible's own statements. Furthermore, in its key passage, the Affirmation declared that the five-point declaration committed the church to "certain theories" concerning inspiration, the Incarnation, the Atonement, the Resurrection, and the supernatural power of Christ. Fellowship within the Presbyterian Chuuch, the signers affirmed, should be broad enough to include any people who like themselves held "most earnestly to these great facts and doctrines," regardless of the theories they employed to explain them.[16]

Although most of the signers apparently held moderate or liberal theological positions, a few were known conservatives.[17] In fact, by 1924 it was becoming evident that there were at least three major parties in the Presbyterian controversy. There were the theological progressives (moderate or liberal) who were clearly a minority party, but with strength in many seminaries and in the church hierarchy. They, of course, took an inclusivist view of the denomination. Joining them was a key swing group who were conservative theologically, yet who took an inclusivist position largely because they did not wish theological issues to destroy the peace, unity, and evangelical outreach of the church. Opposing them were the conservative exclusivists or militants, now generally known as fundamentalists.[18]

From the outset of the 1924 General Assembly, its central feature was the division between the inclusivist conservatives and the exclusivists. The fundamentalist champion, Clarence Macartney was the exclusivist candidate for Moderator. His opponent was Professor Charles R. Erdman of Princeton Seminary. Erdman had all the credentials of a fundamentalist save one. He was conservative theologically, a premillennialist, and a contributor to *The Fundamentals.* But he lacked militancy. The failure to enlist Erdman and his like would in the long run be devastating to the exclusivist cause. In the short run they managed barely enough votes to elect Macartney, but were not able to find leverage in the available constitutional procedures to accomplish much else. The Fosdick question was settled by inviting Fosdick to join the Presbyterian Church—in effect an invitation for him to let himself be tried for heresy. This move, in fact, ensured Fosdick's resignation from his New York pulpit. Even this accomplishment had involved dealing with substantial doctrinal issues only in an indirect manner. Exclusivists found no effective way to challenge the signers of the Auburn Affirmation, and other attempts to impose general doctrinal tests failed.[19]

Despite the wide national interest in and substantial popularity of fundamentalism in 1924, the same problems that were impeding fundamentalist efforts in the Presbyterian Church were also rife among the Northern Baptists. The Baptist fundamentalists had even less leverage for centralized or constitutional control of doctrine, and the extreme demands of many of the premillennialists had apparently forced other "fundamentalists" into a conservative-inclusivist position. In 1923, rather than make any attempt to dominate the Convention itself, most of the extreme militants had turned their attention to the formation of the Baptist Bible Union. When they returned in 1924 they found the original "fundamentalist" party in the middle, conciliatory position, with premillennialist J. C. Massee playing a role similar to that of Erdman among the Presbyterians. As the convention preacher, Massee affirmed the ideals of the revivalist tradition with sentiments reminiscent of Dwight L. Moody, calling for a moratorium on debate in order to get to the main business of soul-winning.[20] Perhaps it was the tension between these two conflicting emphases—the fight against apostasy on the one hand, soul-winning on the other—that kept many potential fundamentalists from full identification with fundamentalist attitudes. Fundamentalism, as a coalition built around anti-modernism, was always a part of a larger evangelical tradition. Even among the most militant fundamentalists, soul-winning or missionary emphasis was mixed with their exclusivistic doctrinal vigilance. Some who might have considered themselves fundamentalists on the basis of their doctrinal commitments found that when all was said and done their doctrinal militancy was not as strong as their zeal for spreading the Gospel. These sentiments, together with strong denominational loyalties, prevented formation of large organized groups willing to purge the denominations even at the cost of major schism.

The Baptists might still combat liberalism in the mission field—clearly an area of denomination-wide concern and practical consequence. At the 1924 Convention the militant Bible Union fundamentalists were prepared to press the case against one particular missionary who had been sent out by the Foreign Mission Board although he had refused to affirm some of the fundamentals. The moderate fundamentalists, however, led by Massee, agreed with the liberals on a compromise in which a committee was appointed to investigate Northern Baptist Missions generally. As is inevitable with the appointment of committees, this blunted the attack of the militants who were by this time thoroughly disillusioned with the moderate fundamentalist leadership.[21] In 1925 the appointed committee reported that, although there were some scattered cases where concern might be justified, the vast majority of the Convention's missionaries were doctrinally sound. Rather than suggesting any specific doctrinal test, the committee proposed that the Convention should ensure that missionaries were, in effect, warm evangelicals.

Pro-fundamentalist sentiments were still strong, and at this point the militant Baptists made their last move that had any reasonable hope of success. Starting from the liberals' 1922 resolution that the New Testament was the sole Baptist creed, they spelled out some of the specific "fundamentals of the faith" (divine creation, supernatural inspiration of Scripture, Virgin Birth of Christ, other aspects of Christ's person and work, and the necessity of regeneration). Following the Presbyterian example, they suggested these as doctrines for testing the orthodoxy of missionaries. A tactical delay in bringing this proposal to a vote may have caused its failure,[22] but at any rate, the move was defeated and the counsels of peace prevailed. Moderate conservatives promoted reconciliation. J. Whitcomb Brougher was especially effective in urging the Convention to get rid of extremists of both kinds. The real work of the Convention, he said in a speech entitled "Play Ball," was evangelism. Again the fear of an all-out internal war destroying the evangelical witness of the denomination stopped the militant advance just when it seemed on the verge of success.[23]

The fury of the militants was now directed against those conservatives who had undermined the movement by yielding to compromise when victory was possible. In a typical statement the fiery T. T. Shields declared that he had more respect for Harry Emerson Fosdick than for J. Whitcomb Brougher. Fosdick, said Shields, at least wore the uniform of the enemy. "Dr. Brougher has worn the uniform of orthodoxy; and while wearing it, has betrayed the Baptist cause absolutely to the enemy."[24] Similarly, Riley said concerning Massee's defection: "This is not a battle; it is a war from which there is no discharge."[25] This issue was dividing the fundamentalist camp, and it revealed some underlying ambivalence within the movement. Both sides had the same goal—the preservation of doctrinal purity and the promotion of evangelism. Both were militant to a degree, although some of the original fundamentalists defected once the consequences for evangelism became apparent. In addition, there was disagreement about whether the movement was sectarian or establishmentarian. Was their goal to create a pure church, even at the expense of becoming outsiders, or was it simply to clean up the traditional, socially acceptable denominations? Most of the fundamentalist leaders tried at first to work within the denominations and if they eventually left they did so only with reluctance when they were convinced that there was no hope.

In the Presbyterian Church also, 1925 was the peak year for fundamentalist strength, and the militants came even closer than their Baptist counterparts to victory. In fact, they seemed to have won some major battles but were then outmaneuvered by the action that proved decisive in the war. The moderates played a decisive role in the defeat of the militants, who reacted as bitterly as their Baptist counterparts.

Between the 1924 and 1925 meetings of the Presbyterian General Assembly this tension grew among the faculty of Princeton Theological Seminary. In that relatively small body were found two conservatives who represented diametrically opposite approaches to dealing with theological liberalism. J. Gresham Machen viewed the new theology somewhat as a medieval Pope or the Puritans in Massachusetts would have viewed the preaching of Mohammedanism in their respective churches. He saw it as another religion and there was no excuse for anyone who claimed to love the faith to tolerate it. At the opposite pole his colleague, Charles Erdman, was the leader of the conservative group who worked for reconciliation. During the school year of 1924–1925, Machen stated in public, as well as privately to a number of dedicated students and correspondents, his opinion of Erdman's willingness to consort with the enemy. Erdman replied indignantly and there followed a protracted, well publicized, and acrimonious dispute. Both sides attempted to enlist sympathetic delegates to the 1925 Assembly, at which Erdman would again be the inclusivist candidate for Moderator. Machen insisted that it was not a matter of personalities, but one of doctrine. "It concerns the question not of this doctrine or that, but of the importance which is attributed to doctrine as such."[26] "Dr. Erdman," Machen added, "despite his personal orthodoxy, had the plaudits of the enemies of the gospel." The exclusivists, on the other hand, "bore the reproach of Christ." They had "laid aside all personal considerations and stood for the defense of the Christian faith."[27]

These attacks were probably counterproductive. At the 1925 General Assembly, Erdman was elected Moderator, despite the fact that the exclusivists seemed to have a slight working majority. The exclusivists used this strength to pass a report of the Judicial Commission dealing with the situation in the New York Presbytery. This measure allowed the Assembly to review the Presbytery's ordination of ministerial candidates who had refused to affirm the five-point doctrinal test. This was precisely the judicial procedure the exclusivists needed to begin uprooting liberalism. The liberal party was dismayed by this Assembly action, which would have severely limited their freedom. By the most dramatic move in the controversy, the threatened defeat was turned into an inclusivist victory. Henry Sloan Coffin of New York, perhaps the best known of the Presbyterian liberals, "rushed to the platform" and read a prepared statement from the Presbytery of New York, declaring in effect that the Assembly's action was unconstitutional and that the New York Presbytery would not comply with it. Here was a scene and an issue that closely resembled that which had split the denomination the previous century. A New School party stood defiant against an Old School effort to force New York Presbyterians into doctrinal conformity. Although much more important theological issues were involved this time, in the 1920s among Presbyterians there was far less willingness to split the denomination even at the expense of important doctrinal questions. In the tense moments that followed Coffin's declaration, the inclusivists made their next carefully planned move. Erdman, leaving the Moderator's chair, proposed that a special commission be appointed to study the spiritual condition of the church and report back to the next Assembly. This motion received wide support, and was seconded by both Coffin and William Jennings Bryan.[28]

It was not immediately obvious that the exclusivist fundamentalist movement in the Presbyterian Church would be killed by referral to a committee. In fact, it was. The working strength of fundamentalism everywhere depended greatly upon the national mood. In the early summer of 1925 fundamentalism was at its peak; by the next year its strength was rapidly sinking.

XXI. Epilogue: Dislocation, Relocation, and Resurgence: 1925–1940

It would be difficult to overestimate the impact of "the Monkey Trial" at Dayton, Tennessee, in transforming fundamentalism. William Jennings Bryan's ill-fated attempt in the summer of 1925 to slay singlehanded the prophets of Baal brought instead an outpouring of derision. The rural setting, so well suited to the stereotypes of the agrarian leader and his religion, stamped the entire movement with an indelible image. Very quickly, the conspicuous reality of the movement seemed to conform to the image thus imprinted and the strength of the movement in the centers of national life waned precipitously.

It was part of the liberals' contention that the issues separating them from the fundamentalists were determined by social forces. As Shailer Mathews put it in *The Faith of Modernism*, "the differences between these two types of Christians are not so much religious as due to different degrees of sympathy with the social and cultural forces of the day."[1] While the fundamentalists argued that the acceptance or rejection of unchanging truth was at issue, the modernists insisted that the perception of truth was inevitably shaped by cultural circumstances. By modernist definition fundamentalists were those who for sociological reasons held on to the past in stubborn and irrational resistance to inevitable changes in culture.

The scene at Dayton in 1925 was unsurpassable as a confirmation of this interpretation. Here were the elements of a great American drama—farce, comedy, tragedy, and pathos. Mark Twain and H. L. Mencken in collaboration could hardly have scripted it better. This bizarre episode, wired around the world with a maximum of ballyhoo, would have far more impact on the popular interpretation of fundamentalism than all the arguments of preachers and theologians.

The central theme was, inescapably, the clash of two worlds, the rural and the urban. In the popular imagination, there were on the one side the small town, the backwoods, half-educated yokels, obscurantism, crackpot hawkers of religion, fundamentalism, the South, and the personification of the agrarian myth himself, William Jennings Bryan. Opposed to these were the city, the clique of New York-Chicago lawyers, intellectuals, journalists, wits, sophisticates, modernists, and the cynical agnostic Clarence Darrow. These images evoked the familiar experiences of millions of Americans who had been born in the country and moved to the city or who were at least witnessing the dramatic shift from a predominantly rural to a predominantly urban culture. *Main Street,* Sinclair Lewis's famous portrait of the dullness of small-town America, had since its publication in 1920 furnished a potent symbol of the rural America from which people of education and culture escaped. Dayton surpassed all fiction in dramatizing the symbolic last stand of nineteenth-century America against the twentieth century.

Since 1923 several Southern states had adopted some type of anti-evolution legislation, and similar bills were pending throughout the nation. The law passed in Tennessee in the spring of 1925 was the strongest. It banned the teaching of Darwinism in any public school. This law was immediately tested by a young Dayton biology teacher, John Scopes. Scopes was brought to trial in that small mountain town in July. For his defense, the American Civil Liberties Union supplied three of the eminent lawyers of the day, headed by Darrow, who had recently served as counsel for the defense in the notorious Leopold and Loeb trial. William Jennings Bryan, seizing the chance to meet the enemy head-on, volunteered his services to the prosecution.

Scopes was found guilty of teaching evolution (the decision was subsequently reversed on a technicality). But in the trial by public opinion and the press, it was clear that the twentieth century, the cities, and the universities had won a resounding victory, and that the country, the South, and the fundamentalists were guilty as charged. No doubt anything Bryan said would have been seized upon by the press and labeled foolishness. Bryan did not, however, make the task especially difficult. He was better at oratory than debate, but at the height of the proceedings he allowed himself to be cross-examined by the greatest trial lawyer of the day on the subject of the precise accuracy of the Bible. Having urged the self-evident superiority of Biblical faith to infidelity before so many audiences, Bryan could hardly refuse such an opportunity. "I want the papers to know, " he said, "I am not afraid to get on the stand in front of him and let him do his worst."[2] The result was a debacle. Darrow forced Bryan into admitting that he could not answer the standard village-atheist type questions regarding the literal inter-pretation of Scripture. Bryan did not know how Eve could be created from Adam's rib, where Cain got his wife, or where the great fish came from that swallowed Jonah. He said that he had never contemplated what would happen if the earth stopped its rotation so that the sun would "stand still." More importantly, Darrow uncovered Bryan's ignorance of the modern literature concerning the origin of ancient religions. Incapable of dealing with many specifics, Bryan was forced to admit that he never had been much

Bryan arrives at Dayton. From *The Memoirs of William Jennings Bryan,* by himself and his wife, Mary Baird Bryan (Philadelphia, 1925).

interested in examining the claims of other religions. Nor had he read critical accounts of the origins of Scripture. In a masterpiece of ridicule Darrow brought the point home. He led Bryan reluctantly to say that he basically accepted Bishop Ussher's chronology as printed in many Bibles. Pressing the advantage, Darrow continued: "When was that flood?"

BRYAN: I would not attempt to fix the date. The date is fixed as suggested this morning.

. . .

DARROW: But what do you think that the Bible itself says? Don't you know how it was arrived at?

BRYAN: I never made a calculation.

DARROW: A calculation from what?

BRYAN: I could not say.

DARROW: From the generations of man?

BRYAN: I would not want to say that.

DARROW: What do you think?

BRYAN: I do not think about things I don't think about.

DARROW: Do you think about things you do think about?

BRYAN: Well, sometimes.[3]

Modern liberal culture was fighting back against the efforts of "bigots and ignoramuses" (as Darrow described them)[4] to retard its progress, and ridicule was perhaps the most effective weapon.

H. L. Mencken revelled in a scene so superbly suited to his talents for derision. In his anti-eulogy to Bryan, who died in Dayton the Sunday after the trial ended, Mencken did not let mere death blunt the sting of his satirical wit. The fundamentalist cause was synonymous with rural backwardness. It was appropriate, he observed, that Bryan had spent his last days in a "one-horse Tennessee village," because Bryan loved all country people, including the "gaping primates of the upland valleys," and delighted in "greasy victuals of the farmhouse kitchen, country smells," and "the tune of cocks crowing on the dunghill." Bryan had made the grade of a country saint. "His place in Tennessee hagiography is secure. If the village barber saved any of his hair, then it is curing gall-stones down there today."

Moreover, Mencken assured his readers, "what moved him at bottom, was simply hatred of the city men who had laughed at him so long, and brought him at last to so tatterdemalion an estate." Bryan "knew all the while that they were laughing at him—if not at his baroque theology, then at least at his alpaca pantaloons." He had "lived too long, and descended too deeply into the mud, to be taken seriously hereafter by fully literate men, even of the kind who write school-books." The heyday of American democracy might have seemed 1896 when Bryan was nearly elected, but Bryan had "lived long enough to make patriots thank the inscrutable gods for Harding, even for Coolidge." Mencken did not dismiss fundamentalism's continuing threat to modern culture. "Heave an egg out a Pullman window" he said, "and you will hit a Fundamentalist almost anywhere in the United States today."

> [Fundamentalists] are thick in the mean streets behind the gas-works. They are everywhere where learning is too heavy a burden for mortal minds to carry, even the vague, pathetic learning on tap in the little red schoolhouses. They march with the Klan, with the Christian Endeavor Society, with the Junior Order of United American Mechanics, with the Epworth League, with all the Rococo bands that poor and unhappy folk organize to bring some new light of purpose into their lives. They have had a thrill and they are ready for more.[5]

Two things had changed in the image of fundamentalism now presented by Mencken. Its meaning had expanded considerably. "Fundamentalism" now applied to almost every aspect of American rural or small-town Protestantism. Only those facets that might include a modicum of intellectual respectability, integrity, or social value were excepted. Fundamentalism thus ceased to refer specifically to groups with identifiable Protestant traditions and organized in opposition to modernism. Nevertheless, there was some justification for the expanded use of the term; extensive national publicity had in fact aroused distinctly fundamentalist concerns in a great many more people and religious groups than the movement had previously encompassed. Moreover, at least temporarily, fundamentalism was a focal point for the real hostility of rural America toward much of modern culture and intellect. This rural element was not entirely new to fundamentalism. Some tent-meeting revivalists had long been capitalizing on anti-liberal sentiments. Yet this element had never before been central to the movement. Fundamentalism had been predominantly urban with its strength in the northern and eastern sections of the country. In the past, when its opponents had tried to discern the social base of the movement, they had not perceived a rural-urban dichotomy but were rather inclined to suspect that fundamentalism was controlled by conservative business and political interests.[6]

Another consequence of the Menckenesque caricature of fundamentalism that held sway after 1925, was the obscurantist label that would ever after stick to fundamentalists. Nor could they raise the level of discourse to a plane where any of their arguments would be taken seriously. Whatever they said would be overshadowed by the pejorative associations attached to the movement by the seemingly victorious secular establishment. This image of fundamentalism was strengthened, for example, by Sinclair Lewis's novel, *Elmer Gantry*, published in 1927. While Gantry was hardly a true fundamentalist, he was in part patterned after New York City's John Roach Straton. Gantry was a charlatan who adopted fundamenalist rhetoric largely because he was not bright enough to understand liberalism and because it served the purposes of his sensational campaigns for moral reform. Lewis was eager to expose any hypocritical use of religion, but he took an especially dim view of fundamentalists. "Men technically called 'Fundamentalists,'" in his account, "saw that a proper school should teach nothing but bookkeeping, agriculture, geometry, dead languages made deader by leaving out all the amusing literature, and the Hebrew Bible as interpreted by men superbly trained to ignore contradictions."[7] "For the first time in our history," declared Maynard Shipley in his *War on Modern Science*, appearing the same year, "organized knowledge has come into open conflict with organized ignorance. "If the 'self-styled fundamentalists' gain their objective of a political takeover," warned Shipley, "much of the best that has been gained in American culture will be suppressed or banned, and we shall be headed backward toward the pall of the Dark Age."[8]

The furious activities of fundamentalists themselves, especially in the two years following 1925, as they scrambled to raise the banner dropped by the fallen Bryan, lent credibility to such assertions. Fundamentalists across the country had been organizing vociferous anti-evolution lobbies under the leadership of such organizations as the World's Christian Fundamentals Association and the related Anti-evolution League. George F. Washburn, a friend of Bryan's, although not previously an active fundamentalist, proclaimed himself "the successor of William Jennings Bryan." He founded the Bible Crusaders of America, inducing a number of fundamentalist leaders to join the fight "Back to Christ, the Bible, and the Constitution." Other friends of Bryan undertook massive money-raising drives, with the intention of creating a William Jennings Bryan University. Meanwhile, in California, evangelist Paul W. Rood reported a vision from God calling *him* to be Bryan's successor, which led to the formation of the Bryan Bible League. Next, Gerald Winrod of Kansas founded the Defenders of the Christian Faith, another organization using the methods of sensationalism to fight evolution and modernism. Winrod sent a squadron of "flying fundamentalists" through the Midwest and elsewhere to promote the anti-evolution cause. Edgar Young Clarke, a former national organizer for the Ku Klux Klan, attempted to cash in on this trend with the foundation of the Supreme Kingdom, which was structured like the Klan but had fundamentalist anti-modernist and anti-evolutionary goals.[9]

All of these efforts either were short-lived or fell far below their founders' expectations. Anti-evolution political agitation in the United States, although major efforts continued until about 1928, was losing as much support from moderates as it gained from extremists. Its real successes remained confined to handful of states, mainly in the South.[10]

The literature of these organizations contained much that was bizarre. The rhetoric of Washburn's Bible Crusaders is a classic example of what Richard Hofstadter has since designated the "paranoid style" in elements of American thought.[11] "Thirty years ago," announced the *Crusaders' Champion* in 1926, "five men met in Boston and formed a conspiracy which we believe to be of

German origin, to secretly and persistently work to overthrow the fundamentals of the Christian religion of this country." Emissaries of this organization, who at times "masqueraded as higher critics" and at others were
"posing as fundamentalists," had led America into a "moral breakdown"
evidenced by "a great tidal wave of crime, . . . Sunday desecration, an
alarming increase in divorces, and a tremendous drop in moral standards
and ideals."[12] With literature of this sort being cranked from presses around
the country, opponents of fundamentalism hardly needed to resort to caricature.

The activities of some of its established national leaders did not help the
fundamentalist image either. J. Frank Norris, the leading fundamentalist
organizer in Texas, had already won such notoriety among his fellow Southern Baptists that he had been successively banned from local, county, and
state organizations. He kept up an ongoing warfare with the Southern Baptist Convention, which he openly despised. Accusing the conservative body of
tolerating modernists and evolutionists, Norris consistently referred to the
Southern Baptist leadership as "the Sanhedrin." He called one leading
Texas pastor "the Infallible Baptist Pope," "the Great All-I-Am," and "the
Holy Father." Another was "the Old Baboon." In Fort Worth, Norris pur-
sued civic reforms with a similar combination of colorful rhetoric and personal attack. He preached, for instance, on the theme, "The Ten Biggest
Devils in Ft. Worth, Names Given." In 1926 such a campaign was directed
against "Rum and Romanism," particularly attacking H. C. Meacham,
Roman Catholic mayor of the city, on charges of channeling city funds to
Roman Catholic institutions. Meacham, said Norris, "isn't fit to be a man-
ager of a hog-pen." In response, D. E. Chipps, a friend of Meacham, threatened Norris by phone, and then came to his study. After a heated exchange,
Norris shot and killed Chipps. The jury readily ruled it self-defense, but the
image of Norris and fundamentalist Christianity was seriously damaged by
the incident.[13]

A few years later T. T. Shields of Toronto, another of the leading figures
in the Baptist Bible Union, became involved in an incident that received
sensational national publicity like the Norris case. In 1927 the Baptist Bible
Union took over the failing Baptist institution, Des Moines University in
Iowa. Fundamentalists at that time were very interested in establishing a
bastion of conservative learning. Shields, the president of the Baptist Bible
Union, came to Des Moines as acting president of the university. In 1928 he
secured H. C. Wayman as the school's president; but almost at once Shields
and Wayman had a falling out. The situation was complicated by charges
that Wayman's academic degrees were phony. The infighting and widespread espionage and accusations by students, faculty, and administration,
culminated when in the spring of 1929 Shields was accused of having an
affair with Miss Edith Rebman, secretary of the Baptist Bible Union and of
the College. Finally, while the college board was meeting, a student riot

against Shields brought about the total collapse of Des Moines University. Shields dropped out of active participation in American fundamentalism, and returned to Canada where he remained a notorious opponent of "modernism and Romanism."[14]

These bizarre developments in fundamentalist activities meant that in the years after 1925 it became increasingly difficult to take fundamentalism seriously. Even those not predisposed to ridicule the movement, could hardly ignore so many aberrations. Walter Lippmann argued in 1929 that the fundamentalists were in fact pointing out the central issues in modern civilization, and described Machen's *Christianity and Liberalism* as "the best popular argument produced by either side in the current controversy." Nevertheless, argument could not be wholly detached from practice. "In actual practice," said Lippmann, "this movement has become entangled with all sorts of bizarre and barbarous agitations with the Ku Klux Klan, with fanatical prohibition, with the 'anti-evolution laws' and with much persecution and intolerance." Such practice, he said, "shows that the central truth, which the fundamentalists have grasped, no longer appeals to the best brains and the good sense of the modern community, and that the movement is recruited largely from the isolated, the inexperienced, and the uneducated."[15]

It would be oversimplification to attribute the decline and the disarray of fundamentalism after 1925 to any one factor. It does appear, however, that the movement began in reality to conform to its popular image. The more ridiculous it was made to appear, the more genuinely ridiculous it was likely to become. The reason was simple. Lippmann was correct that the assumptions of even the best of the fundamentalist arguments were not acceptable to the best educated minds of the twentieth century. Before 1925 the movement had commanded much respect, though not outstanding support, but after the summer of 1925 the voices of ridicule were raised so loudly that many moderate Protestant conservatives quietly dropped support of the cause rather than be embarrassed by association.

The most solid evidence of the dramatic decline in fundamentalist influence is found in the two denominations where the controversies had been fiercest. From 1922 to 1925 fundamentalists were close to gaining control of the Northern Presbyterian and Northern Baptist groups. Suddenly in 1926 they were much weakened minorities. Perhaps members were simply tired of the acrimony of debate, and the national fundamentalist fad had played itself out. There is no sure explanation for the decline. The simplest explanation lies in the sordid and reactionary cultural image it had acquired.

"To many people," observed the *Christian Century* in mid-1926, "so decisive a rout of fundamentalism was unexpected." The prevailing liberal understanding of fundamentalism, that the movement was governed by naturalistic principles of social development, should have anticipated the sudden withering of fundamentalism however. "Looking at it as an event now passed," the victorious *Century* continued, "anybody should be able to see that the whole fundamentalist movement was hollow and artificial. . . . If we may use a biological term, fundamentalism has been a *sport*, and accidental phenomenon making its sudden appearance in our ecclesiastical order, but wholly lacking the qualities of constructive achievement or survival." The luxuriant and grotesque flowering of the movement had been based on nothing more than a temporary and abnormal social environment. Some offshoots would be found here and there for some time, but "it is henceforth to be a disappearing quantity in American religious life, while our churches go on to larger isssues. . . ."[16]

With respect to the major denominations, the *Christian Century*'s estimate appeared to be exactly right. In the Presbyterian Church, the Special Commission—appointed in 1925 as a response to conservative charges against the Presbytery of New York—urged the General Assembly in 1926 and again in 1927 to exercise toleration and rejected Machen's exclusivist definition of the issue. The exclusivists could do nothing to stem the tide, and the reports were adopted overwhelmingly.[17] The inclusivists had mounted a sharp counterattack. In 1926 Machen had been elected by the Princeton Seminary boards to the important chair of apologetics and ethics, and in response to the inclusivist outcry, the Assembly of 1926 delayed his appointment and named a committee to investigate the controversies at Princeton Seminary. As a result, in 1929 the seminary's government was reorganized to ensure a broader representation of theological positions. Machen and his followers immediately withdrew and founded their own institution, Westminster Theological Seminary in Philadelphia.

During the next years the Presbyterian exclusivists beat a bitter retreat. In 1933, unable to inhibit the spread of liberal teachings in the foreign mission fields, Machen inaugurated his own Independent Board for Presbyterian Foreign Missions. With conservative representation reduced to scarcely more than one tenth of the delegates, the Assembly of 1934 moved to ban Presbyterian office-holders from participation on the Independent Board. Machen's refusal to comply led to a trial in 1935 and suspension from the ministry. In 1936 he and a few followers left to found what became known as "The Orthodox Presbyterian Church." At the inauguration of the new group Machen declared with relief that it was a "true Presbyterian church at last."[18] Yet few were willing to follow the principle to this conclusion. Almost all the leading figures of the conservative movement, excepting a few younger men, dropped away as the prospect of expulsion or schism appeared. A number of important leaders such as Clarence Macartney continued to proclaim the conservative cause in strong local congregations within the larger Presbyterian Church, but anti-modernism ceased to be a force at the national level. Machen died of pneumonia in the winter of 1937 while singlehandedly attempting to rally handfuls of supporters in the Dakotas—an ironic end to to a life dedicated to bringing Christianity to the centers of culture.[19]

By 1925 the Northern Baptist fundamentalists, although numerically strong, were seriously divided over the central issue of whether the movement should take an establishmentarian or a sectarian direction. This tension was aggravated by those premillennialists, with more exclusivist and sectarian leanings, as represented by the radical Baptist Bible Union, formed in 1923. The original "fundamentalists," who formed the Fundamentalist Federation, were determined on the other hand to work within the denomination. This split continued to grow as J. C. Massee, President of the Federation, pushed the movement in a moderate direction until late in 1925 he dropped his fundamentalist affiliations altogether.[20] By the 1926 meeting of the Northern Baptist Convention, the militant forces, under the leadership of William B. Riley, were greatly reduced in number. They could now muster less than one fourth of the votes, for the effort to ensure othodoxy in the mission field, and an effort to make immersion a prerequisite for Baptist membership was defeated by a similarly decisive margin.[21] In Canada, T. T. Shields, one of the strongest voices in the Baptist Bible Union, was another victim of the fundamentalist decline of 1926. Censured by the Baptist Convention of Ontario and Quebec, he withdrew to form his own denomination.

By 1927 the Northern Baptist Convention was close to peace. Most of the Baptist Bible Union was beginning to move in a separatist direction, while moderate conservatives worked more quietly from within. In 1932 the Baptist Bible Union changed its name to the General Association of Regular Baptists and became a small denomination.[22] In the new Association (as within many Baptist churches that simply became independent congregations), separation became a new test of faith as it did among Machen's followers. Even among the premillennial militants many were unwilling to make this move. Some remained to fight a rear-guard action in the denomination. In 1947, however, there was a repetition of what had happened among the Presbyterians in the 1930s. A Convention ban on a new conservative missions agency led to the formation of a new denomination, the Conservative Baptist Association of America.[23] The most famous of those militants who resisted separation was William B. Riley. In the 1930s he had continued the fight through his dwindling World's Christian Fundamentals Association. By the 40s, however, the aging Riley gave up the effort to control the denomination, and in 1947, the last year of his life, he resigned his membership in the Northern Baptist Convention. Although he did not know it, he had by this time established the link between his work and the resurgent non-separatist fundamentalism (eventually to be known as neo-evangelicalism or evangelicalism) by securing the young Billy Graham to succeed him as president of the Northwestern School in Minneapolis. In 1947, however, to anyone who equated American religious life with the major denominations, fundamentalism was a bizarre American episode now fast fading into oblivion.

Fundamentalism, while fading from the reputed centers of American life since 1925, was in fact taking solid root in other, less conspicuous areas. The movement had entered into a distinct new phase. The effort to purge the leading denominations having failed, the leadership now re-emphasized working through local congregations and independent agencies, such as Bible schools and mission organizations. Local pastors, often independent from major denominations either formally or simply in practice, built fundamentalist empires both large and small.[24] With all the variety fostered by American religious free enterprise, countless groups were formed to promote the causes that national fundamentalism had recently publicized. Radio, peculiarly suited to the revivalist style, gave new impetus to the movement. Bible schools flourished, with twenty-six new schools founded during the depression years of the 1930s. Other important new institutions of learning, such as Dallas Theological Seminary and Bob Jones University, became significant centers for branches of the movement. Wheaton College was for several years during the 1930s the fastest growing liberal arts college in the nation. A network of similar colleges grew in size and influence. Fundamentalist publications increased in circulation; summer Bible conferences and other youth movements attracted the young; mission agencies continued to grow. In general, although the rest of American Protestantism floundered in the 1930s, fundamentalist groups, or those at least with fundamentalist sympathies, increased. As Joel Carpenter remarks in explaining this upsurge, fundamentalism played a role parallel to that of neo-orthodoxy among intellectuals. It "provided ordinary people with as compelling a critique of modern society."[25]

Among the denominations, fundamentalism had a perceptible impact on many groups that had never been at the center of American religious life. The Southern Baptist Convention, which in the 1920s had manifested substantial affinities to fundamentalism, gained almost one and a half million members during the next fifteen years.[26] At the same time, some explicitly fundamentalist separatist groups flourished in opposition to the more moderately evangelical revivalism of the Southern Baptist Convention. Fundamentalism began to take on more of a Southern accent as such leading figures as Bob Jones and John R. Rice established headquarters in the South. Other groups outside the traditional centers of influence in American cultural life were attracted by the fundamentalist emphases. Holiness and Pentecostal groups, in spite of their different dynamics, shared common background with fundamentalists and were influenced by anti-modernist tendencies. In many places the two traditions began to merge and become part of a discernable new subculture.[27]

Many from immigrant groups were attracted to fundamentalist principles. Perhaps militant anti-modernists' ambivalence toward aspects of American culture resembled theirs. Cutting across a variety of previous traditions, fundamentalist movements and influences grew among a variety of new Americans. Baptists, Methodists, Free Church movements, Lutherans, and Reformed all had fundamentalist offshoots. The Evangelical Free Church and the Swedish Baptists, for example, which came to play important roles in the new movement, lost much of their Scandinavian identity and became Americanized by taking on fundamentalist characteristics. Other denominations, including the Missouri Synod Lutheran and the Christian Reformed, were also Americanized to an extent by adopting some fundamentalist ideals while retaining other distinctive features of their European traditions.[28] Some older sects, such as the Quakers and Mennonites, which had always maintained their own distinctive characteristics, were now affected by some fundamentalist influences, and new groups, like the Evangelical Mennonites and the Evangelical Friends, were formed.[29] The evidence is somewhat sketchy, but there is little doubt that many independent Bible churches attracted considerable numbers of northern European ethnics, who found a congenial form of Americanism there.[30] The loosely organized fundamentalist-evangelical movement was perhaps not the largest in American Protestantism; it now had, however, a solid base of growing institutions which paralleled the older denominational establishments.[31]

The movement took three principal forms. Considerable groups within the major denominations identified themselves with the fundamentalist tradition, although they had now abandoned all hope of excluding the modernists. Second, there were substantial fundamentalist influences outside of the traditional dominant structures of American culture but within denominations that were not purely fundamentalist. In the South, in Holiness and Pentecostal movements, and in immigrant denominations, pietistic traditions were often reshaped by fundamentalist example and influence. Finally, some of the most extreme fundamentalists separated into their own denominations or into independent churches. These were mainly dispensationalists for whom strict separation was an article of faith. By about 1960, this wing of the movement was the only one that still chose to wear the badge of "fundamentalist."[32] Most of the other groups that had been touched by the fundamentalist experience of the 1920s re-emerged in a new post-fundamentalist coalition. Their basic attitude toward culture is suggested by their successful appropriation of the more culturally respectable term "evangelical." Yet, although this new evangelical sub-culture repudiated "fundamentalist" as too exclusivist in implication, "fundamentalistic" remains a useful adjective to describe many of its most conspicuous and controversial traits.

PART FOUR
Interpretations

XXII. Fundamentalism
as a Social Phenomenon

After 1925, the fragmentation and relocation of fundamentalism was taken by many observers for evidence of its disappearance. Fundamentalism, they assumed, was the offshoot of a social adjustment. As the interpretation of the original movement passed into the hands of the historians, this became a recurring theme. On the first page of his *History of Fundamentalism,* published in 1931, Stewart Cole pronounced, "For a half century the church has suffered a conflict of social forces about and within it that accounts for the present babel of witnesses to Christian truth and purpose."[1] H. Richard Niebuhr, writing in the mid-30s, emphasized the "social sources" of fundamentalism "closely related to the conflict between rural and urban cultures in America."[2] Statements like this abounded in textbooks on the 1920s.

After World War II many people were eager to discover the roots of the anti-intellectualism and extreme anti-liberalism prevalent in the McCarthy era. The fundamentalism of the 1920s seemed to provide an obvious precedent. Norman F. Furniss's *The Fundamentalist Controversy,* published in 1954, emphasized the anti-evolution aspect of fundamentalism and its predilection for ignorance in the face of new ideas. Two more popular works of the 50s, *Inherit the Wind,* a play by Jerome Lawrence and Robert E. Lee (1955), and Ray Ginger's popular history, *Six Days or Forever?* (1958), dramatized Bryan's last stand at Dayton. Both stressed the tension between rural and urban as a source of fundamentalist intolerance. The most subtle analysis of fundamentalist intolerance came from Richard Hofstadter in his *Anti-Intellectualism in American Life* and *The Paranoid Style in American Politics,* published in the early 60s. Hofstadter perceived status anxieties among fundamentalists. "By the end of the century," he wrote, "it was painfully clear to fundamentalists that they were losing much of their influence and respectability." Their anti-intellectualism and paranoid style were "shaped by a desire to strike back at everything modern—the higher criticism, evolutionism, the social gospel, rational criticism of any kind."[3]

The interpretation of fundamentalism as a side effect of the passing of an old order intimated that the movement would die away when the cultural transformation was complete and the social causes removed. William McLoughlin, whose outstanding work on American revivalism supplied Hofstadter with much of his material, subscribed to this "consensus" interpretation of American history. According to this view, American society develops toward a consensus of shared cultural values that eventually absorbs alien and dissenting elements. As this happens, the consensus itself gradually changes, leaving once dominant patterns to fade away after a period of upheaval and resistance. In McLoughlin's view fundamentalism represented the "Old Lights" who always appear in a time of religious change, while the more radical fringe-sects were the "inevitable emotional and institutional effluvia of a major alteration within Christendom." Even taken together, they did not constitute a "third force in Christendom" capable of replacing the established order.[4]

By the time McLoughlin published his analysis in 1967, this kind of sociological explanation of fundamentalism was beginning to come under fire. Some interpreters, moreover, were beginning to take the fundamentalists' doctrinal positions seriously. In 1955, in an important reinterpretation of fundamentalism, the neo-orthodox theologian William Hordern stated that "no system of thought can be judged by what fanatics do in its name."[5] According to an important text of the 1960s, "fundamentalism drew a necessary line between historic Christianity and naturalism, but it drew the line at the wrong place."[6] A trend was developing toward more balanced approaches.[7]

Ernest Sandeen provided the most influential critique of the social interpretations of fundamentalism. He pointed out that neither the fundamentalists' predictions of the end of the world nor the liberals' predictions of the end of fundamentalism had as yet come true. Sandeen showed that the roots of fundamentalism lay much deeper than the social upheaval of the 1920s. In refutation of the consensus interpreters, Sandeen pointed to the pluralistic nature of American society, a theme that was becoming increasingly popular in the 1960s: "We exist in a fragmented and divided culture, not in one pervaded by consensus." Therefore it was possible to regard fundamentalism as "an authentic conservative tradition," rather than the temporary aberration or "pseudo-conservative" departure that Hofstadter and other historians had seen.[8]

To arrive at this conclusion, Sandeen had to use an unusually narrow definition of the fundamentalist movement. Sometimes he maintained that fundamentalism before 1918 was an alliance between dispensationalism and Princeton theology.[9] Elsewhere he defined it even more narrowly. "The Fundamentalist movement of the 1920s was only the millenarian movement renamed."[10] This definition, which differentiated between the longer-lived millenarian-fundamentalist movement and the fundamentalist controversy of the 1920s, successfully undercut the social explanation. The social upheaval following World War I might explain the intensity of the denominational controversies or the anti-evolution crusade, but these outbursts were of little significance for understanding the essence of the movement.[11]

Sandeen's work was an important step toward taking fundamentalism seriously as a significant and lasting religious movement with its own types of organization and ways of thought. Moreover, he made important progress in uncovering some of its primary roots. Yet he mistook the roots he uncovered for the source of the entire movement. He failed to see that the lush and complex overgrowth of what was called "fundamentalism" in the 20s sprang from equally complex and tangled roots in the nineteenth-century traditions of revivalism, evangelicalism, pietism, Americanism, and variant orthodoxies.[12] Moreover, Sandeen provided fundamentalism with "an essentially theological definition."[13] His insistence on the integrity of the religious and intellectual aspects of the movement was a valuable corrective to those interpretations that reduced fundamentalism to its social dimensions. In attempting to restore balance, however, he went too far toward the opposite extreme.

What then can be said of the social dimensions of fundamentalism? While the present interpretation maintains that fundamentalism was first of all a religious movement, there is nonetheless no doubt that the sense of cultural crisis following World War I shaped and modified the movement in important ways. Certainly the postwar crisis helped to intensify feelings, increase militancy and harden resistance to change. The distinctive ideologies of the movement came to be waved like flags above the cultural field of battle. Extremism flourished in the midst of the conflicts, and extremists were attracted to the movement.

The cultural crisis of the 1920s was part of a wider movement of truly revolutionary cultural and intellectual change. At the time, the crisis was widely perceived as a conflict between urban and rural culture, but that was perhaps because extreme positions were most visible. The issues at stake had for two generations been affecting every aspect of American life, from the institutions of higher learning to the meanest village. In its later phases the conflict did have a rural-urban dimension; Sandeen is right, however, in asserting that this was not the essential issue.

The peculiarities of the American environment to some extent determined the specific forms the conflicts took. Living in a very large and new country still being settled at the same time that major internal cultural changes were taking place, Americans had an unusual degree of diversity in their acquaintance with new ideas and values. Rural-urban differences accentuated this diversity. The remarkable ethnic diversity was probably just as important. Long after a degree of Americanization had taken place, national groups, and even sub-groups from the same national origin, might have little interaction even when living in close proximity. Social prejudices were reinforced by denominational differences, which often entailed different institutions, including those of higher education.[14] Within ethnic and denominational groups, there might also be wide regional diversities. Northerners, Southerners, Easterners, and Westerners might have their first real encounter with a new idea decades, or even generations, apart.[15]

These circumstances greatly increased the probability of religious conflict when the diverse groups came into contact. World War I and the contemporaneous growth of the mass media accelerated that inevitable contact. Suddenly national consciousness overrode local and parochial concerns. Individuals with wide differences in background and belief were forced by the war to work closely together. Moreover, the overseas experience accentuated the "How-ya-gonna-keep-'em-down-on-the-farm-after-they've-seen-Paree" syndrome. One side effect was national paranoia and a chain reaction of crusades against various cultural enemies. There was a natural tendency to oversimplify the issues, and the media magnified and sensationalized these reactions.

It is thus possible to understand the timing of fundamentalism's rise to popularity, as well as its intensity and some of the accompanying extremism in terms of the social conditions of the day. Yet this is only a partial explanation. As emphasized by Sandeen, and effectively documented by Robert E. Wenger, fundamentalism's first principal centers of strength were urban and Northern. In the light of this fact the common social hypothesis, premised on the conflict between rural and urban, cannot stand.[16] On the other hand, Walter Ellis has presented some good, albeit limited evidence that liberals within a city or town were as a rule of somewhat higher social status than fundamentalists in the same community.[17] A similar pattern emerges in comparisons of fundamentalist and liberal leadership.[18] One might infer that this contrast would generally obtain. Liberal religion was essentially culture-affirming and hence would appeal to more cosmopolitan individuals as a form of Christianity that would not unduly disrupt their established ways of life. The "old" families of a community and those settled in one local church for generations would be most inclined toward such views. The growth of fundamentalist churches, conversely, was largely through conversions. Thus it would more likely come from among young people, recent arrivals in a community, and those outside the power centers of the culture. Unlike the radical Holiness and Pentecostal groups, however, fundamentalism was not likely to exist simply on the fringes of society. Its radicalism was tempered by traditionalist identification with the middle-class ideals of the older Protestant establishment. Fundamentalism appealed to some well-to-do, and some poor, but also and especially to the "respectable" Protestant and northern European working class, whose aspirations and ideals were essentially middle-class Victorian.[19]

One example from Ellis's study of a fundamentalist controversy in the town of Indiana, Pennsylvania, provides one very brief—though perhaps representative—glimpse at what the national movement looked like at the local level. Although this instance is drawn from a small town, the sequence of events and the social patterns involved appear similar to those found in urban centers as well. In 1915 the Reverend William McKee, a graduate of the Nyack Bible Institute (of A. B. Simpson's Christian and Missionary

Alliance) and a dispensationalist, became pastor of the First Baptist Church of Indiana, a Pennsylvania town of some 6,000. During 1916 McKee inspired a considerable revival, adding fifty new members by baptism. In the early 1920s McKee attempted to involve his still growing congregation in the national fundamentalist debates. Some of the more established families in the congregation refused to take a fundamentalist stand against the policies of the Northern Baptist Convention. Ellis demonstrated that the fundamentalists in this struggle, loyal to the Baptist Bible Union, were drawn from the more recently arrived residents of the town, and from the laboring classes. While some well-to-do long-time residents were in this group, most of the business and professional people and the older families remained loyal to the Convention.[20]

This case illustrates the complexity involved in assessing the significance of social factors in religious development. Although Ellis found a clear correlation between social class and religious affiliation, it does not necessarily follow that the religious choices were dictated by class antagonism. The non-fundamentalist group in Indiana had apparently long dominated the church, and would presumably have resisted any new group trying to take control, whether they were rich, or poor, or neither. Ellis points to the significant fact that the non-fundamentalists were not theologically liberal. One should not underestimate, moreover, the force of sheer inertia—of loyalty to the Baptist denomination and comfortable traditional Baptist concerns. The fundamentalists in this case were innovators attempting to drag the congregation into a national debate the local relevance of which was probably not readily apparent to the "old guard."[21]

Virtually every religious group is characterized by a particular social base. Social factors exert a considerable influence on religious life, and, except for explicitly stated commitments, may provide the best means of predicting religious behavior. It is, however, a mistake to reduce religious behavior to its social dimensions, or to assume that these are usually primary. Christianity claims, in various ways, to meet all sorts of human needs. The factors creating a sense of need are extremely complex within a single individual, let alone a group. Needs for order, growth, morality, and survival can be traced to a variety of social, economic, psychological, emotional, intellectual, physical, and spiritual forces, in addition to the inherent insecurities of the human condition. It is usually fruitless to attempt to explain a historical development on the basis of any one of these factors. Moreover, contrary to a common working assumption, those factors most amenable to measurement are not necessarily the most significant. Our analysis, then, must consider the range of human experience—social, economic, psychological, philosophical, symbolic, biological, etc.—and acknowledge that especially for large groups the underlying factors in behavior often can be analyzed only in a subjective way.

In view of this limitation and the difficulties of finding any precise social or class determinants of fundamentalist behavior, we can nonetheless attempt, more impressionistically, to make some sense out of the important psychological-social dimensions of the fundamentalist experience. Given the imprecise nature of the case, it can perhaps be best described by an extended analogy or metaphor, rather than by any more exact analysis.

The fundamentalist experience may be seen as providing American Protestants of English and Scottish ancestry with an analogy to the immigrant experience of other ethnic groups. The fundamentalist leadership came primarily from this "Anglo-Saxon" group, although some were of German origin.[22] Most of these northern European Protestants in America had not personally experienced the shock of crossing the sea and making their way in a new land.[23] They could be said, however, to have experienced a similarly traumatic cultural upheaval. In some respects America after 1918 was a new world as compared with America at the end of the nineteenth century. People who had retained the dominant beliefs of the culture in which they were raised now found themselves living in a society where those same beliefs were widely considered out-dated, or even bizarre.

The well-to-do and the well-educated middle classes often survived the transition with some of their influence intact, at least within their limited sphere. Although their adjustment to the new society might be difficult, normally it could be a gradual transition with no crisis forcing a confrontation between tradition and modernity. The lower middle classes were more likely to experience something akin to the immigrant experience. Raised with middle-class Victorian ideals they might find themselves in new and unsettled situations; "in-migrants" within a pluralistic and not always friendly society, or simply outside centers of cultural influence. Faced by a culture with a myriad of competing ideals, and having little power to influence that culture, they reacted by creating their own equivalent of the urban ghetto. An overview of fundamentalism reveals them building a subculture with institutions, mores, and social connections that would eventually provide acceptable alternatives to the dominant cultural ethos. As in immigrant communities, religion played a central role in shaping their identity. Immigrants combined some innovative religious approaches with the equivalent of old-world social, political, and individual mores, and their communities emphasized doctrines and practices that symbolized separateness from the larger community.[24] While other practical accommodations of immigrants to the new culture may have proceeded smoothly, these symbolic points were not negotiable, so that beliefs and values were often frozen in the form which they had had in the old world prior to the migration.[25] Similarly, among fundamentalists religious and political ideals hardened at about the point they had reached by 1900.

The "immigrant" analogy should not be pushed too far. Immigrants normally come to a new land voluntarily. Fundamentalists, by contrast, experienced the transition from the old world of the nineteenth century to the new world of the twentieth century wholly involuntarily. Thus they not only experienced a sense of alienation, but felt called to a militant defense of the old order; they had a fondness for military imagery and did not hesitate to describe their cause as a holy war.[26] So the metaphor may be extended to picture fundamentalists sheltered behind their ideological ghetto wall, with the wall itself as heavily fortified as the very wall of Zion. Behind this barrier, the possibility of intellectual isolation, extremism, and paranoia was greatly increased.

This immigrant analogy is also inadequate in that fundamentalists' sense of alienation seems to have been in force only selectively. Much of the time they appear to have identified with the old Victorian Protestant establishment. Their struggle was not really that of trying to adjust to a new culture or to break into the centers of influence in the culture. Rather they saw themselves, and the groups with which they identified, being forced out.

Fundamentalism appealed, as we have seen, to a number of actual immigrant groups, especially those who shared a northern European Protestant heritage. Somewhat paradoxically, many from these groups seem to have found fundamentalism an acceptable milieu for their Americanization. In any case fundamentalists and immigrants had some basic affinities. Some of these were important common social denominators—non-urban Protestant origins for example. The importance of such influences is difficult to assess, but one central aspect of their common uprooting and anxiety was explicitly expressed: their sense of finding themselves in a culture that was turning from God. In twentieth-century America many Scottish and English Protestants could sing one of the most popular fundamentalist songs together with newer Americans:

> I am a stranger here,
>   within a foreign land;
> My home is far away,
>   upon a golden strand;
> Ambassador to be
>   of realms beyond the sea—
> I'm here on business for my King.[27]

The widespread defection from traditional Christianity had another important effect that tied fundamentalists' social experience to their intellectual and theological concerns. With the culture less and less dominated by evangelical values, the religion was losing its social base. It was no longer automatically supported by community pressure and the reward of respectability. This was especially true in the cities. With this social base seriously eroded, something else had to give cohesion to the movement. Thus greater stress was placed on personal commitment and belief as the basis for solidarity. Certain key beliefs—inerrancy, anti-evolution, often premillennialism—gained special importance as touchstones to ascertain whether a person belonged to the movement. Exactly correct belief then became proportionately more important to the movement as its social basis for cohesiveness decreased.

XXIII. Fundamentalism
as a Political Phenomenon

Ever since fundamentalism first appeared on the scene, its opponents had suspected the existence of a sinister political dimension to the movement. In World War I, professors at the Divinity School of the University of Chicago suggested that the premillennialists might be supported by German money. When the war was over and fundamentalist patriotism was no longer in question, there came the more plausible accusation of complicity with business interests. In 1921, the *Christian Century* still equated premillennialism with fundamentalism, and it opined that business had initiated "a new courtship" with premillennialism. "When the capitalist discovers a brand of religion which has not the slightest interest in 'the social gospel,' but on the contrary intends to pass up all reforms to the Messiah who will return on the clouds of heaven, he has found just the thing he has been looking for."[1] "It may appear," wrote Kirsopp Lake in *The Religion of Yesterday and Tomorrow* (1925), "to large financial interests that industrial stability can be safe-guarded by Fundamentalists who can be trusted to teach 'anti-revolutionary' doctrines in politics and economics as in theology."[2] Later interpreters suggested similar connections. William McLoughlin in his studies of American revivalism, and Richard Hofstadter in his comments on fundamentalism, both stressed the political leanings of their subjects. Paul A. Carter's "semi-Marxist" interpretation of the Social Gospel written in the 1950s was based on the assumption of business support for fundamentalist conservative politics.[3]

Since the early 1960s, however, most interpreters have agreed that fundamentalists' deepest interests were more ideological and theological than political. In 1968 Paul Carter published a radical revision of the view he had defended in the 1950s. Referring to fundamentalist political interests, Carter now argued that "in deepest essence this was not what the fundamentalist controversy was about." While acknowledging that political interests were sometimes important to fundamentalists, Carter argued that their principal concerns were simple. They were "defending what the Fundamentalists honestly believed was all that gave meaning to life, 'the faith once delivered to the saints.'"[4] In a more detailed study Robert Wenger concurred with Carter that "we cannot adequately explain fundamentalism in terms of social and economic interests." Wenger held that since some fundamentalists could be found on each side of almost every social-political issue, no political stance could be regarded as a test of faithfulness to the movement. Furthermore, he

pointed out that much political conservatism, which was indeed the dominant political tendency in the movement, was little more than a manifestation of commonplace American opinions of the day. Fundamentalist nationalism was, moreover, tempered by a sense of God's judgment, a sense
absent from the patriotism of most Americans. The unity of the movement,
he maintained, "lay in its biblically-based Christian theology." This faith
"helped to shape the fundamentalist's view of his culture far more than his
culture shaped his faith."[5]

Faith and theology were no doubt foremost in determining the general
outlook of fundamentalists; nevertheless their cultural experience had a
great deal to do with shaping their secondary attitudes, especially their
political views. This is obvious if one compares fundamentalism in the later
1920s or the 1930s with the earlier stages of the movement around 1900 or
1910. In the era before World War I expressions of cultural alarm were
infrequent, nationalism was not strong, and progressive political sentiments
were still common, even though conservatism prevailed. By about 1930
politically liberal sentiments had disappeared almost entirely from the movement.[6] As we have seen in Chapter X, the disappearance of progressive
sentiments is a complex phenomenon related explicitly to fundamentalists'
reaction to liberalism's identification with the Social Gospel. But not only
was fundamentalism almost uniformly conservative in politics by the 1920s.
In addition, during the decade following the first world war, leading fundamentalists were commonly found preaching alarmist views of the state of
American culture. They expressed alarm not only about modernism and
evolution, but also about the spread of communism. Occasionally even anti-
Jewish sentiments were incorporated. At the same time the unqualified fundamentalist patriotism was growing rapidly.[7] The marked contrast with the
period before World War I confirms Paul Carter's statement that "fundamentalism may have been not so much one of the causes of that wartime and
postwar intolerance, as has so often been assumed, as it was one of its
victims."[8]

This observation reinforces the point that American fundamentalism was
not simply an expression of theology or of concern about false doctrines (as
it might have been described in 1910). As this work has emphasized, in the
minds of most fundamentalists the theological crisis came to be inextricably
wedded to the very survival of Christian civilization—by which they meant a
Bible-based civilization. One cannot comprehend the character of the movement without recognizing this social and political dimension. Although the
anti-worldly direction taken by revivalist evangelicalism had precluded most
explicitly social programs by World War I, the traditions from which fundamentalism sprang almost always had encouraged some political involvement—whether temperance, Sabbath legislation, anti-Masonry, anti-slavery,
or any of the other evangelical causes. It was therefore not entirely out of
character when the movement was dramatically politicized after World War I,

as in the campaign to legislate against evolution. Nor was it particularly incongruous for a politican to emerge as the chief spokesman for fundamentalism. It does seem a bit anomalous that the premillennial leaders should fall all over themselves in their enthusiasm to enlist Bryan as leader of their organizations; that phenomenon is perhaps the best evidence that premillennial otherworldliness was not decisive in determining fundamentalists' behavior. The belief that America should be a Christian nation founded on God's word was more deeply rooted in their tradition.

Fundamentalism had indeed become politicized in the 1920s, but this politicization was haphazard. Although many fundamentalists supported the anti-evolution crusade, they do not seem to have been very united on other political questions. They did participate in the general conservative Protestant opposition to Roman Catholicism and Al Smith in 1928, and they also joined with most Protestants, conservative and liberal alike, in supporting prohibition.[9] Otherwise, the movement does not appear to have been identified with any political stand. The immediate origins of fundamentalism reveal almost no systematic political thought, except perhaps some inherited wisdom from the days of the nineteenth-century evangelical establishment—which of course tended to be conservative and Republican. For reasons already mentioned, revivalists, premillennialists, holiness teachers, and Baptist and Presbyterian conservatives had concerned themselves relatively little with such such subjects since the Civil War. Certainly they had developed no clear consensus on them, except that the church should not be involved in political affairs. The closest thing to a political principle that most fundamentalists seemed to share was a profession of individualism that paralleled their theological dictum that the individual was the basic unit in the work of salvation. Even this principle was not consistently developed, since many fundamentalists held that God judged whole nations. Seldom, in fact, did fundamentalists work out their political views in any systematic way.[10] In general individualistic, not oriented toward politics, and suspicious of the growing connection between liberal theology and liberal politics, the precursors of fundamentalism had drifted in a politically conservative direction. Yet they were essentially drifting, rather than moving purposefully. Hence after 1917, when social and political issues once again loomed large, they responded to the issues haphazardly and on the basis of inherited prejudices and formulae, with next to no theoretical preparation to guide them.

The emergence of the notorious political extremism of later fundamentalism should be considered in this context. Before World War I the lists of vices illustrating the decline of civilization contained only scattered references to socialism and anarchism. In 1919, fundamentalists, and most Americans, became acutely aware of the Bolshevik threat. The premillennialists' earlier predictions concerning the menacing role of Russia in the end times added a degree of plausibility to such fears. It was not until 1923 or 1924 that

these fears in their most extreme forms began commonly to appear to fundamentalist literature. This development seemed to be connected with their
anti-evolution interests. "As a matter of fact," said *Moody Monthly* in 1923,
citing Frank Norris as an authority, "evolution is Bolshevism in the long
run. . . . It eliminates the idea of a personal God, and with that goes all
authority in government, all law and order."[11] At about this time, William B.
Riley began to stress the connection between socialism and evolutionism as
atheistic threats to "Christian America" and its schools. The *King's Business*
likewise began to emphasize the seriousness of the communist threat.[12]
Increasingly, modernism, evolutionism, and Bolshevism were lumped together as part of the same basic threat to Bible belief. "Christendom reposes
upon a book, the Bible." *Christian Fundamentals in School and Church*
quoted with approval this statement of a Union Seminary (New York) graduate
who in 1926 described his school as linked to the "Socialistic Revolution."

From *The King's Business* (May 1925), p. 197.

"Since these professors deserve high place in socialistic ranks because they are propagators of communism," the magazine added, "how would it do to nominate the very Reverend Harry Emerson Fosdick for president on the Socialistic ticket? Perhaps it would not be amiss to nominate Clarence Darrow as his running mate. What a combination!"[13]

By the 1930s such views of collaboration among the various conspiracies against Christian civilization had generated some really extreme beliefs, especially among the premillennialists. Arno C. Gaebelein in *The Conflict of the Ages* (1933) presented probably the most comprehensive catalog of interrelated conspiracies. Starting with the struggle between God and Satan in the Garden of Eden, Gaebelein compiled a classic list of conspiratorial threats that had faced America, including the Illuminati who promoted the infidelity of the French Revolution, secret societies, Roman Catholics, socialists, and the Jews. The Jews were condemned on the basis of the post-World-War-I publication of the factitious *Protocols of the Elders of Zion*. William B. Riley was not the separatist that Gaebelein was, but he enumerated a similar list of menaces. Roosevelt, he was convinced, was "painting America Red." "Disarmament," "Internationalism," and "Social Gospel," he said, "have become passwords of the secret order which deliberately plots, not alone the downfall of the American Government after the manner of Russia's collapse, but the overthrow of every civilized government in all the world."[14] Riley, like Gaebelein and a few other fundamentalists of the 1930s, was convinced by the spurious *Protocols* of the Jewish aspect of the international threat. This anti-Jewish sentiment, while by no means characteristic of fundamentalists generally, was remarkable in light of the strong pro-Zionist convictions of most premillennialists.[15] Gerald Winrod, editor of the *Defender Magazine,* and sometime publisher of Riley's diatribes of the 1930s, was an especially vocal anti-communist, anti-Semitic, and indeed pro-Nazi fundamentalist leader of the time.[16] Frank Norris, on the other hand, defended the Jewish people.[17] Norris, however, who began his career with militant anti-Catholic attacks, and always represented extreme views in the Southern Baptist Convention, found in anti-communism a cause that exactly fit his mentality.[18] By the 1950s most political fears had coalesced into the communist threat, which would continue to attract considerable audiences for such premillennialist leaders as Carl McIntire or Billy James Hargis.[19]

Even though the political attitudes of most fundamentalists were much like those of their non-fundamentalist Republican neighbors, the development of hyper-American patriotic anti-communism is a puzzle and an irony in the history of fundamentalism. How could premillennialists, whose attention was supposed to be directed away from politics while waiting for the coming King, embrace this highly politicized gospel? It is difficult to account for the phenomenon on simply rational grounds. Perhaps the puzzle can be solved by understanding a type of mentality, or disposition of thought, sometimes associated with fundamentalism. Richard Hofstadter aptly described this mentality as "essentially Manichean." The world, in this view, is "an arena for conflict between absolute good and evil. . . ." This outlook lies behind a view of history that has often appeared on the American political scene. "History *is* a conspiracy, set in motion by demonic forces of almost transcendent power. . . ." This view, says Hofstadter, led to "the paranoid style" often seen in American political thought.[20]

This syndrome has a near affinity to the view of history central to the fundamentalists' outlook. They held, as other Christians often had, that history involved a basic struggle between God and Satan. This premise in itself was not particularly conducive to conspiracy theories. The fundamentalists, however, were disposed to divide *all* reality into neat antitheses: the saved and the lost, the holy and the unsanctified, the true and the false. Moreover, their common sense philosophical assumptions added the assurance that they could clearly distinguish these contrasting factors when they appeared in everyday life. Add to these predispositions the fundamentalist experience of social displacement (which Hofstadter makes much of) and the "Manichean mentality" becomes comprehensible.

Given this mentality it is perhaps possible to shed some light on the paradox of super-patriotic premillennialism. During the half century before World War I premillennialists developed very little in the way of political theory. After the war when communist and other conspiracy theories arose as explanations of what was going wrong, they had little basis for evaluating these theories on their own merits. The conspiracy theories did, however, appeal to their general disposition of thought. Like their premillennialism, the political threats could be placed in the framework of the conflict between the forces of God and of Satan. The two types of conspiracy theory, the political and the religious, might well have appealed to a single mind-set in such a way as to override the difficulty of reconciling specific details.

The paradox involved here was certainly not unique to those premillennialist fundamentalists holding extreme political views. Their experience reflected the tension felt throughout the fundamentalist movement between an otherworldly profession and the lingering conviction that God's kingdom could indeed be found in America itself. After World War I the evidence suggested that Satan was assailing Protestant America on every front. Some maintained that counterattacks should be confined to the theological and ecclesiastical arenas. Others, however, extended the battle to the schools. It seemed consistent then for some fundamentalists to conclude also that Satan's hosts would appear in clearly identifiable political manifestations, just as they appeared so clearly in the churches and schools. In the face of this threat, the political battle to defend God's kingdom could not be entirely postponed until a coming era.

XXIV. Fundamentalism as an Intellectual Phenomenon

Clarence Darrow said in Dayton that his intention was to prevent "bigots and ignoramuses" from controlling the schools. This view of the fundamentalist intellect would continue to prevail in the liberal community. Stewart Cole populated his *History of Fundamentalism* with "religiously disturbed" defenders of "antiquated beliefs," contending against "open-minded seekers for the truth that makes man free."[1] According to H. Richard Niebuhr "inadequate development of educational institutions" and "the distrust of reason and the emphasis on emotion" resulted from the isolation, poverty, and hardships of farm life.[2] Norman Furniss observed that "ignorance . . . was a feature of the movement; it became a badge the orthodox often wore proudly." Fundamentalists' "distorted opinions," said Furniss, were based on "complete misunderstanding" of evolution and modernism. They had to resort to coercion because they "were aligning themselves against ideas that had the weight of fact behind them. . . ."[3] These interpretations gained some stature in the American historical community when Richard Hofstadter identified the "paranoid style" of fundamentalist thought as a species of "anti-intellectualism" reflecting a "generically prejudiced mind."[4]

As Hofstadter showed, anti-intellectualism was a feature of American revivalism, and fundamentalists were certainly not free from this tendency. The suggestion that the ancestors of Ph.D.s were monkeys and baboons was always good for a laugh from an anti-evolution crowd. Likewise the titles of the learned were enumerated "D.D., Ph.D., L.L.D., Litt.D."—ending with "A.S.S." Even the well-educated and usually humorless Reuben Torrey would stoop to this.[5] Moreover, some champions of the Bible school movement were beginning to assert that Bible education was the only proper education, not just an expedient for lay evangelists, as it was originally conceived. There was a strong tradition in America that the Bible in the hands of the common person was of greater value than any amount of education.[6] As William Jennings Bryan often said "It is better to trust in the Rock of Ages, than to know the age of the rocks; it is better for one to know that he is close to the Heavenly Father, than to know how far the stars in the heavens are apart."[7]

If one reads fundamentalist literature, however, it is apparent that such Bible-versus-science themes were usually brought up only as a last line of defense. The Bible was thought to be scientific (in the sense of reporting the facts accurately)[8] whereas evolution was wholly unscientific. Scientists and

Ph.D.s might deserve ridicule, but not *because* they were scientists or Ph.D.s. The joke was that in spite of so much learning they arrived at conclusions that common sense knew to be patently unscientific.

It was endlessly repeated that true science rested on facts, while evolution was mere hypothesis. This was basic to William Jennings Bryan's argument. "It is not scientific truth to which Christians object," he wrote for a speech meant to be the capstone of the trial at Dayton, "for true science is classified knowledge and nothing can be scientific unless it is true." "Evolution," on the other hand, "is not truth; it is merely hypothesis—it is millions of guesses strung together."[9] It was appalling to Bryan that a doctrine so destructive to both Christian belief and civilization was based on guesses that were "absurd as well as groundless."[10]

In several respects the views of Bryan and Darrow were similar. Each considered the other's view ridiculous, and wondered aloud how any sane person could hold it. Each thought that the theories of the other were being imposed by the state on school children and saw the legal issue as the abridgment of traditional American freedoms. Bryan pointed out that Darrow, acting for the defense in the notorious Leopold and Loeb child murder, had suggested the Leopold had taken too seriously the evolutionary views of

From *The King's Business* (August 1923), p. 809.

Nietzsche which he had been taught at the University of Chicago. In response Darrow quoted his own remarks from the transcript of the Leopold trial, to the effect that the university has a duty "to be the great storehouse of the wisdom of the ages, and to let students go there, and learn, and choose."[11] In a parallel statement Bryan affirmed his confidence in free inquiry. "The people will determine this issue," said the Commoner in his last speech in court; ". . . this case will stimulate investigation and investigation will bring out information, and the facts will be known, and upon the facts, as ascertained, the decision will be rendered. . . ."[12]

It is a mistake, then, to regard the fundamentalist controversies as at bottom a conflict between science and religion. It is incorrect to state, as John Dewey did in 1934, that

> the fundamentalist in religion is one whose beliefs in intellectual content have hardly been touched by scientific developments. His notions about heaven and earth and man, as far as their bearing on religion is concerned, are hardly more affected by the work of Copernicus, Newton, and Darwin than they are by that of Einstein.[13]

Indeed, fundamentalists had resisted Darwin and knew little of Einstein, but they were not opposed to science as such. Rather, they were judging the standards of the later scientific revolution by the standards of the first—the revolution of Bacon and Newton. In their view, science depended on fact and demonstration. Darwinism, so far as they could see, was based on neither. The larger objection of course, was that the evolutionary approach to the interpretation of biology and history took only natural causes into account, to the total exclusion of the supernatural. In the Newtonian worldview it had been possible, as indeed it was for Newton himself, to regard the Bible as a repository of facts on a par with the book of nature. To fundamentalists, a worldview that excluded the most important facts in favor of a set of tenuous and speculative hypotheses was patently absurd and disastrous in its consequences.

The issue was a classic instance of what Thomas Kuhn, the controversial historian of science, describes as a "paradigm conflict" of two scientific worldviews. It is not necessary to subscribe to Kuhn's extreme view of the subjective character of knowledge to appreciate the persuasiveness of his argument that scientific thought does not progress by a simple accumulation of new and more advanced theories as more facts are discovered by objective observation. Kuhn maintains that science advances by a series of revolutions. With each revolution comes a change in basic perceptions, models or paradigms, and language. For example, to pre-Copernicans "earth" was, by definition, "a fixed position." To them, therefore, it was nonsense and unscientific to speak of the earth as in motion. The Copernicans reversed the paradigm, and it then became equally nonsensical and unscientific to think of the earth as fixed. The facts, that is, the observable phenomena, had not changed, but there was a different model for perception. Because it was a difference in perception, rather than a matter of facts or logic, the two sides were unable to communicate. Kuhn claims that this process underlies every scientific revolution. He quotes Max Planck: "a new scientific truth does not triumph by convincing its opponents and making them see the light, but rather because its opponents eventually die, and a new generation grows up that is familiar with it." Kuhn adds that "the transfer of allegiance from paradigm to paradigm is a conversion experience that cannot be forced."[14]

The paradigm theory, whatever its validity with respect to the field of natural science,[15] helps to clarify the nature of the fundamentalist experience. Fundamentalists had committed themselves totally to a "normal science." That is, they took one model of perception as normal for all persons. This was a "Baconian" model based on common sense. Almost all their apologetic and interpretation of Scripture rested on this foundation. Their opponents, however, belonged to a philosophical tradition that, especially since Kant, was willing to see perception as an interpretive process. Hence they were more open to speculative theories. They nevertheless considered these theories to be reliable inferences from the facts, and felt that no modern scientific person could seriously doubt them. In fact, they too had accepted perceptual models (for example, naturalism or the assumption that process and change are normal) that limit the theories that may be derived from the perceived facts.

Kuhn argues that the necessity for paradigms can be understood as part of the sociology of knowledge. The scientific community, because of its needs as a community, tends to affirm one set of theories as "normal science," to present these authoritatively in texts, effectually excluding all other theories. Kuhn suggests that this tendency to establish an orthodoxy is more characteristic of the natural sciences than of any other discipline, "except perhaps theology."[16]

In America between 1860 and 1925 something like the general acceptance of a new perceptual model took place in both the scientific and theological communities. Non-Darwinists, of course, were ostracized from scientific circles. Similarly, the modern theological community adopted a model for truth that in effect stigmatized theologians who rejected evolutionary views as neither scientific nor legitimate theologians. The conservatives were equally dogmatic. No compromise could be made with a worldview whose proponents denied the fixed character of supernaturally guaranteed truth. Communication between the two sides became almost impossible. Fundamentalists, excluded from the community of modern theological and scientific orthodoxy, eventually were forced to establish their own community and sub-culture in which their own ideas of orthodoxy were preserved.[17]

This explains something of what gave the fundamentalist coalition its cohesiveness. A simple theological definition of fundamentalism, such as Sandeen's with its emphasis on premillennialism, is too narrow and excludes some key figures, such as Machen and Bryan. There is, however, a common underlying assumption that explains the unanimous militant opposition to liberalism of these conservative Protestants of differing theological emphasis. Despite their differences, they agreed that knowledge of truth was of overriding and eternal significance, that truth was unchanging, and that it could be known by true science and common sense.

The intellectual issue probably was most clearly defined in the thought of J. Gresham Machen, as expressed in his critique of a non-fundamentalist conservative, E. Y. Mullins. Mullins, the distinguished president of Southern Baptist Theological Seminary in Louisville, attempted to bridge the gap between traditional and modern thought in his own defense of supernatural Christianity, published in 1924 as *Christianity at the Cross Roads*. Machen reviewed this work of "a true friend," but took the opportunity to expound his belief that the compromises which Mullins allowed would eventually result in the destruction of Christianity.

Mullins had attempted to save supernatural Christianity from the depredations of modern science by arguing that religion should be held separate from both philosophy and science. Religion, he said, was not governed by the principles of science and philosophy, but rather by its own principle of "personal relation." Such a relation could be confirmed only by "the immediate experience of God."[18]

Machen replied that science, philosophy, and religion all dealt with precisely the same thing—facts. Either persons saw the facts correctly or they did not. Hence, contrary to Mullins's view, only one philosophy could be true. False science and philosophy resulted when sin obscured the facts or led one to accept naturalistic presuppositions that excluded some of the facts. So, said Machen, "We ought to try to lead scientists and philosophers to become Christians not by asking them to regard science and philosophy as without bearing upon religion, but on the contrary by asking them to become more scientific and more philosophical through attention to all, instead of to some, of the facts."

Machen regarded Mullins's position as a dangerous concession in principle to the chief tendency in modern thought—away from direct knowledge of facts to subjective experience. The issue was most clear with respect to the resurrection of Jesus. According to the assumptions of modern thought, Machen pointed out, scientific history could only talk about "the belief of the disciples in the resurrection." Machen, on the other hand, in accordance with Common Sense Realism[19] assumed that what we know about in history is not the *idea* of the event (which is in the present) but the event itself (which is in the past). It would not do to say, as Mullins did, that religion dealt with "spirit," rather than with "matter." "The question of the resurrection of our Lord," said Machen, "in accordance with the common-sense definition of 'resurrection' which Dr. Mullins certainly holds, does concern 'matter'; it concerns the emergence or non-emergence of the body from the tomb." The issue, Machen insisted, was not one of ideas about the event; ultimately it came down to "whether the events really took place."

Machen saw it as a question of scientific Christianity versus "modern anti-intellectualism." Just as those who held to the paradigms of naturalistic science found supernatural Christianity wholly "unscientific" and even "obscurantist," so Machen, holding firmly to the view that science dealt with the facts directly, found modern philosophy and religion equally unscientific. Compromisers like Mullins, he said, seemed to place themselves "in the full current of present-day anti-intellectualism." Some, including Mullins himself, Machen conceded, would not be swept away, even in letting go their firm hold on facts. "But," he added, "it would never be safe for us." In Machen's view, faith without science would soon be dead.[20]

Machen, like Bryan, was something of an anomaly in the fundamentalist movement. Each found his place in it not just because he defended evangelical Protestant supernaturalism (many moderates such as Mullins did so also), but also because of the view of science, philosophy, and the facts that almost all fundamentalists held in common.

The leading premillennialists expressed a similarly firm trust in proper reason and science. A. C. Dixon, assuming the role of Daniel in the lion's den, in a 1920 speech to "an Infidel Club in Chicago," asserted confidently "I am a Christian BECAUSE I AM A THINKER. . . . A RATIONALIST. . . . A SCIENTIST." "I do not mean, " he added, "that I devote all my time to scientific investigations, but I believe in the scientific method of 'gaining and verifying knowledge by exact observation and correct thinking.' An ounce of fact is worth a ton of theory."[21] It is a mistake to suppose, wrote William B. Riley in another typical statement,

> that those of us who represent Christianity have any quarrel with science. We have not. . . . but Christianity like all truth, is not tolerant of error, and it will not harmonize with this pseudo science,—this utterly false philosophy.[22]

With the scientific community in fact regarding fundamentalist views as pseudo-science and false philosophy, the fundamentalist search for scientific confirmations of Christianity seems to have been at times an almost desperate one. Some continued to insist, along the lines suggested earlier by A. T. Pierson, that the Bible contained amazing scientific predications. Riley, for example, claimed that when in Job XXVIII it says "To make weight for the wind," the Bible was predicting air pressure.[23] Others searched the Scriptures for mathematical formulas. In 1922 *Moody Monthly* published an argument correlating the seven days of creation with the seven notes in the octave, relating these to the seven sayings of Christ and the seven parts of Psalm 23 and concluding "what need we of further proof that 'all Scripture is God-breathed.' . . ."[24] Even more elaborate was Ivan Panin's work on "Scripture Numerics." In an incredibly complex scheme, Panin claimed to have demonstrated that if one counts up all the words and letters in any given

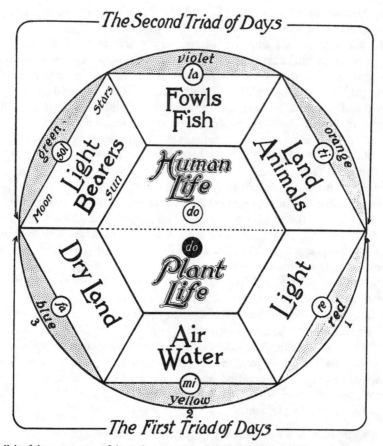

Parallels of the seven notes of the scale, seven colors of the spectrum, and seven days of creation. From E. J. Pace, "The Law of the Octave," *Moody Monthly* (May 1922), p. 1023.

section of the Bible the totals arrived at will be a multiple of seven. *The King's Business,* which published a sample of Panin's work, presented it as "An Unanswerable Proof of the Divine Authority of the Bible," which "no Critic has ever dared answer." "While life is too short," an editorial added, "for the ordinary Bible student to attempt to go into details in following up this system, he can at least take a great deal of comfort in the discovery and can safely rest assured that it cannot be disproven."[25]

This grasping after scientific straws was a side effect of a serious intellectual crisis. The fundamentalists took it to be a crisis in common sense. Their worldview, which until recently had been generally considered both sacred and academically impeccable, was now becoming a laughingstock. This was a key part of the fundamentalist experience of social displacement. Machen and the movement's other able exponents, who saw the underlying philosophical issues as they were, could still present a reasoned defense, at least one respected by critics. Others, however, who accepted the common sense assumptions more naïvely, began to turn to increasingly extreme versions of their view of reality to explain the widespread failure of rationality in the culture.

This phenomenon is nowhere more clearly illustrated than in the life of Charles Blanchard, president of Wheaton College from 1877 to 1925. Blanchard's adult life spanned almost exactly the years of this study and he was a prominent participant in many aspects of fundamentalist development. A friend of Moody, he supported both revivalism and evangelical education, was converted to premillennialism, and adopted Keswick holiness teaching.[26] As we have seen, he carried on the ideals of moral reform inherited from his father, but by the end of his career the focus of these reforms had narrowed considerably and a degree of premillennial pessimism had clouded his hopes for a "Christian America."

Blanchard, perhaps more than any other figure, can be seen attempting to explain the demise of evangelicalism as a cultural force by applying apparently unquestioned assumptions of Common Sense philosophy. The failure of common sense and of the evangelical effort in America was especially poignant for Blanchard because he came from a heritage that had had the highest hopes for national moral reform based on Christianity and sound education. Jonathan Blanchard had established the program at Wheaton in the 1860s on the foundation of Scottish Common Sense philosophy and his son Charles was still propounding these doctrines in the 1920s.[27] In the meantime, however, a most distressing question had arisen, with which many others of Blanchard's generation (B. B. Warfield, for example) had had to wrestle. If each individual is normally endowed with both intellectual and moral senses that enable him to perceive the right, how could almost the whole culture have turned away from common sense and God?

Blanchard's answer, often repeated, was that the twentieth century was simply an "age of insanity."[28] This conclusion followed from Blanchard's premises and was confirmed by his distinctive experience as an heir to the tradition of nineteenth-century American moral philosophy. There was a considerable body of "truths which are always true and which are every where recognized as true by rational minds." This included not only logically necessary truths, but also a whole range of common-sense experience.[29] Blanchard thought, therefore, that arguments for the truth of Christianity could be constructed such that "it is impossible for a rational mind to disbelieve it."[30] In Blanchard's works he constantly appeals to an abstract personage, "the rational man." "This man is omnipresent in Blanchard's writing," remarks a recent observer. "He is the sane man, the honest man, the candid man, the intelligent man, the rational man, the thoughtful man, the fair-minded man."[31] Being a Christian was for Blanchard simply equivalent to using good sense. "It is true today that any man who will use good sense will be religious," he wrote in the early 1890s. "Even if men don't read the Bible, the evidence is sufficient if they will cease to be swine rooting about in the earth."[32]

If one accepted these premises, by the early twentieth century the world must indeed have seemed insane. Blanchard simply could not believe that people really believed, or had clearly thought about, many of the things they professed. For instance, he found the cult of Christian Science utterly baffling. His first objection to the new teaching was "that every man, sane man, knows that it is not true." With arguments such as "if it were true one could not cut off his hand with an ax," he concluded, "I will not say that they do not think that they believe it, but it is obvious that no person can really believe such teaching and, strictly speaking, be in his right mind, for the heavens are overhead and the earth under our feet."[33]

Almost as puzzling were the new philosophies of the day. "The reason why materialists and spiritualists (in philosophy)," wrote Blanchard, "are not shut up in an asylum is because while their fundamental beliefs are irrational, their practical activities are sane."[34] Such irrational philosophies, of course, could soon lead to ruin, as higher criticism and religious infidelity demonstrated.

The common sense principle that seemed to Blanchard most helpful in accounting for the delusions of the age, was that of the intimate connection between religion, rationality, and morality. This connection was readily recognized not only by the ubiquitous "rational man," but also by the common people. "A common sense people know that it is the Bible and Christian teachings which make their children good."[35] Moreover, said Blanchard, "unbelief seems never to have originated with the common man."[36]

How then was mass infidelity and unbelief to be explained? The fault did not lie with the common sense of mankind, but with the moral defects of false teachers. "Ministers and teachers of theology, " Blanchard asserted, "seem to be the ones who lead the Church into error, and the more these are paid, the longer vacations they have, the higher positions they obtain, the more unfaithful to God and his Church they seem to become."[37] Blanchard was saying in effect that intellectual delusions were the inevitable counterparts of the moral decline against which he and his father had so long battled. How else could one account for the many seemingly well-educated and intelligent liberals who came to such insane conclusions? The high pay and extended vacations were possible explanations. Another possibility, Blanchard speculated after studying some of the higher critics, was the "poisoned Brain." Tobacco and alcohol, two great symbols of vice to the American evangelical tradition, might be the culprits. "It is well known," said Blanchard, "that the critics of our time have been usually men who have poisoned their nervous systems and injured their minds by the use of narcotic and other poisons."[38]

In this remark, extreme though it is, many of fundamentalist themes converge. The common sense tradition in America assumed a national consensus of rationality and morality wed to Protestant religion and the revival. This tradition provided a basis for holding on to the Christian faith at all costs—which of course was the principal issue. Yet it provided no fully adequate way to account for the collapse of the consensus. Dispensational premillennialism did offer an explanation of the cultural and religious decline. Yet most fundamentalism, or at least fundamentalism as a movement, was dispensationalist only part of the time. Much of the time it was very typically American. That is, it combined with its Christianity certain nineteenth-century American ideas about truth and morality. These values, as well as a traditional and Biblical Christianity, had to be saved from the delusions of the critics. The intellectual, moral, and religious issues were too intertwined to be sorted out thoroughly.

Although there was a respectable philosophical heritage behind this outlook, it could easily become anti-intellectualism when translated into popular rhetoric. If Blanchard, a college president, had difficulty explaining the prevalence of the new views in Common Sense terms, less distinguished popularizers could only explain the breakdown of common sense as the sinister work of evil men. That is the message of a 1925 statement attributed to Billy Sunday:

> Our country is filled with a Socialistic, I. W. W., Communistic, radical, lawless, anti-American, anti-church, anti-God, anti-marriage gang, and they are laying the eggs of rebellion and unrest in labor and capital and home, and we have some of them in our universities. . . . If this radical element could have their way, my friends, the laws of nature would be repealed, or they would reverse them; oil and water would mix; the turtle dove would marry the turkey buzzard; the sun would rise in the West and set in the East; chickens would crow and the roosters would squeal; cats would bark and dogs would mew; the least would be the greatest; a part would be greater than the whole; yesterday would be after tomorrow if that crowd were in control.[39]

XXV. Fundamentalism as an American Phenomenon

In many respects fundamentalist Christianity was not unique to America. It had affinities with revivalist and pietistic movements around the world, and was often successfully propagated overseas by its vigorous missions. Yet almost nowhere outside of America did this particular Protestant response to modernity play such a conspicuous and pervasive role in the culture.[1]

One of the closest counterparts to American fundamentalism is English evangelicalism and the differences between them are instructive. From the time of the Puritans until Dwight L. Moody, British and American evangelicalism was, to some extent, part of a single transatlantic movement. The British either originated or contributed to revivalism, the modern missionary movement, agencies for evangelism such as the Sunday School, the YMCA and YWCA, and a host of other agencies for moral and social reform. Dispensationalism and the Keswick movement were both largely British in origin. As late as 1910–1915, conservative evangelicals seem to have taken British-American ties for granted. Fully a fourth of the essays in *The Fundamentals* were by British authors. A. C. Dixon, first editor of *The Fundamentals*, left that work to become pastor of the church built by Charles Spurgeon in London. In the 1920s, however, when the American fundamentalists were fighting their spiritual battles, few in England rallied to the battle cry.

Some English evangelicals did try to resist the trend toward liberalism in theology during the 1920s. For the great majority of English Protestants, however, the issues raised by Darwinism and higher criticism had been settled long before, in the two decades of furor over *Origin of Species* (1859) and *Essays and Reviews* (1860). Despite the efforts of Dixon and a few others to drum up a British equivalent of the militant American movement, most conservative evangelicals in England seemed to be of the non-controversialist Keswick variety. Enough conservatism survived to produce a sophisticated and militant "fundamentalist" resurgence after World War II, but from 1900 until 1940, only those closest to the movement could have realized that there was any British counterpart to the American movement.[2]

The Scopes trial apparently seemed totally foreign to the experience of the vast majority of the British public. "Perhaps no recent event in America stands more in need of explanation . . . ," wrote one British observer in 1925.[3] Even those who followed English church life closely saw no counterpart to militant fundamentalism. "Perhaps it was [his] greatest service," observed the *Times* of London in 1929 concerning A. S. Peake, a moderate Biblical critic, ". . . that he helped to save us from a fundamentalist controversy such as that which has devastated large sections of the church in America."[4] To the extent that conservative evangelicalism existed in England at the time, it differed significantly from the American variety in its general lack of militance and impact on the culture.[5]

What was it in the American situation that fostered militant fundamentalism on such a large scale? Any answer to such a broad question must necessarily be speculative, but may, however, illuminate the issue. The following suggestions may be divided into three interrelated categories: social factors, religious-cultural traditions, and intellectual tendencies.

SOCIAL FACTORS

Two social factors especially useful to understanding American fundamentalism may be mentioned again here. The remarkable ethnic and denominational diversity of America, accentuated by new regional diversities, created unique tendencies with respect to the acceptance or non-acceptance of new ideas. Although limited ethnic, denominational, and regional diversity can be seen in England, the extraordinary diversity in America, as well as its sheer size, made this aspect more significant. In America, each group had its own traditions, educational system, and rate of development. In England, however, ethnic groups had long ago stabilized their relation to the larger society. Channels of communication were ancient and well established, and an issue that was discussed in the universities would likely soon be well known throughout the provinces and parishes.

The social-psychological factor of the experience of displacement, as described in Chapter XXI, would seem to apply more or less equally to both Americans and Englishmen living in the period of the 1880s through the 1920s. On each side of the ocean, Bible-affirming evangelicals found that the values of their group had come to appear quaint and almost foreign. Significantly, however, English civilization was solidly grounded in the idea of "Christendom," broadly and tolerantly conceived. In America, on the other hand, the religious base of the culture was perceived as somewhat narrowly evangelical. To be an evangelical in England meant to belong to a respectable minority that had learned over the course of centuries to live with religious diversity. American evangelicals, in contrast, had until very recently been socially dominant. Although many evangelicals were not themselves influential, they identified with a group that could claim notable success in shaping education and professed values in America. Although they did tolerate some internal diversity, evangelicals had not been particularly tolerant of other faiths, as their treatment of Roman Catholics and Mormons in the nineteenth century shows. For this group, until recently identified with dominant cultural influences, the experience of displacement was especially traumatic.

RELIGIOUS-CULTURAL TRADITIONS

To a remarkable degree, American religious experience, and hence American culture, was shaped by what may be called (to modify a phrase of Stanley Elkins) "the dynamics of unopposed revivalism."[6] Revivalism has flourished in many countries since the eighteenth century. In America, however, it encountered little resistance from pre-existing traditions and institutions. Again, a comparison with England is instructive. While revivalism was certainly a transatlantic phenomenon, in England the universities, the established church, and the pre-revivalist traditions of most of the Nonconformist groups were among the powerful and venerable forces for moderation and restraint. In America these forces were either nonexistent or had little effect. Revivalism had little competition when it came to determining the distinctive characteristics of American religious life.[7]

Among these characteristics, the Biblicism and primitivism fostered by revivalism were especially important. In America, for the first two centuries Protestantism dominated overwhelmingly, and the Bible had played a role in shaping the culture for which there was no European parallel. Lacking a strong institutional church and denying the relevance of much of Christian tradition, American Protestants were united behind the principle of *Scriptura sola*. Indeed, the Bible played a major role in America's self-understanding.[8] This Biblicism, strong among the Puritans, gained new significance in the early nineteenth century. In the wake of the Revolution, Americans saw themselves as inaugurators of a new order for the ages. The new order was conceived as a return to a pristine human condition. For Protestants this ideal was readily translated into Biblical primitivism. The true church should set aside all intervening tradition, and return to the purity of New Testament practice. The Bible alone should be one's guide.[9]

Biblicism was closely related to religious individualism, also encouraged by revivalism. The individual stood alone before God; his choices were decisive. The church, while important as a supportive community, was made up of free individuals. The Bible, moreover, was a great equalizer. With Bible in hand, the common man or woman could challenge the highest temporal authority.

This continuity between nineteenth-century revivalism and twentieth-century fundamentalism sustains the contention that fundamentalism is best understood as a sub-species of American revivalism rather than as an outgrowth of the movements espousing millenarianism or inerrancy. It characteristically emphasized doctrinal tendencies which were already strong in American cultural and religious traditions.

Fundamentalism maintained the important distinction between the supernatural and the natural—always a strong revivalist concern. All the key doctrines depended on this. Inerrancy stressed the divine origin of Scripture and tended to subordinate its human authorship. The other traditional fundamentals—the Virgin Birth, the miracles of Christ, his substitutionary atonement, and bodily resurrection—all involved the supernatural. Dispensationalism highlighted the role of divine forces in shaping history, and insisted that the hope for the future lay only in divine intervention, not human effort. Creation versus evolutionism was a straightforward opposition of supernaturalism to naturalism.

The strong revivalist tradition in America doubtless contributed to the tendency to see things in terms of simple antitheses. The revivalist believed that the universe was divided into the realm of God and the realm of Satan, the righteous and the unrighteous. Revivalist hymns were full of simple contrasts between sorrow and joy, turmoil and rest, weakness and strength, darkness and light, defeat and victory, purity and impurity, guilt and forgiveness, the world and heaven.[10] The whole revivalist impulse was based on the perception of an antithesis between the saved and the lost. In this dichotomized worldview, ambiguity was rare. Transitions never occurred gradually, but were, like the conversion experience itself, radical transformations from one condition to its opposite.

This type of thinking left almost no room for the motifs that characterized liberal theology and scientific naturalism in the late ninetenth century. Both Darwinism and higher criticism postulated a natural process of development, and the new theology saw God working through similar means, emphasizing the *synthesis* of the natural and the supernatural, rather than the antithesis. Wherever revivalism had prevailed in American religious life, there was virtually no preparation for the acceptance of the new categories. Indeed, there was hardly a way to discuss them. Many American Protestants reacted by rejecting them outright as incompatible with the faith and by asserting their own views still more strenuously.

Although recognition of the dynamics of revivalism is indispensable to an understanding of the popularity of the militant defense of evangelical doctrine in America, revivalism and pietism in America must themselves be viewed in the context of the older Calvinist religious and cultural tradition. Calvinism in America nearly always demanded intellectual assent to precisely formulated statements of religious truth. Revivalists often modified and simplified the doctrines involved, yet they preserved both the emphasis on simple antitheses and the general principle that assent to rightly stated doctrine was of eternal significance.

The Calvinist tradition helps to explain the disparity between the American reputation for religious tolerance and the actual intolerance of so much of American ecclesiastical practice. The Calvinists and their revivalist heirs eventually accepted and even endorsed civil tolerance of religious diversity. Civil tolerance, however, was quite distinct from intellectual tolerance. One may allow Quakers or Roman Catholics political equality and yet find semi-Pelagianism to be appropriate grounds for fierce theological debate and even separation.

Such Calvinist attitudes were carried over into American revivalism and continued into twentieth-century fundamentalism; fundamentalism arose primarily among groups with Reformed origins, such as Baptists and Presbyterians, and was quite rare on the Methodist side of American revivalism, which emphasized the ethical rather than the intellectual aspects of Christianity.

INTELLECTUAL TENDENCIES

The fundamentalists fought the new ideas with the Bible and with materials from the stockpile of American assumptions and concepts. Much has been said already about the great reverence in America for the Baconian tradition of scientific thought and the related philosophical Common Sense Realism.

Once again, we may use a comparison with England. The relatively easy acceptance of Darwinism, higher criticism, and liberal theology in England seems to stem from the pre-existence in nineteenth-century England of a concept of history as gradual natural development. Darwinism itself was, of course, a product of this climate. In British church life and especially in English constitutional history there was a deeply rooted awareness of the gradual development of traditions. By contrast, the newness of America seemed to demand written and rational definitions, new departures, and a break with the past.

This suggests that American intellectual life was distinguished from that of most western European countries by a distinctly anti-modern view of history. Substantial elements in the late nineteenth- and early twentieth-century America lacked those assumptions central to modern historical thought and scholarship, including the assumption that history was a natural evolutionary development and the corollary that the present can best be understood as a product of the past.

Important aspects of the American experience militated against the acceptance of such assumptions. American historiography had long been dominated by interpretations based on analogies to Biblical history which took for granted direct supernatural, or at least providential, intervention.[11] History was viewed through the lens of Scripture. Obviously, this was incompatible with the higher critical idea that Scripture, like everything else, should be viewed through the lens of history. Additionally, many secular versions of American history emphasized newness and progress toward the future, rather than continuity with the past. Americans had relatively little history of their own, and their national experience often seemed like a new dispensation, totally discontinuous with the past. Primitivism, or the desire to start the new age by returning to a pristine state, was one response to this situation. Dispensationalism embodied all these assumptions and ideals, and no doubt the popularity of this imported British view in America was due in part to its affinities to this distinctive American outlook.[12] Other fundamentalists had various other non-developmental and non-naturalistic views of history, although worked out with less detail.[13]

In America, romanticism did not enjoy the early success that it had in England and most of Europe. America came into being during the Enlightenment, and well into the nineteenth century remained generally content with modes of thought whose origins were no later than the mid-eighteenth century. In Europe, since the 1780s romanticism had fostered suspicion of rational and fixed definitions of experience and stressed the value of the changing and the unique.[14] These ideas certainly helped prepare the way for the second scientific revolution which, starting with Darwinism, saw the primary function of science transformed from the finding of fixed laws into the analysis of the natural processes of change.

Romanticism was not a major movement in America until about the 1830s. Many of its adherents were to be found in New England, the region which would later prove most receptive to naturalistic and historicist analysis. By the middle of the nineteenth century, some important evangelical theologians, including Horace Bushnell, Henry B. Smith, and John Nevin, were introducing romantic ideas; others, however, such as Charles Hodge and Nathaniel William Taylor, remained firmly in the Common Sense tradition. Revivalism itself fostered many popular romantic attitudes by its emphasis on personal sentiment, and the holiness movement was a practical evangelical counterpart to other romantic developments. These, however, did not reflect any deep awareness of the issues at the center of the modern intellectual revolution.

Thus in the second half of the nineteenth century many Americans were only beginning to discover romanticism at the time when the second scientific revolution forced the inclusion of the new historical and developmental views on the theological agenda. Even in the intellectual community, there was little preparation for post-romantic modes of thought. There were some very well educated people among those who fought naturalism with pre-romantic rationalism. So emerging fundamentalism did not entirely lack intellectual leadership. Its thought was not shaped simply by revivalist eccentricities, but also by the substantial pre-romantic Baconian and Common Sense intellectual system that had played a significant role in shaping American life in general.

This philosophical outlook was buttressed by revivalist thought and the American reverence for the Bible as well as by a variety of social, ethnic and geographical circumstances. These influences combined to dispose many people to anathematize every aspect of the new views and to set up rigidly antithetical views in opposition to them. As the influence of the naturalistic developmental views increased until by the 1920s they had become prevalent, the fundamentalists continued to stress their opposing paradigms more and more urgently.

Every modern nation, of course, has experienced religiously defined traumas and contests arising out of the transition to modernity. A comparison of these various "fundamentalist" movements casts a light on the unique characteristics of the religions and the nations involved. Muslim fundamentalism, for example, resembles American Protestant fundamentalism in a number of striking ways. In view of its militant opposition to much of modern culture, it seems appropriate to borrow the American term to describe this Islamic phenomenon.[15] Yet the differences between the two movements are striking also. In Islam there has traditionally been less theoretical tension between religious militancy and actual military force than in Christianity. Moreover, Muslim fundamentalism has arisen and flourished in nations to which modernization was imported from without, via more powerful foreign cultures, and where there remains a memory of golden ages belonging to their distant past. Nevertheless, recent developments in Islam clearly demonstrate, as would surveys of other religious communities as well, that fundamentalism is not a strictly American phenomenon. It is American only in the sense that it was here that it took shape and flourished in its classic Protestant form. In its generic sense fundamentalism refers to phenomena not restricted to America nor to the early twentieth century.

PART FIVE

Fundamentalism Yesterday and Today (2005)

Few of the participants in the fundamentalist struggles of the 1920s would have predicted that the movement would long persist as a major factor in American life. Ernest Sandeen made the classic remark on this point. "Ever since its rise to notoriety in the 1920s," he commented, "scholars have predicted the imminent demise of the movement. The Fundamentalists, to return the favor, have predicted the speedy end of the world."[1] When Sandeen wrote those words in the 1960s, he was contemplating a fundamentalism that, however resilient, was playing a far different role in American life than would the fundamentalism of the later decades of the twentieth century. Much the same was still true when I began this book in the early 1970s. At that time, fundamentalism was essentially a separatist and sectarian movement on the fringes of American church life and society. The conclusion of the last chapter suggests how it looked even near the end of that decade. As an historical phenomenon I thought of it as important not so much for understanding those peripheral groups as for understanding the longer range imprint that the fundamentalist experience of the early twentieth century had on a much larger evangelical movement that came in many varieties. I added my original (now abandoned) subtitle, "The Shaping of Twentieth-Century Evangelicalism 1870-1925," partly because early fundamentalism indeed had a large impact on later evangelicalism, but also because I felt a need to justify a study of fundamentalism in terms of something larger. By the time *Fundamentalism and American Culture* came out in 1980, there was no need to account for a history of fundamentalism except as important in its own right. I received my first copy the morning after Ronald Reagan was first elected president of the United States.

Writing twenty-five years later, the most illuminating question to ask is how the fundamentalism of recent decades differs from that of the 1920s. Answering that question casts light both on the recent and the distant past. One of the intriguing things about fundamentalism in America is that it has been a moving target. The old-time religion has always been changing, innovative, and in many ways up to date. While its core concerns for proclaiming the Gospel, its fundamental doctrines, its concerns for personal piety, and its militant opposition to liberal theology and to secularizing culture remain largely the same as in the 1920s, its ways of expressing those concerns have gone through several transmutations. In order to better understand recent fundamentalism and its differences from its progenitors, we will trace a number of the factors that changed the movement during the twentieth century. Before doing that, let me sound the major theme.

The most striking feature of fundamentalism since the 1970s that distinguishes it from its forebears is its deep involvement in mainstream national politics. This point must be stated carefully. Fundamentalism has always had political implications. One of the several dynamics shaping early fundamentalists was a sense of alarm over the demise of Christian culture. National revival, they urged, was the only adequate response. Salvation of souls, they affirmed, would restore righteousness to the culture.[2] Born-again people, they at least implied, would choose upright leaders who honored God's laws. Occasionally the movement did have some explicitly political components, best exemplified in the crusades against godless evolutionism and godless Bolshevism, but its political interests were haphazard.[3] Prior to World War I, most of fundamentalists' immediate precursors stayed away from most direct political involvement. The premillennial revivalist movement that revered Dwight L. Moody was invigorated by a militant sense of cultural crisis, but the primary response was to mobilize an army of evangelists. The major exception was Prohibition, but that movement had its roots in the old postmillennialism and was as much a mainline Protestant and Progressive cause as a revivalist concern. In the era that followed the 1920s, in the mid-decades of the century, fundamentalism was even less involved in direct political action. After World War II anti-communism became a conspicuous theme but its major function was as a prelude to the old call for national revival, as it was for Billy Graham, as a way of urging individual conversions and enlisting support for evangelism and missions. Some evangelists, such as Fred Schwartz, Carl McIntire, and Billy James Hargis, specialized in anti-communism, and paved the way for the Religious Right. Yet their efforts did not result in large-scale political mobilization and they seemed marginal to the national scene. Through the 1960s the endlessly repeated mainline Protestant critique of fundamentalism was that its "otherworldliness" and emphasis on personal conversion as the only real answer to life's problems had turned Christianity into a "private" and socially irresponsible religion.[4]

The question to be addressed then is: How did a soul-saving revivalistic movement that mostly steered clear of direct political involvement emerge at the end of the twentieth century as known especially for its political stances and influences? That is not to say that political involvement has become the controlling feature of most fundamentalism or related evangelicalism. Concerns for evangelism, missions, and personal spirituality still are the central features of the movement. Many churches that are strongly conservative in theology do not emphasize politics. Nonetheless, there is no doubt that in the past generation political activism has risen dramatically in prominence as one feature of the movement.[5]

FROM FUNDAMENTALIST TO EVANGELICAL AND BACK—AND HOW DEFINITIONS CHANGE

Fundamentalism in the 1920s was a broad coalition drawn from many denominations and traditions. The most dedicated core of this many-faceted movement was made up of dispensational premillennialists, associated with revivalism, Bible institutes, and independent missions. At the same time many other conversionist-oriented, biblicist, and conservative Protestants were influenced and reshaped by the fundamentalist anti-modernist outlook. The diversity and hence decentralization of fundamentalism helped give it remarkable resilience. So, even though in the most publicized denominational and cultural battles of the 1920s fundamentalists might have seemed to be fighting for lost causes, their campaigns took deeper root at the local level, and often they flourished in adversity.

After World War II, the strength of conversionist Protestantism became evident once again with the immense popularity of Billy Graham. The young evangelist was a purebred fundamentalist, but once he became a national celebrity in the 1950s he and his closest supporters began to reclaim the term "evangelical" to describe their movement.[6] While these "new evangelicals" did not abandon their militancy, they tempered it in the interests of evangelism and in the hope to regain influence in the cultural and ecclesiastical mainstream. Usually the new evangelicals, like their fundamentalist predecessors, maintained the so-called "pietist" position that churches and religious leaders should stay out of politics and confine themselves to more strictly "spiritual matters," especially preaching the salvation of souls, which they believed was in any case the most effective solution to social problems. They did not, however, always maintain that stance consistently. Some of the largest financial contributors to the movements in the 1950s were ardent political conservatives who saw revivals as an antidote to liberal trends in church and society. The new evangelicals also included some voices, of whom the most prominent was Carl F. H. Henry, founding editor of *Christianity Today*, challenging the pietist majority among them to reclaim their Reformed heritage of fostering a larger social, political, and intellectual agenda.[7]

Meanwhile and partly in reaction to the new evangelicals, other heirs to the original fundamentalist movement moved in a strict separatist and more purely "fundamentalist" direction. These more rigorous fundamentalists did not differ from the new evangelicals in their implicit political leanings or the dominance of pietist-conversionist social solutions, but they did object to the efforts of Graham and his associates to build alliances with sympathizers in mainstream Protestant denominations, which they regarded as hopelessly liberal in theology. By the late 1950s strict fundamentalists split with Graham and the new evangelicals, insisting that complete separation from any alliance with doctrinal impurity should be a test of true faith. Often they demanded double separation, breaking fellowship not only with liberals but also with those who fellowshipped with liberals. Bob Jones University became a prototype of such separatism. These separatists were almost all strict dispensational premillennialists, while the new evangelicalism included some adherents from other heritages. The break between strict separatists and Billy Graham led to a change in terminology. By the later 1960s a considerable network of ecclesiastical separatists were the only ones to use the term "fundamentalist" as a self-designation (a change from the broader use of the term in the 1920s). "Evangelical" became the usual term to refer not only to the more moderate heirs to the broader fundamentalist coalition, but also to conversionist Protestants of any heritage. For a time a convenient rule of thumb was that an evangelical was anyone who identified with Billy Graham.

Even though "evangelicalism" represented a broad and diverse coalition, most of those who used "evangelical" as their primary self-identification were from groups that had some direct fundamentalist heritage. Such "card-carrying" evangelicals, as we may call them, included a more militant or "fundamentalistic" wing, which typically emphasized the inerrancy of Scripture, and perhaps premillennialism, as among the tests of the faith, but were not strict ecclesiastical separatists as were those who actually called themselves "fundamentalists."[8]

When in the mid-1970s the Religious Right entered the national consciousness as a politically active movement, some of its early core leadership was drawn from separatist fundamentalists, of whom Jerry Falwell and Tim and Beverly LaHaye were fairly typical. As a political coalition, however, the new Religious Right soon drew in many conservative evangelicals who were militant, or fundamentalistic on cultural issues, even if they might be less so on theological or ecclesiastical matters. The Religious Right also included cultural conservatives from other heritages such as Roman Catholics and Mormons. The Protes-

---

19th Century

Evangelicalism

Includes most major Protestant denominations and also newer revivalist groups including holiness and premillennialists. By end of century American evangelicalism is beginning to polarize between theological liberals and conservatives.

1920s

Fundamentalism

A generic name for a broad coalition of conservatives from major denominations and revivalists (prominently including premillennial dispensationalists) who are militantly opposed to modernism in the churches and to certain modern cultural mores.

Related revivalist groups, such as from pentecostal or holiness churches, are also often called fundamentalists although some remain separate from major cultural and theological battles.

tant part of this coalition has often been referred to, especially by those who do not appreciate the internal divisions within conversionist Christianity, as simply "evangelical," or sometimes as simply "fundamentalist." It would be more accurate to say that the Religious Right as a political movement has attracted many separatist fundamentalists and "fundamentalistic" evangelicals. "Fundamentalistic" is here used in about the same way as "fundamentalist" was used in the 1920s: as referring to a broader coalition of militant evangelical Christians drawn from all sorts of denominations. My own unscientific shorthand for this broader usage is that a fundamentalist (or a fundamentalistic evangelical) is "an evangelical who is angry about something."[9]

By this standard, it should be carefully noted, the operational distinction between simply being an evangelical and being what I am calling a fundamentalistic evangelical involves their relative degrees of militancy in support of conservative doctrinal, ecclesiastical, and/or cultural issues. "Evangelical" is broadly defined to include those in traditions that emphasize the Bible as the highest religious authority, the necessity of being "born again" or regenerated through the atoning work of Christ on the cross, pietistic devotions and morals, and the necessity of sharing the Gospel through evangelism and missions.[10] Because the terms are

---

1950s-mid1970s

New Evangelicalism and Fundamentalism

"New Evangelicals" (eventually just "evangelicals"), most of whom have a fundamentalist heritage, form the core of a broad coalition that draws in related theological conservatives, ranging from pentecostals to Mennonites, who emphasize positive evangelism, best exemplified by Billy Graham.

"Fundamentalism," (technically a sub-species of evangelicalism in the 19th century sense) is used as a self-designation almost only by ecclesiastical separatists who break fellowship with Graham. Almost all are dispensational premillennialists, as are some non-separating evangelicals.

Late 1970s to early 21ˢᵗ Century

Fundamentalistic Evangelicalism

The Religious Right (which also includes Catholics and Mormons) includes "fundamentalistic" militants who from not only separatist fundamentalists groups, but also from almost the whole spectrum of evangelicals, even though by no means all evangelicals, including self-styled fundamentalist, are politicized.

used in so many different ways, however, it is nearly impossible to get a clear reading on the size of these groups, although there is no doubt that they have become a significant factor in American politics.[11]

Many of the fundamentalistic evangelicals in the new political coalition were direct heirs to the fundamentalist movement of the 1920s (either by the new evangelical or separatist fundamentalist routes) but many others come from related groups, most notably pentecostals, who were close cousins to the original fundamentalists. One difference between the "new evangelical" coalition of the mid-century and the strict separatist fundamentalists was that the former was more often open to ecclesiastical cooperation with pentecostals. Pentecostalism grew rapidly after World War II. Among its remarkable manifestations was the work of many healing evangelists, of whom Oral Roberts became the best known through nation-wide television broadcasts.[12] In the 1960s and 1970s the related charismatic movement was spreading in many mainline denominations and even into Roman Catholicism. These movements emphasized expressive Christianity and usually avoided politics. By the end of the twentieth century pentecostal and charismatic Christianity had become a major part of American evangelicalism and had made a phenomenal impact in world-wide Christianity, where their adherents were estimated in the hundreds of millions.[13] In the United States these movements tended to set the tone much more widely for evangelical worship, which became more oriented toward expressive spirituality, especially in contemporary praise music, and increasingly emphasized the immediate benefits of faith. Influences, however, moved in both directions. Evangelical Protestantism operates as an open market, so what works for one group quickly spreads to another. At the same time as expressive styles appeared widely among all sorts of evangelical churches, militant or fundamentalistic attitudes toward culture and politics sprang up in many (but certainly not all) pentecostal and charismatic groups. Pat Robertson, for instance, was charismatic in his theology, but fundamentalistic in his politics.

Evangelicals come in countless varieties and their cultural and political attitudes do not always correlate with their church affiliations or theologies. Many hold moderate views or remain apolitical and are not much touched by the "culture wars" attitudes. Some vote Democratic and a few lean to the political left. Nonetheless, recognizing all these qualifications and exceptions, the news in the decades since the 1960s is that a wide variety of evangelical traditions that earlier might have been thought of as culturally marginal and on the "private" or "otherworldly" side of American Christianity have been mobilized into significant mainstream national political force that has shifted their center of gravity by adding a very "this-worldly" or "public" agenda. The intriguing question is: How did this revolution take place?

THE SOUTH RISES AGAIN

One of the most important cultural developments between the 1930s and the 1970s was the rise of the South from a self-consciously separate region to more of an integral part of the national culture. That transformation was not possible until the turmoil of the civil rights movement receded and the South formally joined the rest of the nation in accepting racial integration, at least in principle. During the era of the triumph of civil rights legislation and enforcement of school desegregation in the 1960s, opposition to these causes was a major force in separating many white southerners from the Democratic Party, as was most evident in George Wallace's 1968 campaign for president. Despite religious dimensions in that opposition, piety was probably no more conspicuous there than it was in most other aspects of southern public life, whether conservative or progressive, white or black. In any case, only after white southerners were no longer automatically voting Democratic was it possible to organize a truly national movement of political conservatives. Furthermore, once civil rights receded as the defining political issue so that not everything that southern conservatives did was dismissed by their critics as motivated by veiled racism, the door was open to marshal southern conservative political energies and resentments elsewhere. So it is no accident that almost as soon as the divisive issue of civil rights formally receded, the Religious Right emerged as a national movement with conspicuous southern leadership, best exemplified by Jerry Falwell, Pat Robertson, and James Robison.[14]

It may seem odd that a movement that, as I and others have argued, appears to be primarily northern in its origins should now seem to have its most solid base in the South. Yet it is not new that many fundamentalists should speak with a southern accent. A number of the most influential early proponents of the movement, including William B. Riley, A. C. Dixon, Curtis Lee Laws, John Roach Straton, J. C. Massee, J. Gresham Machen, and J. Frank Norris, were from the South.[15] Fundamentalist militancy typically arises when proponents of a once-dominant religious culture feel threatened by trends in the larger surrounding culture. In other words, to use a non-fundamentalist analogy, it takes two to tango. If organized fundamentalism is to arise not only does there have to be a conservative religious community but also the more liberal-secular culture has to be strong enough to be impinging on the once-dominant religious culture and seem to be threatening to replace it. Accordingly, although transplanted southerners were prominent in northern fundamentalism, for a long time there was very little *organized* fundamentalism in the Deep South. Special fundamentalist organization there would have been redundant. Though people might be aroused against an alien teaching such as evolution, on the whole southern evangelical culture seemed secure. When evangelical white southerners were directly confronted with seemingly inexorable national secularizing trends, some of them, such as the early fundamentalist leaders who had been transplanted to the north, were ready to fight.

Organized fundamentalism, by way of contrast, has long been stronger in the western South and the upper South, where southern culture was less isolated from the national mainstream. Dallas Theological Seminary, founded in 1924, was the most influential seminary promoting dispensationalist theology. J. Frank Norris, born in Alabama, established the major southern outpost of early organized fundamentalism in Fort Worth. John R. Rice, a native Texan, as a young pastor in Dallas followed Norris in breaking with the Southern Baptist Convention in 1927 and in 1934 established *The Sword of the Lord*, which was probably the most influential fundamentalist periodical for the next four decades. Bob Jones, Sr., originally a Southern Methodist, in 1926 established a college, named for himself, which migrated from Panama City, Florida to Cleveland, Tennessee (1933), and Greenville, South Carolina (1946), where it became one of the first centers for organized separatist fundamentalism in the Deep South. Even so, Bob Jones University drew much of its support from the upper and western south, the rust belt Midwest, and California.[16]

During the first half of the twentieth century in much of the South, white evangelical Protestants typically exercised, as Grant Wacker has so nicely put it, "custodial" control over the local culture.[17] So long as their cultural dominance was secure, they could afford to be champions of separation of church and state and of "the spirituality of the church," a popular code phrase for the doctrine, sacred since the days of slavery, that churches should not meddle in political causes. Even though "the spirituality of the church" was transparently a way of protecting the segregated social order and churches did exercise their influence when it came to approved political causes such as prohibition, Sabbath observance, or anti-evolution,[18] most of that influence was informal or taken for granted and did not require special political organization. Jerry Falwell's famous 1965 sermon "Ministers and Marchers," in which he proclaimed that the duty of the church was simply to "preach the Word" and not to "reform the externals" was an expression of this classic southern and fundamentalist stance.[19]

One of the earlier sources of the transition to political fundamentalism was the massive migration out of the South during the 1930s through the 1950s. Transplanted white southerners could be found in fundamentalist churches in every northern city. J. Frank Norris, for instance, established in 1932 a second headquarters in Detroit. By 1970 some seven and a half million white southerners were living outside the South. Many settled in the Midwest.[20] Perhaps the most dramatic impact of the migration, however, was in southern California. Southern migrants, particularly from the Arkansas/Oklahoma region, helped make southern California a center for the old-time religion. Billy Graham's much heralded success in his 1949 Los Angeles crusade, which vaulted him into national prominence, was built on this demographic trend. Other lesser known southern evangelists, such as "Fighting" Bob Shuler, John Brown, J. Vernon McGee, and Bill Bright, all from Oklahoma, Arkansas, or Tennessee, had already laid the groundwork for revivalist Christianity in California. The real story, however, was at the local level. White southerners, used to a friendly custodial environment, were confronting a more diverse and secular American culture. Often the initial confrontations involved what was being taught in the public schools, leading to local political mobilization. By the 1960s such grassroots organizations, often growing out of local churches, had become considerable sources of support for Barry Goldwater in 1964, and then, more significantly, for Ronald Reagan's successful run for governor in 1966. From that time on it would be difficult to find any aspect of the renewed religious and cultural militancy of the emerging Religious Right that did not have a major southern component. By the early 1970s people were talking of the Americanization of the South, and the "southernization" of America, and the "Californization" of Texas.[21] The early Moral Majority emerged from the upper South, but eventually similar attitudes could be found throughout the region, as the conservative takeover of the Southern Baptist Convention best exemplifies. Conservative attitudes were now strong throughout the Sunbelt. That is not to say that latter-twentieth-century fundamentalism was a southern invention or a purely southern product. To the contrary, its roots were firmly entwined with and grafted onto traditions and attitudes traceable to the fundamentalism of the 1920s and its mid-century northern heirs. Nonetheless, the new even more resistant hybrid that emerged after the mid-1970s flourished especially well in the southland sun.

The participation of significant numbers of white southerners in recent fundamentalism in some ways paralleled the experience of some northern ethno-Protestants who played roles in the movement since its beginnings.[22] The Southern Baptist Convention, America's largest Protestant denomination and probably the largest source of the fundamentalistic Religious Right of recent decades, for instance, has some traits like those of ethno-religious groups, such as Missouri Synod Lutherans (German origins), or the Christian Reformed Church of North America (Dutch origins). Each tends to be inward looking in terms of ecclesiastical and theological concerns. Each used its religious commitments to preserve a distinctive outlook throughout the twentieth century. As each came into contact with the mainstream culture it developed both a moderate wing and a strong group of conservatives who made the inerrancy of Scripture a firm test of the faith and who tended to adopt the causes championed by the Religious Right.[23] Others of Protestant ethnic heritage joined fundamentalist or evangelical churches. Especially in the Midwest, one can find alliances between people of Protestant ethnic heritage and transplanted southerners in the Religious Right.

THE COUNTERCULTURE, PATRIOTISM, AND THE FAMILY

As in Reagan's California, the countercultural revolution of the 1960s vastly accelerated a sense of cultural alarm not only for transplanted white southerners but also for many other sorts of Americans. Two sorts of issues energized the backlash that in 1969 was still far enough beneath media radar to be tagged by Richard Nixon "the silent majority." First was patriotism and the Vietnam War. Ever since the Russian Revolution, anti-communism had been a leading theme for evangelists who were evoking a sense of world crisis. Such religious anti-communism supported and sometimes amplified political anti-communism, but evangelists usually left actual political organization to others.[24] In the 1940s and 1950s communism stood not only for atheism, totalitarianism, and a nuclear threat from abroad, but also at least intimated the menace of atheistic secularism promoted by big government at home. During the early Cold War American patriotism was at a peak and not surprisingly often took on a "Manichean" quality. On the "good" side of this dichotomy was "The American Way of Life," often associated with family values and a "Christian," or increasingly "Judeo-Christian" heritage. Fundamentalists, as such, were seldom taken seriously in the cultural mainstream, although everyone knew they were plentiful on the fringes. The immense popularity of Billy Graham, even in his early fundamentalist phase, might have suggested how deeply that religious style, once again with a southern accent, could resonate with a wide segment of Americans. Another significant area where explicitly evangelical influence was growing was the American military. Here again the rise of the South and the prominence of southerners in the military contributed to this trend, which by the 1960s was running counter to the growing secularism of public life.[25] More broadly, when opponents of the Vietnam War seemed to question patriotic anti-Communism and to undermine the military, the backlash, whether from the North, South, or West, had one of its strongest bases in conversionist Christianity.

The cultural revolution of the 1960s and early 1970s, especially the assaults on traditional standards of family and sexuality, had an even larger impact in reshaping fundamentalism. Dramatic changes in standards for public decency, aggressive second-wave feminism, gay activism, and challenges to conventional family structures all generated alarm. These changes were not simply countercultural but in most cases the movements were co-opted by the commercial culture and promoted in its media.[26] Archie Bunker reminded the world each week that conventional views on family and sexuality were both laughable and associated with racism. This revolution in standards for sexuality and gender coincided with aggressive efforts to secularize public culture, of which the 1963 United States Supreme Court ruling against Bible reading in the public schools became the chief symbol. Echoing the reaction to the revolution in mores in the 1920s, the idea that America was a Christian nation that had forsaken its heritage gained new credibility. Campaigns to counter that trend gained new urgency.

Fundamentalism as a backlash against a revolution in morals both suggests a striking parallel to the 1920s and also one of the biggest differences between the two movements. One of the oldest and most common interpretations of the rise of fundamentalism in the 1920s is that it was part of a "Puritanical" reaction to the excesses and changing mores of the 1920s jazz age. *Fundamentalism and American Culture* has been justly criticized for not emphasizing such factors more. My only defense is that since such interpretations were so commonplace, I was both taking for granted the impact of the revolution in mores and trying to show that fundamentalism was considerably more than gut reactions to cultural change.[27] I have long said that fundamentalists were militant evangelical Protestants who were fighting battles on two fronts: They were fighting against the inroads of theological modernism in mainline denominations and they were combating a variety of alarming changes in the culture. Nonetheless, I need to acknowledge that the account would have been fuller and more balanced had I included more detail on the sense of cultural crisis. Particularly, I neglected the alarm of fundamentalists over issues of gender, sexuality, and the family. The book would be better balanced if it included accounts of fundamentalist distress over changing sexual standards, the new woman, women's suffrage, women's ordination, flappers, birth control, divorce rates, and the decline in family authority. It should also have included much more on fundamentalist views concerning women and the roles of women who were fundamentalists. Although fundamentalists typically held that church leaders and public spokespersons should be male, women accepted and defended their subordinate roles and often exercised far more influence in practice than would have been apparent by examining the theory alone. Fortunately these topics have been well covered in the literature since *Fundamentalism and American Culture* first appeared.[28]

Despite continuities in fundamentalist concerns over sexuality, gender, and family from the 1920s to the later decades of the century, the immense difference is that in the former era these issues did not lead to any considerable political mobilization. Fundamentalist editorials may have run more than ten to one against women's suffrage,[29] but that was not an issue over which fundamentalists themselves were organizing a political countermovement. One reason was that the relationship of politics to the revolution of mores of the 1920s was much different from that of the 1960s and 1970s. The era of Wilson, Harding, and Coolidge was as much the era of Prohibition as it was of women's suffrage. Politically the Protestant establishment was still more-or-less in place in the 1920s, while in the 1960s and 1970s it was rapidly disintegrating. The earlier revolution in mores was not perceived as part of a larger secularizing political trend that had to be resisted.

In the 1970s distress over rapidly changing public standards regarding sexuality and the family combined with longstanding anti-communist patriotism to make fundamentalistic evangelicals ripe for political mobilization. Some of the foundations had been laid by conservative financiers of conversionist religious groups. Sun Oil Company's J. Howard Pew, for instance, financed Howard Kershner's Christian Freedom Foundation in the 1950s[30] and the free enterprise journal *Christian Economics*. Pew was also a principal supporter of the influential evangelical journal *Christianity Today*. When during the turmoil of the late 1960s that magazine seemed insufficiently conservative, founding editor Carl F. H. Henry was replaced with a regime that better reflected Pew's very conservative political and economic views. Perhaps typical of this transitional era was Bill Bright, leader of Campus Crusade for Christ, one of the largest parachurch evangelistic agencies. During the 1960s and 1970s Bright, whose theology was essentially fundamentalistic, supported the Christian Freedom Foundation, one of the earliest groups attempting to directly mobilize conservative Christians politically. Bright aided such causes and in return they and their financial sponsors, such as Richard M. DeVos of the Amway Corporation, supported Campus Crusade. Nevertheless, Bright's highly visible evangelistic campaigns, such as the massive youth rally, Explo '72, in Dallas or the much publicized national evangelistic campaign, "Here's Life America," or even his Christian Embassy in Washington, D. C., for evangelizing politicians, remained, technically speaking, non-political, although they blurred the line between evangelism and politics.[31]

The issues of family and sexuality proved the key that unlocked evangelical potential for overt political involvement, but remarkably several of those most responsible for turning that key were Roman Catholics. For conservative Catholics, of course, issues regarding sexuality had long been seen as preeminently political. Phyllis Schlafly was one of the first Catholics to effectively reach across the long-standing divide as she enlisted support against the Equal Rights Amendment, designed to end discrimination against women, which had been easily passed by the U. S. Senate in 1972. Aided by direct mail expert Richard Viguerie, Schlafly's Eagle Forum waged an eventually successful campaign throughout the decade, drawing Protestants and Mormons into alliances against ratification in the states. Schlafly and her allies convinced a large constituency that the amendment was not essentially about legal equality but rather an effort by aggressive feminists to impose their individualistic anti-family agenda on the whole culture. The white South, where the traditional family and sexual purity had long been sensitive issues, was especially susceptible to mobilization in this national campaign.[32]

As late as 1976 it was not at all clear what the evangelical vote might mean. It could not be assumed that conservative evangelicalism would translate overwhelmingly into political conservatism, let alone support for the Republican Party. When Democratic presidential candidate Jimmy Carter announced that he was "born again" many conservative evangelicals were delighted. Meanwhile, it sent reporters on the coasts scurrying to find out what this ominous phrase from the heartland might mean. Carter's election, thanks in part to evangelical support, led *Newsweek* to declare 1976 "Year of the Evangelicals."

Disillusionment with the Carter White House soon set in as it became clear that the president would not forsake core Democratic constituencies to take up the Religious Right agenda on issues of family, sexuality, or religion in public life.[33] Opposition to gay rights emerged as a grassroots political issue as singer and evangelical activist Anita Bryant led a campaign that helped overturn an anti-discrimination law in Florida's Miami-Dade County. An IRS threat to deny tax-exempt status to Christian schools, on the basis that they were de facto segregationist, was the catalyst for widespread and effective mobilization of evangelical, Catholic, and other counterforces in 1978. By 1979 alarm about the nation's perceived continuing drift toward secularism and promiscuity made it an auspicious time for the founding of the Moral Majority. Jerry Falwell, a true fundamentalist connected with the Baptist Bible Fellowship, a group whose lineage went back to Frank Norris, soon became its leading spokesperson. Once again, however, two Catholics, Richard Viguerie and Paul Weyrich, were instrumental in creating the new movement. Supporters of Republican conservatism, especially as embodied in the candidacy of Ronald Reagan, were recognizing the potential usefulness of the Religious Right. The feelings were mutual. Falwell brought with him a large television ministry and soon turned the Moral Majority into a major political lobby. Among charismatics and pentecostals his efforts were paralleled by Pat Robertson, who had an even larger television ministry and was instrumental, along with Demos Shakarian of the Full Gospel Businessmen's Association and Campus Crusade's Bill Bright, in organizing a "Washington for Jesus" prayer rally that attracted 200,000 in April 1980.[34]

Revivalist Protestantism, drawing on two centuries of experience in reaching mass audiences, had proved itself a master of modern media ever since the emergence of commercial radio in the 1920s. By the 1970s that mastery had spread to the use of television both for reaching huge audiences and for massive fund-raising. Robertson, who founded the Christian Broadcasting Network in 1960, was the leading pioneer and innovator in this area. In the 1970s hot-topic issues regarding politics and sexuality proved effective in fund-raising and helped demonstrate that conservative Christian politics had significant grassroots support.[35]

Remarkably, it was not until the end of the 1970s that abortion emerged as a leading evangelical concern. Prior to the 1970s strict opposition to abortion had been viewed primarily as a Roman Catholic position. Earlier fundamentalists and their mid-century heirs viewed abortion with disfavor, largely because it was a manifestation of sexual permissiveness, but it was not unthinkable to discuss exceptions to the general rule. As late as 1968 *Christianity Today*, the leading voice for the new evangelicalism associated with Billy Graham, sponsored a colloquy on abortion at which Carl F. H. Henry, evangelicalism's best-known ethicist, spoke equivocally on the topic[36]—something that would be almost impossible for a card-carrying evangelical to do with impunity fifteen years later. The United States Supreme Court's legalization of abortion in 1973 did not at first spark a major evangelical or fundamentalist reaction. As late as 1976 most regarded it as just one more sad sign of declining public moral standards, but only a few saw it as an issue around which cultural militants should rally, and it was not thought of as a major factor affecting grassroots born-again support for Jimmy Carter. By the early 1980s, however, strict anti-abortion had become the centerpiece of a new Catholic-Protestant political alliance and a virtual test of faith in militant evangelical circles.

NEW ALIGNMENTS

If we think back to the strength of moderate and liberal mainline Protestantism during the fierce controversies of the 1920s, we can get a better sense of how dramatically the cultural upheavals precipitated by the 1960s changed the American religious landscape. As late as the 1950s mainline Protestants could think of themselves as near the center of a cultural consensus that was then expanding to "Protestant, Catholic, and Jew," and which stood for progressively tolerant and scientifically informed thinking and championed laudable causes, most notably civil rights. By the end of the 1970s the major mainline Protestant denominations, such as United Methodist, American (formerly Northern) Baptist, Presbyterian, Episcopal, and United Church of Christ were losing members at alarming rates as older generations died off and they could not attract comparable numbers among the young. As the leadership of these denominations moved toward the moderate left in politics and ethically centered theologies, they had relatively less to offer constituents that could not be found outside the churches. Ironically, to the extent that they identified with the political left they recognized that they themselves had been part of the WASP establishment and that it was discriminatory to speak as white Protestants, hence leaving themselves with a serious identity problem when it came to recruitment. Furthermore, despite these efforts to keep up with the times, after the mid-1960s the permissive left generally found the churches irrelevant.[37]

These developments in mainline Protestantism helped shift the center of gravity of fundamentalism. In the 1920s the liberalizing trend in the mainline churches was a major cause of concern in itself and also helped foster a sense of wider cultural crisis. So what was happening in the mainstream white Protestant denominations was arguably the primary focus of fundamentalist alarm. By the later twentieth century most fundamentalists had already written off the predominantly northern mainline denominations. While each of those denominations (and now Catholics could be included as well) generated activist conservative parties that gained strength toward the end of the century, in opposition to theological liberalism, radical feminism, ordination of gays, and similar causes, those conservatives played a relatively minor role in fundamentalistic Christianity as a whole.

Once again the South provides the striking exception as the conservative (sometimes known as "fundamentalist") takeover of the huge Southern Baptist Convention in the 1980s and 1990s recapitulated the denominational controversies of the 1920s. The remarkable difference, however, is that, contrary to many predictions during the early stages of the Southern Baptist controversies, in this case the fundamentalists did win. In one of the most remarkable developments in American ecclesiastical history, conservatives gained control of the central boards of the denomination and took over its theological seminaries. Although characteristic fundamentalist theological concerns, often encapsulated under the rubric of "the inerrancy of Scripture," were major elements in defining Southern Baptist conservatism, most observers believed that the cultural-political issues were just as important, or perhaps more so, in enlisting popular support.[38]

SECULAR HUMANISM OR A RETURN TO CHRISTIAN ROOTS?

While, with the major exception of Southern Baptist conservatives, alarm over doctrinal erosion in major denominations played a relatively smaller role in the new fundamentalism, opposition to the expansion of the powers of civil government played a far greater role. That in turn related to the times. The decades after 1945 were a time of expansion of government, especially the federal government, in a way the 1920s were not. Alarm over secularizing trends accordingly focused on governmental intrusion on people's lives, as the national trends were toward creating a more pluralistic and inclusive, and hence more secular, society.[39] Once again, opposition to racial integration and continuing bitterness over matters like affirmative action and school busing fueled anti-government resentment. Related concerns focused on the welfare state of "the Great Society." At the same time the courts were taking more aggressive positions in declaring that the First Amendment entailed a "wall of separation" between church and state, most notoriously implemented in the ban on Bible-reading and prayer in public schools. In the same era, the 1960s, courts became far more permissive regarding what had previously been regarded as pornographic in publications, film, and other public entertainment. Fundamentalistic fundraisers could point with alarm to courts that removed the Bible from public life but made *Playboy* available at every corner convenience store. Conservative evangelical alarm over *Roe v. Wade* could be generated initially in part because it fit this permissive pattern. The fierce and often effective opposition to the Equal Rights Amendment for women in the later 1970s grew naturally out of well-established resentments against governmental attempts to alter essential basic patterns of American life.

"Secular humanism" came to be the shorthand framework for understanding the convergence of these cultural and political trends. Francis Schaeffer was the key person in articulating this new comprehensive yet simple paradigm. Schaeffer had studied briefly under J. Gresham Machen at Westminster Theological Seminary and after Machen's death in 1937 followed the more strictly fundamentalist and dispensationalist Presbyterian separatist Carl McIntire. In 1941 McIntire founded the American Council of Christian Churches, made up of small separatist denominations. After World War II he became one of the most widely heard fundamentalist preachers, featuring attacks on communism and the World Council of Churches. In the 1950s Schaeffer split with McIntire and established L'Abri Fellowship in Switzerland, which by the counterculture years become well known as a mission to disillusioned young people. Schaeffer was an effective popularizer of the Reformed idea that Christianity had powerful implications as a cultural critique. In 1976 he brought these ideas to fundamentalist and evangelical churches all over American though a film series, *How Shall We Then Live?* Imitating Kenneth Clark's *Civilization,* Schaeffer provided conversionist Christians with an overview of Western culture and civilization, as illustrated in its art, architecture, and literature, emphasizing the point that the great Christian synthesis that culminated in the Protestant era had been replaced by secular humanism, which had proved empty and destructive in the fragmentation and moral relativism of the twentieth century.[40] Schaeffer was also instrumental in raising *Roe v. Wade* to a position of preeminence as an example of the secular takeover of government to promote an anti-Christian and licentious agenda.[41] In 1979, working with Dr. C. Everett Koop (soon to be surgeon general under Reagan), Schaeffer came out with a follow-up film series, *Whatever Happened to the Human Race?* which focused on abortion-on-demand as the culmination of the secular humanist creed of freedom and self-indulgence that had led to the wholesale murder of the weakest of the human race.[42]

"Secular humanism" quickly became the code word for enemy forces in the dichotomized world of the emerging mentality of culture wars. Tim LaHaye seized on the term and simplified and popularized it further in *The Battle for the Mind* (1980), dedicated to Schaeffer. LaHaye, along with his wife Beverly, founder of Concerned Women for America in 1979, were among the most effective of fundamentalist promoters of the new political consciousness. According to Tim LaHaye, secular humanism was not so much a cultural trend as an organized conspiracy. Hard-core humanists numbered only about 275,000 but they controlled much of American media, entertainment, and education. The estimated sixty million born-again Christians, if properly organized, should be able to defeat the secular humanists, who were supported by naïve moralists and religious liberals.[43]

The times were propitious for mobilizing an army of militants around such rhetoric. At the grassroots level the viewpoints of American schools and textbooks had long been volatile issues, sparking various local controversies over teachings of moral relativism, sex education, and biological evolution. Campaigns to counter the teaching of biological evolution in the public schools, boosted by the "creation-science" movement that claimed a scientific basis for a young earth, reached levels comparable to those of the 1920s. At the local level, anti-evolution was one of the most effective means of enlisting grassroots political support. Now, however, in contrast to the 1920s, it was only one part of a larger anti-humanist political package.[44] In the meantime, since the 1960s and 1970s the Christian School movement had gained immensely in popularity as a practical sort of cultural separatism and as an alternative to government controlled secular education. Especially in the South, one motive was to avoid racial integration, but resistance to other cultural trends soon became more basic to the national movement. The rationale that Christian schools offered an alternative to the threat of government-supported secular humanism provided a way of clearly articulating the positive religious justification for what these schools were already doing.

The separatism of these school movements usually involved a subtle shift in emphasis from that which prevailed among fundamentalists from the 1920s through the 1950s. During that earlier era some fundamentalists founded their own schools, from lower schools to colleges and Bible institutes, as part of their attempt to live the "separated life," teaching people how to stay pure from behavioral and ideological corruptions of the society and how to relate to society primarily through evangelism and missions. While these traditions continued to shape the rapidly expanding Christian school and home school movements, by the 1980s these movements included more explicitly political dimensions dealing with civic and legal issues designed to prepare the next generation not only to resist secular humanism intellectually, but to take back America or at least resist politically.[45]

The larger framework was the necessity of restoring America's original Christian heritage.[46] That the United States was founded as a Christian nation and had abandoned that heritage had long been part of fundamentalist outlook.[47] Even during the mid-century separatist era fundamentalist rhetoric invoked political and social threats, such as communism or declining morals, as urgent concerns. But the solution was essentially the old standard of personal and national religious revival. The implication was that righteous individuals and leaders would turn the nation back to God. But how that would happen usually remained vague.

The dramatic transformation of cultural fundamentalism (as opposed to strictly theological or ecclesiastical fundamentalism) into a major national political power involved more than resourceful evangelical leaders rallying their people around an alternate vision for America. It was also the result of the shrewd leadership of non-evangelicals who were building the new conservative coalition that reshaped the Republican Party in the late twentieth century. In a sense the professional politicians "used" the Religious Right, as became apparent in some of the latter's frustration with the Reagan administration's reluctance to move on the politics of sexuality.[48] Yet the relationship was two-sided. Evangelical leaders "used" the Republican Party and the national perception of their own political power to build their religious movements and spread their cultural ideologies. Being market driven, the greater the perception of potential political power, the more the message of some ministries brought out longstanding cultural themes that readily resonated with their constituencies.

In terms of the longer fundamentalist heritage, the more explicitly politicized fundamentalism of the later twentieth century brought into the center of the movement the older custodial side of the American evangelical impulse that went back to the Puritans and had been best preserved in the South. That custodial side had been apparent in a good bit of the northern fundamentalism of the 1920s, but during the mid-twentieth century it had been overshadowed by the sectarian premillennialist side. In the new cultural-political fundamentalism it reemerged in full force. Jerry Falwell in his 1980 book, *Listen America,* for instance, echoed the Puritans in calling for national repentance to stay God's hand. "While it is true that we are not a theocracy, as was ancient Israel," he conceded, "we nevertheless are a nation that was founded upon Christian principles, and we have enjoyed a unique relationship toward God because of that foundation." In addition to national repentance, Falwell called for Christian voter registration drives. "It is perfectly legal, for example, for a deputy registrar to come right to your local church at a designated time and register the whole congregation."[49] Without much reflection on how practical political campaigns fit in with continuing predictions that the Rapture and end-times would commence in a few years, an ideal of cultural transformation reemerged as one of the most conspicuous traits of the movement.

THE PREMILLENNIAL PARADOX

The central cultural paradox of fundamentalism was thus even more dramatically pronounced than ever. In tandem with massive efforts to transform American politics and culture for the long run, ever more popular dispensational premillennial teachings suggested that for the United States there would be no long run. The Rapture and hence the beginning of the End Times, as countless preachers and writers proclaimed, were very likely to occur at least within the next few decades. America was simultaneously Babylon and God's chosen nation. Countless sermons and fund-raising appeals described in lurid terms how America was under judgment. Doom was inevitable and imminent. Each new crisis in the Cold War, conflict in the Middle East, or development in the European Union proved that the Bible prophecies were fulfilled and the end was near. Yet the United States at the very same time also remained a moral beacon for the ideals of freedom and best hope for defending righteousness against the powers of darkness. The Cold War and opposition to atheistic Communism fueled the idea that America represented a virtuous alternative. Jerry Falwell, for instance, organized "I Love America" rallies at every state capitol.[50] "Love it or leave it" style patriotism remained a hallmark of the movement, as much in the era shaped by 9/11 as it had been in that shaped by Vietnam. America might deserve the wrath of God for its sins, but let an American protester desecrate the flag or criticize the military and such outbursts would be treated as though they were blasphemy.

At the same time as such sentiments were building during the 1970s, Hal Lindsey's *The Late Great Planet Earth* (1970) was America's best-selling nonfiction book, reaching 28 million in print by 1990. Lindsey's tour de force is an arch-typical example of fundamentalism in its apolitical mode. Lindsey predicted that as the end approached, apparently within the generation, the U.S. moral decline would "so weaken law and order" that first the economy and then the military would collapse. Meanwhile institutional churches would be forming "religious conglomerates" and the Pope would become "even more involved in world politics" as the prophesied union of world church and world government moved into place. "Open persecution" was likely "to break out for 'real Christians.'" For America the only hopes were for individual conversions and possibly "a widespread spiritual awakening." In an interview in 1977 Lindsey declared, "God didn't send me to clean the fishbowl, he sent me to fish." [51]

The most striking contrast to such apolitical premillennialism was the militantly political postmillennialism of the Christian Reconstructionist movements. Christian Reconstructionism in its pure form is a radical movement that has never had a wide following. Founded by Rousas J. Rushdoony, an ultra-conservative Presbyterian, Reconstructionism, Theonomy, or Dominion Theology, as it is variously called, advocates ultra-conservative economic theory and calls for a theocracy that would include a reinstitution of Old Testament civil law. The positive proposals of Reconstructionists are so far out of line with American evangelical commitments to American republican ideals such as religious freedom that the number of true believers in the movement is small. Nonetheless Reconstructionists helped formulate the early critiques of secular humanism and their call for a biblically based alternative had considerable influence on the rhetoric of the Christian Right.[52] What might be tagged "Soft Reconstructionism," calling for a Bible-based civilization but not in a literal or thoroughgoing way, thus became a common motif within the Christian Right, so that avowed premillennialists often spoke as though they were postmillennialists. The best-known case was Pat Robertson, who emerged as the leading political figure in the Christian Right with his run for the Republican presidential nomination in 1988 and formation of the Christian

Coalition in 1989. Robertson's books, such as *The Secret Kingdom* (1983) and *The New Millennium* (1990), included seemingly postmillennial themes involving restoration of explicitly Christian influences in American government.[53] The paradox itself is not new. Already in the 1920s mixes of premillennial doctrine and postmillennial rhetoric reflected a longstanding cultural ambivalence in the American evangelical heritage.

It should not be surprising then, even if it remains remarkable, that at the same time as implicitly postmillennial political rhetoric was flourishing, premillennial end-time scenarios became more popular than ever. Beginning in the mid-1990s the *Left Behind* book series by Tim LaHaye and Jerry B. Jenkins surpassed its end-time predecessors and by 2004 had sold over sixty-two million copies.[54] These adventure stories tell of the tumultuous times following the Rapture. The primary task of a brave band of Christians, left behind but converted by recognizing the meaning of the Rapture, is to evangelize others, but they are also deeply involved in political intrigue as they try to subvert the machinations of the Anti-Christ and his sinister world government. The enormous popularity of these books, which sell to audiences far larger than the dedicated fundamentalist or evangelical constituencies, suggests the popular appeal in America of an aura of biblical authority combined with adventure set in an ultimate dualistic clash between a minority with Christ on their side versus a world empire of evil.

The continuing popularity of these themes—at the same time that many of their most ardent fundamentalistic proponents are deeply involved in politics and in establishing, for instance, educational institutions with buildings designed to last for generations—also confirms what appears to be a longstanding pattern. Premillennial end-time views, while important for confirming biblical authority and for promoting evangelism and missions, have not usually been prime determinants of fundamentalist views on other matters.[55] While sincerely held, these do not appear to be the sort of core doctrines (such as the necessity of trusting in Christ's sacrifice for salvation) that are so much at the center of a movement's web of beliefs that they cannot be easily ignored when in conflict with other pressing interests. Less central to the whole system, they are operative in some areas of concern, but not controlling factors for the whole.[56]

The one major area of practical politics where premillennialism is operative is policy toward the state of Israel.[57] A variety of nineteenth- and twentieth-century Protestant biblical interpreters, including Dispensationalists, predicted the return of the Jews to Palestine and such views had some impact in encouraging British and American support for that project. The foundation of the state of Israel in 1948 vastly strengthened the credibility of Dispensationalists, providing them with their most compelling case for the fulfillment of prophecy in contemporary times. They could also tie the Cold War into the scenario as Dispensationalist interpreters almost universally agreed that the USSR would, with Arab support, lead the invasion of Israel in the cataclysmic events of the last times and the fateful Battle of Armageddon. The practical result of these teachings was that American fundamentalists and most evangelicals were among the most ardent promoters of U.S. policies of support for Israel. Even though most prophetic interpreters could not find the United States directly in biblical prophecy, they could offer hope for America on the basis of the promise to Abram in Genesis 12:3 ("I will bless those that bless thee") so long as the United States made the defense of Israel a cornerstone of its foreign policy.[58]

AMERICAN FUNDAMENTALISM AND THE WORLD PHENOMENON

At just about the same time that *Fundamentalism and American Culture* first appeared, fundamentalism was much in the international as well as national news. By 1980, spurred in part by the Iran hostage crisis, journalists and scholars often extended the use of the term "fundamentalist" to include militant anti-modernists of other world religions, especially Islam. It is questionable whether a term, coined as it was in the American Protestant context of 1920, can appropriately be applied to strongly conservative movements in Judaism, Buddhism, Sikhism, Hinduism, or Islam, especially when none of the parties involved are happy with the analogy. Nevertheless, the scholars who have approached these comparisons in the most sensitive and nuanced ways have pointed out that it is still useful to note some illuminating parallels, even while acknowledging essential differences. *"Fundamentalism,"* according to an especially helpful summary, *"refers to a discernible pattern of religious militance by which self-styled 'true believers' attempt to arrest the erosion of religious identity, fortify the borders of the religious community, and create viable alternatives to secular institutions and behaviors."*[59]

Recognizing that fundamentalistic American Protestants fit this generic worldwide pattern of responses to selected aspects of modernity, it is illuminating also to reflect on how they are different, particularly as compared to radical Islamists. Although each of these groups is militant, fundamentalistic American Protestants are distinguished from radical Islamists and some other armed conservatives in world religions in that the warfare in which their group engages is almost always metaphorical rather than literal. Fundamentalistic American Protestants stress those biblical passages that emphasize the warfare between the forces of good and evil. Nonetheless, it has been unusual for them to recommend that church groups or individuals should take it on themselves to engage in physical violence against God's enemies. Occasionally fundamentalistic Christians have physically attacked abortionists or their clinics, but this has been rare.

One overarching difference between fundamentalistic American Protestant and radical militant movements in most other world religions is that American Protestants are shaped not only by their religious heritage but also by the American Enlightenment. Most fundamentalistic Americans are, after all, Baptists who have a heritage that affirms separation of church and state that antedates the Enlightenment. And as Mark Noll has shown most definitively, because they joined forces with champions of more Deistic or liberal Christian Enlightenment outlooks in the American Revolution, most American evangelical Christians were far more open to republican ideology than were their European Christian counterparts. Thus the Common Sense philosophy, with its confidence in the rational judgments of ordinary people, became fused with the American evangelical heritage. Further, as Nathan Hatch has argued, the populist or "democratic" elements in American evangelicalism fostered its remarkable growth in the era of the early republic.[60] In the burgeoning religious marketplace of the Second Great Awakening, separation of church and state seemed a boon to vital Christianity. The overall result was that American evangelicalism, despite its sectarian tendencies and concerns for purity versus cultural corruption, nonetheless usually remained remarkably comfortable with what they see as the ideals of the American Revolution. Even if they romanticize the American founders as working from an essentially Christian worldview, one result of that use of history is that they view many of the early ideals of the American political heritage as sacred. One of their most deeply held beliefs is that individual freedom of choice is central to the American Christian heritage. Although they believe legislation should reflect God's moral law on selected issues such as abortion or gay marriage, their general instinct on most matters is to advocate voluntary persuasion rather than governmental coercion.[61] Above all—and most important in making the comparisons to militant religious movements elsewhere more misleading than clarifying—is that when American evangelicals speak of a "Christian America," the first thing they are likely to speak of is religious freedom as being at the heart of the American experiment.[62]

In the light of American fundamentalists' republican and nationalistic heritage, the comparison with radical militants in other world religions takes on a more complex form. While fundamentalistic American Protestant militancy rarely involves personal undertakings of physical violence as a religious duty, it nonetheless often strongly supports literal warfare on the part of the nation. And although in domestic affairs fundamentalistic American Protestants clearly distinguish between the far-too-secular nation and their churches, in foreign policy they often seem uncritical of American nationalism and treat the United States as though it were unquestionably on God's side in warfare against the forces of evil. Thus while relying on lawfully constituted authorities to wield the sword has something to be said for it morally, both in terms of the Christian tradition and modern Western standards, it cannot be said that the difference between fundamentalistic American Protestants and other religious militants is that the former do not advocate physical violence in the name of a holy cause.[63] Much the same could be said, of course, of any religious Americans who might favor military action for a good cause. But fundamentalistic evangelicals are more likely to advocate state-sponsored warfare than are other Americans.

FUNDAMENTALISM AND EVANGELICALISM FOR REAL PEOPLE

Concentrating on the most striking feature of recent American fundamentalism, its political involvement, is nonetheless likely to lead to an unbalanced view both of fundamentalism itself and the evangelical movement of which it is a part. To understand the core traits of these movements one must look at them at the local and individual levels. Fundamentalism and its evangelical relatives are first of all religious or spiritual movements, more specifically built around variations on longstanding Christian teachings about human sin and guilt and the monumental eternal implications of salvation in Christ. Evangelicals of all sorts have believed that sharing that message is the kindest thing one can do for one's neighbor and such spiritual concerns have long proved infectious, not only in mass revivals, but also in personal relationships.

In order to appreciate the significance of this point—that for most evangelicals and fundamentalist there are things more important than politics—we need to be reminded of interrelationships of the movements we are considering. Fundamentalism, here defined primarily by its degree of militancy, is part of a larger American evangelical or conversionist Protestant movement that goes back to the trans-Atlantic revivalism of the eighteenth century. Since then it has generated countless variations on the fertile American soil and cross-bred with many other traditions. In that light we can appreciate that fundamentalism was part of "an authentic conservative tradition"—conversionist evangelicalism—and not just a reactive militancy against theological and cultural change.[64] It is true that the controversies of the 1920s and their sequels reshaped many types of conversionist evangelicalism. Similarly, political militancy since the 1970s has helped revive "fundamentalistic" attitudes even among many evangelicals who would not call themselves "fundamentalists." Nevertheless, the larger conversionist evangelical movement is shaped by longstanding greater concerns—such as the urgent need for positive evangelism, missions, and spirituality. Since the nineteenth century it has generated a host of parachurch agencies for promoting these goals. So even while theological or political controversies may do the most to make the news and shape later historical analyses, such contests are rarely the largest factors in shaping the everyday character of evangelicalism for its ordinary constituents.

Even in stricter self-styled fundamentalist churches, many other concerns far outweigh politics for most members. Individuals are attracted to these strict Bible fellowships for any number of reasons, but one pattern that consistently becomes conspicuous in local studies is that many converts are attracted to the order that it brings to their previously chaotic lives. In typical fundamentalist churches people who have been distressed by marital difficulties, alcohol abuse, or other disruptive behavior will tell how they came to value fundamentalist discipline. Those who feel disoriented by the mobility and impersonality and plethora of choices of contemporary life are attracted to the stability of a close-knit community with clear values and unambiguous sources of authority.[65]

Looking more broadly at conversionist evangelicalism in recent decades, we must also be reminded that some of the most flourishing groups have little to do directly with politics. Most of the largest mega-churches are built around emphases on evangelism and personal spiritual growth, rather than political action. Rick Warren of the huge Saddleback Church in Lake Forest, California, for instance, is best known for his ideas in *The Purpose Driven Church* (1995) and *The Purpose Driven Life* (2002), emphasizing church growth and discipleship. Bill Hybel's seeker-friendly Willow Creek Community Church in suburban Chicago similarly emphasizes church growth and advocates a non-partisan social agenda. Each of these churches served as models for hundreds of other thriving congregations. The charismatic Vineyard Christian Fellowship likewise grew since its founding in the 1970s to include hundreds of affiliated churches and represents only one of many types of pentecostal and charismatic churches that have thrived on emphasizing experiential Spirit-filled fellowship. Many of these enterprising and growing churches and movements have extensive overseas connections, missions, and charitable programs. By the end of the twentieth century Bible-believing conversionists had by default won the "fundamentalist" battles that had begun on the mission fields, as ninety percent of American missionaries were evangelical. Perhaps the largest story of recent decades, however, is the indigenous wild-fire spread throughout the third world of what was originally American-style evangelicalism. The counterpart in the United States has been the ethnic diversity of those who identify with various forms of evangelicalism, especially among Hispanic and Asian-American populations.

Some of the newer emphases among conversionist evangelicals, including self-styled fundamentalists, have reflected recent American preoccupations with the psychological and the relational. The most truly fundamentalist of these have been authoritarian. Bill Gothard's widely followed Basic Youth Conflict and Basic Life Principle seminars, for instance, teach biblically based male headship and a chain of command for church and family. While such hierarchical teachings had most impact in providing discipline for private and family life, they also had potential to be transformed into overt politics. James Dobson, a PhD in child psychology who first became widely known for his 1970 book, *Dare to Discipline,* provides the classic example. Originating in a holiness tradition, Dobson and his many-faceted Focus on the Family, founded in 1977, soon became one of the most influential forces in the fundamentalistic culture wars, promoting increasingly partisan political views. Other psychologically oriented conservative evangelical movements were both less fundamentalistic and less openly political. One of the largest movements of the 1990s was Promise Keepers, founded by University of Colorado head football coach Bill McCartney. Though criticized as anti-feminist, the major goals of this all male interracial movement were to promote greater spirituality and commitment among men and to help men to act more responsibly and lovingly as husbands and fathers. After a series of massive rallies that attracted national attention for a few years, it settled into a lower-key ongoing ministry.

When looking at relational teachings of recent evangelicalism, including major pentecostal and charismatic strands, one not only again finds countless varieties, but many of them appear to be a characteristically modern American to the degree that their appeal involves the promise of a contemporary form of self-fulfillment. Most religious movements, of course, offer spiritual self-fulfillment, whether by finding true meaning, losing oneself in God, or dedicating oneself to a community. These are still primary motifs in recent evangelicalism. At the same time, however, it is at least arguable that the movement also includes significant elements that are not so much protests against consumer culture as manifestations of it. Although the conservative political rhetoric and the strictly authoritarian branches of the movement echo the ideals of the Protestant work ethic of self-denial more characteristic of the producer economy of industrialism of the nineteenth century, they compete with other promises of the material good life, so ubiquitous in a consumer economy. Granted, there are aspects of the consumerist creed of self-fulfillment and self-indulgence that virtually all evangelical groups decisively reject, especially entertainments and ideologies that make nearly unrestrained sexual freedom and accompanying permissive lifestyles as an essential part of the good life and self-realization.[66] Nonetheless, there are not many other material aspects of the American dream that most adherents are expected to give up. Rather, it is usually assumed, and sometimes advertised, that the comforts of the suburbs, ability to vacation in exotic places, and economic security may well be added benefits of "seeking first the kingdom of God." It is true that evangelicals give considerable amounts to charities and that their spiritual commitments and stewardship often limit participation in the more extreme excesses of American material indulgence. Nonetheless, one also finds, as most notoriously in the giant televangelist ministries of Jim and Tammy Bakker, Pat Robertson, and Oral Roberts of the 1980s, perplexing mixes of the spiritual and the materialistic. Even aside from the influences of large-scale religious marketing, in most cases the difference between the behavior of many ordinary evangelicals and that of most other Americans is not at all dramatic.[67] Furthermore, in this "therapeutic age," Christian bookstores are filled with a vast literature on the superiority of spiritual means for everything from a better sex life, to overcoming depression, to achieving weight loss.[68] Fundamentalistic evangelicals' emphasis on conservative politics as a means of working for a secure and prosperous America are of a piece with this emphasis on this-worldly comforts, even while they also preach the otherworldly message that eternity depends on one's relation to Christ and that the true Christian must give up the pleasures of the world.[69]

Comparing this world of the Christian good life to that of fundamentalists and pentecostals of the 1920s suggests a shift away from a culture in which there was more emphasis on self-resignation and self-sacrifice to a culture in which this-worldly self-fulfillment is a more prominent theme. Although one can find anticipations of the culture of Christianity as an attractive lifestyle in the revivalist religion of the 1920s, and some fundamentalists were well-to-do promoters of modern commerce, it was far more common than it is today that fundamentalists and their pentecostal and holiness cousins were to be set apart, often by the way they were dressed. Women particularly were expected to signal their spiritual commitments by not using makeup and by dressing plainly and modestly in contrast to the fashionable consumerist styles of the day.[70] True discipleship was supposed to involve self-sacrifice, as in giving up worldly amusements, strictly observing the Sabbath, and performing sacrificial service. Sermons more often emphasized the joys of the next world as an explicit alternative to success as the world counted such things. In the 1920s if one was looking for a message that Christianity was the key to this worldly accomplishment and self-fulfillment and to being a responsible citizen, it was more likely to be heard from liberal preachers in mainline Protestant churches, the very clergy whom fundamentalists so strongly opposed.[71]

Much of the difference between the conservative evangelicals of the two eras is related to social class and location. While evangelicalism has always drawn from the whole spectrum of social classes, in recent decades it has flourished especially in the suburbs, as many mega-churches there attest. In this suburbanized setting, the affluence and aspirations to affluence have been unprecedented. Many of the standards of luxury in consumer culture prove nearly irresistible, so it is not surprising that, while the old Gospel of salvation in Christ and a life of discipline and service still speaks to people who are needy in many respects, it sometimes is most popular when it seems also to promise also an economically and psychologically fulfilling lifestyle.

THE LARGER PICTURE

This whole picture of evangelicalism and fundamentalism of recent decades as displaying stronger affinities to the American mainstream than it did in the 1920s suggests some larger patterns. The fundamentalism of the 1920s was one outgrowth of the evangelicalism that in the mid-nineteenth century had been among the major formative forces in American life. In a sense, then, the movement is returning to some of its deepest roots in a tradition that always had a custodial as well as a sectarian dimension. As in the early nineteenth century, when it opposed Enlightenment secularism, it thrives on opposition to modernizing trends. In the early twentieth century the progressive liberalism and modernism seemed inexorably moving to take over the dominant culture. Fundamentalism had an aspect of the desperation of those making a last stand for a dying civilization. By the end of the twentieth century, however, contrary to almost all predictions, fundamentalists had regained at least a self-image of being closer to the sort of relationship to the mainstream that they had held in the nineteenth century. That is not to say that they that they were living comfortably with the mainstream. Rather, as Christian Smith has pointed out in *American Evangelicals: Embattled and Thriving* and as was also true in the nineteenth century, evangelicalism is especially vigorous when it is closely connected with the cultural mainstream yet maintains a sense of being culturally embattled against it. It is a symbiotic relationship that invigorates just because one is so unhappy about it.

The politicization of fundamentalistic evangelicalism in recent decades and its unexpected resilience as a political force points to another larger story in American culture, the weakening of the progressive modern scientific liberal consensus that seemed to be building in the first half of the twentieth century. That was an era of national and cultural consolidation that had been going on since at least the Civil War. By the 1920s that national consolidation (which was resisted in much of the South and in many ethno-religious communities) had entered a predominantly secular stage. During that era most mainstream liberal observers believed that, if the totalitarian extremes could be avoided, it was virtually inevitable that modern scientifically based ideals would bring most people, formerly divided by pre-scientific faiths, together on the basis of universally valid principles. On that basis, many wise commentators predicted that fundamentalism would fade as the nation became more urbanized and universal education advanced. Such predictions proved wrong on two counts. First they underestimated fundamentalist and evangelical staying power even during the hey-day of progressive liberalism. Second, the even bigger story is that they overestimated the ability of science and progressive democratic ideas to provide a coherent and compelling alternative.

To make a long story short, at the end of this era of faith in science and progressive consensus, the countercultural upheaval of the 1960s intervened. Rather than arriving at cultural accord, the culture fragmented. Multiculturalism meant that the old white male establishment could no longer presume to speak for all right-thinking people. Post-modern intellectual motifs that flourished after the 1960s underscored cultural relativism with a vengeance. Science itself lost much of its cultural authority, even among intellectuals, as the popularity of Thomas Kuhn's *Structure of Scientific Revolutions* attested. More important for our purpose, the divisions of the cultural establishment over Vietnam and the stridency of the counterculture, including radical feminists, gays, and champions of the new sexual freedom, undercut the moral authority of progressive scientific liberalism for many working class and middle class Americans.

If we can generalize very broadly, the old progressive liberal side of the culture was saddled with the problems inherent in the pragmatism on which it had largely relied since the New Deal. Pragmatism is a wonderful cultural broker when it can draw on shared moral capital, but it does not provide much means for generating moral ideals of its own or for adjudicating among contending moral claims. When numerous goals and interest groups each presents the principles of its cause as self-evident, as they have done in the post-1960s era, how does the pragmatist choose among them? When the popular media of a consumer economy unrelentingly promote a culture of free choice and self-indulgence as the keys to the good life, how does pragmatism find a moral basis for alternatives? Even if there may be an argument that pragmatic liberalism is preferable to any of the truly ideological alternatives, its inability to generate a widely compelling larger moral vision left a sense of moral disarray that the Religious Right rushed in to try to correct. Not coincidentally, the fact that the secular left wing of the pragmatic liberal establishment had been particularly aggressive in attempting to eliminate distinctive religious voices from public life helped spark the counterattack.[72]

William Allen White once observed of William Jennings Bryan that he was always right in political prognosis and always wrong in prescription.[73] The same might be applied to much of fundamentalistic politics of the past thirty years.

Even those who most dislike the Religious Right and its simple either-or choices might recognize that it has been responding to a real crisis in a culture that has lost its moral compass—or, more precisely, finds itself with too many competing moral compasses. Perhaps most tellingly, the fundamentalistic attacks and their anger itself have pointed to a structural flaw in the attempt to shape society by a liberal pragmatism. "Inclusive pluralism" has been a working principle for pragmatists, one that can bridge the divide between liberals and post-modernists. Yet that principle of inclusion has also served to inhibit the religious expressions in the public domain of many sectarian groups who are not inclusive pluralists.[74] Sometimes such inhibiting has not been so much ideologically motivated as determined by the practical necessities of diverse peoples working together in public settings. Whatever the sources of these problems, so long as they are not resolved it is not altogether surprising that deeply committed people who claim some of the oldest American Protestant heritages should have responded by reasserting—sometimes with far more success than anyone would have predicted in the mid-1960s—their influence in the public sphere.

It is far easier, of course, to identify these peculiar features of American culture than to suggest an effective remedy. A safe bet, however, is that the simplistic and polarizing proposals of alarmists on either the secular left or the Religious Right are more likely to inflame the social tension rather than to provide a cure. One might hope that historical perspective might at least help persons on both sides of these issues to step back and try to assess them in their larger contexts. The cultural conflicts are not simply products of the machinations of the warped minds of one's opponents, but rather reflect deeply embedded cultural patterns. These patterns will need to be understood and taken into account by those who are looking for non-polarizing solutions to the problems of living together peacefully.

AFTERWORD
History and Fundamentalism

As we have seen, the question of history was central to the fundamentalist–modernist controversy. Should Christianity and the Bible be viewed through the lens of cultural development, or should culture be viewed through the lens of Scripture? The fundamentalists and the modernists shared a common assumption on this point. Each assumed that the abandonment, or at least substantial redefinition, of traditional Christian teaching concerning God's acts in history was implicit in the modern historical method which explained events in terms of natural cultural forces.

This assumption concerning history, which was at the heart of the old controversy, seems to me incorrect. It is basic Christian doctrine that there is an awesome distance between God and his creation, and yet that God nevertheless enters human history and acts in actual historical circumstances. The awareness that God acts in history in ways that we can only know in the context of our culturally determined experience should be central to a Christian understanding of history. Yet the Christian must not lose sight of the premise that, just as in the Incarnation Christ's humanity does not compromise his divinity, so the reality of God's other work in history, going well beyond what we might explain as natural phenomena, is not compromised by the fact that it is culturally defined.

The history of Christianity reveals a perplexing mixture of divine and human factors. As Richard Lovelace has said, this history, when viewed without a proper awareness of the spiritual forces involved, "is as confusing as a football game in which half the players are invisible."[1] The present work, an analysis of cultural influences on religious belief, is a study of things visible. As such it must necessarily reflect more than a little sympathy with the modern mode of explanation in terms of natural historical causation. Yet it would be a mistake to assume that such sympathy is incompatible with, or even antagonistic to, a view of history in which God as revealed in Scripture is the dominant force, and in which other unseen spiritual forces are contending. I find that a Christian view of history is clarified if one considers reality as more or less like the world portrayed in the works of J.R.R. Tolkien. We live in the midst of contests between great and mysterious spiritual forces, which we understand only imperfectly and whose true dimensions we only occasionally glimpse. Yet, frail as we are, we do play a role in this history, on the side either of the powers of light or of the powers of darkness. It is crucially important then, that, by God's grace, we keep our wits about us and discern the vast difference between the real forces for good and the powers of darkness disguised as angels of light.[2]

Such a larger vision is, I think, the proper context for understanding the historian's modest task of trying to identify the formative cultural elements that have either properly shaped or distorted our understanding of God and his revelation. Since God's work appears to us in historical circumstances where imperfect humans are major agents, the actions of the Holy Spirit in the church are always intertwined with culturally conditioned factors. The theologian's task is to try to establish from Scripture criteria for determining what in the history of the church is truly the work of the Spirit. The Christian historian takes an opposite, although complementary, approach. While he must keep in mind certain theological criteria, he may refrain from explicit judgments on what is properly Christian while he concentrates on observable cultural forces. By identifying these forces, he provides material which individuals of various theological persuasions may use to help distinguish God's genuine work from practices that have no greater authority than the customs or ways of thinking of a particular time and place.[3] How one judges any religious phenomenon will, however, depend more on one's theological stance than on one's identification of the historical conditions in which it arose.

More specifically, to point out how American fundamentalism was shaped by historical circumstances is not to place that movement in any special category in the history of Christianity. Since God works among imperfect human beings in historical settings, "pure" or "perfect" Christianity can seldom if ever exist in this world. God in his grace works through our limitations; for that very reason we should ask for the grace to recognize what those limitations are. So we may—and ought to—carefully identify the cultural forces which affect the current versions of Christianity.

In American church history many authors have pointed to the intertwining of Christianity with the various "isms" of the times—nationalism, socialism, individualism, liberalism, conservatism, scientism, subjectivism, common-sense objectivism, romanticism, relativism, cultural optimism, cultural pessimism, intellectualism, anti-intellectualism, self-ism, materialism, and so forth. Fundamentalism, as we have seen, incorporated some of these into its vision of Christianity. Yet God can certainly work through some such combinations. Christians' trust in God may be mingled or confused with some culturally formed assumptions, ideals, and values. Inevitably it will. The danger is that our culturally defined loves, allegiances, and understandings will overwhelm and take precedence over our faithfulness to God. So the identification of cultural forces, such as those with which this book is concerned, is essentially a constructive enterprise, with the positive purpose of finding the gold among the dross.

Notes

Introduction

1. Mencken, *Prejudices, Fourth Series* (New York, 1924), pp. 78–79; Lippmann, *A Preface to Morals* (New York, 1929), p. 12; Krutch, *The Modern Temper* (New York, 1956 [1929]), pp. 9, 16.
2. William R. Hutchison, *The Modernist Impulse in American Protestantism* (Cambridge, Mass., 1976) makes a similar point, pp. 257–287. Hutchison's is the most valuable study of the development of modernism in the period of this study.
3. Gray, "Modernism a Foe of Good Government," *Moody Monthly* XXIV (July, 1924), p. 545; Bryan, "The Fundamentals," *The Forum* LXX (July, 1923), from excerpt in Willard B. Gatewood, Jr., ed., *Controversy in the Twenties: Fundamentalism, Modernism, and Evolution* (Nashville, Tenn., 1969), p. 137; Machen, *Christianity and Liberalism* (New York, 1923), p. 6. Gatewood's volume is a very valuable collection of documents with perceptive introductions.
4. While militancy against modernism was the *key distinguishing* factor that drew fundamentalists together, militancy was not necessarily the *central* trait of fundamentalists. Missions, evangelism, prayer, personal holiness, or a variety of doctrinal concerns may often or usually have been their first interest. Yet, without militancy, none of these important aspects of the movement set it apart as "fundamentalist."
5. See Chapters XXII–XXIV below on these interpretive traditions.
6. Sandeen, *The Roots of Fundamentalism: British and American Millenarianism 1800–1930* (Chicago, 1970). I have commented on Sandeen at greater length in "Defining Fundamentalism," *Christian Scholar's Review* I (Winter, 1971), pp. 141–51; cf. Sandeen's reply, I (Spring, 1971), pp. 227–232. See also comments on Sandeen in Chapter XXII of this volume.
7. Cf. George Dollar who in *A History of Fundamentalism in America* (Greenville, S.C., 1973) has this strict separatist fundamentalist perspective of today and agrees basically with Sandeen's definition.
8. LeRoy Moore, Jr., "Another Look at Fundamentalism: A Response to Ernest R. Sandeen," *Church History* XXXVII (June, 1968), pp. 195–202 makes this and other valuable criticisms of an earlier statement of Sandeen's thesis.
9. In this approach I agree with C. Allyn Russell in his worthwhile volume *Voices of American Fundamentalism: Seven Biographical Studies* (Philadelphia, 1976).
10. Sydney E. Ahlstrom writes, "No aspect of American church history is more in need of summary and yet so difficult to summarize as the movements of dissent and reaction between the Civil War and World War I." *A Religious History of the American People* (New Haven, 1972), p. 823.

I. Evangelical America at the Brink of Crisis

1. George L. Prentiss, "The National Crisis," *American Theological Review*, 1st ser., 4 (October, 1862), pp. 674–718; William Adams, "The War for Independence and the War for Secession," *American Presbyterian and Theological Review*, 2nd ser., 4 (January, 1866), p. 92. These quotations are from George M. Marsden, *The Evangelical Mind and the New School Presbyterian Experience* (New Haven, 1970), pp. 207, 209, which provides some background to the present study.

2. *The Kingdom of Christ on Earth: Twelve Lectures Delivered Before the Students of the Theological Seminary, Andover* (Andover, Mass., 1874), p. 2, quoted in Robert T. Handy, *A Christian America: Protestant Hopes and Historical Reality* (New York, 1971), pp. 98–99. Handy's work is a good source on the identification of America with the kingdom.

3. The Rev. W. W. Patton, "Revivals of Religion—How to Make them Productive of Permanent Good," *History, Essays, Orations, and Other Documents of the Sixth General Conference of the Evangelical Alliance, Held in New York, October 2–12, 1873*. Philip Schaff and S. Irenaeus Prime, eds., (New York, 1874), p. 351. (Hereafter cited as *EA 1873*.)

4. Joseph Angus, "Duty of the Church in Relation to Mission," *EA 1873*, p. 583.

5. See John Harris Jones, "Christianity as a Reforming Power," *EA 1873*, pp. 661–62, for an illustration of this argument.

6. "The Relations of Constitution and Government in the United States to Religion," *EA 1873*, p. 527.

7. Paul A. Carter, *The Spiritual Crisis of the Gilded Age* (DeKalb, Illinois, 1971) provides a good portrait of this age.

8. Quoted in Handy, *A Christian America*, p. 84. Handy, pp. 84–88, provides a very valuable account of this concern.

9. "Sunday Legislation," *EA 1873*, pp. 540–43.

10. Both quotations are from Handy, p. 85, the first from a Congregational statement in 1877 and the latter from the Northern Methodists in 1884.

11. Brian Harrison points out that in Sabbatarianism "flourished . . . a genuine coincidence of interest between evangelicals and working men. . . ." *Past and Present*, 38 (Dec., 1967), p. 105, cited in Daniel Walker Howe, ed., *Victorian America* (Philadelphia, 1976), pp. 10–11.

12. William H. Allen, "The Labor Question," *EA 1873*, pp. 670–74.

13. "The Right Use of Wealth," *EA 1873*, pp. 357–61.

14. Anderson says precisely this, *ibid.*, p. 361. Cf. Daniel Walker Howe, "Victorian Culture in America," in Howe, ed., *Victorian America*, p. 24. Howe's essay is perhaps the best brief account of the American Victorian outlook.

15. George P. Schmidt, *The Old Time College President* (New York, 1930).

16. Burton J. Bledstein, *The Culture of Professionalism: The Middle Class and the Development of Higher Education in America* (New York, 1976) explores these trends. Cf. Frederick Rudolph, *The American College and University: A History* (New York, 1962).

17. Cf. G. Stanley Hall's remark in 1879, "there are less than a half dozen colleges or universities in the United States where metaphysical thought is entirely freed from reference to theological formula." Quoted in Herbert W. Schneider, *A History of American Philosophy* (New York, 1946), p. 376.

18. Among the number of very useful summaries of Common Sense Realism which have helped in formulating this account are: Sydney E. Ahlstrom, "The Scottish Philosophy and American Theology," *Church History* XXIV (Sept., 1955), pp. 257–72; Theodore Dwight Bozeman, *Protestants in an Age of Science: The Baconian Ideal and Antebellum American Religious Thought* (Chapel Hill, 1977); George H. Daniels, *American Science in the Age of Jackson* (New York, 1968); Elizabeth Flower and Murray G. Murphey, *A History of American Philosophy* (New York, 1977); S. A. Grave, *The Scottish Philosophy of Common Sense* (Oxford, 1960); Daniel Walker Howe, *The Unitarian Conscience: Harvard Moral Philosophy, 1805–1861* (Cambridge, Mass., 1970); William McLoughlin, ed., *The American Evangelicals, 1800–1900* (New York, 1968); Terence Martin, *The Instructed Vision: Scottish Common Sense Philosophy and the Origins of American Fiction* (Bloomington, Ind., 1961); Henry F. May, *The Enlightenment in America* (New York, 1976); Donald H. Meyer, *The Democratic Enlightenment* (New York, 1976); D. H. Meyer, *The Instructed Conscience, the Shaping of the American National Ethic* (Philadelphia, 1972); Perry Miller, ed., *American Thought: Civil War to World War I* (New York, 1963 [1954]); Herbert W. Schneider, *A History of American Philosophy* (New York, 1946); Douglas Sloan, *The Scottish Enlightenment and the American College Ideal* (New York, 1971); John W. Stewart, "The Tethered Theology . . . ," uncompleted manuscript (1978) Ph.D. dissertation, University of Michigan.

19. Meyer, *Democratic Enlightenment*, pp. 191–92. Cf. Garry Wills, *Inventing America: Jefferson's Declaration of Independence* (New York, 1978).

20. See especially Bozeman and Daniels, cited note 18 above. Also Herbert Hovenkamp, *Science and Religion in America, 1800–1860* (Philadelphia, 1978).

21. Francis Wayland, *The Elements of Moral Science,* Joseph Angus, ed., (London, n. d. [1835]), p. 85 and p. 4.

22. Ahlstrom, cited note 18 above, points out the optimistic, humanistic, and individualistic tendencies of Common Sense philosophy.

23. On the tensions between Calvinism and individualism, see Bozeman. Cf. Marsden, *Evangelical Mind.*

24. See discussion, Chapter XIII below.

25. "Grounds of Knowledge and Rules for Belief," *Princeton Review* 57 (January, 1881), p. 18; for a compendium of Common Sense arguments to cure "honest doubt," see p. 1 and *passim.*

26. Letter to Frederic Hedge, quoted in Francis P. Weisenburger, *Ordeal of Faith: The Crisis of Church-Going America 1865–1900* (New York, 1959).

27. Hitchcock, "Romanism in the Light of History," *EA 1873,* p. 436 (Hitchcock's address is actually a plea for more understanding toward Rome than was generally expressed at the meetings).

28. "Recent Questions of Unbelief," *Bibliotheca Sacra* XXVII (July, 1870), p. 469.

29. William E. Dodge, "Opening Address," *EA 1873,* p. 14.

30. M. Cohen Stuart, "Holland," *EA 1873,* p. 93; Hermann Krummacher, "Germany," p. 80; Christlieb, "The Best Methods of Counteracting Modern Infidelity," p. 207.

31. "American Infidelity: Its Factors and Phases," *EA 1873,* pp. 249–54. The Rev. E. A. Washburn, a New York pastor who followed Warren to the platform, echoed similar sentiments, "Reason and Faith," pp. 255–69.

32. "Religious Aspects of the Doctrine of Development," *EA 1873,* pp. 264–75.

33. *EA 1873,* Appendix, "Discussion on Darwinism and the Doctrine of Development," pp. 317–23.
34. Cf. Bozeman's discussion of "doxological science."
35. This interpretation follows more or less that of James Ward Smith's excellent essay, "Religion and Science in American Philosophy," Smith and A. Leland Jamison, eds., *The Shaping of American Religion* (Princeton, 1961), pp. 402–42.
36. Moderate reconciliations, such as that suggested by McCosh, seem to have been more readily accepted in Great Britain. See George M. Marsden, "Fundamentalism as an American Phenomenon, A Comparison with English Evangelicalism," *Church History* 46 (June, 1977), pp. 215–32.

II. The Paths Diverge

1. This summary is based most immediately on the following: Daniel Walker Howe, ed., *Victorian America* (Philadelphia, 1976); Burton J. Bledstein, *The Culture of Professionalism: The Middle Class and the Development of Higher Education in America* (New York, 1976); Robert H. Wiebe, *The Search for Order 1877–1920* (New York, 1967); Paul A. Carter, *The Spiritual Crisis of the Gilded Age* (Dekalb, Ill., 1971); Howard Mumford Jones, *The Age of Energy: Varieties of American Experience* (New York, 1970); H. Wayne Morgan, ed., *The Gilded Age: A Reappraisal* (Syracuse, N. Y., 1963).
2. As D. H. Meyer says, "The Victorians of the late nineteenth century replaced the medieval alliance of faith and reason with a combination of sentimentalism and intellectualism. . . ." "The Victorian Crisis of Faith," in Howe, ed., *Victorian America,* p. 76.
3. Cf. William G. McLoughlin, *The Meaning of Henry Ward Beecher: An Essay on the Shifting Values of Mid-Victorian America, 1840–1870* (New York, 1970), pp. 185–220 and Henry Ward Beecher, *Patriotic Addresses,* J. R. Howard, ed. (New York, 1887). For an engaging account of the Beecher family see Marie Caskey, *Chariot of Fire: Religion and the Beecher Family* (New Haven, 1978).
4. Paul Carter, *The Spiritual Crisis,* pp. 111–32, has a helpful account of Beecher's reputation.
5. Cf. Sydney Ahlstrom, "Theology in America: A Historical Survey," James Ward Smith and A. Leland Jamison, eds., *The Shaping of American Religion* (Princeton, 1961), p. 294.
6. Cf. Daniel Walker Howe, *The Unitarian Conscience: Harvard Moral Philosophy, 1805–1861* (Cambridge, Mass., 1970).
7. McLoughlin, *Beecher,* pp. 25–26; 134–51. Cf. Clifford E. Clark, *Henry Ward Beecher: Spokesman for Middle Class America* (Urbana, Ill., 1978), who likewise argues for this thesis.
8. McLoughlin, *Beecher,* p. 49.
9. Carter, *The Spiritual Crisis,* p. 125.
10. Quoted in Caskey, *Chariot of Fire,* p. 248.
11. Cf. Perry Miller, "Nature and the National Ego," *Errand into the Wilderness* (New York, 1956), pp. 204–16.
12. Cf. McLoughlin, *Beecher,* pp. 4–5; see also Bledstein, *Culture of Professionalism,* pp. 259–68, on immense popularity of Emerson among students.
13. Quoted in McLoughlin, *Beecher,* p. 67.

14. "Future Punishment," *The Original Plymouth Pulpit, Sermons of Henry Ward Beecher*, vol. V. (Boston, 1871), pp. 99–111.

15. *The Modern Movement in American Theology: Sketches in the History of American Protestant Thought from the Civil War to the World War* (New York, 1939), p. 86.

16. "The Two Revelations," *Evolution and Religion* (New York, 1885), pp. 44–55. For explication of the romantic defense of science see McLoughlin, *Beecher*, esp., pp. 34–54.

17. *Evolution and Religion*, p. 24. Foster quotes this passage with great approval, an indication of the extent to which Beecher enunciated a basic principle of later liberalism.

18. *Yale Lectures in Preaching* (New York, 1872), pp. 76–84, 87–90; reprinted in William R. Hutchison, ed., *American Protestant Thought: The Liberal Era* (New York, 1968), pp. 37–45. Hutchison in *The Modernist Impulse in American Protestantism* (Cambridge, Mass., 1976) points out that many liberals were not as optimistic or as liberal as Beecher, e.g., p. 100.

19. Foster, *Modern Movement*, pp. 16–27. Cf. Daniel Day Williams, *The Andover Liberals: A Study in American Theology* (Morningside Heights, N.Y., 1941).

20. *Old Faiths in New Light* (2nd ed., New York, 1879), pp. 383–91, reprinted in H. Shelton Smith *et al.*, eds., *American Christianity: An Historical Interpretation with Representative Documents*, vol. II, 1820–1960 (New York, 1963), pp. 266–70. Compare this analysis to that of Daniel Day Williams, *Andover Liberals*, p. 173: "Liberal theology has been both attracted and repelled by the possibility of the limitation of human knowledge to that which is scientifically verifiable. It has accepted science as the valid interpretation of certain aspects of nature and has avoided accepting the full consequences of this acceptance."

21. Carter, *The Spiritual Crisis*, pp. 50–55. Abbot quotation from *The Evolution of Christianity* (Boston, 1892), p. 227.

22. "The Law of Growth" (1877), *The Law of Growth and Other Sermons*, Ninth Series (New York, 1902), p. 12.

23. Frances C. Blanchard, *The Life of Charles Albert Blanchard* (New York, 1932), p. 23.

24. *Lectures on Revivals of Religion* (New York, 1835), p. 177, quoted in Richard Hofstadter, *Anti-Intellectualism in American Life* (New York, 1962), p. 94.

25. "A Perfect State of Society," *Sermons and Addresses* (Chicago, 1892), pp. 35–36. Donald W. Dayton, *Discovering an Evangelical Heritage* (New York, 1976), discusses Blanchard, Finney, and other radical evangelical reform of the time.

26. Clyde S. Kilby, *Minority of One: The Biography of Jonathan Blanchard* (Grand Rapids, 1959), pp. 15–102; Richard S. Taylor, "Jonathan Blanchard: Nineteenth Century Evangelical," M.A. thesis, Northern Illinois University, 1970, pp. 20–93. Taylor's work has been revised and expanded in "Seeking the Kingdom: A Study in the Career of Jonathan Blanchard (1811–1892)," Ph.D. dissertation, Northern Illinois University, 1977. References below, however, are to the earlier version.

27. Kilby, *Minority*, pp. 100–102, 120–21, 137–47. Cf. George P. Schmidt, *The Old Time College President* (New York, 1930), p. 210n.

28. "The Kingdom of Christ: And the Duty of American Colleges Respecting It" (1846), *Sermons and Addresses*, p. 114.

29. Taylor, "Blanchard," pp. 103–5; William Delahoyde, "Common Sense Philoso-

phy at Wheaton College (1860–1940)," unpublished paper, Trinity Evangelical Divinity School, 1976.

30. "The Kingdom," pp. 104–5.

31. Cf. Richard S. Taylor, "Millennialism in American Education: Jonathan Blanchard at Knox and Wheaton," paper delivered at the American Society of Church History, December, 1977, pp. 10–11.

32. Finney wrote *The Character, Claims, and Practical Workings of Freemasonry* (Chicago, 1869).

33. "The Spirit of the *Cynosure*," *Christian Cynosure* I (July 11, 1872), p. 154.

34. Blanchard wrote to Finney, Nov. 12, 1868, "The Masons are hunting and hounding me to death—but Christ is with me, and 'I will not fear what man can do.'" Quoted in Taylor, "Blanchard," p. 139. One need not assume, of course, that such active opposition was wholly imaginary, although perhaps exaggerated.

35. See Thomas A. Askew, Jr., "The Liberal Arts College Encounters Intellectual Change: A Comparative Study of Education at Knox and Wheaton Colleges, 1837–1925," Ph.D. dissertation, Northwestern University, 1969, for a fascinating account. See also Timothy L. Smith, "Uncommon Schools: Christian Colleges and Social Idealism in Midwestern America, 1820–1850" (essay printed by the Indiana Historical Society, 1978), which sets such developments in a wider context.

36. Both were active in the National Reform Association which had this goal. Jonathan served as Vice-President for a time. See Jonathan Blanchard, "God in the Constitution," *Sermons and Addresses*, pp. 138–48, delivered at the NRA convention in 1871. Charles Blanchard spoke at the 1874 meeting, *Proceedings of the National Convention to Secure the Religious Amendment of the Constitution of the United States* (Philadelphia, 1874). It is significant regarding the dynamics of the later fundamentalist coalition that Archibald Alexander Hodge of Princeton Theological Seminary also spoke for this cause, *ibid.*

37. *A Brief History of the National Christian Association* (Chicago, 1875), pp. 10–12.

38. Askew, "Liberal Arts College," pp. 81–82.

39. "Henry Ward Beecher," *Christian Cynosure* I (May 9, 1872), p. 118; "The Spirit of the *Cynosure*," p. 154. I am indebted to Paul Carter who points out this controversy, *The Spiritual Crisis*, pp. 113–14, 124, 139.

40. Blanchard had been closest to Edward Beecher. The two co-edited *Secret Societies: A Discussion of their Character and Claims* (Cincinnati, 1867). Edward, however, was in Brooklyn aiding Henry in editorial work at the time of the Blanchard attack. Taylor, "Blanchard," pp. 121, 129; Caskey, *Chariot*, 137–38.

41. Kilby, *Minority*, pp. 182, 190; Taylor, "Blanchard," pp. 139–46. By this time Blanchard was correspondingly more cautious in his optimism for society, seeing each advance in one area accompanied by setbacks in others. In 1886 he saw the immediate prospect as "gloomy," although the long-range outlook seemed good. Taylor, "Millennialism," pp. 16–17.

42. Cy Hulse, "The Shaping of a Fundamentalist: A Case Study of Charles Blanchard," M.A. thesis, Trinity Evangelical Divinity School, 1976, p. 56, convincingly sets the date for Charles Blanchard's shift to premillennialism at around 1885. He did not, however, say much about such views before *Light on*

the Last Days: Being Familiar Talks on the Book of Revelation (Chicago, 1913), a work dedicated to Emma Dryer.

43. Frances Blanchard, *Life*, pp. 65, 73.
44. *Ibid.*, pp. 52–53.
45. Quoted in Askew, "Liberal Arts College," p. 227.
46. Frances Blanchard, *Life*, p. 180.

III. D. L. Moody and a New American Evangelism

1. "Introduction," Dwight L. Moody, *Echoes from the Pulpit and Platform* . . . (Hartford, Conn., 1900), p. 31.
2. *Ibid.*, title page.
3. *Ibid.*, p. 27.
4. Quoted in James F. Findlay, Jr., *Dwight L. Moody: American Evangelist 1837–1899* (Chicago, 1969), p. 412.
5. Cf. the excellent discussion of this issue in Stanley N. Gundry, *Love Them In: The Proclamation Theology of D. L. Moody* (Chicago, 1976), pp. 198–218.
6. "Revivals," *Moody's Latest Sermons* (Chicago, 1900), p. 125.
7. Liberals as well as conservatives claimed the Moody heritage, as is indicated by a long controversy sparked by an editorial, "Where Would Mr. Moody Stand?" *Christian Century* XXXX (July 12, 1923), pp. 870–72. Gundry, *Love Them In*, p. 200, lists twelve publications in the ensuing debate.
8. The following account depends considerably on the outstanding biography of Moody by James F. Findlay. Cf. Richard K. Curtis, *They Called Him Mister Moody* (Grand Rapids, 1962); and J. C. Pollock, *Moody: A Biographical Portrait of the Pacesetter in Modern Mass Evangelism* (New York, 1962).
9. Findlay, *Moody*, pp. 286–87, 337.
10. See Findlay, *Moody*, pp. 306–55 for fine accounts of these works. On the schools see Donald A. Wells, "D. L. Moody and His Schools: An Historical Analysis of an Educational Ministry," Ph.D. dissertation, Boston University, 1972.
11. Gundry, *Love Them In*, pp. 71–86 argues against the charge that "technique had triumphed over truth" in Moody's theology. His argument establishes that Moody was not a pragmatist *in theory* the way Finney was. However, Gundry's own subsequent account shows that Moody tested doctrines on the basis of their suitability to evangelism. See, for instance, p. 185 where Gundry says that "perhaps Moody's major emphasis in his preaching of premillennialism . . . is the practical effect of preaching the doctrine." See also the quotations cited in notes 12 and 14 below. Such pragmatism, of course, does not imply that Moody (or Finney for that matter) did not test his doctrines first by Scripture.
12. W. H. Daniels, ed., *Moody: His Words, Work, and Workers* (New York, 1877), quoted in Gundry, *Love Them In*, p. 88.
13. This scheme is attributed to Moody by Daniels, *op. cit.* Its adequacy is attested by Gundry who organizes his analysis of Moody's theology around this scheme.
14. Quoted in Gundry, *Love Them In*, p. 99.
15. *Moody's Latest Sermons*, pp. 52–60.
16. For example, "Tekel," *Moody: His Words*, Daniels, ed., pp. 415–16.
17. "The Ninety-First Psalm," *Moody's Latest Sermons*, pp. 11–12.
18. For examples, "Sowing and Reaping," *Secret Power* (Chicago, 1896); "Tempta-

tion," *Latest Sermons;* "Tekel," *Moody: His Words.* Cf. Gundry, *Love Them In,* pp. 90–91, who observes from a wider study of Moody's sermons, "In expanding the thought of the sinfulness of humanity, it was common for Moody to speak of acts of sin such as ingratitude to parents, drunkenness, acts of sexual immorality, theater attendance, worldly amusements, Sabbath-breaking, etc."

19. *Latest Sermons,* pp. 27–28. Cf. *Secret Power,* pp. 109–11, where he argues that lotteries, entertainments, dramas, or "unconverted choirs" in churches are signs of the Church descending to the level of the world.

20. All these hymns are found in *Gospel Hymns Nos. 1 to 6,* Ira D. Sankey, *et al.,* eds. (New York, 1894). Sandra S. Sizer, *Gospel Hymns and Social Religion: The Rhetoric of Nineteenth-Century Revivalism* (Philadelphia, 1978), provides a very insightful analysis of the Sankey volume and other aspects of this topic. William G. McLoughlin, Jr., *Modern Revivalism: Charles Grandison Finney to Billy Graham* (New York, 1959), pp. 233–39, also discusses Sankey and these hymns.

21. *Moody: His Words,* Daniels, ed., pp. 431–32. Moody's social views are discussed in Findlay, *Moody,* pp. 272–302, and in McLoughlin, *Modern Revivalism,* pp. 267–79. McLoughlin's work documents similar emphases in other evangelists of the era. Moody's associates, however, were quite divided on the issue; see Chapter IX below.

22. These points are argued at length in Sizer, *Gospel Hymns.*

23. *Moody: His Words,* Daniels, ed., pp. 431–32.

24. This point also is stressed in Sizer, *Gospel Hymns.*

25. *Sowing and Reaping* (Chicago, 1896), p. 83.

26. Ernest Sandeen, *The Roots of Fundamentalism* (Chicago, 1970) has an excellent discussion of the relationship of the premillennial movement to Moody's work.

27. *Secret Power: or, the Secret of Success in Christian Life and Christian Work* (Chicago, 1881); and *The Way to God and How to Find it* (Chicago, 1884). These reflect the influences of Keswick teaching; cf. Chapter VIII below.

28. Gundry, a dispensationalist himself, has examined Moody's sermons carefully on this point and does not find any clear teachings on such dispensationalist positions as the secret rapture of the church, a seven-year interval between Christ's coming and his inauguration of the millennial kingdom, or the view of the church age as "a parenthesis," *Love Them In,* pp. 187–88.

29. Gundry, *Love Them In,* p. 185.

30. "The Second Coming of Christ," *The Best of D. L. Moody,* Wilbur M. Smith, ed. (Chicago, 1971), pp. 193–95.

31. *Ibid.*

32. "Revivals," *Latest Sermons,* pp. 106, 125–26.

IV. Prologue: The Paradox of Revivalist Fundamentalism

1. Stanley N. Gundry, *Love Them In: The Proclamation Theology of D. L. Moody* (Chicago, 1976), although very sympathetic, raises questions about his anti-intellectualism, p. 221. Cf. the rather less sympathetic treatment in Richard Hofstadter, *Anti-Intellectualism in American Life* (New York, 1962), pp. 106–14; 121–22.

2. "What was Christ's Attitude Towards Error? A Symposium," *Record of Christian Work* (November, 1899), pp. 600, 602, quoted in Gundry, *Love Them In,* pp.

217–18. Cf. the response of A. T. Pierson, another fundamentalist precursor, whose response is negative, unlike most of the others, *ibid.*, p. 602.

3. The relationships among Puritanism, pietism, and later evangelicalism are explored in helpful ways by Richard Lovelace, *The American Pietism of Cotton Mather* (Grand Rapids, 1979).

4. Sizer, *Gospel Hymns and Social Religion* (Philadelphia, 1978), esp. pp. 50–82; 112–15.

5. Sizer, *Gospel Hymns*, pp. 48, 111–37, and *passim.*

6. Sizer, *Gospel Hymns*, e.g. p. 129, emphasizes the neglected popular forms, but then neglects the role of the belief system.

7. C. Norman Kraus, *Dispensationalism in America: Its Rise and Development* (Richmond, Va., 1958), develops this relationship. Both Kraus and Ernest Sandeen, *The Roots of Fundamentalism* (Chicago, 1970), trace the development of Darby's views and their importance in America in very helpful detail. On the Brethren, see also H. A. Ironside, *A Historical Sketch of the Brethren Movement* (Grand Rapids, 1942).

8. Sandeen, *Roots,* p. 152; cf. p. 239. Samuel J. Kellogg of Western Seminary, one of the early theologians of the movement, estimated that at the 1878 conference at least 88 percent of those supporting the call to the conference were explicitly committed to Calvinism, Kraus, *Dispensationalism,* pp. 59–60.

9. A notable exception was William E. Blackstone who in 1878 published *Jesus is Coming,* which was the most popular book associated with the movement through World War I. Blackstone and the few other notable Methodists in the movement had very loose associations with the denomination, Sandeen, *Roots,* p. 163.

10. Sandeen, *Roots,* pp. 75–78; James Findlay, *Dwight L. Moody* (Chicago, 1969), p. 127. Moody accepted the outlines of premillennial teaching some time after 1867 largely through contacts with Henry Moorhouse, a representative of the British Plymouth Brethren.

11. One example is the popularity of Hal Lindsey, *The Late Great Planet Earth* (Grand Rapids, 1970). As of 1978 the publisher claimed over 9,800,000 copies in print. In the 1970s most fundamentalists, holiness groups, pentecostals, and other evangelicals held some form of these premillennial views.

12. The importance of the institutional history of the movement has been described in helpful detail by Sandeen, *Roots.*

13. *Modern Revivalism* (New York, 1959), p. 371.

14. Arthur Tappan Pierson (1837–1911) was (as his name suggests) closely related to the New School Presbyterian tradition. J. Wilbur Chapman (1859–1918), another evangelistic associate and successor of Moody, was educated at Oberlin College and Lane Seminary. A. J. Gordon (1836–1895) was always a New Englander with a typical New England clerical education. William J. Erdman (1834–1923) was a graduate of the New School Presbyterian Union Theological Seminary in New York. The Blanchards always considered themselves New Englanders. For a discussion of such affinities see George M. Marsden, "The New School Heritage and Presbyterian Fundamentalism," *Westminster Theological Journal* XXXII (May, 1970), pp. 129–47.

15. Robert Harkness, *Reuben Archer Torrey: The Man and His Message* (Chicago, 1929), p. 10.

16. Interview with Dr. Ernest W. Wordsworth, Torrey file, Moody Bible Institute archives.

17. McLoughlin, *Modern Revivalism,* 371–73.

18. *Modern Revivalism,* p. 375.

19. Daniel Stevick, a particularly acute observer of fundamentalism, pointed out such contrasts continuing in the 1960s. "One observes," he says, "that a good many Fundamentalist churches . . . practice both styles of worship—lecture hall with black gown and immense dignity on Sunday morning, vaudeville with xylophone and frenzied indignity on Sunday evening." *Beyond Fundamentalism* (Richmond, Va., 1964), p. 148.

V. Two Revisions of Millennialism

1. *Sixty Years with the Bible: A Record of Experience* (New York, 1912 [1909]), p. 102.

2. Such secularization, of course, can be found in every age, but has been especially pronounced since the eighteenth century. "Secularization" is not a precise term, and can be used with more positive connotations.

3. *The Modern Schism: Three Paths to the Secular* (New York, 1969), p. 95.

4. Clear distinctions in terminology between "premillennial" and "postmillennial" do not seem to occur before the nineteenth century. A third position, "amillennialism," not so termed until the twentieth century, holds that the prophecies concerning *both* the struggles with anti-Christ *and* the reign of Christ are being partially fulfilled already in the present church age so that the "millennium" does not represent a separate historical period. Robert G. Clouse, ed., *The Meaning of the Millennium: Four Views* (Downers Grove, Ill., 1977), clarifies these distinctions.

5. See, for instance, "History of Opinions Respecting the Millennium," *American Theological Review,* 1st series, I (November, 1859), p. 655. I have summarized postmillennial teaching, as well as pre-Civil-War American premillennialism, in more detail in *The Evangelical Mind and the New School Presbyterian Experience* (New Haven, 1970), pp. 182–98.

6. See Nathan Hatch, *The Sacred Cause of Liberty: Republican Thought and the Millennium in Revolutionary New England* (New Haven, 1977) on the secularization of postmillennialism during the Revolutionary era. For a broader discussion of American millennialism and nationalism, see Ernest Lee Tuveson, *Redeemer Nation: The Idea of America's Millennial Role* (Chicago, 1968).

7. Clarke, *Sixty Years,* pp. 104–5; cf. Clarke, *The Use of Scripture in Theology* (New York, 1905), pp. 102–13.

8. *The Ideal of Jesus* (New York, 1911), pp. 70–72.

9. McGiffert, "The Kingdom of God" (1909), *Christianity as History and Faith,* Arthur Cushman McGiffert, Jr., ed. (New York, 1934), p. 303.

10. For example, see William R. Hutchison, *The Modernist Impulse in American Protestantism* (Cambridge, Mass., 1976), pp. 148–50, on Clarke.

11. This analysis follows roughly the analysis of how changes in ideas take place found in Thomas S. Kuhn, *The Structure of Scientific Revolutions,* 2nd ed. (1970 [1962]). An accepted orthodoxy provides a paradigm into which all data are placed. Eventually, however, this paradigm may become so overburdened

with anomalies that a period of crisis develops. At this point some may produce new paradigms that interpret the data in a radically different framework. Exponents of the two schools of thought then can hardly communicate since their basic perceptions of the data differ. See also the discussion in Chapter XXIV below. I see Kuhn's own model as a useful analogy for discussing changes in other areas of thought, rather than as a precise analytical tool.

12. See Marsden, *Evangelical Mind,* pp. 182–98. For an example of this earlier premillennialism see George Duffield, *Dissertations on the Prophecies Relative to the Second Coming of Jesus Christ* (New York, 1842). The rise of premillennialism in the 1860s is suggested especially by the appearance of many premillennial hymns during this era. Particularly prominent in this respect is the work of Philip P. Bliss, author of "Hold the Fort, For I am Coming," and many other premillennial songs. By the time of the Moody revivals of the 1870s, such hymns seem to have been quite popular. Cf. Sandra Sizer, *Gospel Hymns and Social Religion* (Philadelphia, 1978).

13. Arno C. Gaebelein (1861–1945), a German by birth, relates that this fact initially aroused the suspicion of James H. Brookes (1830–1897) who questioned him carefully to see that he was free from German rationalism and higher criticism. Gaebelein, *Half a Century* (New York, 1930), pp. 39–40.

14. These developments are traced in detail in the works by Sandeen and Kraus, cited Chapter IV, and Dollar, cited Introduction—to name only the best known sources—and so will not be repeated here. Timothy P. Weber, "Living in the Shadow of the Second Coming: American Premillennialism, 1875–1925," Ph.D. disssertation, University of Chicago, 1976, provides one of the best discussions of the cultural attitudes of the movement. Cf. his book of the same title (New York, 1979).

15. *The Scofield Reference Bible,* C. I. Scofield, ed. (New York, 1917 [1909]), pp. 914–15, notes.

16. *Ibid.,* pp. 1334–50, notes.

17. This controversy over whether the rapture would take place before or after the tribulation split the movement and contributed to the demise of the Niagara Bible Conference in 1901. Robert Cameron (ca. 1845–ca. 1922) led the posttribulationist party. A. C. Gaebelein and C. I. Scofield (1843–1921) became the most influential spokesmen for the successful pretribulationist party. See Sandeen and Kraus. Also Talmadge Wilson, "A History of Dispensationalism in the United States of America: The Nineteenth Century," Th.M. thesis, Pittsburgh-Xenia Theological Seminary, 1956; Larry D. Pettegrew, "The Niagara Bible Conference and American Fundamentalism," five parts, *Central Bible Quarterly* XIX–XX (Winter, 1976–Winter, 1977). Richard E. Reiter, "The Decline of the Niagara Bible Conference and Breakup of the United Premillennial Movement," unpublished seminar paper, Trinity Evangelical Divinity School, 1976, points out that the dispute was "a serious 'family quarrel'" but that not all personal connections were severed, as evidenced, for instance, in the cooperation of some posttribulationists in the *Scofield Bible.*

18. *Scofield Bible,* pp. 1002, 1089, notes.

19. See, for instance, W. E. B. [William E. Blackstone], *Jesus Is Coming* (Chicago, 1908 [1878]), pp. 83–97.

20. For example, see the chart, "Degeneration," near the beginning of Chapter VII.

Timothy Weber, "Living in the Shadow," p. 33, lists six schemes of prominent dispensational leaders. That of C. I. Scofield, which became a sort of orthodoxy in his *Reference Bible,* has the following dispensations: (1) Innocence, from the creation of Adam and ending in the Fall; (2) Conscience, from the Fall to the flood; (3) Human Government, from Noah but overlapping other dispensations, ending with various failures (Babel, the captivities of the Jews, and for the Gentiles the judgment of the nations) though continuing today among the Gentiles, who govern for self and not for God (cf. *Reference Bible,* p. 16); (4) Promise, from Abraham to Moses; (5) Law, from Moses to the death of Christ; (6) Grace, from the cross to the second coming; (7) the Kingdom, or millennial age, or personal reign of Christ, ending with "Satan loosed a little season" but quickly defeated. After the millennium are the "new heavens and new earth" of eternity. Scofield, *"Rightly Dividing the Word of Truth,"* Revell paper edition (Westwood, N.J., n. d. [1896]), pp. 12–16.

21. See, for instance, the passage from *The Letters of John Nelson Darby,* 2nd ed. (London, n. d.), 3: 298–301, quoted in Sandeen, *Roots,* pp. 32–34.

VI. Dispensationalism and the Baconian Ideal

1. "The Coming of the Lord: The Doctrinal Center of the Bible," *Addresses on the Second Coming of the Lord: Delivered at the Prophetic Conference, Allegheny, Pa., December 3–6, 1895* (Pittsburgh, 1895), p. 82.

2. Theodore Dwight Bozeman, *Protestants in an Age of Science: The Baconian Ideal and Antebellum American Religious Thought* (Chapel Hill, 1977), is a very important work which points out the widespread appeal to Bacon. See especially his summary of the above themes, pp. 3–31.

3. Cf. Merle Curti, "The Great Mr. Locke: America's Philosopher, 1783–1861," *Huntington Library Bulletin* 11 (1937), pp. 107–51. Bozeman, *Age of Science,* pp. 23–27, argues persuasively, however, that Bacon had replaced Locke by early in the nineteenth century.

4. Cf. Ralph H. Gabriel, "Evangelical Religion and Popular Romanticism in Early Nineteenth Century America," *Church History* XIX (March, 1950), pp. 34–47. Bozeman, *Age of Science,* suggests also the importance of doxology as a conclusion of scientific investigation.

5. These views are clearly presented and documented in Bozeman, *Age of Science,* pp. 8–21. Similar treatment is found in Herbert Hovenkamp, *Science and Religion in America, 1800–1860* (Philadelphia, 1978).

6. *"I Am Coming,":* A Setting Forth of the Second Coming of Our Lord Jesus Christ as Personal—Private—Premillennial, 7th ed., rev. (London, n. d. [ca. 1890]), p. 121.

7. "Questions Concerning Inspiration," *The Inspired Word: A Series of Papers* (London, 1888), pp. 17, 23, cf. p. 20. Cf. Chapter XIII below for similar tendencies toward dictation analogies in *The Fundamentals.*

A. J. Gordon suggests a more balanced image of light through stained glass to describe the divine and human elements in inspiration, *The Ministry of the Spirit* (Valley Forge, 1895), pp. 175–76, quoted in Bruce Shelley, "A. J. Gordon and Biblical Criticism," *Foundations* XIV (January–March, 1971), p. 74.

Shelley points out that Ernest Sandeen overemphasizes the influence of Princeton theologians in formulating fundamentalist views of Scripture, *ibid.,* p. 77n.

Cf. Norman H. Maring, "Baptists and Changing Views of the Bible, 1865-1918," *Foundations* I (July, 1958), pp. 52-75, (October, 1958), pp. 30-62, for similarly rather independent developments among conservative Northern Baptists. Among conservative and "fundamentalist" Baptists views of inspiration varied far more than among dispensationalists or militant conservative Presbyterians. See, for instance, Grant A. Wacker, Jr., "Augustus H. Strong: A Conservative Confrontation with History," Ph.D. dissertation, Harvard, 1978.

8. *The Thousand Years: Studies in Eschatology in Both Testaments* (Fincastle, Va., n. d. [1889]), pp. 339, 343-44.

9. *"Many Infallible Proofs:" The Evidence of Christianity or The Written and Living Word of God* (New York, 1886), pp. 11, 13, 14. Pierson himself appeals to the exact analogy between the design of nature and that of the Bible, p. 110.

10. *Ibid.,* pp. 129-35.

11. Cf. C. Norman Kraus, *Dispensationalism in America: Its Rise and Development* (Richmond, Va., 1958), who perceptively relates dispensationalism to its intellectual context with good observations on this point, e.g., p. 132.

12. Revell paper edition (Westwood, N.J., n. d. [1896]), p. 3.

13. *Ibid.,* p. 34.

14. Kraus, *Dispensationalism,* p. 122.

15. *The Scofield Reference Bible,* C. I. Scofield, ed. (New York, 1917 [1909]), Introduction, p. iii.

16. *What the Bible Teaches: A Thorough and Comprehensive Study of What the Bible has to Say Concerning the Great Doctrines of which it Treats,* 17th ed. (New York, 1933 [1898]), p. 1.

17. E.g., W.E.B. [William E. Blackstone], *Jesus is Coming* (Chicago, 1908 [1878]), p. 21.

18. *Scofield Bible,* p. 1349, notes.

19. William Ames, *The Marrow of Theology,* John D. Eusden, ed. (Boston, 1968 [1623]), p. 188. Cf. the Puritan interest in the "method" of Petrus Ramus. Although this system was deductive, rather than inductive, it reflected the tendencies toward encyclopedic classification based on identifying mutually exclusive categories. Cf. Perry Miller, *The New England Mind: The Seventeenth Century* (New York, 1939).

20. Ernest R. Sandeen, *The Roots of Fundamentalism* (Chicago, 1970), pp. 136-39.

21. I am very much indebted to Harry Stout for pointing out to me this theme in American religious history. On the Puritans, see his "Puritanism Considered as a Profane Movement," The Newberry Papers in Family and Community History (Chicago, 1977).

22. See Stout, "Religion, Communications, and the Ideological Origins of the American Revolution," *William and Mary Quarterly,* 3rd series, XXXIV (October, 1977), pp. 519-41.

23. "Christ's Coming: Personal and Visible," *Premillennial Essays,* Nathaniel West, ed. (Chicago, 1879), pp. 25-26.

24. "Christ's Predictions and Their Interpretation," *Prophetic Studies of the International Prophetic Conference* (Chicago, 1886), p. 46.

25. Quoted in William G. McLoughlin, Jr., *Modern Revivalism* (New York, 1959), p. 372. Original source not clear, from 1906.

26. Richard Hofstadter, *Anti-Intellectualism in American Life* (New York, 1962) provides much documentation of this side of the outlook.

27. These themes are suggested in Joel A. Carpenter, "A Shelter in the Time of Storm: Fundamentalist Institutions and the Rise of Evangelical Protestantism, 1929–1942," ms., cf., *Church History* (March, 1980).

VII. History, Society, and the Church

1. C. Norman Kraus, *Dispensationalism in America* (Richmond, 1958), p. 1.
2. Cf. Lewis Sperry Chafer, *Satan* (Chicago, 1935 [1909]) and Reuben A. Torrey, *What the Bible Teaches* (New York, 1933 [1898]), pp. 513–35.
3. *"Rightly Dividing the Word of Truth,"* Revell paper edition (New York, n. d. [1896]), p. 12.
4. Again, this analysis is based on an analogy to the processes Thomas Kuhn describes in *The Structure of Scientific Revolutions* (Chicago, 1970 [1962]).
5. Karl Dieterich Pfisterer, *The Prism of Scripture: Studies on History and Historicity in the Work of Jonathan Edwards* (Bern, Switzerland, 1975) has helpful insights on the shift to modern historiographical views. See also Ernest Lee Tuveson, *Redeemer Nation: The Idea of America's Millennial Role* (Chicago, 1968), for many examples of supernaturalistic views of history in nineteenth-century America.
6. Theodore Dwight Bozeman, *Protestants in the Age of Science* (Chapel Hill, 1977), pp. 119–24; John C. Greene, "Science and Religion, *The Rise of Adventism: Religion and Society in Mid-Nineteenth-Century America,* Edwin S. Gaustad, ed. (New York, 1974), pp. 50–69; Michael Ruse, "The Relationship between Science and Religion in Britain, 1830–1870," *Church History* 44 (Dec., 1975), pp. 505–22. Orthodox Protestant versions of catastrophism were taught in America by prominent scientists such as Edward Hitchcock, Benjamin Silliman, James Dwight Dana, and Louis Aggasiz. Greene describes Hitchcock's *The Religion of Geology* (1851) as "a resounding success," p. 58. Bozeman finds Presbyterian scholars of the era relating the geological theories to postmillennialism.
7. Scofield, *Rightly Dividing,* pp. 12–16. Of course, catastrophism as such was not wholly novel in Christian apocalyptic views.
8. *The Scofield Reference Bible,* C. I. Scofield, ed. (New York, 1917 [1909]), p. 3, notes.
9. "Condition of the Church and World at Christ's Second Advent; or, Are the Church and the World to Grow Better or Worse Until He Comes?" *Prophetic Studies of the International Prophetic Conference* (held in Chicago, November, 1886) (Chicago, 1887?), pp. 173–76. For another statement of such frequently stated themes see W. G. Moorehead, "The Final Issue of the Age," *"Our Lord Shall Come," Addresses on the Second Coming of the Lord, delivered at the Prophetic Conference, Allegheny, Pa., Dec. 3–6, 1895* (Pittsburgh, 1896), pp. 25–27.
10. "The Second Coming of Christ as Related to the Establishment of the Coming Kingdom," *The Second Coming of Our Lord; Being Papers read at a Conference held at Niagara, Ontario, July 14th to 17th, 1885,* James H. Brookes, ed. (Toronto, 1885), p. 135.
11. Modern Delusions," *Prophetic Studies* (1886), p. 71.
12. *The Thousand Years: Studies in Eschatology in Both Testaments* (Fincastle, Va., n. d. [1889]), pp. 445–452. Again, statements similar to these are not hard

to find. On disillusion with reform movements, see for instance, W.E.B. [William E. Blackstone], *Jesus is Coming* (Chicago, 1908 [1878]), pp. 148–150. Oñ cities, cf. Arthur T. Pierson, in *Addresses of the International Prophetic Conference Held Dec. 10–15, 1901 in the Clarendon Baptist Church Boston, Mass.* (Boston, 1902), p. 157.

13. West, *Thousand Years,* pp. 439–48; *Scofield Bible,* pp. 900–901, 907–13, 1342–43, notes.

14. Howard Mumford Jones, *The Age of Energy: Varieties of American Experience 1865–1915* (New York, 1970), p. 338. Of course, the same might be said of almost any quarter century in modern history.

15. For example, see Frederic Cople Jaher, *Doubters and Dissenters: Cataclysmic Thought in America, 1885–1918* (New York, 1964), which treats this subject rather exclusively in terms of social thought.

16. Frost, "Condition . . . ," *Prophetic Studies* (1886), p. 174; cf. James Brookes, *"I am Coming,"* (London, n. d. [ca. 1890]), p. 118–19; West, *Thousand Years,* pp. 448–53; Arthur T. Pierson, *The Second Coming of Our Lord* (Philadelphia, 1896), pp. 28–29.

17. Blackstone, *Jesus is Coming,* pp. 243–44; Brookes, *"I am Coming,"* p. 119.

18. "How I Became a Premillennialist: Symposium," *The Coming and Kingdom of Christ: A Stenographic Report of the Prophetic Bible Conference Held at the Moody Bible Institute of Chicago, Feb. 24–27, 1914* (Chicago, 1914), pp. 65–79. Cf. Arthur F. Wesley, a defector from premillennialism, who said that his original reasons for adopting it had been the argument that the world population was growing faster than the Christian population as well as the simplicity, clarity, and definiteness of the system, "Why I Became a Post Millennialist," *Winona Echoes: Notable Addresses Delivered at the Twenty-Fourth Annual Bible Conference* (Winona Lake, Ind., 1918). Postmillennialists were still claiming that the motto of the Student Volunteer Association, "the world for Christ in our day," was likely of fulfillment and that soon Christianity would be the dominant world religion, e. g., David Haegle, "Signs of the Times: Is the World Growing Better or Worse," *Winona Echoes* (1918), p. 237.

19. Talmadge Wilson, "A History of Dispensationalism in the United States of America: The Nineteenth Century," M.A. Thesis, Pittsburgh Theological Seminary, 1956. Cf. Ernest Sandeen, *The Roots of Fundamentalism* (Chicago, 1970), pp. 79–80.

20. Sidney Mead, "Denominationalism: The Shape of Protestantism in America," *The Lively Experiment: The Shaping of Christianity in America* (New York, 1963), pp. 103–33 for a helpful discussion of this subject.

21. "Condition . . . ," *Prophetic Studies* (1886), p. 177.

22. *The Truth or Testimony for Christ* XX (Jan., 1894), p. 3; and XXI (Oct., 1895), pp. 522–624, and *passim.*

23. Arno Gaebelein is a notable exception. He left the Methodists in 1899 and established a militant journal, *Our Hope,* in which he preached ecclesiastical separation. Gabelein's career is summarized in Sandeen, *Roots,* pp. 214–17, 220–25.

24. *Jesus is Coming,* p. 95 and p. 87.

25. Timothy P. Weber, *Living in the Shadow of the Second Coming; American Premillennialism 1875–1925* (New York, 1979) provides much helpful material

on almost all the subjects covered in this chapter, as well as on some other important points. As far as I can see, however, he does not question the assumption, which seems to come from Sandeen, that premillennialism was the central category dominating the thought of the movement.

VIII. The Victorious Life

1. Scofield, *Plain Papers on the Doctrine of the Holy Spirit* (New York, 1899), preface, quoted in Donald W. Dayton, "The Doctrine of the Baptism of the Holy Spirit: Its Emergence and Significance," *Wesleyan Theological Journal* XIII (Spring, 1978), p. 120.
2. Donald Dayton, to whom I am greatly indebted for help and insight on this entire subject, has collected enough holiness works from this and surrounding periods to fill from floor to ceiling shelves on all four walls of an office. See, for instance, Dayton, *The American Holiness Movement: A Bibliographic Introduction,* David W. Faupel, *The American Pentecostal Movement; A Bibliographical Introduction,* and David D. Bundy, *Keswick: A Bibligraphical Introduction to the Higher Life Movements,* all published by the B. L. Fisher Library, Asbury Theological Seminary, Wilmore, Ky., 1971, 1972, 1975 respectively.
3. See, for instance, Vinson Synan, ed., *Aspects of Pentecostal-Charismatic Origins* (Plainfield, N.J., 1975).
4. "Holiness" is here capitalized when referring to the Methodistic Holiness movements and the denominations growing from them. When referring to the wider holiness teachings or movement, including that usually associated with fundamentalism, "holiness" will be lower case.
5. Bruce Shelley, "Sources of Pietistic Fundamentalism," *Fides et Historia* V (Fall, 1972; Spring, 1973), pp. 68–78, points out this connection. Ernest Sandeen, *The Roots of Fundamentalism* (Chicago, 1970), provides a good bit of information on the ties, but gives holiness teaching a role more incidental to millenarianism, which he sees as primary.
6. Those actively promoting the holiness movement, almost all of whom wrote works on the Holy Spirit, include Charles Blanchard, James Brookes, J. Wilbur Chapman, A. C. Dixon, William J. Erdman, Henry W. Frost, A. J. Gordon, James M. Gray, I. M. Haldeman, L. W. Munhall, George Needham, Bishop William R. Nicholson, A. T. Pierson, C. I. Scofield, William H. Griffith Thomas, and Reuben Torrey. See also Edith Lydia Waldvogel, "The 'Overcoming Life': A Study in the Reformed Evangelical Origins of Pentecostalism," Ph.D. dissertation, Harvard, 1977.
7. For instance, at the Northfield conferences holiness doctrines were regularly presented, while premillennialism was kept in the background. In the large premillennial conferences, by contrast, the holiness doctrines were often presented. Similarly, in *The Fundamentals* (see Chapter 14 below) holiness teachings were prominent while premillennialism was almost absent.
8. Timothy P. Weber, *Living in the Shadow of the Second Coming* (New York, 1979), describes this and other practical implications of premillennialism.
9. Wesley recognized that if one defined sin as "any coming short of the law of love" Christians could not be sinless, and he admitted that they were not sinless in such a sense. John Leland Peters, *Christian Perfection and American Methodism* (New York, 1956), p. 46.

10. John Wesley, *A Plain Account of Christian Perfection*, Epworth Press edition (London, 1952 [1766]), pp. 106–8; John Peters, *Christian Perfection*, pp. 32–66.

11. *Westminister Confession of Faith*, chapt. XIII, "Of Sanctification;" cf. James Fisher, *The Assembly's Shorter Catechism Explained by way of Question and Answer* (Edinburgh, 1835 [1753]), p. 181–88.

12. On Common Sense philosophy in Taylor see George Marsden, *The Evangelical Mind and the New School Presbyterian Experience* (New Haven, 1970). On Common Sense in the Methodist Holiness tradition of the same period see James E. Hamilton, "Epistemology and Theology in American Methodism," *Wesleyan Theological Journal* X (Spring, 1975), pp. 70–79. On Common Sense in Mahan, see James E. Hamilton, "Nineteenth Century Holiness Theology: A Study of the Thought of Asa Mahan," *Wesleyan Theological Journal* XIII (Spring, 1978), pp. 51–64.

13. Finney, *Lectures on Systematic Theology*, J. H. Fairchild, ed. (New York, 1878 1846]), pp. 115–79; 204–281; cf. Asa Mahan, *Scripture Doctrine of Christian Perfection* (Boston, 1839); J. H. Fairchild in "Oberlin Theology," *Cyclopaedia of Biblical Theological and Ecclesiastical Literature*, John M'Clintock and James Strong, eds. (New York, 1891), vol. II, pp. 277–78 provides a valuable summary; cf. Timothy L. Smith, *Revivalism and Social Reform: American Protestantism on the Eve of the Civil War* (New York, 1965 [1957]), pp. 103–13. See also Smith's very valuable "The Doctrine of the Sanctifying Spirit: Charles G. Finney's Synthesis of Wesleyan and Convenant Theology," *Wesleyan Theological Journal* XIII (Spring, 1978), pp. 92–113.

14. Sandra Sizer, *Gospel Hymns and Social Religion* (Philadelphia, 1978) explores the importance of such gatherings.

15. W. B. Godbey, *Christian Perfection* (Louisville, 1898), p. 14.

16. Vinson Synan, *The Holiness-Pentecostal Movement in the United States* (Grand Rapids, 1971), pp. 59–60. Some of these groups became directly connected with later fundamentalism. See, for instance, Donald W. Dayton, *Discovering an Evangelical Heritage* (New York, 1976).

17. Hannah Whitall Smith, *The Christian's Secret to the Happy Life*, Spire paper edition (Old Tappan, N.J., 1966 [1875]), p. 28; cf. Benjamin Breckinridge Warfield's summary in "The 'Higher Life' Movement," *Perfectionism* vol. II (New York, 1931), p. 512. Warfield, who often was not generous about those with whom he disagreed, attacked Boardman's volume, *ibid.*, pp. 466–94, calling it "a ragtime book," p. 473.

18. Mahan, *The Baptism of the Holy Ghost* (Noblesville, Ind., 1972 [1870]), p. 7. Cf. Charles Finney's similar statements in "The Enduement of Power," (c. 1871). Donald Dayton, "From Christian Perfection to the 'Baptism of the Holy Ghost,'" *Aspects of Pentecostal-Charismatic Origins*, Vinson Synan, ed., pp. 39–54, develops this theme.

19. Sizer, *Gospel Hymns*, pp. 20–49, explores such themes perceptively. The songs of Philip Bliss, "Hold the Fort," and Moody's favorite, "Dare to be a Daniel," and many premillennial hymns are less passive than those of the women writers.

20. Of the several accounts of the origins of Keswick, the most accurate appears to be Steven Barabas, *So Great Salvation: The History and Message of the Keswick Convention* (Westwood, N.J. n. d.), pp. 15–28. Also very valuable is Bundy, *Keswick: A Bibliographic Introduction*. J. C. Pollock, *The Keswick Story: The Authorized History of the Keswick Convention* (London, 1964) is

detailed and based on considerable research. Pollock provides the most detailed account of the Smith scandal. See also Warfield, "'Higher Life,'" *Perfectionism,* II, pp. 463–558, on Keswick origins.

21. H. W. Webb-Peploe, "Sin" (1885), "Grace" (1885), *Keswick's Authentic Voice: Sixty-five Dynamic Addresses Delivered at the Keswick Convention 1875–1957,* Herbert F. Stevenson, ed. (Grand Rapids, 1959), pp. 31–40, 144–50, cf. p. 26. Cf. also Barabas, *So Great Salvation,* pp. 165–69.

22. W. H. Griffith Thomas frequently used these categories in defending Keswick; e.g., "Must Christians Sin?" (tract) (Chicago, n. d., available at Moody Bible Institute archives).

23. Barabas, *So Great Salvation,* pp. 47–51; Arthur T. Pierson, "Unsubdued Sin" (1907), *Keswick's Triumphant Voice: Forty-Eight Addresses Delivered at the Keswick Convention, 1882–1962,* Herbert F. Stevenson, ed. (Grand Rapids, 1963), p. 106.

24. Barabas, *So Great Salvation,* pp. 128–47; Andrew Murray, "The Carnal Christian" (1895), *Keswick's Triumphant Voice,* pp. 84–93. Later in the twentieth century these ideas, especially as formulated by Murray, were given wide publicity by Bill Bright of Campus Crusade for Christ International. See, for instance, their tract "Have You Made the Wonderful Discovery of the Spirit-filled Life?" (San Bernardino, Calif., 1966).

25. Murray, "The Carnal Christian," pp. 84–93.

26. Barabas, *So Great Salvation,* pp. 110–21, 149–50.

27. Reuben Torrey, "Why God Used D. L. Moody," (pamphlet), Sword of the Lord edition (Murfreesboro, Tenn., n. d. [1923]), p. 57. Cf. James F. Findlay, Jr., *Dwight L. Moody* (Chicago, 1969), p. 132.

28. Early Keswick participants received instruction: "Do not dispute with any, but rather pray with those who differ from you." Charles F. Harford, ed., *The Keswick Convention: Its Message, Its Method, and Its Men* (London, 1907), p. 8.

29. Such themes are prominent, for instance, in Ira D. Sankey, *Sankey's Story of the Gospel Hymns,* 3rd Ed. (Philadelphia, 1906), a compilation of stories he used to introduce hymns at revivals.

30. Cf. Findlay, *Moody,* pp. 341–42. Stanley N. Gundry, *Love Them In* (Chicago, 1976), pp. 153–60 has a helpful account of Moody's views.

31. E.g. undated letter A. J. Gordon to his wife; Ernest B. Gordon, *Adoniram Judson Gordon* (New York, 1896), p. 176.

32. *A College of Colleges, Led by D. L. Moody,* T. J. Shanks, ed. (Chicago, 1887), p. 217.

33. Torrey, "Why God Used D. L. Moody," pp. 57–59.

34. Torrey apparently formulated his views on the Holy Spirit somewhat independently of Keswick teachers and persisted in using the phrase "The Baptism with the Holy Spirit." Perhaps because of this terminology, Torrey has sometimes been taken as a precursor of the Pentecostal movement, although in fact he was adamantly opposed to tongues-speaking. Cf. Horace S. Ward, Jr., "The Anti-Pentecostal Argument," *Aspects,* Synan, ed., pp. 108–109. Torrey also did not hold the Holiness idea of the eradication of sin in the believer. In 1904 (when he was on his world-wide tour) he was received with unusual enthusiasm at Keswick. *Keswick's Triumphant Voice,* pp. 320–321. See Torrey, "How to Receive the Holy Ghost," *Ibid.,* pp. 347–363, which indicates his broad agreement

with Keswick teachings. Torrey, *What the Bible Teaches* (New York, 1898), presents a systematic account, pp. 269–280. Among other statements, the most complete is, *The Person and Work of the Holy Spirit* (Grand Rapids, 1968 [1910]).

35. *The Person and Ministry of the Holy Spirit,* A. C. Dixon, ed. (Baltimore, 1890), pp. vi and *passim.*

36. The usual story is that the "Old Guard" at Northfield, including Pierson, Scofield, Erdman, Needham, accused Moody of allowing heresy at the conference by inviting Keswick speaker F. B. Meyer; but then these men were soon won to Meyer's position. Cf. Sandeen, *Roots,* p. 176; Shelley, "Sources," p. 73. The source of this story, however, is a recollection of a recollection of James Gray many years later. William M. Runyan, ed., *Dr. Gray at Moody Bible Institute* (New York, 1935), pp. 5–8. The degree of this conflict, however, must have been overstated in this account. George Needham and W. J. Erdman were prominent in the conference on the Holy Spirit in 1890. Moreover, A. J. Gordon, whose book *The Twofold Life* (New York, 1883) taught with its own terminology a view close to Keswick's (cf. note 37 below), had been a teacher at Northfield in the 1880s. On the other side, there was a definite gain in acceptance of explicit Keswick teachings in these years when Keswick speakers came to Northfield. J. Wilbur Chapman dedicated his book, *Received Ye the Holy Ghost?* (New York, 1894) to F. B. Meyer who "two years ago . . . opened up a new life to me. . . ." A. T. Pierson said he did not appreciate the spiritual force of the teachings until he heard Webb-Peploe at Northfield in 1895, J. Kennedy MacLean, ed. *Dr. Pierson and His Message,* (London, n. d.), p. 35. Scofield's dedication to holiness views dated from this same period, Charles Gallaudet Trumbull, *The Life of C. I. Scofield* (New York, 1920), pp. 66–68.

37. Gordon, like Torrey, apparently developed his view before there were Keswick influences in America. He emphasized two stages in the life of the believer, the second being marked by a definite experience of being filled with the Holy Ghost. This experience imparts "power from God. . . ." He denied perfectionism, saying our sinful natures were only "repressed." He said of Spirit-filled Christians, "if they have not gained full victory, they have at least enjoyed 'the truce of God' for a season." *The Twofold Life: Or Christ's Work for Us and Christ's Work In Us,* 2nd ed. (New York, 1884 [1883]), pp. 47; iv; 143.

38. *Plain Papers on the Doctrine of the Holy Spirit,* p. 73. Torrey said, "The Baptism with the Holy Spirit is absolutely necessary in every Christian for the service that Christ demands and expects of him." *What the Bible Teaches,* p. 278. Torrey emphasizes "power in service" as the result of this baptism. Holiness is the condition for such baptisms, not the result. *Ibid.,* pp. 272–80. Scofield would not use the term "baptism of the Holy Spirit" for such experiences (but rather "fillings") because he took this term to refer to the Pentecost experience of Acts 2 which he placed before this dispensation, when the Gospel was extended to the Gentiles in Acts 10. *Plain Papers,* pp. 39–50.

39. Introduction, *The Person and Ministry of the Holy Spirit,* p. 2; cf. S. D. Gordon, Quiet Talks on Power (Chicago, 1903), p. 164; cf. Paul Rader, *How to Win Victory and Other Messages* (New York, 1919), pp. 16–17.

40. Cf. Hofstadter, *Anti-Intellectualism in American Life* (New York 1966 [1962]), pp. 172–196. See also Henry Adams, *The Education of Henry Adams* (Boston, 1918), pp. 379–90. The fundamentalist movement generally allowed women only

quite subordinate roles. When experiential emphasis predominated, the idea that Pentecost opened a dispensation when women would prophesy (as the prophet Joel suggested) might be accepted. Yet the Baconian Biblicism conflicted with such ideals, due to the Pauline statements about women. Apparently even in Holiness traditions the role of women in the church declined during the fundamentalist era. Cf. Dayton, *Evangelical Heritage*, pp. 85–98.

41. *The Holy Spirit in Life and Service: Addresses Delivered before the Conference on the Ministry of the Holy Spirit Held in Brooklyn, N. Y. Oct. 1894*, A. C. Dixon, ed. (New York, 1895).

IX. The Social Dimensions of Holiness

1. (New York, 1900).
2. "The Holy Spirit in His Relation to Rescue Work" *The Holy Spirit in Life and Service*, A. C. Dixon, ed. (New York, 1895), pp. 116–19.
3. "The Holy Spirit in His Relation to City Evangelization," *ibid.*, pp. 129–30.
4. Aaron I. Abell, *Urban Impact on American Protestantism 1865-1900* (Cambridge, Mass., 1943), p. 249.
5. "Normal Industrial Institute for Colored Young Men and Women," *The King's Business: Proceedings of the World's Convention of Christians at Work and the Seventh Annual Convention of Christian Workers in the United States and Canada . . . Boston . . . 1892* (New Haven, 1893), p. 260. Washington's account of his 1893 trip to the Atlanta convention is in *Up From Slavery: An Autobiography* (New York, 1923 [1900]), pp. 204–5.
6. "Religion a Practical Thing," *King's Business*, pp. 241–42. The reports included a long list of rescue mission workers, Jacob Riis on tenement conditions, and many special ministries.
7. *Revivalism and Social Reform* (New York, 1965 [1957]), pp. 148–77.
8. Stephen Tyng, Sr., in an introduction to his son's book, *He Will Come; Or, Meditations Upon the Return of the Lord Jesus Christ to Reign over the Earth* (New York, 1878), p. 9, remarks that he personally adopted premillennial views "many years hence." The Tyngs were also close friends of George Duffield, Sr. and Jr. (who were prominent premillennial spokesmen at mid-century and also notably progressive on social issues). Cf. George Marsden, *The Evangelical Mind and the New School Presbyterian Experience* (New Haven, 1970), pp. 190–98.
9. Abell, *Urban Impact*, pp. 28–29. Last quotation is from *New York Tribune*, Feb. 25, 1878, p. 2.
10. Stephen Tyng, Jr., *He Will Come*, p. 192; cf. Tyng, Sr.'s, introduction, pp. 10–11, which also stresses holiness.
11. *Revivalism and Social Reform*, p. 172n.
12. Abell, *Urban Impact*, pp. 155–56.
13. *Ibid.*, pp. 157–58.
14. Ernest B. Gordon, *Adoniram Judson Gordon* (New York, 1896), pp. 106–16. In addition Gordon reportedly worked for "the relief of the unemployed, unrestrained freedom of speech, . . . the protection of Chinese immigrants" and for "state-controlled versus Catholic parochial schools." *Ibid.*, p. 116. A. J. Gordon considered Pentecost to open up a new status for women in the church, allow-

ing them to preach. "Ministry of Women," *Missionary Review of the World* VII (December, 1894). I am indebted to Becky Garber for this point.

15. "The Baptism of the Holy Ghost," *The King's Business,* p. 459, cf. pp. 459–70. This was a prominent theme at the Christian Worker's Convention as indicated by speeches in the same volume by Maurice Baldwin, "The Meaning of the Word Christian," and Stephen Merrit, "The Baptism of the Holy Ghost: Christian Work Before and After."

16. Cf. William M. Menzies, "Non-Wesleyan Origins of the Pentecostal Movement," *Aspects of Pentecostal-Charismatic Origins,* Vinson Synan, ed. (Plainfield, N.J., 1975), p. 88. Simpson's "fourfold Gospel" was Christ the Savior, the Sanctifier, the Healer, the Coming King.

17. The Church of the Nazarene fit a very similar pattern of Holiness concern for the poor in its early years. Cf. Timothy L. Smith, *Called Unto Holiness: The Story of the Nazarenes: The Formative Years* (Kansas City, Mo., 1962).

18. Norris Magnuson, *Salvation in the Slums: Evangelical Social Work, 1865–1920* (Metuchen, N.J., 1977), is the best and most thorough account of these movements. Donald W. Dayton, *Discovering an Evangelical Heritage* (New York, 1976), also provides some helpful insights.

19. (New York), pp. 108–27.

20. *Forward Movements,* p. 353. Pierson also wrote a biography of premillennial Brethren philanthropist, *George Müller of Bristol* (New York, 1905).

21. *The Christian Herald and Signs of the Times* XI (1888), *passim.*

22. Magnuson, *Salvation in the Slums,* pp. 25–29 and *passim.*

23. William Bell Riley expressed this opinion in 1910. Ferenc Morton Szasz, "Three Fundamentalist Leaders: The Roles of William Bell Riley, John Roach Straton, and William Jennings Bryan in the Fundamentalist-Modernist Controversy." Ph.D. dissertation, University of Rochester, 1969, p. 97. *The Christian Herald's* shift away from premillennialism seems to have taken place around the turn of the century. For instance, an essay by Mrs. M. Baxter, "The Millennium," XIX (Dec. 23, 1896), is premillennial, while the editorial, XXIV (Jan. 24, 1901), is distinctly optimistic. The tone until World War I seems postmillennial. In any case charitable emphases were a major aspect of the journal by the 1890s before premillennialism disappeared. Cf. Charles M. Pepper, *Life-work of Louis Klopsch: Romance of a Modern Knight of Mercy* (New York, 1910), p. 10 and *passim.*

24. Magnuson, *Salvation in the Slums, passim. Christian Herald* XXIV (1901), XXX (1907), XXXIII (1910), XXXVII (1914), *passim.* On immigration, for instance, pictures had captions as "A Happy Russian Group," "Sturdy Italian Stock," or (July 1, 1914) p. 629, "The more of this kind the merrier," under picture of mother and smiling children.

X. "The Great Reversal"

1. David Moberg, *The Great Reversal: Evangelism versus Social Concern* (Philadelphia, 1972); Donald W. Dayton, *Discovering an Evangelical Heritage* (New York, 1976); Richard V. Pierard, *The Unequal Yoke* (Philadelphia, 1970). All these discuss the subject at some length and give evidence for severe subordination of social concern by about 1930. An account especially ambiguous as to

what was lost is George M. Marsden, "The Gospel of Wealth, the Social Gospel, and the Salvation of Souls in Nineteenth-century America," *Fides et Historia* V (Fall, 1972 and Spring, 1973), pp. 10–21.

2. William G. McLoughlin, ed., *The American Evangelicals, 1800–1900: An Anthology* (New York, 1968), introduction, p. 13, although otherwise helpful, seems to have this implication.

3. Jean P. Miller, "Souls or the Social Order: Polemic in American Protestantism," P.h.D. dissertation, University of Chicago, 1969; Martin E. Marty, *Righteous Empire: The Protestant Experience in America* (New York, 1970).

4. To call the one of these more "Calvinistic" and the other more "pietistic" is to set up a typology to which there are many exceptions. Some Calvinists have held "pietistic" positions and *vice versa*. Yet on the whole, one can say that the Calvinist heritage has been more prone to positively transforming culture, while pietists have been more prone to seeing Christians as living in essential tension with the culture. See, for instance, H. Richard Niebuhr, *Christ and Culture* (New York, 1951).

5. Finney, quoted from "Letters on Revivals—No. 23, " *The Oberlin Evangelist* (n. d.) in Dayton, *Evangelical Heritage*, p. 21. Dayton points out that this letter is left out of modern editions of these letters.

6. Mahan, *Scripture Doctrine of Christian Perfection*, 4th ed. (Boston, 1840[1839]), p. 82. Cf. p. 71, "the doctrine of holiness, as here maintained, is perfect obedience to the precepts of the law." Cf. pp. 79–85 and 192–93. Mahan argues against antinomian perfectionism, such as taught by John Humphrey Noyes, which says that the ten commandments are abrogated by the law of love. Timothy L. Smith's valuable article, "The Doctrine of the Sanctifying Spirit: Charles G. Finney's Synthesis of Wesleyan and Covenant Theology," *Wesleyan Theological Journal* XIII (Spring, 1978), pp. 92–113, points out Finney's emphasis on the covenant. See also Barbara Brown Zikmund, "Asa Mahan and Oberlin Perfectionism," Ph.D. dissertation, Duke University, 1969, which points out the importance of law, e.g., pp. 147–48.

7. Finney, *Lectures on Systematic Theology*, James H. Fairchild, ed. (New York, 1878 [1846]), pp. 214–18. Cf. Mahan, *Abstract of a Course of Lectures on Mental and Moral Philosophy* (Oberlin, 1840), pp. 235–36, and *Science of Moral Philosophy* (Oberlin, 1848), p. 198, for similar positive assessments of government's role. On wider explication of their view of the law see David Weddle, "The Law and the Revival: A New Divinity for the Settlements," *Church History* XLVII (June, 1978), pp. 196–214.

8. Finney, *The Oberlin Evangelist*, I (August 28, 1839), p. 147, quoted in T. Smith, "Doctrine," p. 103.

9. "Once for All" (*c.* 1870), *Gospel Hymns Nos. 1 to 6*, Ira D. Sankey, *et al.*, eds. (New York, 1894), no. 13. Verse 3 contains the holiness line "Surely His grace will keep us from falling."

I am indebted to Donald Dayton for pointing out the change that took place in holiness teaching at this time. See his article, "From Christian Perfection to the 'Baptism of the Holy Ghost,'" *Aspects of Pentecostal-Charismatic Origins*, Vinson Synan, ed. (Plainfield, N. J., 1975), pp. 39–54.

10. Mahan, *The Baptism of the Holy Ghost* (Noblesville, Inc., 1972 [1870]), p. iv, from introduction written after 1870. Donald Dayton, with Methodistic Holiness

groups in mind, observes that "the shift to 'Pentecostal' formulations of holiness teaching usually antedated the adoption of premillennialism by a decade or so." "The Doctrine of the Baptism of the Holy Spirit: Its Emergence and Significance," *Wesleyan Theo. Rev.* XIII, p. 124.

11. E.g., A. J. Gordon, *The Ministry of the Spirit* (Philadelphia, 1894), pp. 15–16.

12. *Plain Papers on the Doctrine of the Holy Spirit* (New York, 1899), esp. pp. 39–69.

13. A. C. Dixon, *Lights and Shadows of American Life* (New York, 1898), p. 103, mentions two associates who took such a position. See also Chapter XV below on the variety of views on "Christianity and culture."

14. Dixon, *ibid.,* pp. 104–8.

15. "'Christian Citizenship' being the notes of an address given by President Blanchard of Wheaton College in Willard Hall October 1897." Manuscript, Wheaton College archives. Cf. his remark on "Christian civilization" in "The American College: an Address on the Day of Prayer for Colleges," pamphlet (n. d., after 1903), p. 12.

16. Similarly dramatic changes took place in fundamentalist leaders William Bell Riley and John Roach Straton. See below.

17. Gray's note here is "The preacher in such references to the Church is not considering her as acting in a collective or corporate capacity. He believes absolutely in the separation of Church and State, and has in mind merely the duty of Christians as individual citizens" (p. 7).

   As this remark indicates, the point at issue at the time was not primarily that of separation of church and state. Most Baptists, Old School Presbyterians, and premillennial-holiness evangelicals—the principals in organized fundamentalism —held that the church as such should stay out of politics. This principle, of course, limited the types of social action they would endorse. Nevertheless, as in Gray's statement here, there was lots of room for political action by individuals or groups.

18. James M. Gray, "Relation of the Christian Church to Civil Government," 2nd ed. (pamphlet) (Chicago, n. d.), pp. 3–10.

19. An important distinction, common by 1900, was that often those who were saying (in reaction to a Social Gospel) that social action should not come *first,* before evangelism, nevertheless thought (as Moody apparently did) it important that social benefits would naturally result from evangelism. Robert Speer, a product of the Student Volunteer Movement, sometimes a Keswick speaker and later the leading Presbyterian missionary spokesman, in 1900 distinguished between the "aim" of foreign missions and the "results." The aim is strictly "a spiritual and a religious work," which missionaries should stick to. The results, however, will touch the body and involve social progress. "The Supreme and Determining Aim," *Ecumenical Missionary Conference New York, 1900,* vol. I (New York, 1900), pp. 74–75. The importance of these results for Speer is indicated in his essay, "Foreign Missions or World-Wide Evangelism," *The Fundamentals: A Testimony,* vol. XII (Chicago, *c.* 1915), p. 73. Arthur Johnson, *The Battle for World Evangelism* (Wheaton, Ill., 1978), pp. 32–33, uses Speer's 1900 remarks in a recent evangelical argument against a Social Gospel.

20. This social characterization is made, among other places, in Sandra Sizer, *Gospel Hymns and Social Religion* (Philadelphia, 1978), p. 139. Sizer argues that

the revivals were a response to the political and social crises of the times. Although there likely is something to this argument, it is difficult to substantiate, since every era has a political and social crisis but not all have revivals. Sizer is correct, however, in pointing out that even the apolitical revivals had political implications, especially in that they were seen as the necessary counteraction to the moral disease that was regarded as the basis of political and social ills, esp. 138–59.

21. Fundamentalist social and political views, before and after World War I, are discussed below in Chapters XV and XXIII.

22. Sizer, *Gospel Hymns*, p. 139. Cf. James F. Findlay, Jr., *Dwight L. Moody* (Chicago, 1969), pp. 262–302. Walter Edmund Warren Ellis, "Social and Religious Factors in the Fundamentalist-Modernist Schisms Among Baptists in North America, 1895–1914," Ph.D. dissertation, University of Pittsburgh, 1974, shows from four local studies that fundamentalists tended to be relatively younger and somewhat lower middle-class than their non-fundamentalist Protestant counterparts, who were more settled. Probably one can assume that middle-class church growth is more likely to occur among the relatively less settled. On Ellis, see below, Chapter XXII.

23. Dayton, *Evangelical Heritage*, pp. 121–35, Moberg, *Great Reversal*, pp. 34–38, and Pierard, *Unequal Yoke*, 29–33, all suggest some social factors in addition to new doctrines and anti-modernism. Dayton emphasizes rising affluence, which probably applies more to Holiness groups than to the more strictly fundamentalist types, who generally were not drawn originally from as far down the social scale.

24. See below, especially Chapters XVI and XVII.

25. Ellis, "Social and Religious Factors," for instance, finds considerable overlap, even though he shows significant overall differences between the two groups.

26. These conflicts are suggested, for instance, in William G. McLoughlin, Jr., *Modern Revivalism* (New York, 1959), pp. 393–99, who claims that Billy Sunday's rise to his greatest prominence after 1912 was on the crest of reaction to the Social Gospel.

27. The two clear exceptions to this are William Jennings Bryan, whose progressivism was too integral a part of his identity to be abandoned; and fundamentalist support for prohibition, which was too sacred and ancient among their causes to be forsaken simply because liberal Protestants supported it also.

28. Rauschenbusch, *Christianity and the Social Crisis,* Robert D. Cross, ed. (New York, 1964 [1907]), p. 6.

29. There is some debate on the degree of the antipathy of the classic Social Gospel to traditional evangelical Christianity. There are, of course, varieties of the Social Gospel and shades that might blend more into compatibility with traditional belief. Yet in Rauschenbusch, at least, the prevailing tendency is to follow William James and John Dewey in regarding ideas as plans of action rather than as mirrors of reality. Traditional theological categories will not fare well in such an approach. James Ward Smith, "Religion and Science in American Philosophy," *The Shaping of American Religion,* Smith and A. Leland Jamison, eds. (Princeton, 1961), pp. 429–30, quotes a long passage from Rauschenbusch, *Christianity and the Social Crisis,* and then comments: "There you have it—the metaphysical heritage of the Christian West shrugged off as 'pagan superstition

and Greek intellectualism'! What could Dewey say that would shock a clergy accustomed to this?" To my mind, the test of a genuine example of the Social Gospel is whether other aspects of Christianity are subordinated to, and in effect incidental to, its social aspects.

30. The impact of fear of liberalism on social questions is suggested in two answers from *Dr. C. I. Scofield's Question Box,* compiled by Ella A. Pohle (Chicago, n. d. [*c.* 1920]), from Moody Bible Institute's *Record of Christian Work* in the preceding decades. In answer to a general question on "the relation of the believer to the present world system and politics," Scofield mentioned that Jesus healed the sick and fed the hungry and that love toward neighbors demanded that "whatever we can do to benefit them or to keep them from harm, we should gladly do." This might include political action, although Scofield (not himself a great champion of social action) mentioned only saving neighbors from "the open bar-room." When a similar question suggested a limited Social Gospel ("Is it not part of the mission of the church to correct the social evils of our day?") Scofield was entirely negative. Christ's only response to slavery, intemperance, prostitution, unequal distribution of wealth, and oppression of the weak was to preach regeneration through the Holy Spirit. "The best help a pastor can bring to the social problems of the community is to humble himself before God, forsake his sins, receive the filling with the Holy Spirit, and preach a pure gospel of tender love," pp. 35–36.

31. Both trends seem to accelerate dramatically after World War I. One good example is John Horsch, *Modern Religious Liberalism: The Destructiveness and Irrationality of Modernist Theology* (Scottdale, P., [1924] 1920). This second edition is introduced by James M. Gray. Horsch characterizes the Social Gospel as teaching that "education and sanitation take the place of personal regeneration and the Holy Spirit. True spiritual Christianity is denied." The most that Horsch has to say in favor of social concern is that "social betterment is excellent as the outgrowth of Christianity . . . ," meaning out of personal regeneration. Social reform is the business of government, he says, not the church. The rest of his account is entirely negative, pp. 127–39.

32. To the extent they did modify these conservative views, as discussed in Chapter XXIII below, they accentuated them by adopting extremist versions of them, such as extreme anti-communism.

XI. Holiness and Fundamentalism

1. Ernest Sandeen, *The Roots of Fundamentalism* (Chicago, 1970), pp. 208–32. See also Chapter V, note 17, above.

2. Helpful surveys of these developments are David W. Faupel, *The American Pentecostal Movement: A Bibliographical Essay* (Wilmore, Ky., 1972); and William W. Menzies, "The Non-Wesleyan Origins of the Pentecostal Movement," *Aspects of Pentecostal-Charismatic Origins,* Vinson Synan, ed. (Plainfield, N.J., 1975), pp. 83–97. Robert Mapes Anderson, *Vision of the Disinherited: The Making of American Pentecostalism* (New York, 1979), is a very complete account of Pentecostal origins.

3. E.g., "Pentecostal Saints and the Tongues Movement," by "a former sympathizer of the Pentecostal movement," *Moody Monthly* XXI (January, 1921), p. 211;

"Fundamentalism Knows No Relation to 'Pentecostalism,'" *Christian Fundamentals in School and Church* VIII (Jan.-March, 1926), pp. 31-35.

4. Frederick Dale Bruner, *A Theology of the Holy Spirit* (Grand Rapids, 1970), pp. 45-46.

5. A. J. Gordon, *The Ministry of Healing: Miracles of Cure in All Ages* (Harrisburg, n. d.). Arthur T. Pierson, *Forward Movement of the Last Half Century* (New York, 1900), pp. 389-408, discusses the growth of belief in divine healing. It was rather common for the associates of Moody to talk of divine healing. They seem, however, to have been somewhat equivocal on the subject, saying prayer could bring miraculous cures, but saying also that God might well have good reasons to continue an affliction; e.g., James M. Gray, "Is any Among you Afflicted? Let Him Pray" (tract) (Chicago, n.d.); Charles Blanchard, "The Bible Teaching Concerning Healing" (tract) (Chicago, n. d.). Discussion of this subject seems to have faded after Pentecostals sensationalized the teaching.

6. Vinson Synan, *The Holiness-Pentecostal Movement in the United States* (Grand Rapids, 1971), p. 206.

7. Walter J. Hollenweger, *The Pentecostals: The Charismatic Movement in the Churches* (Minneapolis, 1972 [1969]) includes considerable discussion of fundamentalist traits of Pentecostals.

8. Anderson, *Vision,* p. 6 and *passim,* argues that Pentecostalism was part of fundamentalism, but qualifies this by saying that the relationship was like that between Quakers and Puritans (which I think is an apt analogy). Synan, *Holiness-Pentecostal,* pp. 221-22, points out that Pentecostals were little involved in the fundamentalist controversies. Synan, who stresses the Holiness roots of Pentecostalism more exclusively than do most interpreters, also says less of fundamentalist influences.

9. This is especially the case in the National Association of Evangelicals, founded in 1942. Synan, *Holiness-Pentecostal,* pp. 205-7. All these topics are elaborated in Edith Lydia Waldvogel, "The 'Overcoming Life': A Study in the Reformed Evangelical Origins of Pentecostalism," Ph.D. dissertation, Harvard, 1977. Waldvogel points out that in the 1920s Pentecostals could readily identify themselves with fundamentalists and that the Assemblies of God especially recommended works of Torrey, Gordon, Simpson, and Keswick writers, even though fundamentalist leaders, including Torrey, explicitly condemned tongues, pp. 205-6.

10. A. M. Hills, *Pentecost Rejected: and the Effect on the Churches* (Titusville, Pa., 1973 [1902]), p. 63.

11. Hills, *Holiness and Power for the Church and the Ministry* (Cincinnati, 1897).

12. Hills, *Pentecost Rejected,* pp. 63-68.

13. *Ibid.,* pp. 30-68. Hills, p. 68, lists a number of other contributions to this growing debate.

14. *Tongues* (Manchester, 1910); *Scriptural Holiness* (Manchester, n. d. [c. 1910]).

15. Quoted from Harmon Alley Baldwin, *Objections to Entire-Sanctification Considered* (Pittsburgh, 1911), in Bundy, *Bibliographical Essay,* p. 45. See Bundy, pp. 42-45 for account of the Keswick-Holiness dispute.

16. (Neptune, N. J., 1912).

17. Anderson, *Vision,* esp. pp. 114-36, documents the overwhelmingly poor economic status of early pentecostals. Walter Edmund Warren Ellis, "Social and Religious Factors in the Fundamentalist-Modernist Schisms among Baptists in

North America, 1895–1934," Ph.D. dissertation, Univ. of Pittsburgh, 1974, suggests more of a lower-middle-class status of early fundamentalists. Holiness groups appear to have stood somewhere between.

18. William R. Hutchison, "Cultural Strain and Protestant Liberalism," *American Historical Review* 76 (April, 1971), pp. 386–411, doucments the relative affluence at least of liberal leadership. Presbyterian conservatives, who like the liberals were drawn from older and well-established American stock, appear most affluent of the fundamentalists.

19. *The Victorious Christ: Messages from the Conferences Held by the Victorious Life Testimony in 1922* (Philadelphia, 1923), pp. 5–7, 249–52; Bruce Shelley, "Sources of Pietistic Fundamentalism," *Fides et Historia* V (Spring, 1973), p. 75.

20. See, for instance, the personal testimonies, pp. 243–48, *The Victorious Christ,* also the "Selected Lists of Literature," pp. 270–72. Cf. *Victory in Christ: A Report of Princeton Conference, 1916* (Philadelphia, 1916), pp. 253–62.

21. Trumbull, "The Sunday School's True Evangelism," *The Fundamentals* XII (Chicago, n. d. [*c.* 1915]), p. 61.

22. *The Victorious Christ,* p. 14.

23. The continuing Keswick ties are indicated by Henry W. Frost, Director for North America of the China Inland Mission, "Consecration," *The Fundamentals* X (*c.* 1914), pp. 79–88.

24. Nelson Hodges Hart, "The True and the False: The World of an Emerging Evangelical Protestant Fundamentalism in America, 1890–1920," Ph.D. dissertation, Michigan State University, 1976, pp. 63–86, has a helpful discussion of evangelical missions activities and attitudes.

25. Timothy P. Weber, *Living in the Shadow of the Second Coming* (New York, 1979), pp. 65–81, has a very helpful discussion of the relation of premillennialism to missions.

26. James Edwin Orr, *The Flaming Tongue: The Impact of Twentieth Century Revivals* (Chicago, 1973).

27. Editorial, "The Keswick Conference," *The Presbyterian* 87 (May 3, 1917), p. 6, and vol. 87 (1917) *passim*. Among Baptist conservatives, the influential president of Rochester Theological Seminary, A. H. Strong, apparently was sympathetic to Keswick views; see Benjamin B. Warfield, *Perfectionism* II (New York, 1931), p. 564.

28. Review of Lewis Sperry Chafer, *He That is Spiritual* (New York, 1918), *Princeton Theological Review* XVII (April, 1919), pp. 322–27.

29. Warfield, "'The Victorious Life'" (1918), *Perfectionism* II, pp. 600–10; cf. review of Chafer, p. 323.

30. W. H. Griffith Thomas, "The Victorious Life," *Bibliotheca Sacra* LXXVI (July, 1919), pp. 267–68 and (October, 1919), pp. 455–67. Quotation is from p. 465.

31. See, for instance, Edwards, "A Divine and Supernatural Light" (sermon) (1734).

32. Keswick teachings reflected some of the intellectual traits found in dispensationalism. (1) It involved a heightened emphasis on the supernatural, picturing the individual as caught in a struggle between a very personal deity and a personal devil. (2) It tended to eliminate ambiguities. People were either "spiritual" or "carnal;" there was no middle ground nor the ambiguities of a life of struggle between constantly conflicting tendencies. (3) It involved a tendency to interpret some Biblical phrases literally. For example, Trumbull says, "At last I realized that

Jesus Christ was actually and literally within me. . . . My body was His, my mind was His, my spirit His . . . Jesus Christ had constituted Himself my life— not as a figure of speech, remember, but as a literal actual fact. . . ." Quoted from "The Life that Wins" (tract) in Warfield's "'The Victorious Life,'" p. 595 (cf. pp. 598–99 on A. B. Simpson's literalism regarding divine healing). Both dispensationalism and Keswick were pessimistic about the state of the organized church, seeing it as insufficiently spiritual.

33. *Ecumenical Missionary Conference, New York 1900,* I (New York, 1900), p. 364.

XII. Tremors of Controversy

1. Donald G. Mathews, *Religion in the Old South* (Chicago, 1977), provides an excellent account of this background.
2. William B. Riley, A. C. Dixon, Curtis Lee Laws, John Roach Straton, J. C. Massee, J. Gresham Machen, and J. Franklin Norris came from the South. Robert Elwood Wenger, "Social Thought in American Fundamentalism 1918–1933," Ph.D. dissertation, University of Nebraska, 1973, pp. 57–72, which looks into this subject carefully, presents a great deal of evidence to demonstrate that fundamentalism in the 1920s had its greatest numerical strength, both in leadership and following, in the Middle-Atlantic and the East-North-Central states, with moderate strength in the rest of the mid-West, in California, and Texas. The South, especially the deep South, was very sparsely represented. In a survey of forty fundamentalist leaders Wenger finds six from the South-Atlantic states south of the Mason-Dixon Line; but only one remained in this part of the South.
3. Southern Methodists, with a strong emphasis on the religion of the heart, subsequently had some room for theological liberalism.
4. Pope A. Duncan, "Crawford Howell Toy: Heresy at Louisville," *American Religious Heretics: Formal and Informal Trials,* George H. Shriver, ed. (Nashville, 1966), pp. 56–88, provides information on both Toy and Whitsitt.
5. Ernest Trice Thompson, *Presbyterians in the South, Volume II, 1861–1890* (Richmond, 1973), pp. 442–90.
6. Theodore Dwight Bozeman, *Protestants in an Age of Science* (Chapel Hill, 1977), and E. Brookes Holifield, *The Gentlemen Theologians: American Theology in Southern Culture 1795–1860* (Durham, 1978), present considerable material on these themes in Southern thought.
7. In 1877 James F. Merriam, of the famous publishing family, was refused installation by a Congregationalist council in Massachusetts for maintaining that the question of future punishment was "open." Frank Hugh Foster, *The Modern Movement in American Theology* (New York, 1939), pp. 16–23.
8. Daniel Day Williams, *The Andover Liberals: A Study in American Theology* (Morningside Heights, N. Y., 1941).
9. Robert E. Chiles, *Theological Transition in American Methodism: 1790–1935* (New York, 1965), pp. 37–75, gives a helpful survey. On the trials see Harmon L. Smith, "Borden Parker Bowne: Heresy at Boston," *American Religious Heretics,* pp. 148–87.
10. Hugh M. Jansen, Jr., "Algernon Sidney Crapsey: Heresy at Rochester," *American Religious Heretics,* pp. 188–224. The small Reformed Episcopal Church, founded

in 1873, had some affinities to fundamentalism; see Paul A. Carter, *The Spiritual Crisis of the Gilded Age* (DeKalb, Ill., 1971), pp. 183–92.

11. Wenger, "Social Thought," p. 54, shows 55 percent of leading fundamentalists from these denominations, with 30 percent from the (Northern) Presbyterian Church in the U.S.A. and 25 percent from the Northern Baptist Convention. No other denomination had nearly comparable representation.

12. Norman H. Maring, "Baptists and Changing Views of the Bible, 1865–1918," *Foundations* I (July, 1958), pp. 53–75, and (October, 1958), pp. 32–61. Cf. Roland Nelson, "Fundamentalism in the Northern Baptist Convention," Ph.D. dissertation, University of Chicago, 1964.

13. Charles Harvey Arnold, *Near the Edge of Battle: A Short History of the Divinity School and the "Chicago School of Theology" 1866–1966* (Chicago, 1966), pp. 28–53.

14. Eri B. Hulbert, "The Baptist Outlook," *The English Reformation and Puritanism: With Other Lectures and Addresses* (Chicago, 1899), p. 441, quoted in Maring, "Baptists" (October, 1958), p. 38.

15. H. C. Vedder, *A Short History of the Baptists* (Philadelphia, 1907), p. 420, quoted in Maring, "Baptists" (October, 1958), p. 53.

16. *Religion in Our Times* (New York, 1932), p. 156.

17. James Edwin Orr, *The Flaming Tongue; The Impact of Twentieth Century Revivals* (Chicago, 1973).

18. *Religion in Our Times,* pp. 118–19.

19. Albert H. Newman, "Recent Changes in Theology of Baptists," *American Journal of Theology* X (October, 1906), pp. 600–609.

20. Cf. Maring, *op. cit.*

21. Augustus H. Strong, "Recent Tendencies in Theological Thought," *American Journal of Theology* I (January, 1897), pp. 133–35. See also the valuable analysis in Grant Albert Wacker, Jr., "Augustus H. Strong: A Conservative Confrontation with History," Ph.D. dissertation, Harvard, 1978.

22. This change occurred in steps between the first edition in 1886 and the eighth in 1907; Maring, "Baptists" (October, 1958), p. 39.

23. Robert Stuart MacArthur, *The Old Book and the Old Faith* (New York, 1900), p. 87, quoted in Maring, "Baptists" (October, 1958), p. 48.

24. Editorial, *Watchman-Examiner* V (February 1, 1917), p. 134.

25. "Recent Tendencies," pp. 120–21.

26. *Systematic Theology,* 8th ed. (Philadelphia, 1907), ix, quoted in Bruce L. Shelley, *A History of Conservative Baptists* (Wheaton, Ill., 1971), pp. 7–8.

27. Donald George Tinder, "Fundamentalist Baptists in the Northern and Western United States, 1920–1950," Ph.D. dissertation, Yale Universtiy, 1969, pp. 364, 405.

28. Maring, "Baptists" (October, 1958), p. 54.

XIII. Presbyterians and the Truth

1. Answer no. 20, *The Westminister Shorter Catechism* (1647).

2. Ethelbert D. Warfield, "Biographical Sketch," introducing Benjamin Breckinridge Warfield, *Revelation and Inspiration* (New York, 1927), p. vi.

3. Cf. Theodore Dwight Bozeman, *Protestants in an Age of Science* (Chapel Hill,

1977). I am especially indebted to John W. Stewart for allowing me to see his uncompleted Ph.D. dissertation, University of Michigan, "The Princeton Theologians: The Tethered Theology." Stewart suggests some of the documentation for the points that follow and also throws considerable light on the points themselves.

4. Quoted in Stewart, "Princeton," VI, p. 10. I am directly indebted to Stewart for this important point.

5. Charles Hodge, "The Inspiration of Holy Scripture," *Biblical Repertory and Princeton Review* XXIX (October, 1857), p. 664, quoted in Stewart, "Princeton," VI, p. 10.

6. Archibald Alexander, "The Nature and Evidence of Truth," *MSS,* Speer Library, Princeton Theological Seminary, Alumni Alcove, quoted in Stewart, "Princeton," VI, pp. 17–18n.

7. Stewart, "Princeton," VI, p. 17, says at least fourteen articles between 1830 and 1860 interpret and endorse works of major Common Sense philosophers.

8. Samuel Tyler, "Sir William Hamilton and his Philosophy," *Princeton Review* XXVII (October, 1855), 553–57 and 564. Despite this high praise here and elsewhere, Princeton theologians were critical of the attempt of Hamilton to fuse principles of Common Sense philosophy with those of Kant. See esp. Charles Hodge, *Systematic Theology,* I (New York, 1874), pp. 335–65. Cf. John C. Vander Stelt, *Philosophy and Scripture: A Study in Old Princeton and Westminster Theology* (Marlton, N.J., 1978), pp. 30–31, 138. Vander Stelt presents a critique of Common Sense influences throughout the history of the Princeton tradition. A similar examination of the Princeton tradition placed in a larger context is Jack Rogers and Donald McKim, *The Authority and Interpretation of the Bible: An Historical Approach* (New York, 1979).

9. See Bozeman, *Protestants.*

10. George H. Daniels, *American Science in the Age of Jackson* (New York, 1968). Herbert Hovenkamp, *Science and Religion in America 1800–1860* (Philadelphia, 1978).

11. Quotations are from Stewart, "Princeton," IV, p. 5. Cf. Bozeman for many other quotations on this theme.

12. *Systematic Theology,* I, p. 18. The taxonomical emphasis had some affinities to the Ramist method, so important to early American Puritans.

13. "Inspiration," *Princeton Review* XXIX (October, 1857), p. 692, quoted Stewart, "Princeton," V, p. 8.

14. Andrew Hoffecker, "Beauty and the Princeton Piety," *Soli Deo Gloria: Essays in Reformed Theology,* R. C. Sproul, ed. (Nutley, N. J., 1976), points out the essential importance that Hodge attached to religious feeling. Most interpreters have been so struck by the Princeton emphasis on intellect as to overlook these crucial elements in the movement.

15. "Professor Park's Sermon," *Princeton Review* XXII (October, 1850), pp. 643, 645, 656. Hodge held, however, as was usual in Common Sense philosophy, that reason rested on intuitive truths and convictions. But these were a matter of apprehending good evidence, not of subjective feeling.

16. "Inspiration," *Princeton Review* XXIX (October, 1857), pp. 675–77. I am indebted to Stewart for pointing out this passage.

17. Dennis Okholm, "Biblical Inspiration and Infallibility in the Writing of Archi-
    bald Alexander," *Trinity Journal* V (Spring, 1976), pp. 79–89.
18. "Inspiration," *The Presbyterian Review* II (April, 1881), pp. 237, 234, 243.
    Ernest Sandeen, *The Roots of Fundamentalism* (Chicago, 1970), pp. 103–31,
    discusses the Princeton view of Scripture at length.
19. *Systematic Theology*, I, p. 10.
20. Stewart, "Princeton," VI, pp. 34–35, shows this to be the position of Thomas
    Reid. He also cites S. A. Grave, *The Scottish Philosophy of Common Sense*
    (Oxford, 1960), pp. 34ff.
      Princeton and fundamentalist defenses of Scripture almost always argued that
    the testimony of honest people must be accepted and hence the Scripture writers'
    own claims as to the inspired nature of Scripture should be believed.
21. Often today the more relativistic perspective can tolerate almost any divergent
    point of view except that which denies its premise and insists on an objectively
    knowable and universally normative fixed body of truth. Such claims, at least
    when given religious backing, are anathema to most modern liberal thought.
22. Introduction to Francis R. Beattie's *Apologetics: or the Rational Vindication of
    Christianity* (Richmond, Va., 1903), *Selected Shorter Writings of Benjamin B.
    Warfield*, vol. II, John E. Meeter, ed. (Nutley, N.J., 1973), pp. 98, 99–100.
23. Beattie's *Apologetics*, pp. 100, 101. Cf. "A Review of De Zekerheid des Geloofs,
    by H. Bavinck (Kampen 1901)" (1903), *Selected Writings*, II, pp. 106–23. I am
    indebted to John Wiers, "Scottish Common Sense Realism in the Theology of
    B. B. Warfield," unpublished paper, Trinity Evangelical Divinity School, 1977,
    for a very helpful discussion of these and other passages cited.
24. "A bad man," said Archibald Alexander, "stands scarcely any chance of reaching
    the full truth." Alexander and Abraham Grosman, "Newman's Hebrew Com-
    monwealth," *Princeton Review* XXII (April, 1850), p. 250, quoted in Stewart,
    "Princeton," V, p. 4.
25. "Darwin's Arguments Against Christianity and Against Religion" (1889), *Se-
    lected Writings*, II, pp. 137, 141. Cf. "Charles Darwin's Religious Life: A Sketch
    in Spiritual Autobiography" (1888), *Studies in Theology* (New York, 1932),
    pp. 541–582.
26. "The Question of Miracles" (1903), *Selected Writings*, II, pp. 176, 181. In 1911
    Warfield published a much more subtle analysis of this whole subject, in a less
    polemical setting. In it he described the Augustinian position (closely following
    William Hamilton's explanation) that reason itself ultimately rests on "beliefs or
    trusts." Trust, however, still rested on good evidence, so that "reason as truly
    underlies faith as faith reason." Faith, Warfield always maintained, was not
    simply assent to compelling evidence, although he emphasized that aspect. "In
    every movement of faith . . . from the lowest to the highest, there is an intellec-
    tual, and emotional, and a voluntary element, though naturally these elements
    vary in their relative prominence in the several movements of faith." "On Faith
    in its Psychological Aspects" (1911), *Studies in Theology*, pp. 325–29, 341.
27. Cf. editorial, "Opinion and Fact," *The Presbyterian* 81 (May 31, 1911), p. 3.
    "To jumble opinion, hypothesis and fact together in thinking is pernicious to
    intelligence and morals." This is what Darwinism, higher criticism, and the
    liberal theologians do, said the editorial. On the other hand, "with true science,

there is no admittance for anything but facts." Likewise the fundamental doctrines of Christianity "are not opinions, nor theories, though men may hold
theories about them." All these "are self-evident or completely sustained by
testimony. . . . If men knew more perfectly what the Scriptures taught, its
truths would bear witness of themselves."

28. In 1903 a less substantial revision was accomplished.
29. See Lefferts A. Loetscher, *The Broadening Church: A Study of Theological
Issues in the Presbyterian Church since 1869* (Philadelphia, 1957), pp. 18–82, for
the best account of these controversies. On the important Briggs cases see also,
Carl E. Hatch, *The Charles A. Briggs Heresy Trial: Prologue to Twentieth-
century Liberal Protestantism* (New York, 1969), and Channing Renwick Jeschke,
"The Briggs Case: The Focus of a Study in Nineteenth Century Presbyterian
History," Ph.D. dissertation, University of Chicago, 1966.
30. The usual form made "the deity of Christ" point no. 2 and combined the resurrection with the second coming as point no. 5. Ernest Sandeen, *Roots,* pp. xiv–
xv, exposes the error of the first historian of fundamentalism, Stewart G. Cole,
The History of Fundamentalism (New York, 1931), p. 34, who attributed this
form to the Niagara Bible Conference of 1895. During the 1920s "the five points
of fundamentalism" sometimes referred to the Presbyterian points and sometimes to the Presbyterian points with the premillennial return of Christ substituted for the miracles as point no. 5. E.g. editorials, *Christian Century* XXXIX
(April 20, 1922), p. 486, and LX (August 16, 1923), p. 1040. Also a sermon by
Walter Benwell Hinson (1860–1926) opposes Shailer Mathews's attack on each
of these five points. John W. Foster, *Four Northwest Fundamentalists* (Portland, Ore., 1975), p. 63. On the original adoption of the Presbyterian five points
see Loetscher, *Broadening Church,* pp. 97–99.
31. Sandeen, *Roots,* pp. 162–207, emphasizes the development of this alliance and
shows some evidence for it at least by the 1890s. For reasons that seem to me
obscure, he sees this alliance as declining, rather than growing, during the first
decades of the century so that *The Fundamentals* is "the last flowering of a
millenarian-conservative alliance." The alliance, however, was certainly still
intact in the 1920s and was still a factor among conservative Presbyterians in
the mid-1930s. Likely it grew up and was held together because of common anti-
modernist interests as well as some common intellectual traits.
32. Sandeen, *Roots,* pp. 201–3, provides a good summary of these activities, carefully noting the role of the dispensationalists.
33. Editorial, "The Bible League of North America," *The Bible Champion* XVI
(August, 1913), pp. 35–36. Board members are listed on the inside covers. In
1913 seven were Methodist, five Presbyterian, four Baptist, three Lutheran,
three Congregationalist, and one Reformed Church in America. Of these, five
were prominent premillennial leaders. (The denomination is not indicated for
some board members, all from New York City.)

XIV. The Fundamentals

1. Lyman Stewart to Milton Stewart, October 26, 1909, Stewart papers, quoted in
Ernest Sandeen, *The Roots of Fundamentalism* (Chicago, 1970), p. 195. I am

indebted to Sandeen for his fine account of the Stewarts' role as well as for his other observations on *The Fundamentals.*

2. Lyman Stewart to A. C. Dixon, July 29, 1915, quoted in Sandeen, *Roots,* p. 188.

3. One fourth of the authors were British, indicating the continuing trans-Atlantic character of evangelicalism.

Of the 37 most prominent authors (that is those whose names appear in library catalogs) still living in 1910 (who contributed over two thirds of the essays) the average birth date was 1850. By 1913, the mid-year of publication, 16 of these authors were in their seventies (this would include two recently deceased), 4 in their sixties, 12 in their fifties, and 4 in their forties. Only 9 of the 37 were still living in 1925 and of these 3 were not sympathetic to the more militant fundamentalism. Ernest Sandeen, *Roots,* pp. 208–32, notes a similar pattern of older leadership among millenarians at this time. Fourteen of the millenarian leaders he lists (p. 209) appear among the 37 authors here considered.

4. *The Fundamentals: A Testimony to the Truth* (Chicago, 1910–1915), XII, p. 4. Other references to *The Fundamentals* in this chapter will be by volume and page only.

5. A mailing list of about 100,000 was built up of those who had requested the volumes, XII, p. 4. In 1917 the publishers thought the demand sufficient for a new four-volume edition. *The King's Business,* a magazine published at the Bible Institute of Los Angeles, which was to continue the work of *The Fundamentals,* p. 213.

6. Cf. William R. Hutchison, *The Modernist Impulse in American Protestantism* (Cambridge, Mass., 1976), p. 198.

7. Only two articles dealt primarily with premillennialism and these were by Charles R. Erdman and John McNicol, both moderates; Sandeen, *Roots,* pp. 205–6. Erdman says that despite differences with postmillennialism "the *points* of *agreement* are far *more important.*" XI, p. 98. In the same volume Arno C. Gaebelein, pp. 55–86, and C. I. Scofield, pp. 43–54, present dispensationalist views, although in restrained ways. The editors appear to be trying gently to introduce this teaching in this late volume. Scofield's essay also presents Keswick teaching rather explicitly.

8. Sandeen, *Roots,* pp. 190–91.

9. Sandeen, *Roots,* p. 197, citing Stewart correspondence, shows that these later concerns were the promoter's intention. Sandeen, pp. 203–6, provides a perceptive brief classification of the topics covered.

10. Charles Erdman, "The Church and Socialism," XII, pp. 108–19. The several essays by Philip Mauro, suggest some alarm regarding communism and anarchy, e.g. II, p. 92. The Sabbath is dealt with by Daniel Hoffman Martin, "Why Save the Lord's Day?" X, pp. 15–17. This volume, pp. 39–47, contains the only other essay on an ethical issue, a rather conventional piece by the late Arthur T. Pierson, "Our Lord's Teachings About Money."

11. On Trumbull's views, XII, pp. 45–63, see Chapter XI above, note 21. Speer, "Foreign Missions or World-Wide Evangelism," XII, p. 73. Cf. above Chapter X, note 19, on Speer's views.

12. "My Experience with the Higher Criticism," III, pp. 102–3. Reeve was from the Southwestern Baptist Theological Seminary, Fort Worth.

13. "Old Testament Criticism and New Testament Christianity," VIII, p. 6.
14. Sir Robert Anderson, "Christ and Criticism," II, p. 70.
15. "The History of Higher Criticism," I, p. 90. Cf. A. W. Pitzer, "The Wisdom of the World," IX, p. 24, who cites Bacon and Newton among the "immortal names" of leaders in "human progress."
16. "The Certainty and Importance of the Bodily Resurrection of Jesus Christ from the Dead," V, pp. 104, 83, 105.
17. All the essays cited in the five preceding notes make this point, often with reference to David Hume.
18. Ten essays deal with the Wellhausen thesis concerning the multiple authorship ("J", "E," "D," "P") of the Pentateuch.
19. E.g. Pitzer, IX, pp. 22–30. Cf. Thomas Whitelaw (of Scotland), "Is there a God?" VI, pp. 22–36, and Prof. F. Bettex (of Germany), "The Bible and Modern Criticism," IV, pp. 72–90, James Orr (of Scotland), "Science and Christian Faith," IV, pp. 91–104, and J. J. Reeve (note 12 above) regarding Christianity itself as based on presuppositions.
20. "Modern Philosophy," II, p. 87.
21. "The Deity of Christ," I, pp. 22–23, 27, 28.
22. "God in Christ the Only Revelation of the Fatherhood of God," III, pp. 61–75. Cf. James Orr, "The Virgin Birth of Christ," I, pp. 7–20, and John Stock, "The God-Man," VI, pp. 64–84, which confine themselves to the Scriptural evidence. Hutchison, *Modernist Impulse,* p. 199, suggests that Speer quoted the liberal William Newton Clarke in his essay, XII, pp. 64–84 but the editors probably removed the citation.
23. "The Testimony of Christian Experience," III, p. 84. On the differences between this approach and that of the more militant Reformed, see Chapter XXIV below on J. Gresham Machen's criticisms of Mullins.
24. The essays in the volumes by James Orr, Robert Speer, and Charles Erdman in various ways fit this category. Cf. the essays on evolution discussed below.
25. C. Norman Kraus observes that "the mediating position of Mullins was blown aside" by the emerging forces of fundamentalism. "Authority, Reason, and Experience: The Shape of the Liberal-Orthodox Debate in Twentieth Century America 1900–1936," unpublished manuscript (1971). Kraus's work is a detailed and valuable exposition of the theologies of leading conservative and liberal voices.
26. "The Inspiration of the Bible," III, pp. 14–15. Cf. p. 33, ". . . we are dealing not so much with different human authors with one Divine Author."
27. "The Testimony of the Scriptures to Themselves," VII, pp. 42–43. Cf. L. W. Munhull, "Inspiration," VII, p. 22, "The original writings, *ipsissima verba,* came through the penmen direct from God. . . ."
28. He nonetheless saw no conflict between true science and Christianity, VIII, pp. 27–35. One essay, by the late Howard Crosby (d. 1891), "'Preach the Word,'" VIII, p. 108, argues that science is largely a waste of time that "has nothing to do with the soul's salvation." Much more typical of the general attitude is A. W. Pitzer, "The Wisdom of this World," IX, p. 23, who says the Christian "hails with joy each new discovery as affording additional evidence of the wisdom, power, and goodness of God." H. M. Sydenstricker of Mississippi, the only author residing in the deep South, applied natural science to conversion

in terms reminiscent of Charles Finney, observing that it is not "supposable that God is less scientific in this the very greatest of all his works than He is in the lesser things of His government." "The Science of Conversion," VII, p. 67.

29. Orr was also known to oppose the Princeton emphasis on inerrancy, e.g., Orr, *Revelation and Inspiration* (New York, 1910), pp. 197–98. In *The Fundamentals* all he said on the subject was that he would not enter into "questions about inerrancy in detail" that have "divided good men." "Holy Scriptures and Modern Negations," IX, p. 46.

30. "The Passing of Evolution," VII, p. 9, cf. pp. 5–20. Orr, "Science and Christian Faith," IV, pp. 91–104. The other article on Darwinism, Henry H. Beach, "Decadence of Darwinism," VII, pp. 36–48, argues against evolutionism more generally as "marvellously unscientific," p. 47. Both he and Wright emphasize that belief in naturalistic evolution is beginning to die out.

31. William James Morison, "George Frederick Wright: in Defense of Darwinism and Fundamentalism 1838–1921," Ph.D. dissertation, Vanderbilt University, 1971, develops these interesting themes. Wright was also active in the Bible League of North America.

32. In 1922 it passed to M. G. Kyle, a contributor to *The Fundamentals*, and was published under the auspices of the faculty of Xenia Theological Seminary in Ohio. It moved to the Dallas group in 1934.

XV. Four Views *circa* 1910

1. See, for instance, the *Missionary Review of the World* for examples of such cooperation.

2. Virtually all of Haldeman's signs can be found in *Our Hope* XVII–XIX (1910–1912), *passim*. A similar position and list of signs are found in Philip Mauro's well-informed volume, *The Number of Man: The Climax of Civilization* (New York, 1909). It is difficult to estimate the popularity of these views. A similar work by Mauro, *Man's Day* (London and New York, 190?), ran a second edition in 1910 of 18,000. Mauro, who wrote many books, later published a notable attack on dispensationalism, *The Gospel of the Kingdom: with an Examination of Modern Dispensationalism* (Boston, 1928).

3. Isaac M. Haldeman, *The Signs of the Times,* Third Edition (New York, 1912 [1911 (?), preface is dated Nov. 1910]), p. 12.

4. *Ibid.,* pp. 340–63.

5. *Ibid.,* p. 21.

6. *Ibid.,* pp. 199–200.

7. *Ibid.,* pp. 280–81 (he also considered socialism a violation of the law of nature since "human life is individualized by its inequality"); p. 287 (the characterization of Judas is based on his wanting to give money for Jesus' anointing the poor); and p. 299.

8. *Ibid.,* pp. 12–13.

9. *Ibid.,* pp. 30, 155, and 160.

10. *Ibid.,* pp. 14, 106–7.

11. *Ibid.,* pp. 294–95.

12. Ernest Sandeen, *The Roots of Fundamentalism* (Chicago, 1970), p. 244.

13. "The Present-Day Apostasy," *The Coming and Kingdom of Christ: A Steno-*

graphic Report of the Prophetic Bible Conference Held at the Moody Bible Institute of Chicago Feb. 24-27, 1914 (Chicago, 1914), p. 154.

14. "The Significant Signs of the Times," *ibid.,* p. 107.

15. Riley, *Messages for the Metropolis* (Chicago, 1906), p. 48, cf. pp. 9–11, 24–27, 31, 35, 165–77, 190–95, 224–27, and *passim.* These themes do not show up nearly so much in his later books. *The Crisis of the Church* (New York, 1914) and *The Evolution of the Kingdom,* revised ed., (New York 1913 [1907]). Good accounts of Riley's views are found in C. Allyn Russell, *Voices of American Fundamentalism: Seven Biographical Studies* (Philadelphia, 1976), and Ferenc Morton Szasz, "Three Fundamentalist Leaders: The Roles of William Bell Riley, John Roach Straton, and William Jennings Bryan in the Fundamentalist-Modernist Controversy," Ph.D. dissertation, University of Rochester, 1969. For Riley's dramatically different and reactionary social views later in life see below, Chapter XXIII.

16. This conclusion agrees with evidence presented by Timothy P. Weber, *Living in the Shadow of the Second Coming: American Premillennialism, 1875-1925* (New York, 1979), who finds that premillennialists' behavior was not actually much different from that of other evangelicals, although the reasons they gave were sometimes different. Weber, pp. 82–104, presents a valuable discussion of both moderate and radical premillennialist social views.

17. S. A. Witmer, *The Bible College Story: Education with Dimension* (Manhasset, N.Y., 1962). Gene Getz, *MBI: The Story of Moody Bible Institute* (Chicago, 1969), p. 45. Daniel B. Stevick, *Beyond Fundamentalism* (Richmond, Va., 1964) suggests a "half-serious" definition of fundamentalism as "all those churches and persons in communion with Moody Bible Institute," p. 45.

18. *The Institute Tie* VIII (September, 1907–August, 1908).

19. Editorial, *Institute Tie* VIII (November, 1907), p. 165. Prophetic speculations of this sort are relatively rare in the Institute's publications in this period. In 1911 James M. Gray did comment that the proposal for direct election of senators "looks like another illustration of the development of the clay part of the image . . ." editorial, XI (March 1911), p. 585.

20. Getz, *MBI,* pp. 95–99. The first exception was a course in writing English, introduced in 1913.

21. Editorial, *Institute Tie* VIII (August, 1908), p. 884.

22. William G. McLoughlin, Jr., *Billy Sunday Was His Real Name* (Chicago, 1955), pp. 44 and 123.

23. Quoted in William G. McLoughlin, Jr., *Modern Revivalism* (New York, 1959), p. 419 (original not clear).

24. McLoughlin, *Billy Sunday,* p. 44.

25. McLoughlin, *Modern Revivalism,* p. 408.

26. Letter to Faculty, July 29, 1908, Gray file, Moody Bible Institute archives. Another indication of respect for intellect is that Torrey had a son at Princeton. In a letter in the Gray file from 1912, as I recall, Torrey says he wants his son to spend a year at MBI, since he regards Gray as the greatest Bible teacher in the world.

27. McLoughlin, *Modern Revivalism,* p. 415.

28. McLoughlin, *Modern Revivalism,* p. 419, quotes the *Watchman-Examiner's* approval of Sunday in 1913.

29. By 1915 even the faculty of Princeton Theological Seminary invited Sunday to speak there. See Ned B. Stonehouse, *J. Gresham Machen; A Biographical Memoir* (Grand Rapids, 1954), pp. 225–28.

30. McLoughlin, *Billy Sunday*, p. 262.

31. See Russell, *Voices,* for pictures which suggest this. See also the picture of Scofield and Trumbull in a Bible conference setting, Chapter XI. Even in the 1970s fundamentalist Carl McIntire preached on Sunday mornings in tails, although he was capable of great informality on other public occasions.

32. Gray, *Prophecy and the Lord's Return* (New York, 1917), p. 109, quoted in Weber, *Living in the Shadow,* p. 98.

33. Editorial, *The Institute Tie* X (July, 1910), p. 856, cited by Weber, *Living in the Shadow,* p. 167.

34. Quoted from the *Institute Tie* X (March, 1910), pp. 536–37 and see *Our Hope* XIX (February, 1913) pp. 461–62, both from Weber, "Living in the Shadow of the Second Coming: American Premillennialism, 1875–1925," Ph.D. dissertation, University of Chicago, 1976, p. 172.

35. Editorial, *The Institute Tie* VIII (January, 1908), p. 345.

36. Bryan, "The Prince of Peace," *The Prince of Peace* (New York, 1909), pp. 5–6. This lecture was first given in 1904.

37. Szasz, "Three Fundamentalist Leaders," pp. 110–11. Cf. Russell's account in *Voices.*

38. Lawrence W. Levine, *Defender of the Faith: William Jennings Bryan: The Last Decade, 1915–1925* (New York, 1965), p. 26. These four assumptions (especially the latter three) are strikingly similar to those characteristic of American evangelicalism in the first half of the nineteenth century as suggested in George Marsden, *The Evangelical Mind and the New School Presbyterian Experience* (New Haven, 1970), pp. 230–44, and as ascribed to American thought of that era generally in Ralph Gabriel, *The Course of American Democratic Thought* (New York, 1956), pp. 14–39.

39. *Winona Echoes: Containing Addresses Delivered at the Seventeenth Annual Bible Conference, Winona Lake, Indiana, August 1911* (Winona Lake, Ind., 1911), p. 4.

40. Peter Ainsley, "Federation and Union," *ibid.,* p. 280.

41. *Ibid.,* pp. 280, 181, and *passim.*

42. Willard H. Smith, "William Jennings Bryan and the Social Gospel," *Journal of American History* LIII (June, 1966), pp. 41–74, shows that Bryan maintained cordial relations with advocates of the Social Gospel.

43. The leadership for this movement—itself only a moderate success—was largely conservative. Gary Smith, "An Attempt to Build a Christian America: The Men and Religion Forward Movement 1911–1912," unpublished paper, Gordon-Conwell Divinity School, 1977.

44. Bryan, "The Old Time Religion," *Winona Echoes 1911,* pp. 50–63.

45. McLoughlin, *Billy Sunday*, p. 157.

46. McLoughlin, *Modern Revivalism*, pp. 432–33.

47. On Sunday's career see McLoughlin, *Billy Sunday,* and also his *Modern Revivalism,* pp. 399–449.

48. Nelson Hodges Hart, "The True and the False: The Worlds of an Emerging Evangelical Protestant Fundamentalism in America 1890–1920," Ph.D. disserta-

tion, documents the outlook of mainstream conservatives from the conservative Baptist *Watchman* and from more general periodicals such as *The Missionary Review of the World* and *The Sunday School Times.*

49. The *Watchman,* for instance, was against the theater, saloons, and Sabbath-breaking. It opposed socialism as too materialistic, but was for Christian social reform, remarking for instance, "If socialism meant the absolute and direct application of the teaching of Jesus Christ . . . we would be willing to be called socialists." Editorial, XCIII (January 5, 1911), p. 7. The editors (Edmund F. Merriam and Joseph S. Swain) also found some merit in the "New Thought," such as in the vitality of Walter Rauschenbusch's social emphasis. This moderation was consistent with the more experience-oriented philosophy common among conservative Baptists, as noted earlier. Yet the editors simultaneously warned about the New Thought that false ideas "may fix the fate of a soul forever." Editorial XCI (January 7, 1909), p. 7. The editors also found evolution irreconcilable with Christianity. Editorial XCIII (January 26, 1911), p. 7. They considered William Blackstone's *Jesus is Coming* unconvincing, although of interest since it "has inspired such marvellous evangelism." Editorial XCI (May 20, 1909), p. 16. The overall attitudes seem similar to those found in the non-denominational weekly, *The Christian Herald,* of this era, which is also moderate conservative, although less oriented toward doctrine and more toward social questions than was the *Watchman.*

50. See George Marsden, "The New School Heritage and Presbyterian Fundamentalism," *Westminster Theological Journal* XXXII (May, 1970), pp. 129–47. For an excellent discussion of the New School contribution to theological liberalism, see Lefferts A. Loetscher, *The Broadening Church* (Philadelphia, 1959).

51. "The Millennium and the Apocalypse" (1904), *Biblical Doctrines* (New York, 1929), pp. 662–63.

52. *Ibid.,* p. 647. By this conquest the moral evil of the world would be at least subdued, p. 664. Warfield himself early in his career pled strongly for at least one reform effort, "to raise and educate the blacks to take their proper place in our Christian civilization." "A Calm View of the Freedmen's Case" (1887), *Selected Shorter Writings* II (Nutley, N.J., 1973), p. 739. Cf. a similar essay from 1888, *ibid.,* pp. 743–50.

53. "Report of the Permanent Judicial Commission [of the General Assembly of the Presbyterian Church in the U.S.A.] May 27, 1910, re complaint against the Synod of New York," in *The Presbyterian* LXXX (June 1, 1910), p. 20. *The Presbyterian,* the leading popular conservative voice, admitted that this declaration was "rather more anxious than is necessary." Editorial, *ibid.,* p. 4. *The Presbyterian* at this time showed strong interest in the moral condition of the country as well as in doctrinal purity. It especially favored the temperance crusade and Sabbath-keeping, although it included some qualified endorsements of progressive social causes. The attempt to stay out of "politics" (though prohibition and Sabbath legislation seemed excepted) limited them somewhat, as in the following: "It is the duty of the Church to oppose all sin and oppression, and to cultivate, foster and demand righteousness among men. But the Church cannot decide questions of civil and commercial rights among men. She cannot determine the number of hours in a day's labor. She cannot say what per cent

of margin must be allowed in business transactions." Editorial LXXXI (November 8, 1911), p. 4. Cf. LXXIX–LXXXI (1909–1911), *passim.*

54. E.g., Machen, *The Origin of Paul's Religion* (New York, 1921), p. 161, ". . . in Jesus and Paul the Kingdom appears partly as present and partly as future."

55. On Machen's career see Stonehouse, *Machen,* and Russell, *Voices.*

56. "Christianity and Culture," *Princeton Theological Review* XI (January, 1913), pp. 1–15.

57. Quoted from Stonehouse, *Machen,* p. 232, from a letter.

58. Stonehouse, *Machen,* pp. 225–28.

59. Machen papers, Westminster Theological Seminary, Gray file. Machen also kept up a correspondence with Billy Sunday.

60. Stonehouse, *Machen,* pp. 424–29.

XVI. World War I, Premillennialism, and American Fundamentalism: 1917–1918

1. For example, in 1913 the Federal Council of Churches appointed William E. Biederwolf secretary of their new commission on evangelism. George W. Dollar (whose standards for "Fundamentalist" are not loose) calls Biederwolf a "solid influential Fundamentalist." *A History of Fundamentalism in America* (Greenville, S. C., 1973), p. 305.

2. Nelson Hodges Hart, "The True and the False: The Worlds of an Emerging Evangelical Protestant Fundamentalism in America, 1890–1920," Ph.D. dissertation, Michigan State University, 1976, especially pp. 87–110, documents this ideal from a variety of sources.

3. Lawrence W. Levine, *Defender of the Faith: William Jennings Bryan: The Last Decade 1915–1925* (London, 1965), pp. 3–131. Bryan saw the German government as "just the antithesis of ours" and noted that the spirit of the war encouraged charity, prohibition, and women's rights. "The Book of Books," *Winona Echoes: Notable Addresses Delivered at the Twenty-Fourth Annual Bible Conference* (Winona Lake, Ind., 1918), pp. 42–43.

4. William G. McLoughlin, *Modernism Revivalism* (New York, 1959), p. 426.

5. Quoted in McLoughlin, *Modern Revivalism,* p. 444.

6. Quoted in Ray H. Abrams, *Preachers Present Arms* (New York, 1933) p. 79.

7. William McLoughlin, *Billy Sunday Was His Real Name* (Chicago, 1955), p. 260; cf. pp. 255–60 and McLoughlin, *Modern Revivalism,* pp. 426–27, 444–45. John Roach Straton endorsed the war with extravagance similar to Sunday's. Ferenc M. Szasz, "Three Fundamentalist leaders," Ph.D. dissertation, University of Rochester, 1969, pp. 121–22.

8. Editorial "A United Country," *Watchman-Examiner* V (March 15, 1917), p. 327.

9. E.g. an editorial in VI (April 18, 1918), p. 493, warns against "hysteria concerning disloyalty." Cf. V, VI (1917–1918), *passim.*

10. Editorial "Pacifism," LXXXVII (April 12, 1917), p. 12. *The Presbyterian,* (David James Burrell, editor).

Correspondingly, by the war's end, as in most of the American Press, the patriotism of *The Presbyterian* was extravagant. The war was a "Crusade" and it was proper to "Smite until Germany is Consumed," said the titles of editorials,

LXXXVIII (October 31, 1918), p. 7 (David S. Kennedy and Samuel G. Craig, eds.). Cf. John W. Dinsmore, "Is it Right to Hate the Hun," LXXXIX (January 23, 1919), pp. 9–11, which answers "yes" and suggests that the Kaiser is head of "a huge embodiment of diabolism, . . . like the legion that went out of the man into the swine." Though cf. also, editorial LXXXVIII (June 20, 1918), p. 7 which condones fairness toward the German people as distinguished from "the autocratic militarists."

11. *Our Hope* XX (August, 1913), p. 103.

12. *Our Hope* XXIV (July, 1917), p. 111. James M. Gray used this argument in "Why Germany Cannot Rule the World," *Winona Echoes 1918*, pp. 216–19, since the former Roman Empire nations now fighting Germany were more likely to be preparing the way for the revival of the Roman Empire.

13. *Our Hope* XXIII (July, 1916), p. 44. Gray, probably writing in 1916, argued also that Russia would likely have to drop out of the Triple Entente because she was not a Roman Empire nation. He predicted home rule for Ireland on the same grounds. *Prophecy and the Lord's Return* (New York, 1917), p. 27. Gray also viewed Russia as the predicted power of the North. "The Regathering of Israel in Unbelief," *Light on Prophecy: Philadelphia Prophetic Conference, 1918* (New York, 1918), p. 27.

14. S. Ridout, "Should a Christian Go to War?" *Our Hope* XXIV (September, 1917), pp. 165–69.

15. *The King's Business* XII (March, 1921) claimed paid subscriptions of 25,000 and by November 1921 was running an edition of 34,000 (cover). T. C. Horton and Keith L. Brooks were the editors during this era.

16. Editorial *King's Business* VII (March, 1917), p. 216.

17. Editorial *King's Business* VI (August, 1915), p. 653.

18. June, 1916, pp. 485–86.

19. *Ibid.,* and August, 1916, pp. 693–98.

20. *Christian Herald* XXXVII (March 4, 1914), p. 218.

21. Editorial *Christian Herald* XL (January 10, 1917), p. 34.

22. In addition to regular premillennial features, the *Christian Herald* promoted the important Philadelphia Prophecy Conference of 1918 and published its book of addresses (note 13 above). In 1920 Charles M. Sheldon (famed for *In His Steps*) became editor, at which time the premillennialist features disappeared. During the fundamentalist-modernist debates Sheldon maintained that Jesus would not have participated in them, e.g. editorial XLVI (June 9, 1923), p. 458. At the height of the fundamentalist furor of 1925 Sheldon's journal was preoccupied with a "Christian Conscience Crusade," XLVIII, *passim*.

23. This created considerable debate *within* the conservative evangelical camp as well. For example the Winona Bible Conference of 1918 included important conservative representatives of both premillennial and postmillennial positions. *Winona Echoes 1918*, pp. 199–285.

24. William R. Hutchison, *The Modernist Impulse in American Protestantism* (Cambridge, Mass., 1976) says "modernism" generally meant these three things.

25. Hutchison, *Modernist Impulse,* pp. 226–56, while acknowledging strong liberal enthusiasm for the war, emphasizes that many liberal Protestants worked to be moderating influences on wartime patriotism. Abrams, *Preachers Present Arms,*

pp. 15–231, documents many extreme expressions by liberals and conservatives alike.

26. Shailer Mathews, "Will Jesus Come Again?" (Chicago, 1917) (pamphlet). The account is in *The King's Business* IX (April, 1918), p. 176. Among replies are Reuben A. Torrey, "Will Christ Come Again? An Exposure of the Foolishness, Fallacies and Falsehoods of Shailer Mathews" (Los Angeles, 1918) (pamphlet); I. M. Haldeman, "Prof. Shailer Mathews' Burlesque on the Second Coming of our Lord Jesus Christ" (New York, 1918) (pamphlet); William B. Riley, "Christ Will Come Again: A Reply to a Darwinian Seminary Professor" (n. d. [1918]) (pamphlet).

27. Case, *Millennial Hope* (Chicago, 1918), pp. v–vi and *passim*.

28. Quoted from the Chicago *Daily News*. January 21, 1918, in *The King's Business* IX (April, 1918), p. 276.

29. During the two years there were fifteen issues and nine features on the subject (some being parts of series). There were also two features on premillennialism in the latter part of 1917 and several in 1920.

30. Editorial comment prefacing William E. Hammand, "The End of the World," *Biblical World* LI (May, 1918), p. 272.

31. Case, "Premillennial Menace," *Biblical World* LII (July, 1918), pp. 21, 16–17. *The King's Business* IX (April, 1918), p. 277, mentions that one of their brethren had been arrested for preaching premillennialism and accused of treason, but had been immediately discharged by federal authorities. They mention no other such problems.

   Ernest Sandeen, *The Roots of Fundamentalism* (Chicago 1970), says that "although Mathews did not relent in his campaign against the millenarian threat, the contributions he published in later months practically disowned Case's diatribe and censured his attitude." This is inaccurate except with regard to the one short essay that Sandeen cites, T. Valentine Parker, "Premillenarianism: An Interpretation and an Evaluation," *Biblical World* LIII (January, 1919), pp. 37–40. This essay is introduced only to balance some of the more strident attacks, one of which immediately precedes it, pp. 26–36. Cf. the series by Harris F. Rall, "Premillennialism," especially part II, (November, 1919), pp. 618–19, where the charge of subversiveness to the democratic war aims is repeated. Cf. also the essay of March, 1919, pp. 165–73. See also George Preston Mains, *Premillennialism: Non-Scriptural, Non-Historic, Non-Scientific, Non-Philosophical* (New York, 1920) for another non-sympathetic liberal account.

32. Szasz, "Three Fundamentalist Leaders," pp. 123–24, documents the *Christian Century*'s and other liberal attacks on premillennialism.

33. *The King's Business* IX (April, 1918), p. 277.

34. Thomas, "Germany and the Bible," *Bibliotheca Sacra* LXXII (January, 1915), pp. 49–66, already makes strongly-worded attacks.

35. Thomas, "German Moral Abnormality," *Bibliotheca Sacra* LXXVI (January, 1919), pp. 84–104.

36. Editorial *Our Hope* XXV (July, 1918), p. 49. The quotations are from *The Baptist Temple News* of Grand Rapids, Michigan.

37. Greene, "The Present Crisis in Ethics," *Princeton Review* XVII (January, 1919), esp. pp. 2–8. Cf. the strident attack in *The Presbyterian* LXXXVIII (August 1,

1918), p. 10, George W. McPherson, "German Theology Also Must Go From America."

38. Kellogg, "'Kultur'—Applied Evolution," *The King's Business* X (February, 1919), . p. 155.

39. *The King's Business* as early as December, 1917, VIII, p. 1065, was pointing out the connections among evolution, "might is right," and Germany. Torrey in his reply to Mathews, "Will Christ Come Again?" makes a similar point, pp. 28–29. Cf. William B. Riley, "The Last Times," *Christ and Glory: Addresses Delivered at the New York Prophetic Conference, Carnegie Hall, November 25-28, 1918* (New York, 1919?), pp. 161–75. Of the roles of A. C. Dixon and William Jennings Bryan in applying the argument to the American situation, Chapters XVII–XVIII below.

40. These ideas were not strictly contradictory since one might well believe that in the long run there is no hope but in the meantime it is worth engaging in limited actions to "hold the fort." Robert Elwood Wenger, "Social Thought in American Fundamentalism 1918–1933," Ph.D. dissertation, University of Nebraska, 1973, pp. 147–48 gives examples of this explanation, including James M. Gray's use of "hold the fort." The same tension can be seen in premillennialist and later fundamentalist thought regarding the prohibition crusade, which some endorsed enthusiastically and others virtually ignored, Wenger, pp. 241–48.

41. Norris Magnuson, *Salvation in the Slums* (Metuchen, N.J. 1977), p. 157; *Christian Herald* XLI (1918), *passim*.

42. *Our Hope* XXIV (April, 1918), p. 629.

43. "Current Events and Signs of the Times," *Our Hope* XXV (July, 1918), p. 48.

44. Gray, "What the Bible Teaches About War," *Christian Workers Magazine* XVIII (October, 1917), pp. 856–61.

45. *Ibid.* In his very perceptive observations on this theme, Paul A. Carter quotes this essay, adding the remark, "Fundamentalism may have been not so much one of the causes of that wartime and postwar intolerance, as has so often been assumed, as it was one of its victims." Carter, "The Fundamentalist Defense of the Faith," John Braeman, *et al.,* eds., *Change and Continuity in 20th-Century America: The 1920's* (Columbus, Ohio, 1968). This is an outstanding essay.

46. Editorial *Christian Workers Magazine* XVIII (June, 1918), p. 775.

47. Editorial *The King's Business* VIII (June, 1917), pp. 485–86.

48. Editorial *The King's Business* IX (January, 1918), pp. 5–7, IX (April, 1918), p. 280.

49. *The King's Business* IX (May, 1918), pp. 365–66. This quotation is from Henry Watterson in a Christmas editorial in the Louisville *Courier-Journal. The King's Business* editor adds, "This certainly was a very appropriate Christmas message," and he adds the observation that evolutionary teaching and higher criticism will lead in the same direction for America.

50. E.g., editorial *The King's Business* IX (January, 1918), p. 2.

51. *The King's Business* IX (July, 1918), pp. 546–47 (editorial written before May 30).

52. Editorial *The King's Business* IX (August, 1918), pp. 642–43.

53. Editorial *The King's Business* IX (December, 1918), pp. 1026–27. By contrast, John Roach Straton found the fast day largely ignored in New York City and

predicted the imminent destruction of the city. "Will New York Be Destroyed if it Does Not Repent?" (sermon) [Summer, 1918], *The Menace of Immorality in Church and State* (New York, 1920), p. 176.

54. A. E. Thompson, "The Capture of Jerusalem," *Light on Prophecy*, pp. 144–75; Arno C. Gaebelein, "The Capture of Jerusalem and the Glorious Future of that City," *Christ and Glory*, pp. 145–60.

55. Riley, "Is Our Part in this War Justifiable," sermon manuscript for October 21, 1917, Riley Collection, Northwestern College, Minnesota.

56. Riley, "The Gospel for War Times," *Light on Prophecy*, pp. 329–42. Wenger, "Social Thought," p. 148, after noting the disagreement within premillennialism over political involvement, observes in passing that the "activist viewpoint" came to dominate fundamentalism in the 1920s.

57. Riley himself continued to wrestle with this subject. In criticizing the Interchurch Movement for identifying the Kingdom with political goals, he says: "Personally I cannot find a place in my Bible that even remotely hints a civilization of any sort as an object of the Church of God." "The Interchurch and the Kingdom by Violence" (pamphlet) (n. p., n. d. [*c.* 1920]), p. 7 and *passim*. However, at the 1918 prophecy conference in Philadelphia he says: "I vote with a vengeance. . . . I have had three debates in my life. One was a liquor fight in my city. We won . . . and I would to it again. . . . When I read articles from brethren saying we have another and a higher mission, I confess to you I hardly know who is the right man. We are citizens of this earth, and yet at the same time we have a citizenship in heaven. . . ." Question period, *Light on Prophecy*, p. 349.

58. See Chapter XXIII below.

59. For instance, this is a central point made by Clarence E. Macartney in a pamphlet, "Truths Tested by the World War" (Philadelphia, 1919), pp. 14–17. Cf. *The Presbyterian*, LXXXIX (May 29, 1919), Editorial p. 3, "This is a time when emphatically he who exalts himself shall be abased." On reaction of non-dispensationalist Baptists, who do not seem to fit well any one of these four types, see Chapter XVII.

XVII. Fundamentalism and the Cultural Crisis: 1919–1920

1. Robert K. Murray, *Red Scare: A Study in National Hysteria, 1919–1920* (Minneapolis, 1955), gives a detailed account that leans heavily toward this interpretation.

2. Cf. David Burner, "1919: Prelude to Normalcy," John Braeman, *et al.*, eds., *Change and Continuity in Twentieth-Century America: The 1920's* (Columbus, Ohio, 1968), pp. 3–31.

3. *King's Business* X (June, 1919), p. 588.

4. The editors in the same issue suggest both these themes in their comment that "until Jesus Christ comes to 'rule with a rod of iron,' there is just one way to really get at the problem of reconstruction: *by a vigorous presentation of the Gospel of salvation to the individual.*" A long series of editorials deals with anti-Christian elements in schools and universities, the churches, home life, crime, the social crisis, apostacies and the sects, and possible closings of mission fields. *Ibid.*, pp. 588–99.

5. The Philadelphia College of the Bible, for instance, where C. I. Scofield was

the dominant voice, confined its occasional comments on the world situation basically to confirmations of prophecy. E.g., Harry Framer Smith, "The Biblical Sequence of our Imperiled Civilization," *Serving and Waiting* IX (July, 1919), pp. 127–31, 136, emphasizes that the crisis confirms premillennial pessimism.

6. *The Christian Workers Magazine* XIX (July, 1919), pp. 787–88.

7. Editorial *The Moody Monthly* (*Christian Workers Magazine*) XXI (Sept., 1920), p. 7; cf. editorial XXI (Dec., 1920), p. 151 which indicates that most religious liberals voted for the League and most Bible teachers against it. Cf. attack on the League, *Our Hope* XXVI (July, 1919), pp. 48–51; but cf. also the more moderate view of A. C. Dixon, "The League of Nations," *King's Business* X (May, 1919), pp. 402–5.

8. *Our Hope* XXIII (July, 1916), p. 44.

9. Editorial *Our Hope* XXVI (July, 1919), pp. 50–51, cf. editorials XXVI (Sept., 1919), pp. 168–69, and (October, 1919), pp. 229–31.

   The Moody Bible Institute published a full two-page advertisement in *The Watchman-Examiner* VIII (July 15, 1920), entitled "The Answer to Labor Unrest," showing students of twenty-six nationalities at MBI and contrasting this melting pot to radical revolutionaries preaching class hatred.

10. Editorial *Our Hope* XXVII (July, 1920), p. 40. Cf. Chapter XXIII below, "Fundamentalism as a Political Phenomenon."

11. E.g., editorials *The King's Business* X (June, 1919), p. 592, and *Our Hope* XXVI (Sept., 1919), p. 168.

12. Editorial *The King's Business* X (April, 1919), p. 295; cf. editorial "Corruption among the Youth," *Our Hope* XXVII (July, 1920), p. 43.

13. Editorial XI (March, 1920), p. 244.

14. From sermon, Nov. 27, 1919, *Baptist Temple News* IX (Jan. 3, 1920).

15. Sandeen, *The Roots of Fundamentalism* (Chicago, 1970), p. 243–47 describes the formation of the WCFA.

16. *God Hath Spoken: Twenty-five addresses delivered at the World Conference of Christian Fundamentals* (Philadelphia, 1919), pp. 7–8.

17. This Fundamentals Conference was not the first organized by Bible teachers and designed primarily for the defense of the faith. Arthur T. Pierson, *The Inspired Word* (London, 1888), is the record of the conference held in Philadelphia in 1887 on the doctrine of Scripture. Apparently, the impact was much less than that of the Fundamentals Conference.

18. *The Presbyterian* XC (January 8, 1920), p. 3. In *The Presbyterian* the Red menace does not seem to have been a large issue.

19. "Convention Side Lights," *Watchman-Examiner* VIII (July 1, 1920), p. 834.

20. Call to the conference, reprinted in *Watchman-Examiner* VIII (May 20, 1920), p. 652. "Rationalism" was at this time used very widely to describe the opposition's position. *The Watchman-Examiner* says "Rationalism fully developed denies that there is any authority over a man external to his own mind or any revelation of truth except through science," X (June 15, 1922), p. 745. Cf. the very similar definition, editorial *The Presbyterian* XCII (Jan. 12, 1922), p. 6.

21. This is essentially the thesis of Paul Carter's excellent essay, "The Fundamentalist Defense of the Faith," in Braeman *et al.*, eds., *Change and Continuity.*

22. Editorial *King's Business* XII (March, 1921), p. 217, and editorial XI (Dec., 1920), p. 1111.

23. Cf. William B. Riley, "Modernism in Baptist Schools," *Baptist Fundamentals: Being Addresses Delivered at the Pre-Convention Conference at Buffalo, June 21 & 22, 1920* (Philadelphia, 1920), pp. 165–88.

24. J. C. Massee, "Opening Address," *ibid.,* pp. 5 and 8. A good bit of the rhetoric of Baptist fundamentalism in this period attacks ecclesiastical centralization, particularly the interdenominational Inter-Church World Movement and efforts to organize the Northern Baptist denomination more centrally, especially its publications. Decentralization as such, however, does not seem to have been much of an issue, because fundamentalists expressed desires for strong denominational controls regarding doctrinal issues, particularly in relation to the schools. Massee, for instance (*ibid.,* p. 6), laments the lack of central control over Baptist schools.

25. Dixon presented the same theme to the WCFA meeting of 1920, Norman F. Furniss, *The Fundamentalist Controversy, 1918–1931* (New Haven, 1954), p. 51. Willard B. Gatewood, Jr., *Controversy in the Twenties* (Nashville, Tenn., 1969), pp. 117–24 reprints a 1922 version of the same speech. Gatewood's volume is an excellent collection of sources on fundamentalism, modernism, and evolution.

26. Cf. Chapter XVIII below.

27. See C. Allyn Russell, *Voices of American Fundamentalism* (Philadelphia, 1976), pp. 20–46, and below, Chapter XXI.

28. Straton certainly preached a doctrine of traditional salvation at this time, but the degree to which he might also be classified as a progressive social reformer is a matter of some debate. See Hillyer H. Straton, "John Roach Straton: Prophet of Social Righteousness," *Foundations* V (Jan., 1962), pp. 17–38; Ferenc M. Szasz, "Three Fundamentalist Leaders," Ph.D. dissertation, University of Rochester, 1969, esp. pp. 70–71; Walter Ross Peterson, "John Roach Straton: Portrait of a Fundamentalist Preacher," Ph.D. dissertation, Boston University, 1961, esp. pp. 210–18, 226–27; C. Allyn Russell, *Voices,* pp. 47–78.

29. See, for instance, the quotation in Russell, *Voices,* p. 57, where Straton says that the future "will be a time of individualism so far as individualism is essential to progress, yet a time of more cooperation and less strife. It will be a time of less injustice and more truth . . ." etc. This progress is related to the advance of the Gospel.

30. Szasz, "Three Fundamentalist Leaders," p. 212, says Straton's arrival in New York heralded the end of his progressive social emphases.

31. *Watchman-Examiner* VI (July 25, 1918), pp. 953–54. Also in Straton, *The Menace of Immorality to Church and State* (New York, 1920).

32. Straton was not among the speakers at the New York prophecy conference of 1918. In addition to continuing WCFA connections, he was on the planning committee for the Baptist Fundamentals conference of 1920. I know of no study of his apparent shift to premillennialism.

33. Quoted from Stanley Walker, "The Meshuggah of Manhattan," *The New Yorker,* April 16, 1927, in Russell, *Voices,* p. 50.

34. *Fighting the Devil in Modern Babylon* (Boston, 1929), pp. 266, 269. Szasz, "Three Fundamentalist Leaders," pp. 215–16, indicates this was written in 1920. In the preface to this book Straton indicates his disillusion with reform and "social service," p. ii. This later book indicates a tendency, common in fundamentalism after 1925, toward increasing frustration and extremism. Straton

supported several unsuccessful attempts to found major nationwide fundamentalist agencies (such as George Washburn's Bible Crusaders) prior to his death in 1929. Cf. Szasz, pp. 286–95.

35. *Fighting the Devil*, p. 18.

36. Straton gained national prominence in 1923–24 in a series of debates with Charles Francis Potter, a Unitarian minister. These debates were on the fundamental doctrines of the Bible, creation, the Virgin Birth, and the Incarnation. A fifth on premillennialism was cancelled. See Russell, *Voices,* pp. 66–75, for a good account.

XVIII. The Fundamentalist Offensives on Two Fronts: 1920–1921

1. Ernest R. Sandeen, *The Roots of Fundamentalism* (Chicago, 1970), pp. 152 and 239.

2. *Watchman-Examiner* V (January 18, 1917), p. 101.

3. Norman H. Maring, "Baptists and Changing Views of the Bible, 1865–1918," *Foundations* I (October, 1958), pp. 39 and 55.

4. *Watchman-Examiner* V (January 18, 1917), pp. 101–2.

5. Grant A. Wacker, Jr., "Augustus H. Strong: A Conservative Confrontation with History," Ph.D. dissertation, Harvard University, 1978, presents a valuable account of Strong's intellectual struggles. Strong wrote Rauschenbusch in 1912 that *Christianizing the Social Order* was "a great book." Yet in 1917 when Rauschenbusch dedicated *Theology for the Social Gospel* to Strong, Strong expressed his disagreement with its main themes. Wacker, p. 230.

6. Strong, *A Tour of the Missions: Observations and Conclusions* (Philadelphia, 1918), p. 192.

7. The story seems never to have appeared.

8. E.g., George F. Pentecost, "The Interchurch Movement and Revival," *The Presbyterian* XC (May 20, 1920), p. 8.

9. Sydney E. Ahlstrom, *A Religious History of the American People* (New Haven, 1972), pp. 896–98, based on Eldon Ernst, "The Interchurch World Movement," Ph.D. dissertation, Yale University, 1967. The Baptist wing of the movement was called the New World Movement. The Presbyterian wing was called the New Era Movement. These struggled on with inadequate support.

10. Lefferts A. Loetscher, *The Broadening Church* (Philadelphia, 1957), p. 101.

11. See C. Allyn Russell, *Voices of American Fundamentalism* (Philadelphia, 1976), pp. 107–34, for a good account of Massee's role in Baptist fundamentalism.

12. Stewart G. Cole, *The History of Fundamentalism* (New York, 1931), p. 77.

13. Ronald Nelson, "Fundamentalism and the Northern Baptist Convention," Ph.D. dissertation, University of Chicago, 1964, pp. 271–72; cf. *Watchman-Examiner* IX (August 4, 1921), pp. 974–75, on "Politics at Des Moines."

14. Sandeen, *Roots,* pp. 249–50. Loetscher, *Broadening Church,* p. 104, says that within three years the Bible Union claimed some 2,200 members.

15. E.g., ed., "The Conflict of Christianity and Modernism," *Presbyterian* XC (January 1, 1920), p. 3.

16. Loetscher, *Broadening Church,* pp. 104–8.

17. Obadiah Holmes, "The Threat of Millennialism," *Christian Century* XXXVIII (April 28, 1921), pp. 10–13.

18. Editorial "We are on the March," *The Baptist* II (July 9, 1921), p. 717.

19. For this creed see Willard B. Gatewood, Jr., ed., *Controversy in the Twenties* Nashville, 1969), pp. 74–75.

20. Editorial "The Baptist on the Rampage," *Watchman-Examiner* IX (August 4, 1921), pp. 973–74.

21. Lloyd C. Douglas, "Mr. Bryan's New Crusade," *Christian Century* XXXVII (Nov. 25, 1920), pp. 11–13; Ferenc Morton Szasz, "Three Fundamentalist Leaders," Ph.D. dissertation, University of Rochester, 1969, p. 176.

22. Bryan, "The Origin of Man," *In His Image* (New York, 1922), pp. 86–135, quotations from pp. 93, 94, 125, 122.

23. E.g., editorial "The Evils of Evolution," *Presbyterian* XCII (March 30, 1922), p. 3, "The conflict between Rationalism and Christianity grows in intensity. Just now it centers in evolution." But see the following note on the Baptists.

24. Norman Maring, "Conservative But Progressive," *What God Hath Wrought: Eastern's First Thirty-Five Years,* Gilbert L. Guffin, ed. (Chicago, 1960), p. 24, observes that among Northern Baptists the more militant and largely premillennial Baptist Bible Union (see below) took up anti-evolution, while the moderates such as Laws paid it little attention. Nelson, "Fundamentalism," pp. 310–21, shows interests of *The Watchman-Examiner* and other moderates not favoring the stand Bryan in 1925.

25. Szasz, "Three Fundamentalist Leaders," p. 180. Szasz says that in the WCFA "the evolution issue had risen to the forefront by 1923," p. 199.

26. Szasz, "Three Fundamentalist Leaders," pp. 184–85. *The King's Business,* for instance, was promoting efforts to secure Bryan's leadership for a "Laymen's League" during this period. Bryan expressed sympathy for such efforts, and spoke for WCFA events, but declined an official role in the organization.

27. Ferenc Szasz, "William Jennings Bryan, Evolution, and the Fundamentalist-Modernist Controversy," *Nebraska History* LVI (1975), pp. 159–278, makes a similar point, but then attributes the change almost entirely to the entrance of WJB into the fundamentalist movement. So he argues that Bryan was far from typical of fundamentalists and "by no means their main leader," p. 259. This conclusion, however, is misleading in the light of the strong tendencies for fundamentalists to be moving in the direction of anti-evolution before Bryan came on the scene.

28. The wider extent of the interest is suggested by the fact that in 1922 the other leading book on anti-evolution, beside Bryan's *In His Image,* was *God—Or Gorilla How the Monkey Theory of Evolution Exposes Its Own Methods, Refutes Its Own Principle, Denies Its own Inferences, Disproves Its Own Case* (New York, 1922), by Alfred W. McCann, a Roman Catholic.

XIX. Would the Liberals Be Driven from the Denominations? 1922–1923

1. Comparing various citations, it seems to have appeared in at least the following: *The Christian Century,* June 8, 1922; *The Baptist,* June 10, 1922; *Christian Work,* June 10, 1922; and in pamphlet form as, "The New Knowledge and the Christian Faith" (New York, 1922).

2. E.g. editorial "The Capitalists and the Premillenarians," *Christian Century* XXXVIII (April 14, 1921), p. 3; editorial "Fundamentalism and 100 Per Centism," XXXIX (Nov. 2, 1922), 1117–18.

3. These points follow the description in the *Christian Century* XXXIX, editorial

"New Denominational Alignments" (April 20, 1922), p. 486. The "five points of fundamentalism," in the classic form they were given in Stewart Cole's history (see above, Chapter XIII, note 30) seem to appear first in the *Christian Century* XL (August 16, 1923), p. 1040. The classic five points, then, appear to have been formulated by liberals, while fundamentalsts' own lists varied in number and content.

4. Ferenc M. Szasz, "Three Fundamentalist Leaders," Ph.D. dissertation, University of Rochester, 1969, p. 179.

5. Reprinted from *Christian Work* CXII (June 10, 1922), pp. 716–22 in William R. Hutchison, ed., *American Protestant Thought: The Liberal Era* (New York, 1968), pp. 170–82.

6. Norman Maring, "Conservative But Progressive," *What God Hath Wrought*, Gilbert L. Guffin, ed. (Chicago, 1960), pp. 32–33; Norman F. Furniss, *The Fundamentalist Controversy, 1918–1931* (New Haven, 1954), pp. 112–13.

7. Ernest R. Sandeen, *The Roots of Fundamentalism* (Chicago, 1970), p. 264.

8. Maring, "Conservative But Progressive," pp. 15–49, sympathetically describes this wing of Baptist fundamentalism and its sequel. Sandeen, *Roots,* p. 263, points out that this division "did not occur between millenarians and non-millenarians, but between moderates and radicals of both camps." However, the tendency was for dispensationalists to be more radical and for moderates to be non-dispensationalist.

9. E.g., editorial *Presbyterian* LXXXIX (Feb. 20, 1919), p. 6. This was a response to an attack on traditional teaching on the part of Fosdick.

10. Clarence E. Macartney, "Shall Unbelief Win? An Answer to Dr. Fosdick," *The Presbyterian* XCII (July 13, 1922), p. 8. Here, as was often the case among militant conservative Presbyterians, Macartney hesitated to apply "fundamentalist" to himself, because of its premillennialist associations, e.g. p. 9. During the next few years, however, "fundamentalist" became the most commonly accepted designation for the party.

11. The factual information in the following account can be found in a number of places. Some of the best are Lefferts A. Loetscher, *The Broadening Church* (Philadelphia, 1957); the chapters on Macartney and Machen in C. Allyn Russell, *Voices of American Fundamentalism* (Philadelphia, 1976); and the very helpful and detailed thesis by Delwin G. Nykamp, "A Presbyterian Power Struggle: A Critical History of Communication Strategies Employed in the Struggle for Control of the Presbyterian Church, U.S.A., 1922–1926," Ph.D. dissertation, Northwestern University, 1974.

12. A Bryan proposal on this theme was adopted only in a very weak form by this Assembly, Loetscher, *Broadening Church,* p. 111.

13. He also declined to write on evolution, "*New York Times*" file, May and June 1925, Machen papers, Westminster Theological Seminary.

14. Machen, *Christianity and Liberalism* (New York, 1923), pp. 2, 7, 5, 47, 7, and 10–15. On Machen's political connections see Russell, *Voices,* pp. 146–50.

15. *Christianity and Liberalism,* pp. 8, 160.

16. Glenn Frank, "Liberalizing the Fundamentalist Movement," *Christian Century* XL (August, 1923), pp. 637–40.

17. *The Nation,* Dec. 26, 1923, p. 729. *The New Republic* XXXVII (Jan. 9, 1924), pp. 161–62, reprinted in Eldred C. Vanderlaan, ed., *Fundamentalism versus Modernism* (New York, 1925), pp. 353–59.

18. Editorial "Fundamentalism and Modernism: Two Religions," *Christian Century* XL (Jan. 2, 1924), pp. 5–6.

XX. The Offensive Stalled and Breaking Apart: 1924–1925

1. William E. Leuchtenburg, *The Perils of Prosperity, 1914–32* (Chicago, 1958), p. 153. The date of Mencken's remark is not clear.
2. Eldred C. Vanderlaan's excellent collection, *Fundamentalism versus Modernism* (New York, 1925), contains numerous defenses of the modernist position, largely from 1924. Virtually all of the sentiments found in Mathews (below) could be duplicated in these essays. Another especially important defense of the modernist position in 1924 was Harry Emerson Fosdick, *The Modern Use of the Bible* (New York).
3. Mathews, *The Faith of Modernism* (New York, 1924), p. 18.
4. *Ibid.*, pp. 35, 51, 61, 102.
5. *Ibid.*, pp. 16, 22.
6. *Ibid.*, pp. 12, 32.
7. *Ibid.*, pp. 9, 34, 124, 180, 80.
8. James Brownlee North, "The Fundamentalist Controversy Among the Disciples of Christ, 1890–1930," Ph.D. dissertation, University of Illinois, 1973; Stewart G. Cole, *The History of Fundamentalism* (New York, 1931), pp. 132–62; Norman F. Furniss, *The Fundamentalist Controversy, 1918–1931* (New Haven, 1954), pp. 170–76.
9. Furniss, *Fundamentalist Controversy*, pp. 162–69; cf. Cole, *History*, pp. 193–225.
10. Furniss, *Fundamentalist Controversy*, pp. 148–55; Cole, *History*, pp. 163–92.
11. Furniss, *Fundamentalist Controversy*, pp. ·156–61.
12. This is evident, for instance, in the work of the leading Southern Methodist conservative, Bishop Warren A. Candler. See, for instance, his *Great Revivals and the Great Republic* (Nashville, 1904), which strongly ties evangelical and nationalistic interests. Bob Jones, Sr. likewise related fundamentalism to Southern political conservatism, including racial segregation.

    John Lee Eighmy, *Churches in Cultural Captivity: A History of the Social Attitudes of Southern Baptists* (Knoxville, Tenn., 1972), relates fundamentalism to attacks on the Social Gospel. Probably the best general account of the relationship of fundamentalism to other cultural issues in the South is found in Kenneth K. Bailey, *Southern White Protestantism in the Twentieth Century* (New York, 1964).
13. Robert E. Wenger, "Social Thought in American Fundamentalism," Ph.D. dissertation, University of Nebraska, e.g., p. 72, shows by a number of tests that originally fundamentalism was not based substantially in the South.
14. Furniss, *Fundamentalist Controversy*, pp. 119–26, 142–47; Bailey, *Southern White Protestantism*, pp. 44–71. Of the major Southern denominations, the Southern Baptists have had the greatest affinities to fundamentalism. Nevertheless, their Southernness had often kept them from close contacts with any Northern evangelicalism. In the 1920s and since, moderates have prevented strong fundamentalist measures, so separatists such as J. Frank Norris have flourished in opposition to the Convention. Southern Presbyterians took steps to ensure doctrinal conservatism during the fundamentalist era, but subse-

quently (in 1944) also condemned dispensationalism. Ernest Trice Thompson, *Presbyterians in the South: Vol. III: 1890-1972* (Richmond, 1973), p. 488.

15. Robert T. Handy, *A History of the Churches in the United States and Canada* (New York, 1977), pp. 354-76; 389-90. On the Canadian Baptist splits the best account is Walter Ellis, "Social and Religious Factors in the Fundamentalist-Modernist Schisms among Baptists in North America, 1895-1934," pp. 1-3, 14-17, 132-78, 211-34. On Shields see, C. Allyn Russell, "Thomas Todhunter Shields, Canadian Fundamentalist," *Ontario History* (December, 1978), pp. 263-79.

16. "AN AFFIRMATION: Designed to safeguard the unity and liberty of the Presbyterian Church in the United States of America," reprinted in *The Presbyterian* XCIV (January 17, 1924), pp. 6-7. Cf. Charles E. Quirk, "Origins of the Auburn Affirmation," *Journal of Presbyterian History* LIII (Summer, 1975), pp. 120-42.

17. Quirk, "Auburn Affirmation," p. 132.

18. Delwin G. Nykamp, "A Presbyterian Power Struggle," Ph.D. dissertation, Northwestern University, 1974, and Quirk "Auburn Affirmation," use this inclusivist/exclusivist terminology.

19. Lefferts A. Loetscher, *The Broadening Church* (Philadelphia, 1957), pp. 121-24.

20. George W. Dollar, *A History of Fundamentalism in America* (Greenville, S.C., 1973), p. 157.

21. Ronald Nelson, "Fundamentalism and the Northern Baptist Convention," Ph.D. dissertation, University of Chicago, 1964, pp. 285-92.

22. Cole, *History,* p. 72.

23. Nelson, "Fundamentalism," pp. 300-302.

24. T. T. Shields, *Gospel Witness,* May 27, 1926, quoted in Nelson, "Fundamentalism," p. 304.

25. Quoted in Cole, *History,* p. 81.

26. "Dr. Machen Replies to Dr. Erdman, *The Presbyterian* XCV (Feb. 5, 1925), p. 20, quoted in Nykamp, "Power Struggle," p. 346. Nykamp's detailed analysis of this episode includes helpful observations regarding Machen's personality. Machen was by this time encouraging a movemental spirit especially among his student followers. To those who were on his side he seemed to be the warmest and most gentlemanly of friends. To opponents he appeared cold and aloof. See pp. 487-93. See also Ned B. Stonehouse, *J. Gresham Machen: A Biographical Memoir* (Grand Rapids, 1954).

27. Machen, "The Present Situation in the Presbyterian Church," *The Presbyterian* XCV (May 14, 1925), p. 6. Billy Sunday at the time wrote to Machen about Erdman's alleged modernism since he had "always counted him with the orthodox folk." Machen's explanation brought the agreement from Sunday that "I think the fact that we have been tolerant is the reason the weed has already grown so noxious." Machen papers, Westminster Theological Seminary, Sunday file, May 14, 16, 23, and 29, 1925.

28. Nykamp, "Power Struggle," pp. 390-407; Loetscher, *Broadening Church,* pp. 125-28.

XXI. Epilogue: Dislocation, Relocation, and Resurgence: 1925-1940

1. Mathews, *The Faith of Modernism* (New York, 1924), p. 18.

2. *The World's Most Famous Court Trial: State of Tennessee v. John Thomas Scopes: Complete Stenographic Report* . . . (New York, 1971 [Cincinnati, 1925]), p. 199.

3. *Ibid.*, p. 287.

4. *Ibid.*, p. 299.

5. Mencken, *Prejudices: Fifth Series* (New York, 1926), in Henry May, ed., *The Discontent of the Intellectuals: A Problem of the Twenties* (Chicago, 1963), pp. 25–30. In Robert S. and Helen Merrell Lynd's study of Muncie, Indiana, conducted in 1924 and 1925, *Middletown: A Study in Contemporary American Culture* (New York, 1929), it is clear that the majority held a very traditional American evangelical belief in the Bible and Christianity. Although conscious identification with fundamentalism does not seem to have been a large issue, a number of respondents did mention the importance of holding to "the fundamentals" when questioned about religious change, p. 328.

6. This is especially true regarding premillennialism. Obadiah Holmes, "The Threat of Millennialism," *Christian Century* XXXVIII (April 28, 1921), p. 11; editorial "The Capitalists and the Premillenarians," *ibid.* (April 14, 1921), p. 3. Editorial "Fundamentalism and 100 Per Centism," *Christian Century* XXXIX (Nov. 2, 1922), p. 3, ties "reactionary theology to reactionary politics." Kirsopp Lake, *The Religion of Yesterday and To-morrow* (London, 1925), p. 161, identifies fundamentalism with industrial interests and "anti-revolutionary" politics.

7. Lewis, *Elmer Gantry,* American Library edition (New York, 1970 [1927]), pp. 374–75.

8. Shipley, *The War on Modern Science: A Short History of Fundamentalist Attacks on Evolution and Modernism* (New York, 1927), pp. 3–4. Shipley estimated the anti-science "fundamentalist" forces in America as "more than twenty-five millions," p. 3.

9. Norman F. Furniss, *The Fundamentalist Controversy, 1918–1931* (New Haven, 1954), pp. 42–43, 57–70.

10. Furniss, *Controversy,* pp. 83–95, summarizes anti-evolution efforts, concluding that by 1928 nine states had adopted some sort of measure. Willard B. Gatewood ed., *Controversy in the Twenties* (Nashville, 1969), p. 36, says that between 1921 and 1929 thirty-seven anti-evolution measures were introduced in twenty state legislatures. Of these, five won approval (Oklahoma, Florida, Tennessee, Mississippi, Arkansas). In California, North Carolina, Louisiana, and Texas, less binding anti-evolution rulings were enacted at least for a time. See also Gatewood, *Preachers, Pedagogues and Politicians: The Evolution Controversy in North Carolina, 1920–1927* (Chapel Hill, 1966).

11. Hofstadter, *The Paranoid Style in American Politics, and Other Essays* (New York, 1963).

12. "The Bible Crusaders' Challenge," *The Crusaders' Champion* I (Feb., 5, 1926), pp. 12–13, reprinted in Gatewood, ed., *Controversy,* pp. 243–47. Cf. Furniss, *Controversy,* pp. 56–75, for similar concerns.

13. This account is based on C. Allyn Russell, *Voices of American Fundamentalism* (Philadelphia, 1976), pp. 20–46. Cf. George W. Dollar, *A History of Fundamentalism in America* (Greenville, S.C., 1973), pp. 122–34.

14. Dollar, *History,* pp. 169–71, 110–11; cf. Stewart G. Cole, *The History of Fundamentalism* (New York, 1931), pp. 292–93; cf. Furniss, *Controversy,* pp. 107–8.

15. Lippmann, *A Preface to Morals* (New York, 1929), pp. 31-32.

16. Editorial "Vanishing Fundamentalism," *Christian Century* XLIII (June 24, 1926), p. 799.

17. Lefferts A. Loetscher, *The Broadening Church* (Philadelphia, 1957), pp. 130-36.

18. *The Presbyterian Guardian* II (June 22, 1936), p. 110.

19. Edwin H. Rian, *The Presbyterian Conflict* (Grand Rapids, 1940), provides a responsible, although highly partisan, sympathetic account of the Orthodox Presbyterian movement. Cf. Loetscher, *Broadening Church,* pp. 148-55, and Russell, *Voices,* pp. 135-61, 190-211. After Machen's death, Carl McIntire led a schism from the new group to found the Bible Presbyterian Church. See George Marsden, "Perspective on the Division of 1937," *Presbyterian Guardian* XXXIII (January to April, 1963).

20. On Massee see Russell, *Voices,* pp. 107-34. See also Norman H. Maring, "Conservative But Progressive," in Gilbert L. Guffin, ed., *What God Hath Wrought, Eastern's First Thirty-Five Years* (Chicago, 1960?), on the foundation of Eastern Theological Seminary by moderate conservative Baptists in 1925.

21. Ronald Nelson, "Fundamentalism and the Northern Baptist Convention," Ph.D. dissertation, University of Chicago, 1964.

22. Dollar, *History,* 162-72.

23. Bruce L. Shelley, *A History of Conservative Baptists* (Wheaton, 1971); Dollar, *History,* pp. 226-33. John W. Foster, *Four Northwest Fundamentalists* (Portland, Ore., 1975), illustrates some of the differences among fundamentalist leaders on separation.

24. Foster, *Northwest,* provides a number of examples. Paul A. Carter, *Another Part of the Twenties* (New York, 1977), p. 51, points out that fundamentalists, while losing on the national level, could quite plausibly claim to be winning on the local level.

25. Joel A. Carpenter, "A Shelter in the Time of Storm: Fundamentalist Institutions and the Rise of Evangelical Protestantism, 1929-1942," ms., cf., *Church History* (March, 1980). Carpenter documents the activities described above. See also Dollar, *History,* esp. pp. 213-62, and Louis Gasper, *The Fundamentalist Movement* (The Hague, 1963).

26. Statistics from Carpenter, "Shelter."

27. Donald Dayton, *Discovering an Evangelical Heritage* (New York, 1976), provides some good examples of fundamentalist transformations in Holiness groups. Edith Lydia Waldvogel, "The 'Overcoming Life': A Study in the Reformed Evangelical Origins of Pentecostalism," Ph.D. dissertation, Harvard University, 1977, points out some of the affinities between the traditions. Robert Mapes Anderson, *Vision of the Disinherited* (New York, 1979), shows fundamentalist influence on Pentecostals.

28. Milton L. Rudnick, *Fundamentalism and the Missouri Synod: A Historical Study of Their Interaction and Mutual Influence* (St. Louis, 1966). Joseph H. Hall, "The Controversy over Fundamentalism in the Christian Reformed Church, 1915-1966," Th.D. dissertation, Concordia Seminary, St. Louis, 1974.

29. Stanley Nussbaum, "You Must be Born Again," a study of the Evangelical Mennonite Church, unpublished manuscript, 1976, portrays a classic case of a transformation from an Anabaptist to a fundamentalist Protestantism. Other examples of such groups are found in the lists of denominational affiliates of the

National Association of Evangelicals and the American Council of Christian Churches, in Gasper, *Fundamentalist Movement*, pp. 38–39.

30. One clear instance is schism from the Reformed Church of America and the formation in Grand Rapids, Michigan, of the Calvary Undenominational congregation, led in 1929 by Martin R. DeHaan, a prominent fundamentalist radio preacher. See James R. Adair, *M. R. DeHaan: The Man and His Ministry* (Grand Rapids, 1969), pp. 79–89. DeHaan's congregation attracted Dutch-Americans from several denominational backgrounds. I thank Herbert J. Brinks for this and other suggestions of fundamentalism's attractiveness to Dutch-Americans. On the larger subject, see Timothy L. Smith, "Religion and Ethnicity in America," *American Historical Review* LXXXIII (December, 1978), pp. 1155–85.

31. Ernest R. Sandeen, "Fundamentalism and American Identity," *The Annals of the American Academy of Political and Social Science*, vol. 387 (January, 1970), pp. 56–65, develops the idea of "parallelism" in post-1920s fundamentalism.

32. See Dollar, *History*, for best examples.

XXII. Fundamentalism as a Social Phenomenon

1. Stewart G. Cole, *The History of Fundamentalism* (New York, 1931), p. xi.

2. H. Richard Niebuhr, "Fundamentalism," *Encylopedia of Social Sciences*, vol. VI (New York, 1937), pp. 526–27. Niebuhr originally formulated this interpretation in *The Social Sources of Denominationalism* (New York, 1929). Later in life he repudiated such exclusively sociological explanations. Examples of the rural-urban theme in two standard histories are, William Leuchtenburg, *The Perils of Prosperity: 1914–1932* (Chicago, 1958), p. 223, and George E. Mowry, *The Urban Nation: 1920–1960* (New York, 1965), p. 28.

3. Richard Hofstadter, *Anti-Intellectualism in American Life* (New York, 1962), p. 121.

4. McLoughlin does note, however, that they did embody aspects of pietist and political conservative traditions that are permanent aspects of the American way of life. "Is there a Third Force in Christendom?" *Daedalus* XCVI (Winter, 1967), p. 45 and pp. 43–68, *passim*.

5. William E. Hordern, *A Layman's Guide to Protestant Theology*, rev. ed. (New York, 1968 [1955]), p. 69.

6. H. Shelton Smith, Robert T. Handy, Lefferts A. Loetscher, *American Christianity: An Historical Interpretation with Representative Documents, Vol. II, 1820–1960* (New York, 1963), pp. 316–17.

7. Willard Gatewood's works, *Preachers, Pedagogues and Politicians* (Chapel Hill, 1966) and *Controversy in the Twenties: Fundamentalism, Modernism, and Evolution*, Gatewood, ed. (Nashville, 1969), are important contributions to this trend. See also the discussion of Paul A. Carter's works in Chapter XXIII below. Sydney E. Ahlstrom, *A Religious History of the American People* (New Haven, 1972), exemplifies this balance in a most significant text.

8. Sandeen, *The Roots of Fundamentalism* (Chicago, 1970), p. 9; quotation from "Fundamentalism and the American Identity," *The Annals* 387 (January, 1970), pp. 63–64.

9. "Toward a Historical Interpretation of the Origins of Fundamentalism," *Church History* XXXVI (March, 1967), p. 67.

10. "American Identity," *Annals* 387, p. 59; cf. *Roots*, p. xix.

11. *Roots*, pp. 247–69.

12. Cf. George M. Marsden, "Defining Fundamentalism," *Christian Scholar's Review* I (Winter, 1971), pp. 141–51, and Sandeen's reply, *Christian Scholar's Review* I (Spring, 1971), pp. 227–32. LeRoy Moore, Jr., "Another Look at Fundamentalism: A Response to Ernest R. Sandeen," *Church History* XXXVII (June, 1968), pp. 195–202, offers a critique similar to my own.

13. Moore, "Another Look," *Church History* XXXVII, p. 195.

14. An excellent study of differences in patterns of Americanization within a single ethnic group, even among those with similar immigrant experiences, is found in Herbert J. Brinks, "Ethnicity and Denominationalism: The Christian Reformed Church and the Reformed Church of America," paper delivered at the Trinity College conference on "The Shaping of American Christianity," April 18, 1979.

    The degree to which aspects of fundamentalism had ethnic social bases is indicated by the fact that the staunchest support for Princeton theology in the early twentieth century still came from persons of Scotch-Irish heritage. When Machen, in turn, split from Princeton, he found like-minded allies from the Christian Reformed Church, an American alliance of separatist Dutch groups.

15. Albert H. Newman, "Recent Changes in Theology of Baptists," *The American Journal of Theology* X (1906), pp. 600–609, made essentially this point at the time.

16. Sandeen, *Roots*, esp. pp. ix–xix. Robert E. Wenger, "Social Thought in American Fundamentalism, 1918–1933," Ph.D. dissertation, University of Nebraska, 1973, pp. 51–75. It is possible, of course, to argue that living in a city does not necessarily make one "urban" since city dwellers may hold on to rural attitudes of their earlier days.

17. Walter Edmund Warren Ellis, "Social and Religious Factors in the Fundamentalist-Modernist Schisms among Baptists in North America 1895–1934," Ph.D. dissertation, University of Pittsburgh, 1974. Ellis finds similar and significant patterns of difference in four detailed studies of local schisms: that involving William B. Riley's church in Minneapolis, around 1900; the schism at T. T. Shield's church in Toronto in the 1920s; a "non-urban" schism in the First Baptist Church of Indiana, Pennsylvania, in the 1920s; and a similar split in the First Baptist Church in "non-urban" Orilla, Ontario. Ellis presents scattered evidence that these patterns were more general, which there is every reason to expect they would be.

18. William R. Hutchison, "Cultural Strain and American Protestantism," *American Historical Review* LXXVI (April, 1971), pp. 386–411, which compares liberal and conservative religious leaders. Ellis, "Social and Religious," pp. 52–95, suggests similar conclusions in comparing specifically fundamentalists (as opposed to Hutchison's broader category of religious conservatives) to liberals. Ellis points out that fundamentalists seldom had any socially established lineage. Also the support of many fundamentalists for Bible institutes suggests their willingness to have a less educated ministry. At the same time, however, they seemed to have valued higher education.

19. These observations are based especially on Ellis, "Social and Religious," who

says that "Fundamentalism fostered a revival among young persons of lower-middle-class backgrounds who were subject to socio-economic strains," p. iv. Confirmation of the somewhat unsettled lower-middle-class, non-professional, status of disporportionately many (although far from all) fundamentalists is provided in Sam Wanner, "Requested Re-evaluation: Wealthy Street Baptist Church Retrospectively Re-examined," senior seminar thesis, Calvin College, 1974. Wanner shows that this Grand Rapids church, which in 1909 led an early schism of dispensationalist churches in Michigan from the Northern Baptist Convention, in the late nineteenth century drew from a rapidly changing suburban neighborhood of a wide variety of social classes, but predominantly non-professional. The church always remained more modestly middle-class socially than its elite parent church, Fountain Street Baptist, which by 1909 had become the center of Baptist liberalism in the city.

20. Ellis documents this very thoroughly, pp. 192–210. A similar pattern appears in the urban cases he examines in Minneapolis and Toronto. Also the Baptist case in Indiana, Pa., is strikingly similar to a Presbyterian schism in the 1930s in Middletown, Pa., where I was raised. In that case a new pastor, Robert S. Marsden, from Westminster Theological Seminary, came to town in 1930, built up the church, drawing especially from the young and the laboring classes, and in 1936 led a schism mostly of such recent members to form an Orthodox Presbyterian Church. Business and professional people from the older families of the town as a rule remained in the First Presbyterian Church (U.S.A.). As in the case of the Baptists in Indiana, these people seem not to have been especially liberal in theology so much as not interested in doctrinal debate or in making religion into a disruptive issue. The schism caused some social resentment and petty ostracism of the one established family to join it, that into which the leader of the exodus had married. My own interests in the relationship of fundamentalism to American culture undoubtedly arise from growing up in such a setting.

21. This interpretation disagrees considerably with that of Ellis, who sees more significance in the social forces than I see warrant for. Ellis suggests that fundamentalists were "locals" and non-fundamentalists "cosmopolitans," e.g., p. 56. This, however, is not so clearly the case. The fundamentalists, after all, demanded involvement in the larger national controversies. In a sense, in cases such as this, the non-fundamentalists appear to be the real conservatives and the fundamentalists the innovators. In fact the civil courts (though perhaps predisposed to favor the social establishment) ruled this way in settling the property case in favor of the non-fundamentalists, p. 200. A further point is that in a setting such as this the rural/urban interpretation is quite inappropriate, cf. note 16, above.

22. Wenger, "Social Thought," pp. 294–314, lists forty "Prominent Fundamentalists, 1918–1933." Their names are: Biederwolf, Boddis, Burrell, Buswell, Chafer, Conrad, Craig, Dixon, Gaebelein, Goodchild, Gray, Haldeman, Horsch, Kennedy, Keyser, Kyle, Laws, Macartney, Machen, Magoun, Massee, Mathews, Munhall, Norris, Pettingill, Philpott, Price, Rader, Riley, Rimmer, Rood, Shields, Shuler, Sloan, Straton, Thomas, Torrey, Trumbull, Tucker, Wilson.

23. Of Wenger's forty, five were born in England or Germany, a figure similar to that found among modernists of the era, *ibid.,* p. 58.

24. Timothy L. Smith, "Religion and Ethnicity in America," *American Historical Review* LXXXIII (December, 1978), pp. 1155–85, gives a particularly illuminating account of the dynamic role of religion in defining new immigrant identity and subcultures.
25. There are, of course, many exceptions to such broad generalizations. Two well-known essays in which points such as these are made are Oscar Handlin, "The Immigrant in American Politics," in David F. Bowers, ed., *Foreign Influences in American Life* (Princeton, 1944), pp. 84–98, and Milton Gordon, "Assimilation in America: Theory and Reality," *Daedalus* (Spring, 1961), pp. 263–85.
26. Military imagery pervades fundamentalist literature in the 1920s. A good example is T. T. Shields, "The Necessity of Declaring War on Modernism," (pamphlet), an address delivered in New York City in 1925. "For myself," says Shields, "I have resigned from the diplomatic service and have joined the army in the field," p. 11.
27. E. T. Cassel, "The King's Business" (copyright, 1902), *Great Revival Hymns,* Homer Rodeheaver and B. D. Ackley, eds. (New York, 1911). Themes of wanderers in unfriendly lands were already common in the gospel hymns of the Sankey era, so their significance probably should not be taken too literally. Cf. Sandra Sizer, *Gospel Hymns and Social Religion* (Philadelphia, 1978), pp. 29, 140. One evidence, however, of the role of such a hymn is that it appears in the 1934 edition of the *Psalter Hymnal* of the Christian Reformed Church, a Calvinist group whose theology had little emphasis on such themes, but who had experienced immigration from the Netherlands. Significantly, this song was absent from the 1959 edition. James D. Bratt, in an entertaining and perceptive Ph.D. dissertation, "Dutch Calvinism in Modern America: The History of a Conservative Subculture," Yale, 1978, points out that military imagery was common in defining the Dutch-American's relation to American culture, although their thought was never dominated by the categories of the fundamentalist-modernist debates, pp. 414–17. Joseph H. Hall, "The Controversy over Fundamentalism in the Christian Reformed Church 1915–1966," Ph.D. dissertation, Concordia Seminary, St. Louis, presents a more detailed account of the very ambivalent relationships of this group to American fundamentalism.

XXIII. Fundamentalism as a Political Phenomenon

1. Editorial "The Capitalists and the Premillenarians," *Christian Century* XXXVIII (April 14, 1921), p. 3.
2. (London, 1925), p. 161. Norman F. Furniss, *The Fundamentalist Controversy, 1918–1931* (New Haven, 1954), p. 27, cites this and three other quotations to the same effect.
3. Paul A. Carter, *The Decline and Revival of the Social Gospel: Social and Political Liberalism in the American Protestant Churches 1920–1940* (Ithaca, N.Y., 1954), pp. 47–49. McLoughlin, on the other hand, did not suggest that political issues were primary, even if prominent.
4. Carter, "The Fundamentalist Defense of the Faith," *Change and Continuity in 20th-century America: the 1920's,* John Braeman et al., eds. (Columbus, Ohio, 1968), pp. 193, 212. In my opinion, this article is one of the best analyses of fundamentalism.

5. Robert E. Wenger, "Social Thought in American Fundamentalism, 1918–1933," Ph.D. dissertation, University of Nebraska, 1973, pp. 286, 290–91.

6. Carter, "Fundamentalist Defense," makes exactly this point. Wenger, on the basis of what seems to me to be fragments of evidence of fundamentalist work for progressive social legislation, suggests that some balance was maintained through the 1920s; e.g., "Social Thought," p. 237. I can not find a significant amount of such evidence compared with the innumerable fundamentalist attacks on social reform as associated with the Social Gospel, which seems to have reduced vastly their enthusiasm for such projects. Wenger himself presents much evidence on fundamentalist anti-liberal political views.

7. Examples of fundamentalist American patriotism are found in Wenger, "Social Thought," e.g., pp. 118–20, 129, 158. My impression from these and other samplings is that strongly patriotic sentiments became more common after about 1926.

8. Carter, "Fundamentalist Defense," p. 196.

9. Wenger, "Social Thought," pp. 167–76, on Roman Catholicism, and pp. 241–49, on prohibition.

10. Here J. Gresham Machen, who defended political individualism with the same relentless logic that he employed for conservative theology, is a striking exception. See C. Allyn Russell, *Voices of American Fundamentalism* (Philadelphia, 1976), pp. 146–50.

11. Editorial "Will Christian Taxpayers Stand for This?" *Moody Monthly* XXIII (May, 1923), p. 409.

12. Riley, "Socialism in Our Schools" (pamphlet), Minneapolis, n. d. [1923]). Cf. Riley in *King's Business* XIV (October, 1923). The same number contains the first really alarmist editorial on communism in the *King's Business*. Cf. also Riley's statement, "*The Product of Evolution Theory is Bestial Bolshevism,*" in "The Theory of Evolution—Does it Tend to Anarchy?" (pamphlet) (n. p., n. d.). Cf. editorial *Our Hope* XXX (October, 1923), pp. 204–5, which had kept up a steady anti-communist barrage since World War I. Willard B. Gatewood, ed., *Controversy in the Twenties* (Nashville, 1969), p. 24, cites similar quotations.

13. R. S. Beal, "The Eternal Searchlight Turned on Modern Socialism," *The Christian Fundamentals in School and Church* VIII (January, 1926), pp. 44–45. William B. Riley was editor.

14. Riley, "Protocols and Communism" (pamphlet), (n. p., n. d. [1934]), p. 17. Cf. "Painting America Red" (pamphlet) (Wichita, Kansas: Defender Tract Club, n. d. [1939]). Riley did attack Hitler in "Hitlerism or the Philosophy of Evolution in Action" (pamphlet) (n. p., n. d. [1941–1942?]). *The Protocols* were given wide circulation in the early 1920s by Henry Ford's *Deerborn Independent.* Cf. the ambivalent response, blaming the Protocols on the Roman Catholics (!), Charles C. Cook, "The International Jew," *The King's Business* XII (Nov., 1921), pp. 1084–88.

15. Wenger, "Social Thought," pp. 176–92. David A. Rausch, *Zionism within Early American Fundamentalism, 1878–1918: A Convergence of Two Traditions* (New York, 1979), presents a very positive picture of early fundamentalist Zionism and tends to minimize suggestions of later anti-Semitism. However, fundamentalists between the wars could be both pro-Zionist and somewhat anti-Semitic, favoring the return of the Jews to Israel, which would lead eventually to their conversion;

yet in the meantime especially distrusting apostate Jews. Rausch points out that Gaebelein in *Our Hope* deplored Jewish persecutions in Europe and was appalled by the Holocaust, "*OUR HOPE*: An American Fundamentalist Journal and the Holocaust, 1837–1945," *Fides et Historia* CXII (Spring, 1980), pp. 89–103.

In *Zionism,* pp. 32–41, Rausch provides an advance critique of the overall approach of the present volume, based on my earlier exchange with Sandeen (cf. above, Intro., note 6).

16. Wenger, "Social Thought," pp. 176–92, on Winrod's and other's anti-Semitism. Cf. Ralph Lord Roy, *Apostles of Discord: A Study of Organized Bigotry and Disruption on the Fringes of Protestantism* (Boston, 1953), pp. 26–58.

17. So did John Roach Straton, Wenger, "Social Thought," p. 184.

18. Roy, *Apostles,* pp. 350–57. Cf. Russell, *Voices,* pp. 20–46. Norris dropped his anti-Catholicism during the later part of his career.

19. Cf. Erling Jorstad, *The Politics of Doomsday: Fundamentalists of the Far Right* (Nashville, 1970); John H. Redekop, *The American Far Right: A Case Study of Billy James Hargis and Christian Crusade* (Grand Rapids, 1968); Roy, *Apostles.*

20. Richard Hofstadter, *Anti-Intellectualism in American Life* (New York, 1962), p. 135; *The Paranoid Style in American Politics, and Other Essays* New York, 1963), p. 29.

XXIV. Fundamentalism as an Intellectual Phenomenon

1. Leander S. Keyser in a review of Cole in *Christian Faith and Life* XXXVII (June, 1931), pp. 328–31, compiles a long list of such prejudicial statements.

2. H. Richard Niebuhr, "Fundamentalism," *Encylopedia of Social Sciences,* vol. VI (New York, 1937), pp. 526–27.

3. Norman Furniss, *The Fundamentalist Controversy, 1918–1931* (New Haven, 1954), pp. 39, 19–20, 56–57.

4. Richard Hofstadter, *Anti-Intellectualism in American Life* (New York, 1962), p. 133.

5. Reuben A. Torrey, *The Importance and Value of Proper Bible Study* (New York, 1921), p. 45, quoted in Robert E. Wenger, "Social Thought in American Fundamentalism, 1918–1933," Ph.D. dissertation, University of Nebraska, 1973, p. 79. Cf. William G. McLoughlin, Jr., *Modern Revivalism* (New York, 1959), p. 288, for similar quotation from Southern revivalist Sam Jones.

6. This theme is very well developed by Nathan O. Hatch, "Reaping the Whirlwind: The American Revolution, Social Change, and Theology," unpublished paper, 1978.

7. William Jennings Bryan, *In His Image* (New York, 1922), p. 93.

8. Another line of defense sometimes was that science is fully competent to deal with natural subjects, but has no competence with respect to the supernatural, e.g. John Horsch, *The Failure of Modernism* (pamphlet) (Chicago, 1925), pp. 20–21. Horsch also claimed, however, that evolution or any science in conflict with Scripture was unscientific. *Modern Religious Liberalism* (Chicago, 1920). These works were published by Moody Bible Institute.

Another common defense was that "the Bible is not a scientific treatise." *Dr. C. I. Scofield's Question Box,* compiled by Ella E. Pohle (Chicago, n. d.), p. 147.

This meant only that the Bible did not speak on many scientific subjects, and was compatible with holding that the Bible was fully scientific (i.e. accurate as to facts) on subjects on which it spoke.

9. "Text of Bryan's Proposed Address in Scopes Case," *The World's Most Famous Court Trial: State of Tennessee v. John Thomas Scopes: Complete Stenographic Report* . . . (New York, 1971 [Cincinnati, 1925]), p. 323. Cf. *In His Image*, pp. 86–135, esp., p. 94.

10. *In His Image*, p. 95.

11. *World's Most Famous Trial*, p. 182.

12. *Ibid.*, p. 317. Cf. Bryan's common sense view of truth: "His [Jesus'] philosophy is easily comprehended and readily applied. His words need no interpretation; they are the words of the people and the language of the masses." *In His Image*, p. 142.

13. John Dewey, *A Common Faith* (New Haven, 1934), p. 63.

14. Thomas S. Kuhn, *The Structure of Scientific Revolutions*, second edition, enlarged (Chicago, 1970 [1962]), p. 151 and *passim*.

15. For discussion of Kuhn, see Imre Lakatos and Alan Musgrave, eds., *Criticism and the Growth of Knowledge* (London, 1970).

16. *Structure*, p. 136. Actually the model seems to apply in a wide variety of areas. See, for instance, Robert W. Friedrichs, *A Sociology of Sociology* (New York, 1970).

17. Bryan could name no living and respected scientist who supported his views, *World's Most Famous Trial*, p. 297. His move toward separatism is indicated in his undelivered closing address, "Christians must, in every state of the Union, build their own colleges . . . ," p. 322.

18. E. Y. Mullins, *Christianity at the Cross Roads* (New York, 1924), pp. 32, 56.

19. Machen very explicitly endorsed Common Sense philosophy in *What is Faith* (New York, 1933), pp. 27–28, cited also in John C. Vander Stelt, *Philosophy and Scripture: A Study in Old Princeton and Westminster Theology* (Marlton, N.J., 1978), p. 209, cf. p. 215.

20. J. Gresham Machen, "The Relation of Religion to Science and Philosophy," *Princeton Theological Review* XXIV (January, 1926), pp. 38–66. Baconianism pervades Machen's thought. See George Marsden, "J. Gresham Machen, History, and Truth," *Westminster Theological Journal* XLII (Fall, 1979), pp. 157–75.

21. A. C. Dixon, "Why I Am a Christian," *The King's Business* XI (November, 1920), pp. 261–62.

22. Riley defined "science" as "knowledge gained and verified by exact observation and correct thinking; especially as methodologically formulated and arranged in a rational system." This, he said, excludes, "theory," "hypothesis," and "assumption." "Are the Scriptures Scientific?" (pamphlet) (Minneapolis, n. d. [after 1925]), p. 5. For equally definite statements of the Baconian ideal, see Harry Rimmer, *The Theory of Evolution and the Facts of Science* (Grand Rapids, 1935), p. 15; and John Roach Straton, *The Famous New York Fundamentalist Modernist Debates: The Orthodox Side* (New York, 1924), p. 56.

23. Riley, "Are the Scriptures Scientific?" p. 23.

24. E. J. Pace, "The Law of the Octave," *Moody Monthly* XXII (May, 1922), pp. 1022–25. Pace worked with the Extension Department of MBI.

25. Ivan Panin, "Scripture Numerics," *The King's Business* X (May, 1919), pp.

407-10. Cf. editorial "CAN Inspiration be Proven Scientifically?" *ibid.,* pp. 800-801. L. T. Townsend, "Verbal Inspiration," *The Bible Champion* XXVIII (January, 1922), p. 3, refers to Panin approvingly.

26. See Cy Hulse, "The Shaping of a Fundamentalist: A Case Study of Charles Blanchard," M.A. thesis, Trinity Evangelical Divinity School, 1977, on the various sides of Blanchard's career.

27. William Delahoyde, "Common Sense Philosophy at Wheaton College (1860-1940)," unpublished paper, Trinity Evangelical Divinity School, 1976, clearly documents the explicit influences of Common Sense philosophy at Wheaton throughout this period. Cf. Hulse, "Shaping," pp. 66-85. I am indebted to the excellent work of these two students on this subject. Cf. the nearly unbounded confidence in science and rationality in the works of Wheaton professor, Hervin U. Roop, e.g., *The Fundamentals of Christianity* (n. p., 1926), pp. 13, 49, 93.

28. Hulse, "Shaping," p. 85.

29. Charles Blanchard, "Psychological Foundations," unpublished book manuscript, Wheaton College archives, p. 28 and *passim.*

30. "The Bible and the Word of God," sermon manuscript, June 10, 1883, Wheaton archives, cited Hulse, "Shaping," p. 76.

31. Hulse, "Shaping," p. 78.

32. Sermon notes, n. d. (1891?), Wheaton archives, cited Hulse, "Shaping," p. 77.

33. Christian Science and the Word of God" (pamphlet), (n. p., n. d.), pp. 9-13, cited Hulse, "Shaping," p. 80.

34. "Psychological Foundations," p. 39.

35. Charles Blanchard, *President Blanchard's Autobiography* (Boone, Iowa, 1915), p. 160.

36. "The Coming of the Lord Draws Near," in *Prophetic Conference Addresses Given at the Winona Lake Bible Conference* (Winona Lake, Ind., 1918), p. 207.

37. *Ibid.*

38. *Method in Biblical Criticism* (Chicago, 1922), p. 21, cited in Hulse, "Shaping," pp. 91-92.

39. Quoted in H. L. Mencken, ed., *Americana 1925* (New York, 1925), p. 232, from an address by Billy Sunday in Nashville, "as reported by the celebrated *Banner.*"

XXV. Fundamentalism as an American Phenomenon

1. Ulster appears to be an exception—one that would offer another illustration of the relationship of fundamentalism to relatively unique cultural experiences. Canada developed some fundamentalist movements paralleling those in the United States. In many nations, confessionalists and churchly conservatives survived and in some, such as the Netherlands, they had considerable influence; but these lacked the revivalist ties and some of the intellectual emphases characteristic of fundamentalists. Evangelical or pietistic revivalism, sometimes with genuinely fundamentalist traits and connections, could be found throughout the world in the twentieth century, but seldom with a substantial role in their culture comparable to that of fundamentalism and its evangelical heirs in America.

2. I have discussed this comparison in more detail in "Fundamentalism as an American Phenomenon, A Comparison with English Evangelicalism," *Church History* XLVI (June, 1977), pp. 215-32. J. I. Packer, *"Fundamentalism" and the*

Word of God (London, 1958), and James Barr, *Fundamentalism* (Philadelphia, 1977), present respectively pro and con views of recent militant British "fundamentalism." Barr's attacks indicate the considerable influence of such views since World War II, although this British fundamentalism has generally been of a more scholarly sort than most of its American counterparts. I am indebted also to Ian S. Rennie of Regent College, Vancouver, for his discussions with me on this subject.

3. Willard B. Gatewood, Jr., ed., *Controversy in the Twenties* (Nashville, 1969), pp. 409–14.

4. *Times,* August 20, 1929, obituary of Dr. Arthur Samuel Peake, quoted in David G. Fountain, *E. J. Poole-Connor (1872-1962): "Contender for the Faith,"* (London, 1966), p. 91.

5. See "Fundamentalism as an American Phenomenon," *Church History* XLVI (June, 1977), for speculative explanations.

6. Stanley Elkins, *Slavery: A Problem in American Institutional and Intellectual Life* (Chicago, 1959), refers to "the dynamics of unopposed capitalism."

7. Cf. Donald G. Mathews, "The Great Awakening as an Organizing Process 1780-1830: An Hypothesis," *American Quarterly* XXI (1969); *Rise of Adventism: Religion and Society in Mid-Nineteenth-Century America,* Edwin S. Gaustad, ed. (New York, 1974), pp. 119–54, who goes so far as to suggest that revivalism is the key to understanding American life generally.

8. Cf. Sacvan Bercovitch, *The Puritan Origins of the American Self* (New Haven, 1975).

9. Nathan O. Hatch, "Reaping the Whirlwind: The American Revolution, Social Change, and Theology," paper delivered at the Trinity College (Ill.) history conference, April, 1978, suggests and develops this theme of *Sola Scriptura* and *Novus Ordo Seclorum.*

10. These are the dominant themes as summarized by Sandra Sizer, *Gospel Hymns and Social Religion* (Philadelphia, 1978), p. 25.

11. Ernest Lee Tuveson, *Redeemer Nation: The Idea of America's Millennial Role* (Chicago, 1968), gives many examples of this point.

12. In England dispensationalism had relatively few adherents except among the Plymouth Brethren.

13. George Marsden, "J. Gresham Machen—History and Truth," *Westminster Theological Journal* XLII (Fall, 1979), pp. 157–75, deals with this question. Grant A. Wacker, "Augustus H. Strong: A Conservative Confrontation with History," Ph.D. dissertation, Harvard University, 1978, presents a very sophisticated discussion of this issue in the thought of one of the many conservatives caught between liberal and fundamentalist extremes.

14. Cf., for instance, Franklin L. Baumer, *Modern European Thought: Continuity and Change in Ideas, 1600-1950* (New York, 1977), pp. 262, 268–301.

15. See, for example, R. Stephen Humphreys, "Islam and Political Values in Saudi Arabia, Egypt and Syria," *The Middle East Journal* XXXIII (Winter, 1979), pp. 1–19.

16. A recent Gallup survey estimates the number of "evangelicals" at 44 million, or about one fifth of the population. *Christianity Today* XXIII (Dec. 21, 1979), p. 1671. George W. Dollar, *A History of Fundamentalism in America* (Greenville, S.C., 1973), p. 248, estimates the number of "fundamentalists" at "near four million."

Afterword: History and Fundamentalism

1. Richard F. Lovelace, *Dynamics of Spiritual Life: An Evangelical Theology of Renewal* (Downers Grove, Ill., 1979), p. 256.
2. I am indebted to Joy L. Johnson, "The Theology of Middle-earth," M.A. dissertation, Trinity Evangelical Divinity School, 1978.
3. I have discussed these points in greater detail in "A Christian Perspective for the Teaching of History," *A Christian View of History?* George Marsden and Frank Roberts, eds. (Grand Rapids, 1975).

Fundamentalism Yesterday and Today (2005)

1. Ernest R. Sandeen, *The Roots of Fundamentalism: British and American Millenarianism, 1800–1930* (Chicago, 1970), p. ix.
2. I am grateful especially to Joel Carpenter for his emphasis on this point, both in his *Revive Us Again: The Reawakening of American Fundamentalism* (New York, 1997) and in personal comment on this essay. In the latter he quotes Andrew Walls, *The Missionary Movement in Christian History* (New York, 1996), p. 79, who writes, "Historic evangelicalism is a religion of protest against a Christian society that is not Christian enough. . . ." Walls's statement is a reminder that even though, as argued below, conversionist evangelicalism has been shaped most by positive concerns for evangelism, missions, and spirituality, it has since its origins included a sense of crisis in Christendom.
3. See Chapter XXIII.
4. A revealing example is that Marty E. Marty, perhaps the most astute observer of the religious scene of the era, in his *Righteous Empire: The Protestant Experience in America* (New York, 1970), esp. pp. 177–187, wrote of a "two-party system" that emerged in the early twentieth century between a "public" Protestantism associated with the social gospel and a "private" Protestantism associated with revivalism.
15. Christian Smith, *American Evangelicals: Embattled and Thriving* (Chicago, 1998), p. 37, shows that self-identified evangelicals and fundamentalists are somewhat more likely than mainline or liberal religious people to call for changing society according to God's will. But Christian Smith, *Christian America? What Evangelicals Really Want* (Berkeley, CA, 2000), p. 200. also documents that their views are far from monolithic. For instance, only about half (though twice the percentage of all other Americans) of self-identified evangelicals and fundamentalists will agree that "Christian morality should be the law of the land even though not all Americans are Christian." About one-third affirm the view that religion should be essentially a "private matter." See Smith's entire discussion for the many nuances and qualifications of what people mean by their survey answers.
6. In the mid-nineteenth century "evangelical" had been a term that well-described trans-Atlantic conversionist Protestantism that was flourishing in America, but by the 1920s it had become a generic term without clear content, since it was claimed by liberals and conservatives alike.
7. I am here using "pietist" and "Reformed" cultural outlooks in the senses described in the Introduction to this book. These are ideal types and it is easy to find exceptions to these general tendencies.

For fundamentalism in the 1930s to the birth of neo-evangelicalism in the 1950s the indispensable work is Carpenter, *Revive Us Again*. Also see Leo P. Ribuffo, *The Old Christian Right: The Protestant Far Right from the Depression to the Cold War* (Philadelphia, 1983). On the 1940s to 1960s see also George Marsden, *Reforming Fundamentalism: Fuller Seminary and the New Evangelicalism* (Grand Rapids, 1987).

8. Ways of interpreting Scripture were often the most substantial issue in distinguishing fundamentalistic evangelicals from more moderate evangelicals in doctrinal matters. Both affirmed that the Bible was the highest authority and that God would not err in any teaching. More fundamentalistic evangelicals, however, were more prone to interpret Scripture according to the principle of "literal when possible" so that any seeming historical or prophetic narrative (as opposed to unmistakable metaphor) should be interpreted as literally and exactly true. Moderate evangelicals, in the meantime, allowed more leeway in interpreting what the Bible meant to say or teach. In general they distanced themselves from elements in their fundamentalist past that they considered too rigid but affirmed what they saw as the essential doctrinal teachings of the heritage.

My essay, "Fundamentalism and American Evangelicalism," in *The Variety of American Evangelicalism* (Knoxville, TN, 1991), Donald W. Dayton and Robert K. Johnston, eds., pp. 22–35, delineates these relationships more fully. The Dayton and Johnston volume is especially helpful for appreciating the complexity of evangelicalism.

9. Quoted in Richard N. Ostling, "Jerry Falwell's Crusade: Fundamentalist Legions Seek to Remake Church and Society," *Time* 126 (September 2, 1985), p. 48. Falwell subsequently adopted and popularized this quip.

10. This roughly follows the four–fold definition of D. W. Bebbington, *Evangelicalism in Modern Britain: A History from the 1730s to the 1980s* (London, 1989), pp. 2–17, which has become more-or-less canonical.

When I use "fundamentalist or evangelical" or the like below I am referring to the ecclesiastical distinction between separatists and non-separatists, even though separatist fundamentalists are a sub-type of evangelical. For a fuller discussion of the definitional issues see George M. Marsden, *Understanding Evangelicalism and Fundamentalism* (Grand Rapids, 1991), pp. 1–6.

11. Just for one example, political scientist Corwin Smidt estimated that in 2000 twenty-five percent of the electorate were whites who were active in evangelical churches, a predominately Republican group. Richard Ostling, "Religion Today, Surveying the religio-political landscape for hints of November," (AP), 2000 (no exact date) on Beliefnet. The various works by Smidt, Lyman Kellstedt, James Guth, and John C. Green are the most reliable for identifying evangelical influences in electoral politics.

Equally sophisticated is the analysis of Christian Smith in *American Evangelicals and Christian America*. Based on survey data and interviews from the mid-1990s, he concludes that 11.2% of the American population self-identify as "evangelical" and another 12.8% self-identify as "fundamentalist," counting only churchgoing Protestants. Including these, a total of 29% of the American population can be classified as "conservative Protestant," *Christian America*, pp. 16–17. One problem with self-identification is that "fundamentalist" is the more familiar term and by this method self-identified fundamentalists are slightly less conservative than self-identified evangelicals (suggesting the "fundamentalist" population is more likely to include misidentifications). Smith also points out that the populations of these groups is not as monolithic on political issues as their most vocal spokespersons might suggest, see Part 5, note 5, above.

Many African-American Christians qualify as evangelical in terms of their belief, but the term is seldom applied to them due to the segregationist heritage which kept most African-Americans from identifying with the "evangelical" movement. While some African-Americans are militant regarding conservative doctrinal or cultural issues, "fundamentalist" has seldom been a self-designation and relatively few have identified with the conservative Republican politics that dominate recent fundamentalism. See Michael O. Emerson and Christian Smith, *Divided by Faith: Evangelical Religion and the Problem of Race in America* (New York, 2000).

12. David Edwin Harrell, *All Things Are Possible: the Healing and Charismatic Revivals in America* (Bloomington, IN, 1975) and *Oral Roberts: An American Life* (Bloomington, IN, 1985).

13. Edith L. Blumhofer, *Restoring the Faith: The Assemblies of God, Pentecostalism, and American Culture* (Urbana, IL, 1993). On world patterns see, for instance, David Martin, *Pentecostalism: The World Their Parish* (London, 2002) and Philip Jenkins, *The New Christendom: The Coming of Global Christianity* (New York, 2002).

14. Since drafting this I have seen Paul Harvey's *Freedom's Coming: Religion Culture and the Shaping of the South from the Civil War through the Civil Rights Era* (Chapel Hill, 2005), which provides the best account of this transition. The fact that Harvey has a sentence almost identical to the above provides reassuring confirmation. Harvey writes (p. 248): "It was no accident that religious conservative came to national prominence following the demise of race as the central issue of southern life. Underlying their political movements were philosophical positions that updated venerable defense of social order as necessary for a properly ordered society." Elsewhere (p. 219) he succinctly puts it that "the terrain of battle in the southern culture wars had shifted, in effect, from race to gender." These insights seem to me very helpful but at the same time to hide some parts of the picture that are more immediately parts of the specifically *religious* heritage and not reducible to hierarchy or gender. The popularity of creation science is the clearest example. Furthermore, the prominence of concerns over abortion, end-of-life issues, gay rights, pornography, and sexual permissiveness, although including elements concerning hierarchy and gender, also reflect some other longstanding Christian concerns.

Some will argue that racism remained the primary sub-text for the Religious Right even after the era of civil rights battles. Doubtless racism did remain a significant issue, but it is far too simplistic to reduce to that factor the major motivation for a movement with so many dimensions. Many conservative evangelical movements, moreover, made a point of integrating their ministries, even when they had very small African-American constituencies to draw from. My point is that southerners could not be heard on other issues until the civil rights issues were settled in formal ways.

15. Cf. Chapter XII, note 2, above, on the northern predominance of explicit fundamentalist organization.

16. William Glass, *Strangers in Zion: Fundamentalists in the South, 1900–1950* (Macon, GA, 2001). Barry Hankins, *God's Rascal: J. Frank Norris and the Beginnings of Southern Fundamentalism* (Lexington, KY, 1996); Mark Taylot Dalhouse, *An Island in the Lake of fire: Bob Jones University, Fundamentalism, and the Separatist Movement* (Athens GA, 1996); Daniel L. Turner, *Standing Without Apology: The History of Bob Jones University* (Greenville, SC, 1997).

17. Grant Wacker, "Uneasy in Zion: Evangelicals in Postmodern Society," in *Evangelicalism and Modern America* (Grand Rapids, 1984), pp. 17–28.

18. Edward J. Larson, *Summer of the Gods: The Scopes Trial and America's Continuing Debate over Science and Religion* (New York, 1997). In effect the Scopes Trial was part of the triumph of anti-evolution in the South, since some anti-evolution laws remained in place and during the next decades biological evolution was seldom taught in public schools, even in the North.

19. Quoted in Susan Friend Harding, *The Book of Jerry Falwell* (Princeton, 2000), p. 22. During the 1980 election Bob Jones, Jr. and Bob Jones III criticized Falwell for politicizing the Gospel via the Moral Majority. Jeffrey Haddon and Charles E. Swann, *Prime Time Preachers: The Rising Power of Televangelism* (Reading, MA, 1981), p. 155. In 2000 Bob Jones III invited George W. Bush to campaign on the campus of Bob Jones University.

20. Darren Dochuk, "From Bible Belt to Sunbelt: Plain Folk Religion, Grassroots Politics, and the Southernization of Southern California, 1935–1969," PhD dissertation, University of Notre Dame, 2005, p. 11, citing James N. Gregory, "The Southern Diaspora and the Urban Dispossessed," *Journal of American History* 82 (June 1995), p. 112. My interpretation in this section is heavily indebted to Dochuk's impressive work.

21. See Dochuk, "From Bible Belt to Sunbelt," pp. 18–33. Bruce J. Schulman, *The Seventies: The Great Shift in American Culture, Society, and Politics* (Cambridge, MA, 2002), 102–117, provides an overview. On California see also Linda McGirr, *Suburban Warriors: The Origins of the New American Right* (Princeton, 2001).

22. Such experiences are, of course, not confined to peoples who have emigrated to America relatively recently. Many early fundamentalists appear to have been people of many sorts who were attempting to preserve religious and social ideals reminiscent of small-town America in the face of modernizing urban culture. Joel Carpenter, *Revive Us Again*, pp. 9–11, provides a nice overview of what we know of the social locations of early fundamentalists.

23. Many smaller southern denominations and northern ethno-religious groups divided into comparable wings, although the controversies in the three mentioned provide particularly close parallels.

24. Sara Diamond, *Roads to Dominion: Right-Wing Movements and Political Power in the United States* (New York, 1995), pp. 92–106, provides a helpful overview of these developments. As Dochuk, "From Sun Belt to Bible Belt" and McGirr, *Suburban Warriors*, show however, in Southern California the line between religion and direct political mobilization was blurring.

25. Anne C. Loveland, *American Evangelicals and the U. S. Military* (Baton Rouge, 1996).

26. See, for instance, Thomas Frank, *The Conquest of Cool: Business Culture, Counterculture, and the Rise of Hip Consumerism* (Chicago, 1997).

27. Frederick Lewis Allen's *Only Yesterday* (New York, 1931) was the classic work that put fundamentalism in that context, although H. L. Mencken et al. had already firmly established that image.

28. Betty DeBerg, *Ungodly Women: Gender and the First Wave of American Fundamentalism* (Minneapolis, 1990) is especially to be commended for pointing out the continuities between first-wave and second-wave fundamentalists on the above issues and others. She goes so far as to claim, however, that "It was not so much traditional theology they were defending as it was traditional gender ideology." (p. 141) That

surely overstates the case, but still the point is well taken. Theology cannot be entirely separated from its cultural embeddedness, including factors of gender, race, class, and nationality. Margaret Lambert Bendroth, *Fundamentalism and Gender, 1875 to the Present* (New Haven, 1993), also provides an excellent account of fundamentalist views of women and gender within fundamentalism, See also Janette Hassey, *No Time for Silence: Evangelical Women in Public Ministry around the Turn of the Century* (Grand Rapids, 1986). Michael Hamilton, "Women, Public Ministry, and American Fundamentalism, 1920–1950," *Religion and American Culture* 3 (Summer 1993), pp. 172–196, points out that fundamentalist women were more influential in practice than in theory and did not differ from mainline Protestant women as is often supposed. James Ault, *Spirit and Flesh: Life in a Fundamentalist Baptist Church* (New York, 2004) confirms that pattern in his study of fundamentalist women in a small church in the 1980s.

29. DeBerg, *Ungodly Women*, p. 51.
30. Diamond, *Roads to Dominion*, pp. 98–99.
31. John G. Turner, "Selling Jesus to Modern America: Campus Crusade for Christ, Evangelical Culture, and Conservative Politics," PhD dissertation, University of Notre Dame, 2005, pp. 286–331. In the 1980s and 1990s Bright became less fundamentalistic in his theology. For instance, he allowed pentecostals and charismatics on the staff of Campus Crusade and was generally more open to other evangelical perspectives. *Ibid.,* pp. 449–454.
32. Donald Mathews and Jane Sherron DeHart, *Sex, Gender, and the Politics of ERA: A State and the Nation* (New York, 1990), pp. 222–225. William Martin, *With God on Our Side: The Rise of the Religious Right in America,* (New York, 1996), pp. 162–167.
33. Martin, *With God on Our Side,* pp. 148–178. Disillusion with Carter's White House Conferences on the Family was a major source of disaffection.
34. Martin, *With God on Our Side,* pp. 168–220. esp. pp. 172–73, and 212.
35. Quentin Schultze, *Televangelism and American Culture: The Business of Popular Religion* (Grand Rapids, 1991), provides a helpful overview.
36. Scott Flipse, "Below-the-Belt Politics: Protestant Evangelicals, Abortion, and the Foundation of the New Religious Right," pp. 127–141. In David Farber and Jeff Roche, eds., *The Conservative Sixties* (New York, 2003). For earlier views see DeBerg, *Ungodly Women,* p. 115.
37. Douglas Sloan, *Faith and Knowledge: Mainline Protestantism and American Higher Education* (Louisville, KY, 1994) provides an insightful analysis of these developments which are here summarized very broadly.
38. Barry Hankins, *Uneasy in Babylon: Southern Baptist Conservatives and American Culture* (Tuscaloosa, AL, 2002). Nancy Taton Ammerman, *Baptist Battles: Social Change and Religious Conflict in the Southern Baptist Convention* (New Brunswick, NJ, 1990). The split in the Southern Baptist Convention, however, should underscore the point that fundamentalistic attitudes of recent decades have not involved only cultural-political fundamentalism. Rather concerns over the inerrancy of Scripture and about trends away from traditional evangelical doctrines and emphases have been genuine concerns for many militant conservative. Often, though these were connected with cultural issues, for instance, many conservatives opposed women's ordination as inconsistent with taking the inerrancy of Scripture seriously.

The split from the Presbyterian Church in the United States (Southern Presbyterian) in 1973 to form the Presbyterian Church in America more closely followed the pattern and example of J. Gresham Machen in separating from the larger denomination over concerns about toleration of liberalism and a pending merger with the northern Presbyterian Church in the USA.

39. This follows the interpretation of Robert Wuthnow, *The Restructuring of American Religion* (Princeton, 1988).

40. Francis A. Schaeffer, *How Shall We Then Live? The Rise and Decline of Western Thought and Culture* (Old Tappan, NJ, 1976).

41. On the raising of Schaeffer's consciousness regarding abortion see Martin, *With God on Our Side*, pp. 193–94.

42. Francis A. Schaeffer, *Whatever Happened to the Human Race?* (Old Tappan, NJ, 1979). On the raising of Schaeffer's consciousness regarding abortion see Martin, *With God on Our Side*, pp. 193–94. Tim LaHaye remarked to the author in an informal conversation that Schaeffer was crucial to alerting him to the abortion issue. Cf. LaHaye, *The Battle for the Mind* (Old Tappan, NJ, 1980), p. 69.

43. LaHaye, *Battle for the Mind*, pp. 181–82.

44. For a fuller analysis of this see Marsden, *Understanding Fundamentalism and Evangelicalism* (Grand Rapids, 1991), pp. 153–181.

45. I have been aided by the 2004 graduate paper of Danielle DuBois on "Home Schooling," which documents these points especially in the writings of Michael Farris, as in his *Future of Homeschooling* (Washington, D.C., 1997).

46. This standard teaching, which tends to gloss over the anomaly that "Christian" America included racially based slavery, has been among the reasons that the Religious Right has had relatively little appeal to African-Americans who are evangelical in other ways. Turner, "Selling Jesus to Modern America," pp. 425–427, shows that this issue strained relationships between Campus Crusade and some African-Americans. In 2005 the National Summit: Race to Unity organized a video critical of the Christian America theme for a convention of African-American pastors.

47. For instance, Peter Marshall and David Manuel, *The Light and the Glory* (Grand Rapids, 1977), which argues for a providential role for America, was a best-selling account and widely used in Christian schools. For a far less popular critique of such views, including Francis Schaeffer's somewhat more subtle version, see Mark A. Noll, Nathan O Hatch, and George M. Marsden, *The Search for Christian America* (Colorado Springs, 1989 [1983]).

48. Martin, *With God on Our Side*, 226–237.

49. Jerry Falwell, *Listen America* (New York, 1980), pp. 251–252; 258.

50. Steve Brouwer, Paul Gifford, and Susan D. Rose, *Exporting the American Gospel: Global Christian Fundamentalism* (New York, 1996), pp. 15–16.

51. Hal Lindsey (with C. C. Carlson), *The Late Great Planet Earth* (Grand Rapids, 1970), 183–185. In his Introduction (n. p.) he listed politics as among the false solutions offered to human problems, even though, he added in passing, "electing honest, intelligent men to positions of leadership" was "terribly important." Number in print is from Paul Boyer, *When Time Shall Be No More: Prophetic Belief in American Culture* (Cambridge, MA, 1992), p. 5. Interview quotations, "The Great Cosmic Countdown: Hal Lindsey on the Future," *Eternity* (January 1977), p. 21, quoted in Boyer, *Time Shall be No More*, p. 299. By way of contrast, in Lindsey's best-selling *The 1980s: Countdown to Armageddon* (New York, 1981), he was very strongly nationalistic and anti-Soviet and argued that the "Bible supports building a powerful military force," p. 157, as quoted in Boyer, *Time Shall be No More*, p. 145.

52. Francis Schaeffer shared some assumptions with Rushdoony but did not envision a future Christian civilization and was careful to reject suggestions of theocracy. In 1981 Schaeffer, not long before his death, published *The Christian Manifesto,* a work that Michael Lienesch in his careful study of the literature of the religious right, *Redeeming America: Piety and Politics in the New Christian Right* (Chapel Hill, NC, 1993), p. 177, describes as "the single most significant statement of Christian conservative political thinking." In his *Manifesto* Schaeffer provided not only a resounding call to arms, but also a rationale for why politics was OK and Christians should resist the tyranny of government-sponsored secularism. At L'Abri Fellowship in the 1960s, visitors were encouraged to listen to Schaeffer's taped expositions of Rushdoony's views, especially on the antithesis between secular and biblical worldviews. Both men were influenced by Cornelius Van Til of Westminster Theological Seminary, although Van Til's views of the antithesis between Christianity and all sorts of secularism were theological and not political. On the connection of Schaeffer and Rushdoony see also Diamond, *Roads to Dominion,* pp. 246–49.

53. Lienesch, *Redeeming America,* provides extensive coverage of these themes in Robertson's writings. See also David Edwin Harrell, Jr., *Pat Robertson: A Personal, Religious, and Political Portrait* (1987). Boyer, *When Time Shall be no More,* p. 241, concludes that "few prophetic popularizers embraced Robertson's politicized postmillennialism."

54. *Newsweek* Cover Story "The New Prophets of Revelation," May 16, 2004, http://msnbc.msn.com/id/3668484/site/newsweek.

55. Timothy P. Weber, *Living in the Shadow of the Second Coming: American Premillennialism, 1875–1925* (New York, 1979).

56. This is a somewhat different from the valid observation of Grant Wacker in *Heaven Below: Early Pentecostals and American Culture* (Cambridge, MA, 2001) that early pentecostals (and by implication almost all evangelicals) are pragmatists as well as principled biblicists, so that virtually any belief may be temporarily ignored in the light of sufficiently pressing practical considerations. It is also not the same as saying that fundamentalists do not consistently apply their avowed principles such as following the Bible in all of life or in doing what Jesus would do. My point is that, in addition, some beliefs in a belief system are less central than others and are hence more likely to be ignored in certain circumstances. For instance, specific prophetic claims, which are used to bolster the doctrine of the inerrancy of Scripture, can be abandoned, while the doctrine of inerrancy (however flexible in how it may be interpreted) remains.

57. Other exceptions are more rare. James Watt, President Reagan's secretary of the interior, was widely reputed to be unfriendly to the environment in part because of his belief that Jesus would return soon. In his testimony before the House Interior Committee in February 1981 he said, "I do not know how many future generations we can count on before the Lord returns, whatever it is, we have to manage with a skill to leave the resources needed for future generations." As quoted Planet Jackson Hole, http://www.planetjh.com/, in a March 2, 2005 posting. Journalist Bill Moyers's widely cited and criticized 2004 misquotation: "After the last tree is felled, Christ will come back," for which he eventually apologized, reflected common perceptions of critics as to Watt's meaning.

In another exception, Jerry Falwell, who urged an aggressive anti-Communist foreign policy in the 1980s, argued that we did not need to fear an imminent nuclear holocaust that would destroy the world, since the prophesied end-time events had not yet happened. Falwell, "Nuclear War and the Second Coming of Christ" (1983), cited in Boyer, *When Time Shall be No More,* p.137. Boyer, *idem.,* contrasts this view, however, to Falwell's statement as late as 1980 which follows the more common premillennial prediction (as in Hal Lindsey's work) of an imminent nuclear war with the USSR.

58. For valuable accounts of these views see Boyer, *When Time Shall Be No More,* esp. pp. 152–253, and Timothy P. Weber, *On the Road to Armageddon: How Evangelicals Became Israel's Best Friend* (Grand Rapids, 2004).

59. Gabriel A. Almond, R. Scott Appleby, and Emmanuel Sivan, *Strong Religion: The Rise of Fundamentalisms around the World* (Chicago, 2003), p.17. See also the multivolume *Fundamentalism Project,* Martin E. Marty and R. Scott Appleby, eds. (Chicago, 1991–1995).

It is possible that as a result of the use of "fundamentalist" as a term to describe radicals, including terrorists, in other religions, since 9/11 the term is becoming less popular among Americans as a self-designation.

60. Mark Noll, *America's God: From Jonathan Edwards to Abraham Lincoln* (New York, 2002). Nathan O. Hatch, *Democratization of American Christianity* (New Haven, 1989).

61. Christian Smith, *American Evangelicals: Embattled and Thriving,* pp. 210–217, provides very helpful documentation and discussion of the paradox between their absolutistic rhetoric and their strong commitments to voluntarism.

62. Christian Smith, *Christian America?* pp. 26–27, documents that forty percent of self-identified evangelicals give this response to the question of what "Christian America" actually means and that, upon questioning, respondents give mixed responses that typically undercut ideas of "Christianizing" the nation in any strong sense. See also Part 5, note 5, above.

63. For instance, James L. Guth, Lyman A. Kellstedt, John C. Green, and Corwin E. Smidt, "Onward Christian Soldiers? Religion and the Bush Doctrine," *Books and Culture,* 11:4 (July–August 2005), pp. 20–21, documents that evangelicals were considerably more likely to endorse George W. Bush's foreign policy, including unilateral and preemptive wars such as in Iraq, than were any other religious grouping other than Mormons. While evangelicals have always been strongly disposed to support Israel, their partisan identification with the second Bush administration appears to have contributed to a widening gap among conservative and other religious believers on such broader foreign policy issues. In general, I would add that the perception that the Bush administration takes evangelical concerns seriously appears to have strengthened evangelical identification with mainstream politics (even if deploring the nation's overall secularism) and, at least for the time being, lessened their tendency to play the role of outsiders, a tendency that was more apparent in their political efforts of the preceding decades.

Fundamentalist proneness to military solutions is consonant with their end-time scenarios in which they emphasize the cataclysmic warfare led by Christ himself that will destroy history's most insidious and potent coalition of the forces of darkness.

64. See the first pages of Chapter XXII. The quotation, cited there, is from Ernest Sandeen, but as I point out, he defined the essentials of this movement too narrowly in terms of a couple of its distinctive features.

65. For instance, Nancy Tatom Ammerman, *Bible Believers: Fundamentalists in the Modern World* (New Brunswick, NJ, 1987). Ault, *Spirit and Flesh*. Bendroth, *Fundamentalism and Gender*, pp. 108–113, also emphasized this point.

66. Sometimes fundamentalist prophesies retrain a populist tone of critique of business culture and especially of commercialism as parts of the corrupt hedonistic culture that will be associated with the anti-Christ. Boyer, *When Time Shall be No More*, pp. 288–89.

67. Robert Wuthnow, *Poor Richard's Principle: Recovering the American Dream through the Moral Dimension of Work, Business, and Money* (Princeton, 1996), pp. 315–324. Wuthnow's observations on this point apply to other seriously religious Americans as well as evangelicals and fundamentalists, but he does not observe essentially different behavior on their part. By the same token, since these traits apply to most religious and non-religious people, one should keep that in mind in criticizing these shortcomings.

   Ronald J. Sider, *The Scandal of the Evangelical Conscience: Why Are Christians Living Just Like the Rest of the World* (Grand Rapids, 2005), documents some of this lack of difference as does Alan Wolfe, *The Transformation of American Religion: How We Actually Live Our Faith* (New York, 2003). One caution is that sociological aggregates based on the nearly forty percent of the American population who will affirm: "would you describe yourself as a 'born again' or evangelical Christian," include many who would not be classed as evangelicals by other standards and such averages obscure the many for whom their religious belief does make a great difference. Figures based on The Princeton Religious Research Center data since 1976 as reported on the website of the Institute for the Study of American Evangelicalism.

68. R. Marie Griffith, *Born Again Bodies: Flesh and Spirit in American Christianity* (Berkeley, 2004) provides an especially helpful account of Christian culture of dieting.

69. Some of the ideas of this paragraph are suggested by John B. Judis, "Value-free: How Capitalism Redefines Morality," *The New Republic*, April 26 and May 3, 1999, pp. 53–56. For a more recent example see the highly successful *Your Best Life Now* (Nashville, TN, 2004), by Joel Osteen, a Houston megachurch pastor and televangelist, which begins with a man who saw a gorgeous house set high on a hill in Hawaii and came to realize that he need not think he could not have such if he started "believing better of himself and believing better of God" (p. 3).

70. Bendroth, *Fundamentalism and Gender*, pp. 114–15, citing John R. Rice, C. Stacey Woods, and Bob Jones. The emphasis on modesty in these cases was not a protest against consumerism as such but a warning to not unduly arouse men's sexual desires.

71. The issue is closely related to social class and the success-oriented evangelicalism of today reflects the vastly greater affluence of many adherents.

   Gary Scott Smith, "Evangelicals Confront Corporate Capitalism: Advertising, Consumerism, Stewardship, and Spirituality, 1880–1930," in *More Money, More Ministry: Money and Evangelicals in Recent North American History* (Grand Rapids, 2000), pp. 39–80, shows that evangelicals' emphases on stewardship, moderation, and self-control provided some resistance to the juggernaut of consumerism in the early decades of the twentieth century. Timomy Gloege, who is working on a dissertation on Reuben A. Torrey comments that quite a few of the major financial supporters of evangelicalism were also promoters of consumerism.

72. On the crisis in liberalism see the ninetieth anniversary issue of *The New Republic* with a forum "To Liberalism: Embattled . . . and Essential," which is a combination

of obituary and call for resuscitation. "Ask yourself," writes Martin Peretz in a tone characteristic of the whole issue, "Who is a truly influential liberal mind in our culture?"

73. Ferenc Morton Szasz, *The Divided Mind of Protestant America, 1880–1930* (University, AL, 1982), pp. 122–23.

74. Stephen Carter, *The Culture of Disbelief: How American Law and Politics Trivializes American Devotion* (New York, 1993), provides a notable analysis of such themes.

Bibliographical Indexes

Since many of the notes contain bibliographical comments or listings of secondary works, they may fill one of the main roles of an annotated bibliography. The following indexes indicate by chapter and number such notes or related bibliographical comment in text ("t"). The rest of the notes, of course, constitute a working bibliography of sources, topically arranged, and may be surveyed accordingly.

The Introduction and the opening sections of Chapters XXII, XXIII, and XXIV contain the equivalent of a bibliographical essay on the historiography of fundamentalism. C. Allyn Russell, *Voices of American Fundamentalism* (Philadelphia, 1976), and Ernest R. Sandeen, *The Roots of Fundamentalism* (Chicago, 1970), each contain an excellent bibliography with comment.

1. SUBJECTS (on which there is bibliographical comment or a listing).
America and kingdom, I:2; V:5; VII:6 (see also politics)
anti-communism, XXIII:19
anti-intellectualism, IV:1; XXIV:1-4t
anti-Semitism, XXIII:15-17

Baptists (and fundamentalism), VI:7; XII:12; XV:48; XVIII:5, 11; XIX:8; XX:15; XXI:23
Beecher, H. W., II:7, 16-18
Bible, view of, VI:7; XII:12; XIII:8; XIV:25; XXIV:6 (see also Princeton theology)
Blanchard, Charles, XXIV:26, 27
Blanchard, Jonathan, II:26
Brethren (Plymouth), IV:7
British evangelicalism and fundamentalism, I:36; XXV:2
Bryan, Wm. J., XV:37, 38, 42; XVIII:27

Canadian fundamentalism, XX:15
church (views of), VII:20
Common Sense philosophy, I:18-20, 22, 25; VIII:12; XIII:3, 7, 8, 20, 23; XXIV: 27

Disciples of Christ (and fundamentalism), XX:8
dispensationalism III:26, 28; IV:7; V:14, 20; VI:11; VIII:8; XV:16 (see also premillennialism)

ethnicity XXI:28, 30; XXII:14, 16t, 24, 27
evolution (Darwinism), Intro.:3; XIV:31; XVII:25; XXI:10; XXII:7t

"five points" of fundamentalism, XIII:30

2. SECONDARY WORKS (on which there is comment).

Abrams, R. H., *Present Arms,* XVI:25
Anderson, R. M., *Vision of Disinherited,* XI:2, 8, 17; XXI:27
Askew, T. A. "Liberal Arts," II:35

Bailey, K. K., *Southern Protestantism,* XX:12
Barabas, S., *Keswick,* VIII:20
Barr, J., *Fundamentalism,* XXV:2
Bledstein, B. J., *Professionalism,* I:16; II:12
Bozeman, T. D., *Protestants . . . Science,* VI:2-5; XII:6
Bratt, J. D., "Dutch Calvinism," XXII:27
Brinks, H. J., "Ethnicity," XXII:14
Bundy, D. D., *Keswick,* VIII:20; XI:15

Carpenter, J. A., "Shelter," VI:27; XXI:25t
Carter, P. A., "Fundamentalist Defense," XVI:45; XVII:21; XXIII:4t, 6t, 8t
Carter, P. A., *Gilded Age,* I:7; II:4
Carter, P. A., *Social Gospel,* XXIII:3t
Caskey, M., *Beecher Family,* II:3

Lovelace, R., *Dynamics,* Aft.:1t
Lovelace, R., *Mather,* IV:3

McLoughlin, W. G. (ed.), *American Evangelicals,* X:2t
McLoughlin, W. G., *Beecher,* II:3
McLoughlin, W. G., *Billy Sunday,* XV:47
McLoughlin, W. G., *Modern Revivalism,* III:20, 21; X:26; XV:47; XXII:4t; XXIII:3t
McLoughlin, W. G., "Third Force," XXII:4t
Magnuson, N., *Salvation in Slums,* IX:18
Maring, N. H., "Baptists," VI:7
Maring, N. H., "Conservative," XIX:8; XXI:20
Marty, M., *Modern Schism,* V:2t, 3t
Marty, M., *Righteous Empire,* X:3t
Mathews, D. G., *Old South,* XII:1
Mead, S. M., "Denominationalism," VII:20
Miller, J. P., "Souls or Social," X:3t
Moberg, D., *Great Reversal,* X:1t, 23
Moore, L., "Another Look," Intro.:8, XXII:12, 13t
Murray, R. K., *Red Scare,* XVII:1

Nelson, R., "Northern Baptist," XII:12
Niebuhr, H. R., "Fundamentalism," XXII:2; XIV:2t
Nykamp, D. G., "Presbyterian Power," XIX:11; XX:26

Packer, J. I., "Fundamentalism," XXV:2
Pfisterer, K. D., *Prism of Scripture,* VII:5
Pierard, R. V., *Unequal Yoke,* X:1t, 23
Pollock, J. C., *Keswick Story,* VIII:20

Rausch, D. A., *Zionism,* XXIII:15
Rian, E. H., *Presbyterian Conflict,* XXI:19
Reiter, R. E., "Niagara Bible Conference," V:17
Rogers, J. and McKim, D., *Authority,* XIII:8
Russell, C. A., "Shields," XX:15
Russell, C. A., *Voices,* Intro.:9; XV:15, 37, 55; XVII:27, 36; XVIII:11; XIX:11;
    XXIII:10

Sandeen, E. R., "American Identity," XXI:31; XXII:10t
Sandeen, E. R., "Origins," XXII:9t
Sandeen, E. R., *Roots,* Intro.:6t; III:26; IV:7, 12; V:14, 17; VI:7; VII:23; VIII:5;
    XIII:18, 31, 32; XIV:1, 9; XVI:31; XXII:8–12t, 16t; XXIII:15
Shriver, G. H. (ed.), *Religious Heretics,* XII:4, 9, 10
Shelley, B., "A. J. Gordon," VI:7
Shelley, B., "Pietistic Fundamentalism," VIII:5
Sizer, S. S., III:20, 22, 24; IV:4t, 5t, 6; V:12; VIII:14, 20; X:20; XXII:27; XXV:10
Smith, H. S. et al., *American Christianity,* XXII:6t
Smith, J. W., "Religion and Science," I:35; X:29
Smith, T. L., "Ethnicity," XXII:24
Smith, T. L., "Finney's Synthesis," VIII:13; X:6
Smith, T. L., *Revivalism,* IX:7t

Index

350